The New Military in Russia

Other Publications by Richard F. Staar

Arms Control: Myth versus Reality (editor)
Aspects of Modern Communism (editor)
Communist Regimes in Eastern Europe, 5th revised edition
East-Central Europe and the USSR (editor)
Effects of Soviet Political Fragmentation on the Energy Infrastructure (co-author)
Foreign Policies of the Soviet Union
Future Information Revolution in the USSR (editor)
Long-Range Environmental Study of the Northern Tier of Eastern Europe, 1990–2000
Poland, 1944–1962: Sovietization of a Captive People
Public Diplomacy: U.S.A. versus USSR (editor)
Soviet Military Policy since World War II (co-author)
Transition to Democracy in Poland (editor)
United States–East European Relations in the 1990s (editor)
USSR Foreign Policies after Detente, 2d revised edition
Yearbook on International Communist Affairs: Parties and Revolutionary Movements (editor of 22 volumes)

THE
New Military
IN
RUSSIA
Ten Myths That Shape the Image

Richard F. Staar

Naval Institute Press • Annapolis, Maryland

© 1996 by Richard F. Staar
All rights reserved. No part of this book may be reproduced without written permission from the publisher.

Library of Congress Cataloging-in-Publication Data
Staar, Richard Felix, 1923–
   The new military in Russia : ten myths that shape the image / Richard F. Staar.
       p.   cm.
   Includes bibliographical references and index.
   ISBN 1-55750-798-8 (hc : alk. paper). — ISBN 1-55750-740-6 (pbk. : alk. paper)
   1. Russia (Federation)—Armed Forces. 2. Russia (Federation)—Military policy. I. Title.
UA770.S7897   1996
355'.00947—dc20   95-49877

Printed in the United States of America on acid-free paper ∞

03 02 01 00 99 98 97 96   9 8 7 6 5 4 3 2
First printing

for Jadzieńka

Contents

List of Tables, Charts, and Maps	ix
List of Acronyms	xi
Preface and Acknowledgments	xvii

Myth No. 1:	The Military Is Outside Politics	1
Myth No. 2:	Russia Has Only Friends	24
Myth No. 3:	Reform Remains on Course	47
Myth No. 4:	Military-Industrial Complex Is Dead	76
Myth No. 5:	Export of Defensive Weapons Only	94
Myth No. 6:	Peacemaking Equals Peacekeeping	112
Myth No. 7:	Commonwealth Armies Support Russia	133
Myth No. 8:	Arms Treaties Are Observed	150
Myth No. 9:	A National Security Concept Exists	166
Myth No. 10:	The Future Is Ours, Comrades!	186

Appendixes
   A: Biographical Information on Key Military
      Figures — 209
   B: Russian Newspapers and Journals — 227
Bibliography — 233
Name Index — 239
Subject Index — 243

Tables, Charts, and Maps

Tables

1.1.	Government Committee for the State of Emergency (1991)	3
1.2.	Officers Implicated or Removed after 1991 Coup	10
1.3.	Key Rebels with Military Rank (1993)	13
1.4.	Weapons Brought into the White House	16
2.1.	Armed Forces' Comparison	36
2.2.	Group to Implement Decree of 30 November 1994	42
3.1.	Fleets and Flotillas	52
3.2.	Estimated Deployment of Military Equipment and Personnel (1992)	54
3.3.	Russian Forces Previously Deployed Abroad	56
3.4.	Armed Forces High Command	58
3.5.	Military Districts	59
3.6.	Active Duty Military Personnel	64
3.7.	Ranks of Army and Navy Officers, Russia and the United States	66
3.8.	Defense Budget for 1994	68
4.1.	Russia's Hidden Cities	78
4.2.	Attitudes toward Work Abroad by Age Group	81
5.1.	Prices for Conventional Weapons	96
5.2.	Selected Weapons for Sale	100
5.3.	Costs for Modernizing Equipment	102

5.4. Russian Arms Sales in 1993	103
5.5. Soviet/Russian Arms Exports, 1986–1995	105
6.1. Demise of the Ruble Zone	114
6.2. Commonwealth Leaders	117
6.3. Russian Peacemaking Forces	119
6.4. Percentages of Russians in SNG Countries	129
7.1. Defense Ministers in Near Abroad	135
7.2. Azeri and Armenian Heavy Weapons	140
7.3. Conventional Military Power: Russia versus Ukraine	146
8.1. Disparity between Forces in the Reduction Area (1 January 1981)	152
8.2. Soviet CFE-Limited Equipment in East-Central Europe	153
8.3. Maximum Levels for CFE Treaty-Limited Equipment (Tashkent, 15 May 1992)	155
8.4. CW Stockpiles in Russia	157
10.1. Regular and Other Armed Forces (1995)	199
10.2. Ethnic Composition of Military Officers	202

Charts

2.1. Fundamental Armed Forces Doctrinal Concepts	25
2.2. Principles of Armed Forces Force Generation	28
2.3. Security Council Apparatus	40
3.1. Structure of the Russian Armed Forces	50
3.2. Basic Organization of Mobile Forces (end of 1995)	62
5.1. Restructured Arms-Export Mechanism	97

Maps

3.1. Future Unified Strategic-Operational Commands	61
4.1. Russia's Secret Cities	80
6.1. Commonwealth of Independent States	115
6.2. Russian Troops in Moldova	121
6.3. The Caucasus and Central Asia	123
6.4. Nagorno-Karabakh	127
10.1. Russia's Ethnic Republics	188
10.2. Caucasus and Trans-Caucasus	190
10.3. Fault Lines in the Russian Federation	193

Acronyms

ABM	Antiballistic Missile Treaty, 26 May 1972
Al'fa	Spetsnaz group attached to Office of the President; transferred to FSB on 14 August 1995
ASW	Antisubmarine Warfare
AWACS	Airborne Warning and Control Systems
AZhV	*Agentsvo zheleznodorozhnykh voisk* (Agency for Railroad Troops)
Beta	Similar to *Al'fa*, when both were KGB; disbanded
blizhnee zarubezh'e	The Near Abroad (all former Soviet republics outside Russia, including the three Baltic States)
BMD	*Boevaia mashina desanta* (airborne assault vehicle)
BMP	*Boevaia mashina pekhoty* (infantry combat vehicle)
BTR	*Bronetransporter* (armored personnel carrier)
BW	Biological (and Toxin) Weapons Convention, 10 April 1972
C^3	Command, Control, and Communications
CEP	Circular Error Probable
CFE	Conventional Forces in Europe (successor to MBFR) Treaty, 19 November 1990
CIA	Central Intelligence Agency
CIS	Commonwealth of Independent States (see SNG)
CO	Commanding Officer

CPSU	Communist Party of the Soviet Union
CSCE	Conference on Security and Cooperation in Europe (1975–94); see OSCE
CW	Chemical Weapons Treaty, 13 January 1993
dal'nee zarubezh'e	The Far Abroad (former members of WTO)
DVK	*Desantno-vysadochnyi kater* (amphibious landing craft)
EBRD	European Bank for Reconstruction and Development
ELINT	Electronic Intelligence
FAPSI	*Federal'noe agentstvo pravitel'stvennoi sviazi i informatsii* (Federal Agency for Government Communications and Information)
FBIS	Foreign Broadcast Information Service
FDSU	*Federal'noe dorozhno-stroitel'noe upravlenie* (Federal Road Construction Administration)
FPS	*Federal'naia pogranichnaia sluzhba* (Federal Border Service)
FSB	*Federal'naia sluzhba bezopasnosti* (Federal Security Service)
FSK	*Federal'naia sluzhba kontrrazvedki* (Federal Counter Intelligence Service); name changed to FSB, 12 April 1995
GIU	*Glavnoe inzhenernoe upravlenie* (Main Engineering Directorate); transformed into *Oboroneksport*
GKChP	*Gosudarstvennyi komitet po cherezvychainomu polozheniiu v SSSR* (Government Committee for the State of Emergency in the USSR)
Goskomoboronprom	*Gosudarstvennyi komitet oboronnoi promyshlennosti* (State Committee for Defense Industry)
GRU	*Glavnoe razvedyvatel'noe upravlenie* (Main Directorate for [Military] Intelligence)
GTU	*Glavnoe tekhnicheskoe upravlenie* (Main Technical Directorate); renamed *Spetsvneshtekhnika*
GUO	*Glavnoe upravlenie okhrany* (Main Directorate for Protection)
GULAG	*Glavnoe upravlenie lagerei* (Main Directorate for Labor Camps)
GUSK	*Gosudarstvennoe upravlenie po sotrudnichestvu i kooperatsii* (State Directorate for Collaboration and Cooperation); sells licenses abroad
ICBM	Intercontinental Ballistic Missile

IMF	International Monetary Fund
INF	Intermediate-Range Nuclear Forces Treaty, 8 December 1987
JPRS	Joint Publications Research Service
JSTARS	Joint Surveillance and Target Attack Radar Systems
KGB	*Komitet Gosudarstvennoi Bezopasnosti* (Committee for State Security); disbanded in late 1991
MBFR	Mutual and Balanced Forces Reduction negotiations (1973–89); superseded by CFE
MChS	*Ministerstvo po delam grazhdanskoi oborony, cherezvychainym situatsiiam i likvidatsii posledstvii stikhiinykh bedstvii* (Ministry for Civil Defense, Emergencies, and Disasters)
MD	Military District
MI-6	British Foreign Intelligence Service
MO	*Ministerstvo oborony* (Ministry of Defense)
MTCR	Missile Technology Control Regime
MVD	*Ministerstvo vnutrennykh del* (Ministry of Internal Affairs)
NATO	North Atlantic Treaty Organization
NKAO	Nagorno-Karabakh Autonomous *Oblast'*
NPT	Non-Proliferation (of nuclear weapons) Treaty, 1 July 1968
NZ	*Neprikosnovennye zapasy* ("untouchable" supplies)
Oboroneksport	Defense export association responsible for 90 percent of arms sales under the Foreign Economic Relations Ministry; absorbed by *Rosvooruzhenie*
Oboronka	Diminutive for VPK
OMON	*Otriady militsii osobogo naznacheniia* (Special Purpose Militia Detachments)
OMRI	Open Media Research Institute (Prague, Czech Republic); succeeded RFE/RL in January 1995
OSCE	Organization for Security and Cooperation in Europe (new name of CSCE since January 1995)
PfP	Partnership for Peace
PVO	*Voiska protivo-vozdushnoi oborony* (Troops for Air Defense)
RFE/RL	Radio Free Europe/Radio Liberty (Munich, Germany); superseded by OMRI
RKA	*Rossiiskoe kosmicheskoe agentstvo* (Russian Space Agency)
RMA	Royal Military Academy, Sandhurst, UK
Rosvooruzhenie	State Company for Export and Import of Arms and Military Equipment; established in December 1993
RSFSR	Russian Soviet Federated Socialist Republic

Russkoe oruzhie	"Russian weapons" foreign trade company; absorbed by *Rosvooruzhenie*
RVSN	*Raketnye voiska strategicheskogo naznacheniia* (Strategic Missile Forces)
SALT	Strategic Arms Limitation Treaty, 26 May 1972 (I) and 18 June 1979 (II)
SBPR	*Sluzhba bezopasnosti prezidenta Rossii* (Russian President's Security Service)
SBR	*Sily bystrogo razvertyvaniia* (Rapid Deployment Forces)
SK	*Storozhovoi kater* (patrol boat)
SLBM	Submarine Launched Ballistic Missile
SNG	*Sodruzhestvo nezavisimykh gosudarstv* (Commonwealth of Independent States)
SNR	*Sily nemedlennogo reagirovaniia* (Immediate Reaction Forces)
spetsnaz	*Spetsial'noe naznachenie*, elite military and police units, for "special designation"
Spetsvneshtekhnika	Special equipment export committee, for delivery of spare parts and defense infrastructure abroad; absorbed by *Rosvooruzhenie*
SPG	*Sily postoiannoi gotovnosti* (Permanent Readiness Forces)
SR	*Strategicheskie rezervy* (strategic reserves)
SSBN	Nuclear-powered submarine, carrying SLBMs
SSMO	*Spetsial'noe stroitel'stvo Ministerstva oborony* (Special Defense Ministry Construction)
START	Strategic Arms Reduction Treaty, 31 July 1991 (I), and 3 January 1993 (II)
SV	*Sukhoputnye voiska* (Ground Troops)
SVR	*Sluzhba vneshnei razvedki* (Foreign Intelligence Service)
Tekhsnabeksport	Technical Supply Export (organization for weapons sales)
TMD	Theater Missile Defense
TVD	*Teatr voennykh deistvii* (Theater of Military Operations)
UAE	United Arab Emirates
VAT	Value added tax
VMF	*Voenno-morskoi flot* (Navy)
Voentekh	Defense ministry office for sale of excess weapons to SNG countries
VPK	*Voenno-promyshlennyi kompleks* (military-industrial complex)

VVS	*Voenno-vozdushnye sily* (Air Forces)
Vympel	"Victory pennant"—Ministry of Interior *spetsnaz* antiterrorist unit; disbanded
WTO	Warsaw Treaty Organization (1955–90)

Preface and Acknowledgments

The idea for this book originated with a thirty-six-page monograph entitled *The New Russian Armed Forces: Preparing for War or Peace?* written by the author and published at the Hoover Institution on War, Revolution and Peace in 1992. Thanks are expressed to the anonymous colleagues whose comments helped to improve the draft version. Many of the sections have been expanded into chapters. The completed manuscript includes one appendix with descriptions of most Russian newspapers and periodicals that were cited. Brief biographic data on eighty-two admirals, generals, and two civilians also appear in the other appendix. Transliteration from Russian into English follows standard Library of Congress guidelines, except for Yeltsin (rather than El'tsin) and Chechnya (instead of Chechniia).

The author is grateful to Gustav Weber at Radio Free Europe/Radio Liberty (RFE/RL) in Munich, Germany; Robert Orttung at the Open Media Research Institute (OMRI) in Prague, Czech Republic; and Michael Neubert at the Library of Congress in Washington, D.C., for their assistance in obtaining photocopies from Russian articles and other data not available elsewhere.

Slavic Reference Librarian Molly Molloy at the Hoover Institution went beyond the call of duty in helping to find original source materials and esoteric data. Viktor G. Bortnevski, postdoctoral research fellow, kindly read footnotes and other citations for errors in transliteration. Research assistant Anne Garvey tracked down many leads and organized certain materials. Margit N. Grigory, who has worked as a colleague since 1977, meticulously supervised preparation of the manuscript for publication and arranged the index. Jadwiga M. Staar proofread several drafts of the typescript and the page proofs.

The undersigned also expresses his gratitude to Robert V. Barylski (University of South Florida), Stephen J. Blank (U.S. Army War College), Susan L. Clark (Institute for Defense Analyses), Mary C. FitzGerald (Hudson Institute), Maj. Gen. Nicholas S. H. Krawciw, U.S. Army (ret.) (Trevor N. Dupuy Institute), Benjamin S. Lambeth (Rand Corporation), Carl A. Linden (George Washington University), James H. Noren (Central Intelligence Agency, ret.), Bruce Parrott (School for Advanced International Studies, Johns Hopkins University), Brad Roberts (Institute for Defense Analyses), Harriet Fast Scott (Southwest Missouri State University), who also allowed access to her unique biographic data files, and William F. Scott (Joint Military Intelligence College) for reading and commenting on draft chapters.

Special thanks are due to Lester W. Grau, Jacob W. Kipp, Timothy L. Thomas, and Graham H. Turbiville (Foreign Military Studies Office, Fort Leavenworth, Kansas); Roman Laba and Mikhail Tsypkin (Naval Postgraduate School), the latter for organizing a series of conferences that brought together Russian and American military specialists. Suggestions and comments by three anonymous outside readers for the Naval Institute Press helped to improve the text. The manuscript editor, Therese D. Boyd, was a joy to work with, as was the staff of the Naval Institute Press. Their contributions to the final product are gratefully acknowledged.

The author also thanks the Earhart Foundation of Ann Arbor, Michigan, especially Richard A. Ware, and also the Sarah Scaife Foundation of Pittsburgh, Pennsylvania, for supporting this project. Finally, this book could not have been written without the stimulating atmosphere at the Hoover Institution—colleagues, administrators and, above all, the past and present dedicated curators, archivists, and librarians who have built the world's preeminent collection of source materials on Russia.

The New Military in Russia

Myth No. 1
The Military Is Outside Politics

> The army should be a nonpolitical organization.
> *Defense Minister Grachëv over Moscow Radio*
> (3 July 1995)

Generals became involved with domestic politics, prior to the war in Chechnya, during the course of two violent upheavals. The first took place in August 1991, when flag officers in key positions refused to obey their defense minister's orders. Disobedience paradoxically led to promotions for many of these men who were subsequently absorbed by the new armed forces of the Russian Federation.

The second such incident occurred during September/October 1993, when the high command initially made a collective decision to remain outside of politics in the midst of a mutiny to unseat the commander-in-chief. Only specific written orders by the president of Russia brought the military to his defense at the last moment.

Civil-military relations were not exactly peaceful during the Soviet period. The most traumatic experience for the officers' corps began on 11 June 1937, when the entire high command was described as consisting overwhelmingly of traitors.[1] The purge, which lasted fourteen months, included 489 general/admiral equivalents and half of the lower-ranking officers either being shot or sent to the GULAG.

The devastating consequences of Stalin's paranoia could be seen in the 1939–40 winter war against Finland and the lack of preparedness for the subsequent German invasion of the USSR on 22 June 1941. The latter forced the generalissimo to restore some of those officers who had survived the forced labor camps to their former positions.

After the end of World War II, Stalin demoted Marshal of the Soviet Union Georgii K. Zhukov by sending him from Moscow to command military district headquarters in Odessa. The marshal could have been considered a potential rival, due to his popularity. After the death of Stalin, Zhukov became defense minister and a member of the CPSU political bureau. In October 1957, Nikita S. Khrushchëv retired the marshal, perhaps as a prophylactic measure.[2]

In the USSR, neither military officers nor civilian bureaucrats remained immune from arbitrary decisions by the ruling autocrat. It remains to be seen whether a future Russia will resemble its predecessor in this respect. Detailed summaries of the August 1991 and the September/October 1993 attempts to seize power may offer some clues. The most recent data come from the war in Chechnya, which commenced with the Russian invasion on 11 December 1994.

The August Coup

To understand the origins of Russia's new armed forces and their changing role in domestic politics, one must look back to the military's involvement with the abortive attempt by hardliners to establish a "state of emergency" during the coup of 19–21 August 1991. Early reports and conventional wisdom suggested that flag officers played only a minor role in these events, a conclusion that seemed to be supported by the fact that of the sixteen principals arrested (the seventeenth having committed suicide) only two held the highest army ranks. On the contrary, the evidence suggests that military involvement in planning and implementation of the coup included large numbers of high-ranking officers.

Marshal of the Soviet Union Dmitrii T. Iazov (defense minister) and General of the Army Valentin I. Varennikov (commanding officer of ground forces and deputy defense minister) were subsequently indicted for high treason and faced possible death penalties. Marshal of the Soviet Union Sergei F. Akhromeev (military advisor to USSR President Mikhail S. Gorbachëv) hanged himself before he could be detained.[3] (See Table 1.1.) Article 64 of the Russian Soviet Federated Socialist Republic (RSFSR) criminal code defined high treason as "conspiracy aimed at seizing power."

Official Testimony

During the aftermath of the coup, hearings were conducted by a civilian investigative commission of the Supreme Soviet or parliament. It included

TABLE 1.1
Government Committee for the State of Emergency (1991)

Name	Last Position (appointed)
Gennadii I. Ianaev	USSR vice-president (December 1990)
Valentin S. Pavlov	Prime minister (January 1991)
Dmitrii T. Iazov	Defense minister (May 1987)
Vladimir A. Kriuchkov	KGB chairman (October 1988)
Boris K. Pugo[a]	Interior minister (December 1990)
Oleg D. Baklanov	First deputy chairman, Defense Council (March 1991)
Vasilii A. Starodubtsev[b]	USSR Peasant Union chairman (June 1990)
Aleksandr I. Tiziakov	Association for State Enterprises and Industrial Construction, Transport and Communication Facilities president (1990)
Gennadii E. Ageev	KGB first deputy chairman (May 1983)
Valerii I. Boldin	President Gorbachëv's chief of staff (May 1991)
Viacheslav A. Generalov	KGB Kremlin Guards deputy chief (September 1990)
Viktor F. Grushko	KGB first deputy chairman (February 1991)
Anatolii I. Luk'ianov	USSR Supreme Soviet chairman (March 1991)
Iurii S. Plekhanov	KGB Kremlin Guards chief (September 1990)
Oleg S. Shenin	CPSU general secretary Gorbachëv's chief of staff (July 1990)
Valentin I. Varennikov	Ground forces commander (February 1989) and deputy defense minister

Sources: Wendy Slater, "The Trial of the Leaders of Russia's August 1991 Coup," RFE/RL *Research Report*, no. 48 (3 December 1993), especially table on p. 27; "Court Case Against '91 Coupists Abandoned," Moscow Radio, 10 May 1994, in FBIS-SOV-94-090 (10 May 1994), 9.

Note: Col. Gen. Vladislav A. Achalov, deputy defense minister, also would have been indicted had the investigation not been suspended.

The court proceedings were closed on 10 May 1994 against all defendants except for Col. Gen. Valentin I. Varennikov, who refused to accept the amnesty voted by parliament. He was subsequently acquitted of all charges. Kronid Liubarskii, "Sud v zazerkal'e," *Novoe vremia*, no. 22 (August 1994): 6–8.

[a] Pugo shot himself on 22 August 1991; Nikolai L. Kruchina, administrator of CPSU financial affairs, jumped to his death from a seventh floor apartment on 26 August 1991.

[b] Starodubtsev finished reading all documents on the case against him and was the first to be released from prison on parole. See Valerii Rudnev, "Osvobozhdenie Vasiliia Starodubtseva," *Izvestiia*, 8 June 1992, 3.

USSR and RSFSR people's deputies plus representatives of the Soviet defense ministry and the Russian committee for defense. Marshal of Aviation Evgenii I. Shaposhnikov (air force commander in August 1991) testified that the USSR defense ministry previously had established its own group to investigate military participation in the attempted coup. That commission worked over a period of two months, until 5 November 1991. It sought to establish the extent of complicity by members of the General Staff as well as other high-ranking officers.

Air Marshal Shaposhnikov, who only recently transferred from defense minister of the USSR to become commander-in-chief of the armed forces for the Commonwealth of Independent States (SNG), described military operations during the coup.[4] He testified that Iazov had convened a meeting of the defense ministry's collegium (all deputy ministers as well as chiefs of central directorates) at 0600 on 19 August to announce establishment of the so-called Government Committee for the State of Emergency (GKChP). Iazov had also ordered the armed forces to be placed on alert.[5]

Shaposhnikov next revealed that during the three-day coup approximately 5,000 military personnel, about 350 tanks, plus 270 armored personnel carriers and some heavy equipment had been ordered to augment the Moscow garrison. The airborne component brought an additional 380 combat and 700 other military vehicles into the city as a show of force.[6]

Responding to a question from one of the parliamentary deputies concerning culpability of those obeying orders, Shaposhnikov explained that the Moscow Military District commander (Maj. Gen. Nikolai V. Kalinin) had been exonerated of any criminal responsibility by the prosecuting attorney for the Russian Federation. Although this officer implemented orders from Iazov's office, Kalinin subsequently became chief of an armored forces academy. The same exoneration also extended to then–First Deputy Interior Minister Boris V. Gromov, who had been transferred to that position from the regular army. His signature on a letter in support of the Government Committee for the State of Emergency did not prove an obstacle to subsequent appointment as one of the Russian deputy defense ministers.[7] Gromov had changed sides at the right moment.

General of the Army Konstantin I. Kobets, chairman of the above-mentioned defense ministry Commission for Analysis of Activities by the Leadership of the USSR Armed Forces, then summarized the findings of this investigation. He stated that thirty-one generals subsequently had been dismissed from their positions on the high command staff. This represented only 10 percent of the 316 generals and other high-ranking officers recommended for discharge.[8] After his brief statement and a few remarks about the commission's work, there were questions, many of which Kobets did not answer satisfactorily. This mediocre performance should have disqualified him from any position on the new high command. And yet, presumably because he had defended Yeltsin at the White House during the coup, Kobets became the fifth deputy defense minister the following year.[9]

The next witness to testify before the parliamentary commission was Aleksandr V. Frolov, who represented the prosecutor's office for the Russian Federation. Having been charged with investigating the GKChP, he provided the parliamentary commission with a detailed chronology of established events during the coup. The following summarizes the information offered by Frolov.[10]

5 August 1991. The principal conspirators, including KGB Chairman Vladimir Kriuchkov and Defense Minister Iazov, met at a KGB safehouse near the Garden Ring Road, which is a beltway around Moscow. They decided to prevent the Union Treaty from being signed on the twentieth, using any means necessary to do so. That agreement would have recognized the de facto secession of six republics and curtailed central government power.

5–16 August. This period was set aside to prepare orders for the attempted coup d'état.

14 August. A three-member specialized team including airborne forces commander Col. Gen. Pavel S. Grachëv was assigned the task of analyzing preparatory measures required before a state of emergency could be introduced.

17 August. A larger group, including Iazov, Varennikov, and Deputy Defense Minister Achalov, convened during the afternoon and collectively decided to seize power by replacing USSR President Gorbachëv (then vacationing at Foros, Crimea) with Vice-President Gennadii Ianaev under Article 127 (7) of the Soviet constitution, if the former did not agree to declare martial law and postpone signing of the Union Treaty.

18 August. Gorbachëv claims that he refused to join the conspirators when they presented their demands to him at Foros. He was then detained at his vacation dacha until the collapse of the coup. General Varennikov subsequently proceeded to Bil'bek airport in the Crimea, where he met with several military district commanders. Also present at this meeting was General Gromov, representing the minister of internal affairs. Varennikov next flew to Kiev, where he tried unsuccessfully to enlist the Ukrainian leadership's support for the coup.

The overt attempt to seize power took place during the night of 18–19 August. Iazov and Achalov arrived at Prime Minister Valentin S. Pavlov's office in the Kremlin to hear a report from the delegation that had visited

6   MYTH NO. 1

Gorbachëv. The march of troops into the capital commenced at 0400, after Iazov had telephoned Moscow Military District commander Kalinin and ordered him to transfer elements of two divisions into the city.[11]

19 August. At 0500, Achalov passed on Iazov's command that General Grachëv alert elements of the 106th Airborne Division at Tula, which was ready to move within 90 minutes. Iazov ordered that it be concentrated at Tushino airport outside Moscow. Grachëv told his deputy, Maj. Gen. Aleksandr I. Lebed', to supervise this last movement.[12] Then, at 0700, Maj. Gen. Valerii I. Marchenkov commenced movement of units from his 2nd Taman (motorized rifle) Guards Division. At the same time, other units from the 4th Kantemirov (Armored) Guards Division, under Maj. Gen. Vladimir P. Chizhikov, began to execute their orders.

Achalov, at about 0800, next ordered Grachëv to deploy his airborne units around the National Bank, State Repository of Precious Metals, and the Ostankino radio and television stations in Moscow.

20 August. Iazov issued an order that elements of the 98th Airborne Division be flown from Bolgrad in Moldova and deployed at the Kubinka and Chkalovskii airfields near Moscow. General Kalinin, newly promoted from city commandant to commander of the Moscow Military District,

Poster in Moscow commemorating the 19 August 1991 attempt to seize power in that city with tanks. *(Photograph courtesy of Prof. Roman Laba, Naval Postgraduate School, Monterey, California.)*

announced a curfew beginning at 2300. It would have taken an estimated ten divisions to enforce this order throughout the city.[13]

Frolov next testified about preparations to assault the so-called White House, where parliament met, and which had been occupied by Yeltsin and those who opposed the plotters. On 20 August, a group that included Iazov, Achalov, Varennikov, Grachëv, and Gromov met to plan a coordinated attack by airborne, interior, and KGB units. They were to storm the White House and detain all Russian leaders located in that building complex.

Information about the planned assault, code-named "Thunder" (*grom*), is available from interrogation transcripts of the coup leaders.[14] The 20 August meeting included Col. Gen. Gennadii E. Ageev, deputy KGB chairman, as well as commanders of *spetsnaz* Group "Al'fa" (Maj. Gen. Viktor E. Karpukhin) and Group "Beta" (Col. Boris P. Beskov).

During this coordinating session, retired Marshal of the Soviet Union Akhromeev entered the room, accompanied by Defense Minister Iazov. Whether the former addressed the meeting remains uncertain from the Frolov testimony.[15] However, the record shows that Grachëv, as well as his deputy General Lebed', strongly opposed storming the White House, due to the high probability of failure and unwillingness by soldiers to fire on civilians. At this point, Grachëv and Lebed' changed sides. Lebed', under new orders from Grachëv, attempted to notify Yeltsin that the attack on the White House was to be launched at 0300 on 21 August. However, he could not make his way through the huge crowds surrounding the White House.[16]

Plan of Action

Airborne assault units to be commanded by Lebed', together with elite special purpose (OMON) interior ministry police detachments, were assigned to block White House entrances opposite the U.S. embassy and the Krasnopresnenskaia Naberezhnaia Boulevard, forming a pincer movement. Karpukhin would command both Groups Al'fa and Beta, with support by augmentation from the Moscow city and province KGB offices as well as the OMON units. This plan called for a reported total of 15,000 men.

Al'fa would then blast through the heavy White House doors with grenade launchers, fight its way up to Yeltsin's offices on the fifth floor, and capture the president of Russia, dead or alive. Beta would suppress all points of resistance. Other KGB units would secure the twenty entrances to the building and screen all detainees, including the executive leadership of the Russian Federation. Nevertheless, the officers refused to order the killing of other Russians. "I could not, nor was I about to, defy the will of my men," said General Karpukhin, in explaining his decision against leading the assault with his Al'fa group.[17]

In the meantime, Varennikov's attempts to move a rocket-launching helicopter squadron from Tula to the Podol'sk airfield near Moscow and two companies of tanks into the city were ignored by their commanding officers due to the absence of written orders. Both deputy airborne commanders, Maj. Gen. Aleksandr A. Chindarov and the above-mentioned Lebed', briefed Achalov on the unfeasibility of capturing the White House because of civilian crowds on the outside and a well-armed defense inside the building. Then at 2300, Grachëv and Gromov agreed not to move their airborne and interior troops, respectively, to assault positions.[18] Finally, that same night, Achalov personally inspected the crowds surrounding the White House and reported to Iazov on the impossibility of a successful attack without considerable bloodshed.

21 August. Iazov told Grachëv and Kalinin at 1000 in his office at the defense ministry building that the collegium had recommended two hours earlier to withdraw all troops to their home bases and cancel the curfew. He then ordered that this be done.[19] For all practical purposes, the coup had ended.

During the question period after his testimony, Frolov outlined for the parliamentary deputies the abortive attempt by the KGB's 9th Main Directorate (Kremlin service guards) to detain Yeltsin before the coup, which had been agreed upon in the defense ministry at a meeting chaired by Achalov around noon on 17 August. Varennikov reportedly had telephoned from Kiev and asked, "Why hasn't Yeltsin been shot yet?"[20] Two days later, on 19 August, the chief of the general staff, General of the Army Mikhail A. Moiseev, received an order calling him back from annual leave. Moiseev signed the telegrams that notified military commands throughout the country about martial law. Frolov also confirmed that Marshal Akhromeev had become a member of the staff for the Government Committee for the State of Emergency.[21]

Frolov next discussed military districts, navy fleets, and groups of forces, all of which had been contacted by Moiseev through coded telegrams and by Iazov over the telephone. These military formations were placed on combat alert status. The Volga-Ural Military District commander, Col. Gen. Al'bert M. Makashov, set up road blocks and dispatched columns of his steel-helmeted troops in armored vehicles through the cities of Samara, Sverdlovsk, and Perm, presumably to discourage civilian demonstrations.[22] In gathering the above information, Frolov stated that his team had questioned approximately 2,000 individuals (about half from the military), which resulted in almost 40,000 printed pages of testimony. He also revealed that about 300 potentially criminal cases were being investigated, including those stemming from KGB activities, which did not always implicate the military.[23]

A most revealing report came toward the end of these hearings from Vladimir N. Lopatin, at the time deputy chairman of the parliamentary defense committee as well as member of the defense ministry's commission headed by General Kobets. Lopatin criticized the latter for not having treated the military investigation seriously and for rejecting all of his suggestions.[24] In response to specific questions, Lopatin promised to release names of the high-ranking officers who should have been dismissed or, at the very least, retired.

Among those mentioned specifically by Lopatin was Adm. Vitalii P. Ivanov, at the time commander of the Baltic Fleet, later superintendent of a naval academy. The file on the Siberian Military District commander, Col. Gen. Boris E. P'iankov, also had been sent to Air Marshal Shaposhnikov for disciplinary action. Not having been reprimanded, P'iankov served as commander of all Russian peacekeeping forces in Tajikistan during much of 1994. Finally, Col. Gen. Viktor F. Miruk, who commanded the 6th Independent Air Defense Army, received promotion to first deputy commander-in-chief of all air defense troops.

For the record, Lopatin submitted a letter to Shaposhnikov. It ended with the following words: "Despite available information about their actions during the coup, more than 50 generals and admirals…remained at their posts or improved their positions."[25]

Several of those cited in the foregoing, who had supported the August 1991 coup, joined in the mutiny directed out of the parliament building between 21 September and 4 October 1993. Former Deputy Defense Minister Achalov was appointed "defense minister" of Russia by the Supreme Soviet, "replacing" Grachëv for a few days at least inside the surrounded White House. The former Siberian Military District commander, Makashov, became shadow "deputy minister" of defense. Grachëv, on the other hand, had earlier offered "acting president" Aleksandr V. Rutskoi the opportunity to return to active duty with his rank of major general in the air force reserve.[26] (See Table 1.2.)

The October Mutiny

Although the procurator general, security minister, and minister of internal affairs had been ordered by President Yeltsin to investigate the mutiny

TABLE 1.2
Officers Implicated or Removed after 1991 Coup

Vladislav A. Achalov (Colonel General)
  Commander, Airborne Troops; deputy defense minister
Sergei F. Akhromeev (Marshal of the Soviet Union)
  Member, general military inspectors group; military advisor to President Gorbachëv
Aleksei A. Demidov (Colonel General)
  Deputy commander (for combat training), Ground Troops
V. G. Denisov (Colonel General)
  Chief, Operations Directorate of General Staff
Viktor F. Ermakov (General of the Army)
  Chief, Main Directorate for Cadres; deputy minister of defense
Vladimir L. Govorov (General of the Army)
  Chief, USSR Civil Defense
Dmitrii T. Iazov (Marshal of the Soviet Union)
  Minister of Defense
Vitalii P. Ivanov (Admiral)
  Commander, Baltic Sea Fleet
Nikolai V. Kalinin (Colonel General)
  Commander, Moscow MD; Commandant, Moscow city during coup
Mikhail N. Khronopulo (Admiral)
  Commander, Black Sea Fleet
Konstantin A. Kochetov (General of the Army)
  First deputy minister of defense
Fëdor M. Kuz'min (Colonel General)
  Commander, Baltic States MD
Al'bert M. Makashov (Colonel General)
  Commander, Volga-Ural MD
Fëdor I. Mel'nichuk (Lieutenant General)
  First deputy commander, Baltic States MD
Viktor F. Miruk (Colonel General)
  Commander, 6th Independent Air Defense Army
Mikhail A. Moiseev (General of the Army)
  First deputy minister of defense
Vladilen P. Nekrasov (Vice Admiral)
  Chief, Political-Military Directorate for Black Sea Fleet
Viktor D. Ovcharov (Lieutenant General)
  Deputy Commander, Baltic States MD
Boris E. P'iankov (Colonel General)
  Commander, Siberian MD
Nikolai G. Sadovnikov (Colonel General)
  Chief, Main Trade Directorate of General Staff
Viktor N. Samsonov (Colonel General)
  Commander, Leningrad MD and city of Leningrad
Nikolai I. Shliaga (Colonel General)
  First deputy minister of defense; chief, Main Political-Military Directorate

Ivan M. Tret'iak (General of the Army)
  Commander, Air Defense Troops; deputy minister of defense
Valentin I. Varennikov (General of the Army)
  Commander, Ground Troops; deputy minister of defense

Sources: Foreign Broadcast Information Service, *Directory of Military Organizations and Personnel* (Washington, D.C.: U.S. Government Printing Office, November 1992), 192–95, 7, 69, 114, 142, 150; Andrei Vasilevskii and Vladimir Pribylovskii, *Kto est' kto v rossiiskoi politike* (Moscow: Panorama, December 1993), 1: 51–52.

(*miatezh,* in Russian) as early as 7 October 1993, no full disclosure of results had been released at the time of this writing. Approximately 140 key figures were incarcerated at the former KGB prison in Lefortovo—only about 10 percent of the 1,452 armed individuals who had been arrested after suppression of the violence. The chronology of events that follows has been assembled from different sources.

Within one hour after President Yeltsin had declared a state of emergency, the decision was made to use the army as well as interior and security troops in a joint operation. At 1700 on 3 October 1993, Minister of Defense Grachëv issued orders for movement toward Moscow of more than 2,000 men from elements of the 2nd Taman (motorized rifle) Guards Division, with combat vehicles (1,000 men); 4th Kantemirov (Armored) Guards Division, with tanks (400 men); 119th Airborne Regiment of the Naro-Fominsk Division (450 men); 27th Motorized Infantry Brigade (200 men); and 218th *Spetsnaz* Airborne Battalion, one company with motor transport (102 men). All rode to their staging areas during the night and received further instructions upon arrival.[27]

The 27th Brigade reached the Ostankino television station in time to witness about 500 interior and OMON *spetsnaz* troops confronting a hostile crowd approximately ten times their size as well as perhaps 100 armed men led by Col. Gen. Al'bert M. Makashov and Lt. Gen. Boris V. Tarasov. These men had served together in the past, the latter as chief political officer of the Volga-Ural Military District. Interior ministry militia had only twenty-one armored personnel carriers at its disposal. Other reinforcements arrived, and the mutineers were expelled from Ostankino without having made any broadcasts.[28]

The army had received orders from General Grachëv to protect major installations, including the defense ministry. A crowd of approximately 500 people blocked that building at about 1800. Before any troops could be dispatched, however, a group of civilians (who were, in fact,

Afghanistan war veterans) convinced the crowd to disperse. Later that evening, the collegium met at the defense ministry building, together with the president and prime minister. According to an excerpt from Yeltsin's memoirs, a final decision could not be made to storm the White House (parliament building) until early the following morning.[29]

Tanks and armored personnel carriers began moving into position at 0700 on 4 October. About the same time, the government offered those in the parliament building an opportunity to surrender. Three hours later, after another such appeal had been rejected, main battle tanks began shelling the rebel command center located on the sixteenth floor. At 1100, a ceasefire allowed women and children to be evacuated.[30]

Before noon, eighty officers from the Al'fa *spetsnaz* group (transferred from the security ministry to President Yeltsin's office the previous month) and about 100 men from a similar interior ministry *Vympel* unit had infiltrated the White House and quietly occupied the first four floors. Rather than storm the rest of the multistory building, with a substantial number of likely casualties, the commanders of these two elite units were able to convince the opposition to surrender. Following several ceasefire pauses, the former parliamentary deputies and supporters began filing out from the White House with arms raised at about 1650.[31] Until amnestied, together with the August 1991 conspirators, rank-and-file prisoners from the 1993 mutiny faced up to fifteen years in prison for organizing mass disorders.

A report on defections to the rebels from the armed forces suggests that these were infrequent. Former assault helicopter pilot and "acting president" Aleksandr V. Rutskoi had appealed to military aviators in September/October 1993 for support with air strikes; none responded. He also made several contacts with Deputy Interior Minister Boris V. Gromov as well as with air force chief Col. Gen. Pëtr S. Deinekin.[32] "Defense minister" Vladislav A. Achalov, former commander of airborne troops, sent messages to all military districts and fleet commands, requesting assistance. No one offered help or even bothered to reply. (See Table 1.3.) Rebel leaders apparently had misjudged the degree of support they enjoyed with the armed forces.

The only isolated attempts to join the mutiny appear to have been the following:[33]

- The commander of a navy combat unit stationed at Noginsk convinced seventeen sailors to defend the White House. Intercepted only 31 kilometers from Moscow by interior ministry *spetsnaz,* the officer shot himself and the enlisted men were returned to their unit.

TABLE 1.3
Key Rebels with Military Rank (1993)

Name	Position and Rank
Vladislav A. Achalov	"Defense minister"; former deputy minister (1991) and colonel general
Viktor P. Barannikov	"Security minister"; former interior minister (1991) and general of the army
Andrei F. Dunaiev	"Interior minister"; former first deputy minister (1991) and colonel general
Al'bert M. Makashov	"Deputy defense minister"; former Volga-Ural MD commander (1991) and colonel general
Aleksandr V. Rutskoi	"Acting President of Russia"; former vice-president (1991) and reserve major general in the air force
Aleksandr N. Sterligov	Chairman, Russian Assembly; former KGB major general
Boris V. Tarasov	Former Volga-Ural chief political officer (1991) and lieutenant general
Stanislav N. Terekhov	Chairman, radical nationalist Officers Union; former staff member of Lenin political academy (1991) and lieutenant colonel; dismissed from armed forces after mutiny (1993)
Vasilii P. Trushin	Replaced Dunaiev as "interior minister" (1993); former acting minister (1991) and lieutenant general

- The commander of a training company for antiair defense at Podol'sk recruited seventeen others and almost reached the White House. The entire group was arrested and the unit dissolved.
- The officer in charge of chemical warfare for the airborne assault division at Tula attempted to subvert those under his command, without success.
- Among defenders of the White House were two officers from the Humanitarian (formerly Political Indoctrination) Academy, where Lt. Col. Stanislav N. Terekhov had been employed.
- Twelve of the career military officers, who were members of parliament, refused to obey Defense Minister Grachëv's orders and remained in the White House.

This response was not what Maj. Gen. Rutskoi had expected. He completely misjudged his previous influence in the Russian officers' corps as a decorated "Hero of the Soviet Union" for service in Afghanistan.[34]

Yeltsin had wisely courted the military by promoting to flag rank in a single year about 200 instead of the usual 50 officers. Despite this largess, and raising officers' pay several times during the year, the defense ministry's collegium voted unanimously on 22 September 1993 to observe complete neutrality in the struggle between parliament and the president. Grachëv supported that sentiment.[35] However, at a meeting with President Yeltsin, held in the defense ministry during the night of 3–4 October, "a decision was made to call in individual units to impose order around the parliament building for the purpose of assisting interior ministry forces." From among the high command, only Grachëv and his chief of staff attended.[36]

A written order had to be issued by the Russian president as commander-in-chief before the generals would act. It took until 0300 on 4 October before the defense minister issued a command to move main battle tanks into position for shelling the parliament building, according to Yeltsin's memoirs. General Grachëv claims that he convinced all those attending the meeting that the assault should be delayed until daybreak.[37]

Commenting on the above, Maj. Gen. Aleksandr I. Vladimirov, former 28th Army chief of staff, stated categorically that Grachëv had *not* hesitated to back the president and supported with enthusiasm the democratic transformation of Russia.[38] General Staff functionaries at high levels, on the other hand, may want to restore the former Soviet Union, according to Vladimirov, because they "bear no direct responsibility to the people."

On 23 February 1994, the newly elected State *Duma* (lower house of parliament) voted 253 to 67 with 28 abstentions to pardon the leaders of the August 1991 coup attempt as well as those who had been arrested after the armed mutiny in September/October 1993.[39] Most of these legislators who supported an amnesty were not friends of Yeltsin.

Comparison

The two attempts to seize power espoused similar objectives: to turn back the clock and restore the old USSR system within its former geographic boundaries.[40] Gorbachëv had intended to sign a Union Treaty on 20 August 1991 that would have effectively dissolved the Soviet system. The conspirators agreed upon the coup two weeks in advance of that date, taking for granted that the armed forces would obey their orders. After all, the defense minister as well as the commander of ground troops belonged to their cabal.

Two years later, Yeltsin no longer represented a symbol of the democratic spirit in Russia. Economic and social tensions threatened to split the country. Desperate attempts by insurgents to capture the Moscow city mayor's office, military headquarters for the Commonwealth of Independent States, the ITAR-TASS news agency building, the Ostankino television station, and even the defense-ministry complex occurred spontaneously or with little planning. To have a former military district commander (General Makashov) at the head of a mob break into Ostankino only gave developments a "Keystone cops" quality during the night of 3–4 October 1993. Such reckless acts of violence probably alienated most inhabitants of Moscow.

By contrast, the first coup had been carefully planned. Although only the first of the following actions could actually be implemented on 19 August 1991, when more than 5,000 troops were brought to Moscow, documentation had been prepared for

- movement of troops into Moscow, which required the consent of both the defense minister and the city commandant;
- an assault on the parliament building, where the opposition had established its headquarters;
- arrest of legislators and political leaders, such as President Yeltsin; and
- action by elite airborne forces, the KGB Al'fa and Beta teams, and interior ministry OMON *spetsnaz* units.

Leaders of the mutiny in 1993 had no heavy equipment or regular forces, other than a few hundred men armed with light weapons. Newly appointed "defense minister" General Achalov announced from inside the White House that an infantry regiment with about 1,000 men was being formed to defend the legislature and that a special military unit was en route from Siberia. He ordered army commanders in Moscow to place their troops at his disposal. None complied. "Acting President" Rutskoi even appealed to military school cadets, also without success.

Only about forty men, led by "security minister" Vadim G. Shevtsov, from the so-called Trans-Dniester Republic in Moldova, set out for Moscow with a truckload of weapons. Shevtsov is a Russian who previously had commanded an OMON *spetsnaz* unit of the USSR interior ministry in the Latvian capital of Riga. The 14th Army's commanding officer, Lt. Gen. Aleksandr I. Lebed', later told a reporter that two local generals as well as other volunteers from Trans-Dniester had participated in defense of the White House.[41]

To support such an attempt to overthrow the government, the rebels had smuggled large quantities of arms into the parliament building prior to and after 21 September. (See Table 1.4.) These 6,000 weapons could have armed at least four times the 1,452 armed militants, as official figures show actually to have been detained. Casualties included 147 persons killed and 878 wounded, according to the deputy health minister.[42]

Two theories regarding what really happened during the 1993 mutiny are worth considering. The first suggests that insufficient armed units were available in Moscow to put down the insurrection. That is why calls from

TABLE 1.4
Weapons Brought Into the White House

Category	Before 21 Sept 93	After 21 Sept 93	Brought in by Individuals	Totals
Submachine guns	340	1,600	300	2,240
Pistols	1,679	2,000	—	3,679
Machine guns	10	18	30	58
Grenade launchers	—	12	Several	15
Sniper rifles	2	18	—	20
Portable ground-to-air missile launchers	1	—	—	1
Total				*6,013*

Sources: "Raspushchënnyi Verkhovnyi Sovet—samyi vooruzhënnyi parlament mira," *Segodnia*, no. 60 (2 October 1993): 1; press conference with Vladimir Pankratov, head of the Moscow-city main administration for internal affairs.

the Kremlin to the three "power" ministries (defense, interior, and security) remained unanswered. Grachëv then allegedly forced Yeltsin to accept certain conditions before ordering the army to enter Moscow.[43]

The other theory asserts that unidentified government authorities precipitated the assault on the mayor's office as well as the Ostankino television station. By doing so, the mutinous nature of Rutskoi and parliamentary speaker Ruslan Khasbulatov would be revealed as having been involved with a grand provocation. Yeltsin allegedly permitted armed men to leave the house of parliament unchallenged.[44] Subsequent developments would appear to support the first theory, at least in part.

The War in Chechnya

The 1994–95 events in the northern Caucasus had their origins almost three years earlier, when large quantities of weapons were stolen from Russian stockpiles. During 6 February 1992, armed men attacked the 566th Convoy Regiment of interior ministry troops stationed in Chechnya. This reportedly resulted in the theft of more than 3,000 rifles and 3 million rounds of ammunition. Two days later, an army aviation school became the object of assault and plunder of 554 automatic weapons, 494 pistols, two machine guns, 46 tons of equipment, 186 vehicles, 40 tons of gasoline, and 20 wagons loaded with food.[45] Such raids continued.

Finally on 31 May 1992 Maj. Gen. Pëtr Sokolov, who commanded the Russian motorized rifle division in Groznyi, received an ultimatum from his local counterpart to leave the republic. By early the following month, the last Russian officers departed. All weapons, equipment, and ammunition left behind had been recorded by General Sokolov. It may never be established who actually approved these gifts to Pres. Djokar M. Dudayev.[46] The defense minister at the time was Gen. Pavel S. Grachëv.

Once the Chechens had proclaimed their independence in November 1991, it should have been obvious that these huge amounts of military hardware might be used for defensive purposes against a Russian invasion. Before the decision to attack was made, Moscow began a series of covert military operations in mid-1992 under the auspices of the Foreign Counter-Intelligence Service, headed by Col. Gen. Sergei V. Stepashin.[47] These operations included assassination attempts against President Dudayev who previously had attained the rank of major general in the Soviet air force as a bomber pilot.

After four unsuccessful covert operations, the fifth and last took place on 26 November 1994 when Russian tanks and aircraft supported an abortive attempt by opposition forces to capture the capital city of Groznyi. Three days later Boris Yeltsin convened a rump session of his Security Council, at which a unanimous vote to invade Chechnya was adopted *before* any discussion took place.[48] Since a state of emergency or martial law had not been proclaimed, Yeltsin violated Articles 8 and 88 of the Russian constitution which require that both the Federation Council and the State *Duma* be informed of military actions.

Furthermore, only an attack or the threat of aggression can justify the use of armed force. Combat operations in Chechnya involved blatant violations of human rights, written into the Russian constitution (Articles 20, 21, 35, and 40) as well as into international treaties.[49] The 1949 Geneva Convention and 1977 protocols to that treaty guaranteed protection of civilians during a military conflict, especially against indiscriminate bombing, the execution of noncombatants, and destruction of hospitals and schools.

The Three-Pronged Invasion

According to information available to the General Staff in Moscow, as of June 1994, the Chechens disposed of the following armaments:[50]

T-62 and T-72 main battle tanks	40–50
BMP-1 and BMP-2 armored personnel carriers	30–40
BTR-70 and BRDM-2 transport and reconnaissance vehicles	30–35
Antitank weapons	90–100
Grenade launchers	620–630

Artillery and mortars	150–160
Grad multiple rocket launchers	20–25
122mm D-30 howitzers	30
Rifles	42,000
Machine guns	678
Large-caliber machine guns	319
Antiaircraft weapons	40

(plus bullets, shells, bombs, mines, and grenades sufficient to conduct military operations during six or seven months by 40,000 men).

Despite the availability of such information, Defense Minister Grachëv stated at a press conference on 28 November 1994 that one regiment of paratroopers could "solve the problem" within two hours. Perhaps this man, a former airborne officer, had not been briefed by his own military intelligence chief concerning the above information. The invasion, launched on 11 December 1994, with an 8-to-1 advantage in manpower, came from three directions: Russia itself, Dagestan, and Ingushetia. It has been estimated that an absolute majority of officers in the defense ministry and General Staff held a negative attitude toward the invasion.[51]

Three deputy defense ministers (Gromov, Georgii G. Kondrat'ev, and Valerii I. Mironov), who voiced their opposition to the war against Chechnya, were dismissed on 19 January 1995. Others, like 14th Army commander Lebed' and chief of airborne forces Col. Gen. Evgenii N. Podkolzin, suffered no repercussions at first. Even the deputy commanding officer of ground forces, Col. Gen. Ed'uard A. Vorob'ev, requested transfer to the reserves after refusing to lead the invasion. His case, among others, was investigated by the military prosecuting attorney, who concluded that there would be no charges against Vorob'ëv.[52]

The assault on Groznyi involved failures in planning, information gathering, tactics, and operations. Refusal to obey orders extended to lower levels and indicates dissatisfaction with the role assigned to the army. It took less than three weeks before the attack against Groznyi itself commenced on 31 December 1994, even though the troops were not ready. The 131st Motorized Rifle Brigade from Maikop in southern Russia lost almost all of its officers, 20 of its 26 tanks, and 102 of the 120 armored combat vehicles. All six of its *Tunguska* gun and missile truck complexes were destroyed. Seventy-four men, together with the operations officer, were taken prisoner.[53]

Within a week after this crushing defeat, new forces were thrown into battle (the total came to 58,000) with similar results: almost complete destruction of the 255th and 33rd Regiments from Volgograd. In eighteen days of fighting, the Russians lost about 1,000 killed and another 500 wounded.[54] By then, there were only 80,000 civilians left in Groznyi from an original population of 400,000. The rest had fled or been killed. On 19 January 1995, the Russian flag was raised over the burned-out presidential palace. At month's end, just one-third of the city's rubble had been captured by the invaders. Artillery bombardment and air attacks continued to destroy what remained standing.

Chechen fighters withdrew from the ruins of Groznyi and took up new positions in other areas of the country. They appeared resolved to continue the struggle in the mountains from which their ancestors had fought against the tsars. A puppet regime, headed by Salambek N. Khadzhiev (former Soviet petroleum minister), was being supported by Russian interior troops. The regular army and border guards were prepared to pursue native guerrillas throughout the rugged terrain possibly for years to come.

Before moving into the mountains, military authorities apparently sanctioned the destruction and massacre of civilians at the village of Samashki. An eyewitness provided a report on what took place. Russian troops had waited from January until 7 April 1995, when Chechen forces left the area. The assault came unexpectedly. Teams of young soldiers threw grenades into basements and living quarters, set fire to houses with flame throwers, and had orders "to kill everyone between fourteen and sixty-five." At least thirty children from the local school, some only in the third grade, were hanged or strangled by wire.[55]

Such atrocities probably led to the raid into the Stavropol region and seizure of a hospital at Budennovsk, about seventy miles inside of Russia proper by 100 well-disciplined Chechen fighters on 14 June 1995. Two assaults failed to free the 1,100 hostages, even though the first attempt involved *spetsnaz* group "Al'fa."[56] The following day, Prime Minister Viktor S. Chernomyrdin (President Yeltsin was at the G-7 summit in Halifax) agreed to grant safe passage for Shamil Basaev and his men back to Chechnya as well as begin peace talks at Groznyi in return for release of hostages.

In the meanwhile, the high command has undertaken an assessment of what went wrong and why. President Yeltsin announced that he personally would supervise a thorough-going reform of the armed forces. Nothing was mentioned about revising the military doctrine, which is discussed in the next chapter.

Notes

1. Dmitrii A. Volkogonov, "Zagovor Tukhachevskogo," *Triumf i tragediia: Politicheskii portret I. V. Stalina* (Moscow: Novosti, 1989), vol. 1, pt. 2, 254–79. See also listing of 180 from among 305 Jewish generals who were shot during the Great Purge in Fëdor D. Sverdlov, *Evrei-generaly Vooruzhënnykh sil SSSR* (Moscow: Moskovskaia tipografiia no. 9, 1993), 262–69.

2. Nikolai N. Iakovlev, *Zhukov* (Moscow: "Molodaia gvardiia," 1992), 446–50. See also Sergei Pavlenko, "Posledniaia okhota Marshala Pobedy," *Krasnaia zvezda*, 28 July 1994, 4.

3. Biographic sketches of these three military conspirators appear in appendix A.

4. Evgenii I. Shaposhnikov, *Vybor: zapiski glavnokomanduiushchego* (Moscow: PIK, 1993), 18–19.

5. At his trial, Iazov testified that Gorbachëv had agreed to the state of emergency on 18 August; hence, there could not have been any coup. Aleksandr Pel'ts, "Delo GKChP," *Krasnaia zvezda*, 22 January 1994, 1. The same claim is made by Valentin S. Pavlov in his book, *Gorbachëv-putch: Avgust iznutri* (Moscow: Delovoi mir/Business World, 1993), and by Anatolii I. Luk'ianov in *Perevorot mnimyi i nastoiashchii* (Voronezh: Soiuz zhurnalistov Rossii, 1993). See also Arkadii Zheludkov, "Sobiralsia li Gorbachëv vvesti voennoe polozhenie?" *Izvestiia*, 22 June 1994, 2.

6. Verkhovnyi sovet, Komissiia po rassledovaniiu prichin i obstoiatelstv gosudarstvennogo perevorota, *Stenogramma* (Moscow, 18 February 1992), 4–5. This 220-page transcript of hearings in the Russian language can be found at the Hoover Institution archives under the entry: Russia (Federation), *Verkhovnyi Sovet, Komissiia po rassledovaniiu . . .* (henceforth cited as *Stenogramma*).

7. Ibid., 52. See also "Posle putcha: Generaly ni v chëm ne vinovaty...," *Novoe vremia*, no. 10 (3 March 1992): 6–7.

8. *Stenogramma*, 71.

9. "Naznacheniia," *Krasnaia zvezda*, 4 June 1993, 1.

10. *Stenogramma*, 111–17.

11. Ibid., 120. Some thought reportedly had been given to the distribution of army food supplies among the population, according to Iazov. See Valentin G. Stepankov and Evgenii K. Lisov, *Kremlëvskii zagovor* (Moscow: Ogonëk, 1992), 167–68.

12. Lebed', commander of the 14th Army two years later, had been considered for the post of defense minister by "acting president" Aleksandr Rutskoi. See Iuliia Ul'ianova, "O svoëm 'naznachenii' v pervyi raz slyshu," *Rossiiskie vesti*, 29 September 1993, 1.

13. *Stenogramma*, 122–24.

14. Summarized in Stepankov and Lisov, *Kremlëvskii zagovor*, 160–61.

15. *Stenogramma*, 125. See the interview with Akhromeev, only four months before the coup, by Aleksandr Pumpianskii, "Armiia zashchishchaet sebia?" *Novoe vremia*, no. 15 (April 1991): 12–17, esp. 15. There exist two documents that prove Akhromeev indeed did serve as adviser to the Committee and accepted this role voluntarily, according to Leonid Radzikhovskii, "Glas vopiiushchego v pustyne," *Stolitsa*, no. 7 (July 1992): 8–10.

16. See Aleksandr I. Lebed', *Spektakl' nazyvalsia putch* (Tiraspol': Izdatel'stvo

"Lada," 1993), which suggests that this commander of an airborne division did not know the reason for his orders.

17. Note the interview with Karpukhin in "Ia poluchil prikaz arestovat' El'tsina," *Slovo Kyrgyzstana,* 5 September 1991, 2. Beta group commander Beskov is quoted by Vladimir Snegirëv, "V te trevozhnye dni," *Trud,* 13 September 1991, 1, 2.

18. For an account that begins only with 18 August, see Gen. Pavel S. Grachëv, "Desantniki protiv naroda ne poshli...," *Krasnaia zvezda,* 31 August 1991, 3.

19. Lt. Gen. Leonid G. Ivashov, *Marshal Iazov: Rokovoi avgust 91-go* (Moscow: Biblioteka zhurnala "Muzhestvo," 1992), 96–97.

20. Quoted in a summary of Yeltsin's press conference by V. Kononenko and V. Mikheev, "El'tsin obeshchaet...," *Izvestiia,* 24 August 1992, 1–2. See also the 19 August message to Ianaev from Varennikov, urging that "B. N. Yeltsin's group of adventurers be liquidated as soon as possible." Document reproduced by Stepankov and Lisov, *Kremlëvskii zagovor,* 149–50.

21. *Stenogramma,* 142–44.

22. Ibid., 156, 163–64. Two years later, this same Makashov led an armed assault on the Ostankino television station in Moscow.

23. Ibid., 184–86. See also Vadim V. Bakatin, *Izbavlenie ot KGB* (Moscow: Novosti, 1992), 20–21.

24. Shaposhnikov, almost two years later, claimed in an interview that he had warned the coup plotters against storming the White House. If they did so, as air force chief, he threatened to bomb the Kremlin. Aleksei Vorob'ëv, "On sobiral'sia bombit' Kreml'," *Rossiiskaia gazeta,* 17 June 1993, 1.

25. *Stenogramma,* 196.

26. Nikolai Burbyga, "General armii Pavel Grachëv predlagaet general-maioru Aleksandru Rutskomu stat' v stroi," *Izvestiia,* 28 September 1993, 1. See also A. I. Podberëzkin et al., comps., *Neizvestnyi Rutskoi: politicheskii portret* (Moscow: Agentstvo "Obozrevatel'," 1994), 22–40.

27. Dmitrii Kholodov, "Oktiabr' tsveta khaki: ministr oborony otvechaet na voprosy," *Moskovskii komsomolets,* 8 October 1993, 1, 4.

28. Tat'iana Akkuratova, "Uroki shturma Ostankino," *Rossiiskie vesti,* 14 October 1993, 2.

29. Boris El'tsin, *Zapiski prezidenta* (Moscow: Izdatel'stvo "Ogonëk," 1994), 386–87.

30. For an eyewitness account, see Seda Pumpianskaia, "Den', kogda proizoshël obval," *Novoe vremia,* no. 41 (5 October 1993): 7–11. A list of specific units, army and special forces, which participated is given by Mark Galeotti, "Another *Shtorm*—Forces of the 1993 Moscow Coup," *Jane's Intelligence Review* 5, no. 12 (December 1993): 539–40.

31. Sergei Mostovshchikov, "U gruppy 'Al'fa' byl prikaz streliat' na porazhenie," *Izvestiia,* 8 October 1993, 2; "Tragicheskie sobytiia v Moskve," *Krasnaia zvezda,* 5 October 1993, 1. See also Maria Dement'eva and Mikhail Leont'ev, "Vladislav Achalov: Takoe vpechatlenie...," *Segodnia,* 7 February 1995, 10.

32. Radio Moscow, ITAR-TASS, 6 October 1993, in FBIS-SOV-93-192-S of

same date, 19. See also Igor' Cherniak, "Generaly prodolzhaiut boi," *Komsomol'skaia pravda,* 8 October 1993, 2.

33. Nikolai Burbyga, "V armii predatelei schitaiut na edinitsy," *Izvestiia,* 7 October 1993, 2.

34. Nikolai Gul'binskii and Marina Shakina, *Afganistan...Kreml'...Lefortovo...* (Moscow: Izdatel'stvo "Lada-M," 1994), 293–316.

35. D. Makarov, "Armiia mezhdu vchera i zavtra," *Argumenty i fakty,* no. 44 (November 1993): 8.

36. Pavel Fel'gengauer, "Real'noe sokrashchenie armii operezhaet zaplanirovannoe," *Segodnia,* 29 December 1993, 9; interview with chief of the General Staff, Col. Gen. Mikhail P. Kolesnikov.

37. Boris Yeltsin, *The Struggle for Russia* (New York: Random House, 1994), 278–79, 287. See the interview with Grachëv by Savik Shuster, "Boris? Dopo di lui, il massacro," *L'Espresso* (Rome), 9 December 1994, 103.

38. Maj. Gen. (reserve) Aleksandr I. Vladimirov, "Ne delaite iz nas pugala," *Argumenty i fakty,* no. 44 (November 1994): 8.

39. Postanovlenie Gosudarstvennoi Dumy, "Ob ob'iavlenii politicheskoi i ekonomicheskoi amnistii," *Rossiiskaia gazeta,* 26 February 1994, 5.

40. For an analysis of both attempts (1991 and 1993) to seize power, see James H. Brusstar and Ellen Jones, *The Russian Military's Role in Politics,* McNair Paper No. 34 (Washington, D.C.: National Defense University, 1995), 13–29.

41. Svetlana Gamova, "General Lebed' vyiasniaet, kto iz Pridnestrov'ia voeval v Moskve," *Izvestiia,* 12 October 1993, 2.

42. Moscow Radio, Interfax, 5 October 1993, in FBIS-SOV-93-192-S (6 October 1993), 12, for detainees. Moscow Radio, ITAR-TASS, 26 November 1993, in FBIS-SOV-93-227 (29 November 1993), 28, for casualties.

43. Iurii Afanas'ev, "Revansh," *Novoe vremia,* no. 4 (January 1994): 11.

44. See also Alexander Rahr, "The October Revolt: Mass Unrest or Putsch?" RFE/RL *Research Report,* no. 44 (5 November 1993): 1–4.

45. Vadim Belykh and Nikolai Burbyga, "Kto vooruzhal Dzhokhara Dudaeva?" *Izvestiia,* 12 January 1995, 4.

46. Iurii Bespalov, "Oruzhie sdali po prikazu Moskvy," *Izvestiia,* 14 January 1995, 4.

47. Stephen J. Blank, "Yeltsin's Folly: The Russian Invasion of Chechnya," *Mediterranean Quarterly* 6, no. 3 (Summer 1995): 91–107.

48. Aleksandr Gromov, interview with former Minister of Justice Iurii Kh. Kalmykov, "V Sovete bezopasnosti snachala golosuiut...," *Komsomol'skaia pravda,* 20 December 1994, 2. Kalmykov, who opposed the invasion (even though he voted for it), was dismissed.

49. Igor Petrukhin, "The Chechen War Is Unlawful," *Moscow News,* no. 2 (13–19 January 1995): 3.

50. Sergei Surozhtsev, "Legendarnaia v Groznom," *Novoe vremia,* no. 2–3 (January 1995): 14.

51. Ibid., 15.

52. Viktor Litovkin, "General Vorob'ëv: chest' imeiu!" *Izvestiia,* 24 December 1994, 1, 4; Litovkin, *Izvestiia,* 18 January 1995, 2; and *Izvestiia,* 27 January 1995, 1, where the prosecutor general dropped charges.

53. Viktor Litovkin, "Rasstrel 131 brigady," *Izvestiia,* 11 January 1995, 4.

54. Boris Vinogradov, "Zdes' soldaty umiraiut ne s ulybkoi…," *Izvestiia,* 24 January 1995, 2.

55. Aminat Gunasheva, "I Just Wanted to Die without Pain," *Moscow News,* no. 21 (2–8 June 1995): 3.

56. Vitalii Strugovets, "Al'fa shla na vernuiu gibel'," *Krasnaia zvezda,* 28 June 1995, 3.

Myth No. 2

Russia Has Only Friends

> The Russian Federation...does not regard any state as its enemy.
> *Military Doctrine* (2 November 1993)

Prior to 1990, even a draft of the Soviet military doctrine could not be found in a single published document. What had been described by then-President Mikhail S. Gorbachëv as a new defensive strategy merely represented declaratory policy. This was revealed as the USSR was collapsing by Army Gen. Vladimir N. Lobov, chief of the General Staff, who used the term *maskirovka* (deception) to describe declaratory statements of the past,[1] and especially those found in the May 1987 Warsaw Treaty Organization document. All such statements, including Soviet leader Leonid I. Brezhnev's "no first strike" pledge in 1982, were of a similar nature and should not have been taken seriously.

Although the monthly journal of the USSR defense ministry published a draft of a new military doctrine in a special issue of that magazine at the end of November 1990, this document[2] became obsolete following dissolution of the Soviet Union only thirteen months later. Establishment of Russian armed forces on 7 May 1992 required a different concept to fit the altered set of circumstances.

Discussions concerning a new military doctrine for the USSR had taken place both inside the government and among outside military and civilian analysts. The basic tenets were summarized by a deputy director at the Institute of the U.S.A. and Canada in Moscow (see Chart 2.1 on "Fundamental Armed Forces Doctrinal Concepts").[3] He also presented an analysis of a new draft military doctrine, prepared at the military academy of the General Staff.

This document represented the views of the high command, since it

CHART 2.1
Fundamental Armed Forces Doctrinal Concepts

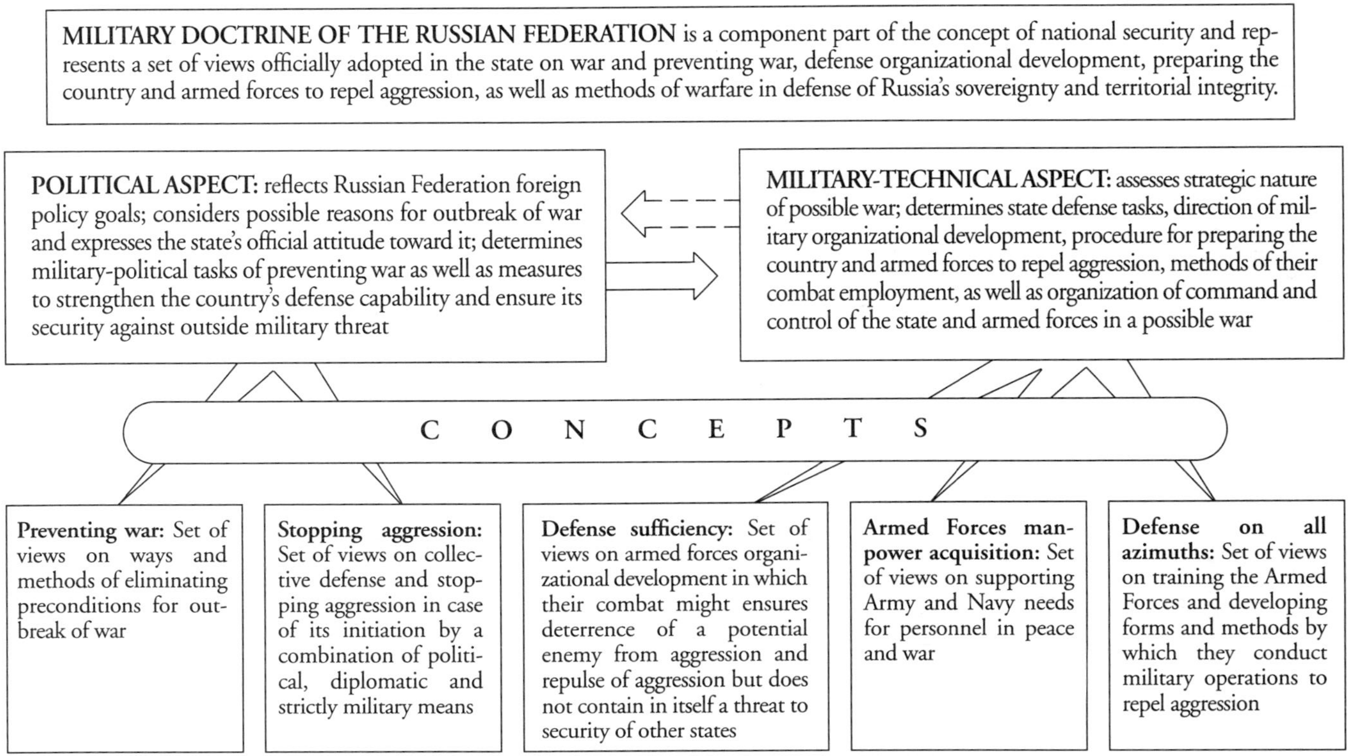

MILITARY DOCTRINE OF THE RUSSIAN FEDERATION is a component part of the concept of national security and represents a set of views officially adopted in the state on war and preventing war, defense organizational development, preparing the country and armed forces to repel aggression, as well as methods of warfare in defense of Russia's sovereignty and territorial integrity.

POLITICAL ASPECT: reflects Russian Federation foreign policy goals; considers possible reasons for outbreak of war and expresses the state's official attitude toward it; determines military-political tasks of preventing war as well as measures to strengthen the country's defense capability and ensure its security against outside military threat

MILITARY-TECHNICAL ASPECT: assesses strategic nature of possible war; determines state defense tasks, direction of military organizational development, procedure for preparing the country and armed forces to repel aggression, methods of their combat employment, as well as organization of command and control of the state and armed forces in a possible war

CONCEPTS

Preventing war: Set of views on ways and methods of eliminating preconditions for outbreak of war

Stopping aggression: Set of views on collective defense and stopping aggression in case of its initiation by a combination of political, diplomatic and strictly military means

Defense sufficiency: Set of views on armed forces organizational development in which their combat might ensures deterrence of a potential enemy from aggression and repulse of aggression but does not contain in itself a threat to security of other states

Armed Forces manpower acquisition: Set of views on supporting Army and Navy needs for personnel in peace and war

Defense on all azimuths: Set of views on training the Armed Forces and developing forms and methods by which they conduct military operations to repel aggression

Source: *Voennaia mysl'* (May 1992), special issue, 14.

appeared in the defense ministry's official monthly journal in May 1992. The brief seven-page statement is prefaced with several questions that were to be answered by those preparing the final version:[4]

- Is war considered appropriate as a means for implementing policy?
- Does a military threat exist?
- What are the objectives and missions of the armed forces during wartime?
- What preparations should be made for and which methods should be used in a possible war?
- What kind of armed forces will be needed to conduct a successful war?

The political fundamentals of this abbreviated draft doctrine specified that Russia "will not be the first to use nuclear or any other weapons of mass destruction." In other words, a "no first strike" pledge had been suggested. This was superseded by the exact opposite statement in the final version signed by President Yeltsin toward the end of the following year.

Equally notable, a new possible cause of war would involve "a violation of the rights of Russian citizens…in former USSR republics," according to the May 1992 draft.[5] This refers to the 25 million ethnic Russians living in the post-Soviet, newly sovereign countries in the Commonwealth of Independent States (SNG).

Furthermore, the same document stated that "Russia considers it legal to employ armed forces to reestablish and maintain peace" among SNG members, when all other efforts toward conflict resolution have proven unsuccessful. Special peacemaking forces are preferable for such purposes, and Russia would take part in establishing them. Joint operations of this type have already taken place in Tajikistan, where three other Central Asian republics promised or actually contributed about one battalion each under SNG (meaning Russian) command.

In the section on preparations to defeat an attack, the proposed military doctrine specified the following:[6]

- Permanent readiness forces (SPG—*Sily postoiannoi gotovnosti*) in theaters of military operations to repel local aggression.
- Rapid reaction forces (SBR—*Sily bystrogo reagirovaniia*), capable of being dropped into any region during the shortest time…to repel medium-sized aggression, in concert with SPG above.
- Strategic reserves (SR—*Strategicheskie rezervy*), mobilized during the threat period and in the course of war, to conduct large-scale military operations.

Finally, the last section of the May 1992 draft document dealt with administration of defense matters. A Security Council, headed by the supreme commander-in-chief (president of Russia), and consisting mainly of civilians, was recommended as the principal politico-military organ to direct defense, military policy, development of the armed forces, economic support, and social protection of servicemen. Ultimately, this same group ended up writing the final version approved in November 1993. (See Chart 2.2.)

The military was hardly of one mind, however. Other views within the establishment were expressed when the defense ministry organized a conference during 27–30 May 1992 at the military academy of the General Staff. Opening remarks were made by Army Gen. Pavel S. Grachëv, the newly appointed defense minister. Grachëv promoted the new concept of defense embodied by the draft doctrine and presented himself as solidly anchored in the reform camp. He was followed by Col. Gen. Igor' N. Rodionov, chief of the military academy since 2 November 1989. In his presentation,[7] the latter speaker did not attempt to camouflage his strong feelings against downsizing, which would affect morale adversely. These thoughts were undoubtedly shared by many of the other former Soviet army officers present.

Rodionov asserted that the Baltic States must recognize Russia's right of access to their seaports, on commercial terms, and that membership in military blocs (such as NATO) would be precluded for these three countries. He also stressed the unconditional rights of ethnic Russians living in Lithuania, Latvia, and Estonia. Rodionov next branded as erroneous the contention that all former enemies had become friends. "A military threat to Russia's national interests exists and will hardly disappear in the near term." Wars that may have to be fought, asserted Rodionov, would be caused by the following:[8]

> The global nuclear danger, which will continue so long as states have such weapons.
> Major aggression, with the use of conventional weapons.
> Local military conflicts, both near the borders of Russia and those of other SNG members.
> Internal destabilization from ethnic and religious differences or civil war.

Regarding the future organization of Russia's armed forces, Rodionov suggested a capability of waging three wars simultaneously as desirable. He argued that western, southern, and eastern military concentrations of troops should be staffed and equipped to accomplish strategic missions independently, if necessary. No cognizance was taken of financial costs or changed world conditions.

The final version of the new military doctrine reflects the positions of

CHART 2.2
Principles of Armed Forces Force Generation

C O N C E P T S

Preventing war	Stopping aggression	Defense sufficiency	Armed forces manpower acquisition	Defense on all azimuths

P R I N C I P L E S

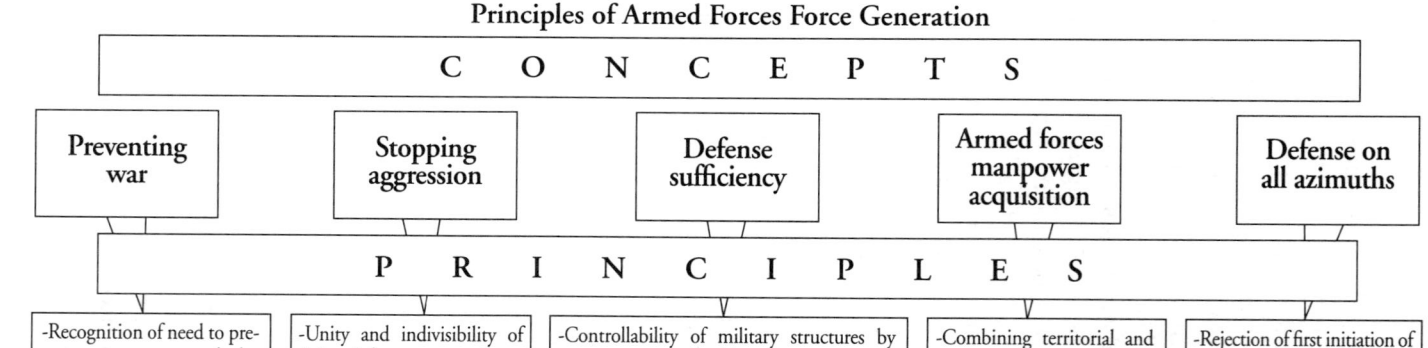

-Recognition of need to preserve peace as a priority goal; -Unacceptability of war as a means of achieving political and other goals; -Nonintervention in other states' internal affairs; -Recognition of inviolability of existing borders; -Openness of military activities; -Cooperation of states and their alliances to settle interstate contradictions and strengthen stability within the framework of regional and global security structures.	-Unity and indivisibility of joint defense; an attack on one CIS member is viewed as an attack on all; -Russia's proportional participation in maintaining and upgrading CIS defense capability and armed forces combat effectiveness; -Nonuse of armed forces to accomplish internal political missions; -Decisiveness of operations to repel aggression from outside by military means; -Readiness for political dialogue to stop military operations and restore a just, firm peace on mutually acceptable terms.	-Controllability of military structures by supreme state authorities; -Conformity of organizational structure, order of battle, and numerical strength of forces to the State Security Concept; -Multiethnic regular army; -Centralization of direction of state defense; -One-man command on legal basis; -Necessary sufficiency for defense; -Maintaining military-strategic balance with consistent lowering of the nuclear potential right down to its total destruction; -Capability for adequate buildup of armed forces might with an increased military threat; -Maintaining combat and mobilization readiness adequate to existing situation; -Consideration for national and historical traditions, rules of international law, and world experience of military organizational development.	-Combining territorial and extraterritorial principles of manpower acquisition; -Force elements of member states; -Combination of universal military obligation with voluntary acceptance for military service under contract; -Social justice and equality of all citizens before the law; -Assurance of a sufficient level of armed forces professionalization.	-Rejection of first initiation of military operations against any state; -Rejection of first use of nuclear weapons; -Readiness to repel aggression on a local scale on any axis (defense on all azimuths); -Timely concentration of efforts on threatened axes; -Combination of defensive and offensive forms and methods of military operations to defeat enemy groupings which have penetrated; -Training troops in what is necessary in war.

Source: *Voennaia mysl'* (May 1992), special issue, 15.

both sides as well as political developments during the intervening months. In mid-1993 then-secretary (apparatus director) of the Security Council Iurii V. Skokov gave an interview about the working group that had spent considerable time developing a military doctrine acceptable to civilian officials as well as to the armed forces high command. The group had come to the conclusion that the document must comprise an aggregate of officially accepted views on the formulation, application, and utilization of military force to guarantee security and defense of vitally important national interests. It should also take into consideration the 1992 law on defense as applied to the triad of individual, society, and state.[9]

Such a military doctrine would consist of several parts, including: (1) a clear definition of the concept, "military force"; (2) an outline for organization of this military force, including its structure; (3) a framework for supplying this military force with equipment, weapons, and ammunition; and (4) a proposed section that would center on civil rights, guaranteeing social protection for the individual enlisted person. Skokov noted that opposition existed to this last recommendation.

It is noteworthy that the means to accomplish what the doctrine would promise were not discussed at this time. For example, the changing nature of the defense budget and the safeguards to guarantee soldiers' civil rights apparently were not taken into consideration. A mechanism to implement and defend the latter apparently was not even considered.

The chairman of the Supreme Soviet (parliament) committee for defense and security, Sergei V. Stepashin, criticized so comprehensive a plan as being too optimistic. He wrote in August 1993 that "without political stability, a healthy economy and a combat-ready army, a premature concept of national security would remain an illusion."[10] He probably had come to the conclusion that the national legislature would never agree to the new military doctrine as worded at that time.

Events during the fall of 1993 broke this apparent stalemate, because the Supreme Soviet was forcibly dissolved on 21 September. As a result, a final version of the new military doctrine could be prepared within a period of only four weeks. The document was signed on 2 November 1993 by President Yeltsin and not submitted to the new State *Duma* or parliament that emerged after the 12 December 1993 national elections. Hence, it does not have the force of law.

Defense Minister Grachëv held a news conference on 3 November and revealed that the doctrine prohibits use of nuclear weapons against nonnuclear countries, parties to the 1968 nonproliferation treaty, unless they are allied with a nuclear-armed country. "As for the states that have nuclear weapons, the doctrine says nothing," according to Grachëv. He also stated that the twenty-three-page document would not be published.[11] Grachëv further explained that this military doctrine would be considered applicable during the transitional period until the year 2000 or until domestic and international security had been established.

The final document envisages territorial-ethnic conflicts as the main threat to Russia, in contrast to the 1990 and 1992 drafts. Some 180 potential flashpoints throughout the former USSR had been identified by the Geography Institute at the Russian Academy of Sciences.[12] For this reason, the immediate military focus would remain on development of lighter rapid-deployment forces rather than on heavily armed troops.

The doctrine reportedly went a long way toward fulfilling the defense ministry's proposals. The General Staff's draft represented the basis for final deliberations.[13] The new military doctrine allows deployment of troops beyond Russia's borders and their stationing at bases in "foreign" countries. No limitation on the future size of the military establishment is mentioned in the document. The former parliament's law on defense of 24 September 1992 had specified a final ceiling equal to one percent of the total population, that is, approximately 1.5 million at the turn of the century.[14] However, a newly elected legislature could lift that restriction by amending the law on defense.

At the above-cited press conference, General Grachëv stated that "Russia reserves the right to use all means at its disposal to repulse aggression and crush aggressors." The new military doctrine also asserts that Russia's military mission is primarily defensive, which is not the position of the officers' corps. In addition, the document provides for military intervention during a domestic crisis "to protect the constitutional system," according to Grachëv.[15] Although regular army units had been sent into Tbilisi, Georgia (April 1989), then Baku, Azerbaijan (January 1990), and the Baltic States (January 1991), upon oral orders of USSR President Gorbachëv, nothing about crushing unarmed civilian demonstrations had ever appeared in a document before.

The New Doctrine

Despite the fact that the high command planned to keep the military doctrine secret, Yeltsin must have overruled Grachëv, because the same summarized version appeared simultaneously in two Moscow newspapers and a day later in a third.[16] Apparently just one and one-half pages were not released to the press, although it remains unknown what exactly was withheld. One of the deputy prime ministers, Sergei M. Shakhrai, explained on the *Slavianka* radio program of the defense ministry that preliminary versions of both the Russian constitution and the military doctrine had been drawn up by the same individuals. Hence, there could be no contradiction between the two documents.[17]

The new constitution, reportedly approved by 58.4 percent of those who voted in a referendum on 12 December 1993, is accepted as the basic law of the land. Article 59 specifies three points relevant to the military:

- Defense of the fatherland is the duty and obligation of every citizen.
- A citizen performs military service as required by federal law.
- Alternative civilian service may be chosen by conscientious objectors.

Article 83, subparagraph "l" provides the president of Russia with authority to "appoint and remove the high command of the armed forces." Article 87 names the president as supreme commander-in-chief of the armed forces, and it gives him the power to introduce martial law in case of an attack or threat of aggression.[18]

The military doctrine itself proclaims that the "Russian Federation…does not regard any state as its enemy." The military obviously does not believe this. Russia undertakes not to use strategic (nuclear) arms against any country that is a party to the 1968 Treaty on Non-Proliferation of Nuclear Weapons, except in cases of an armed attack against Russia, its territory, armed forces, other troops, or its allies by any state that is linked through alliance with another state that does possess nuclear weapons. The other exception involves joint actions by such a state with another state possessing nuclear weapons in carrying out or in support of an invasion or armed attack upon the Russian Federation, its territory, armed forces, other troops, or allies.[19]

The doctrine establishes various levels of conflict and *potential sources of military danger,* which are identified as follows:

Territorial claims by other states
Local wars, especially in the vicinity of Russian borders
The use of nuclear or other weapons of mass destruction
Proliferation of such weapons
Undermining of strategic stability through violation of arms control
   agreements and arms build-ups by other countries
Attempts to destabilize the Russian Federation
Suppression of rights, freedoms, and legitimate interests of Russian
   citizens in foreign countries

Attacks on Russian military installations located on the territory of foreign states

Expansion of military alliances to the detriment of Russia's military security, and

International terrorism.

In short, while no actual enemies of Russia are named, the list of potential ones against whom the doctrine may apply is probably too long to enumerate.

The above-mentioned dangers could be transformed into *immediate threats* by

A military buildup of forces on the Russian border which would disrupt the correlation of forces

Attacks on installations along Russia's borders or those of its allies

Training of armed groups in other states with the intention of transferring them to the territory of Russia or of its allies

Actions by other states which hinder the functioning of Russian strategic nuclear forces, military command and control and, above all, [activities in] space

Introduction of foreign troops into neighboring states by the United Nations or a regional organization, without Russian agreement.

Under "Basic Principles in the Field of Security," the new military doctrine lists maintenance of stability in regions bordering on the Russian Federation, in neighboring countries, and the world as a whole. The first two of these refer specifically to former Soviet republics in the "near abroad" and to neighboring states in East-Central Europe that had once belonged to the now-defunct Warsaw Treaty Organization (WTO).

The implicit reference to East-Central European countries as falling within the Russian sphere of influence probably represents the most important reason for these former WTO states to pursue admission into NATO. The potential conflict between national interests vis-à-vis loyalty to the Western alliance may have caused Russia to qualify its willingness to implement Partnership for Peace objectives (see chapter 9, "National Security Concept Is Known").

The armed forces received a deadline to withdraw completely all units stationed outside Russia through the end of 1996. During the period from then until the year 2000, priority tasks are listed as the following:

- Establish mobile forces, capable of being redeployed within a short period of time, to conduct operations in any region where a threat

to the security of the Russian Federation may arise.
- Interests and security of other members of the SNG may require that [Russian] troops and resources be deployed outside the territory of Russia.
- Forces of the Russian Federation may be stationed outside its territory together with troops of other states or as Russian formations at separate bases.

A section of the doctrine is devoted to military-technical support for the Russian armed forces, including development and implementation of a long-term (between ten and fifteen years) weapons and military hardware program as well as of state defense procurement financed by the government. Apart from cooperation with defense industries of other SNG countries, the Russian military-industrial complex must ensure the following:

- Basic and applied research, advanced scientific and technological developments, experimental testing, and a production base.
- Development of the defense industry's potential and its infrastructure.
- Establishment of capabilities to produce and repair weapons as well as other equipment, in order to maintain a full cycle of production.
- A package of measures for mobilization readiness and maintenance of state mobilization reserves.

Discussion

One should always distinguish between the sociopolitical and the military-technical parts of the doctrine. The former include declaratory statements for Western consumption, such as the current one that Russia has no enemies. The latter should be studied carefully, because the military seems to have obtained exactly what Colonel General Rodionov had demanded in May 1992: repudiation of the "no first use" of nuclear weapons, a definition of domestic missions for the army, and a statement concerning Russian responsibilities in the "near abroad."

Several commentaries appeared throughout Russia after a detailed summary of the military doctrine had been released to the press. First Deputy Defense Minister Andrei A. Kokoshin explained the use of Russian troops outside of their own country as already having been defined and approved by the SNG collective security treaty. These decisions allegedly stem "more from the most insistent requirements—even requests—by the leaders of various states, former republics of the Soviet Union, than from our own wishes."[20]

That may certainly be true of Tajikistan. On the other hand, the government of Moldova never invited Russia to continue stationing its 14th Army (redesignated a "limited contingent" in June 1995) on the territory of the breakaway Trans-Dniester province.

An important caveat has been raised in connection with the lack of constitutional oversight. The military doctrine remains unmentioned in the new constitution and will not be submitted to the State *Duma* (lower house of parliament) for approval, although the president announced that he would show it to the Federation Council (upper house). Defense Minister Grachëv may have been only half-facetious when he reportedly raised the possibility of "correcting parliament," if the latter attempted to correct the doctrine.[21]

Nuclear aspects of the new doctrine were addressed by the director of the Center for Geopolitical and Military Forecasting, a civilian think-tank in Moscow. Aleksei G. Arbatov expressed concern at the reversal from a "no first use" policy announced in 1982 which, henceforth, envisages the use

"Unbreakable union of free republics": Russian army belt holding together the Commonwealth of Independent States. *(Poster in Moscow; photograph courtesy of Prof. Roman Laba, Naval Postgraduate School, Monterey, California.)*

of such weapons against other nuclear powers, their allies, and states that have not signed the nuclear nonproliferation treaty. This scholar destroys the official argument that nuclear weapons are regarded as a political deterrent against aggression and not primarily as a means of conducting warfare. "A first strike strategy can not serve to restrain nuclear aggression, since it presupposes the unleashing of a nuclear war," writes Arbatov.[22]

The same defense analyst went on to suggest that a conflict with any of the former Soviet republics or East-Central European states could be handled with conventional weapons. The same is true regarding Turkey, Iraq, Iran, or Afghanistan, should intervention occur from any of those directions. Only one power remains, namely China, whose nuclear forces over the next ten or fifteen years will still remain inferior to those of Russia. Chinese conventional superiority may indeed develop, however, if Moscow continues to supply Beijing "with the latest Su-27 and MiG-31 fighters, the outstanding S-300 [anti-missile systems]; technology for [production of] medium-range bombers and aircraft carriers [*sic*]; communications and missile-targeting systems; etc."[23]

Reportedly, a struggle between "doves" and "hawks" at the defense ministry resulted in the latter winning out regarding the new military doctrine. That supposedly explains why the preemptive-strike concept appeared in the document and why it makes no mention of a possible civilian head of the defense ministry. Several high-ranking reserve officers were interviewed about other parts of the doctrine. Maj. Gen. Gennadii Dmitriev is reported to have warned that if any East-Central European countries join NATO, they will be targeted by Russia's nuclear weapons.[24] These intercontinental ballistic missiles had been pointed in the direction of Western Europe, Japan, and the United States. However, in mid-January 1994, Russian agreements with American and British heads of government provided for mutual detargeting by 30 May of that year.[25]

Lt. Gen. Dmitrii Evsienko suggested in one of the articles already mentioned that the reference to exporting military power really camouflages full-scale aggression. Dmitriev, also cited above, concluded that the more Russian bases are established in former Soviet republics, the sooner one can anticipate restoration of a single economic and military union. Examples can be found in Russia's relations with Georgia, Armenia, and Tajikistan; Georgia's civil wars in Abkhazia and South Ossetia; the Azeri-Armenian conflict over Nagorno-Karabakh; and defense of Tajik borders from infiltration by Tajiks who had fled to Afghanistan. Russia, thus, has had a number of opportunities to project its military power. (See chapter 6, "Peacemaking Equals Peacekeeping.")

Provisions in the military doctrine for army assistance to interior ministry troops and other forces sanction retroactively what had occurred during 3–4 October 1993. Paradoxically, should a third consecutive attempt to seize power take place, the military high command may turn against the president of Russia. Another observer, Col. Dmitrii Kharitonov, concluded that the army already controls the situation in the country,[26] although he did not offer any evidence to support that assertion. See Table 2.1 for dramatic growth of interior and other armed formations that are not part of the army.

The only active-duty officer quoted in the same article is employed by the General Staff. Col. Konstantin Ivanov observed that "never as yet have the power ministers [defense, interior, security, and counter-intelligence] drawn so closely to the helm of political power" and, if President Yeltsin ever becomes objectionable to them, "illusions about his power functions will be dispelled at once."[27] It should not necessarily be assumed that these remarks had been cleared in advance by the General Staff.

A Western analysis of Russia's military doctrine, by the director of the Conflict Studies Research Center at the Royal Military Academy in Sandhurst, concludes that the document reflects a growing trend to ignore the sovereignties of former Soviet republics in the "near abroad" as well as an assumption of military spending in accordance with need and not the state of the economy.[28] Both of these conclusions should be

TABLE 2.1
Armed Forces' Comparison
(in millions)

Categories	1991 USSR	1991 USA	1995 Russia	1995 USA
Population	287.0	253.0	148.0	260.0
Regular Troops[a]	4.0	2.1	1.9	1.6
Other Troops	0.6	—	1.9	—
Organized Reserves	—	1.2	—	1.0
Inactive Reserves	9.0	—	6.0	—

Sources: Estimates from Russia's defense ministry and U.S. Department of Defense; cited by Vladimir Lopatin, "Manevry generalov," *Izvestiia*, 27 April 1995, 4.

[a] See Table 3.6 for estimates of actual manning levels in six components of Russia's armed forces.

taken seriously by decisionmakers in the United States. They seem to point toward a desire to reestablish in some sense the old Soviet empire and redirect the course of Western-style economic reform. Clearly, if successful, either attempt would have disastrous consequences both for the Russian military and for society.

Security Council

The organization that prepared the final version of the new military doctrine is primarily composed of civilians, although many of its secretariat staff appear to have been drawn from military ranks. The Security Council (*Sovet bezopasnosti*) had been directed by Iurii V. Skokov until 10 May 1993. It included initially the ministers of foreign affairs, defense, interior, justice, nationalities and regions, and civil defense, as well as directors of foreign intelligence and federal counterintelligence.[29] Subsequently the prime minister, commander of border troops, and chairmen of the Federation Council and of the State *Duma* were added to that body.

Skokov was succeeded by Marshal of Aviation Shaposhnikov as secretary of the Security Council. The latter assumed this position on 16 June 1993, only after receiving approval from the presidents of Kazakhstan, Ukraine, Armenia, and other SNG member states for whom he had worked as SNG commander-in-chief.[30]

Two weeks later, President Yeltsin appointed Lt. Gen. Valerii L. Manilov as a deputy secretary of the Security Council and Col. Vladimir Markin to head its administrative secretariat. Manilov's military service in the USSR had involved positions as deputy commanding officer for political affairs, that is, communist party "watchdog" over indoctrination of troops. He never commanded an army unit at any level.

At the beginning of August 1993, a new series of regulations outlined a much larger staff with functional responsibilities within the Security Council. Whereas under Skokov there had been only ten individuals working on the secretariat, the number increased to 150 under Shaposhnikov, many of them drawn from the military. The air marshal justified this expansion by the need to draw on experts who would prepare a national security concept. The secretary of the Security Council in effect became ex-officio chief of staff to the president, and three new administrations covered expanded functions. Interdepartmental commissions were also established to deal with the military-industrial complex, the environment, and crime—all headed by presidential advisors.[31]

Only a few days after this reorganization, on 10 August Shaposhnikov resigned. He complained that he had been unable to meet with President Yeltsin since 30 June and was never given authority to convene the Security Council without the latter's presence. Shaposhnikov also claimed to have been frustrated by the breakdown of cooperation between the legislative and executive branches of government in working out a national security concept.[32]

Even without a new secretary, the Security Council continued the process of restructuring. Yeltsin approved establishment of an Interdepartmental Commission for Scientific and Technical Questions in the Defense Industries. It would develop priorities for military-technical policy that apparently duplicated the oversight function the government's defense industry commission had already been providing.[33] Several more commissions were formed toward the end of October.

Designation of a new secretary for the Security Council was announced on 18 September 1993, when Oleg I. Lobov took the position. He had served in the Sverdlovsk *oblast'* communist party apparatus with Yeltsin during the 1960s and 1970s, and his loyalty was considered unquestionable. Until this new appointment, Lobov had been first deputy prime minister in charge of economic affairs. He also maintained access to the president, meeting weekly with him for 30 or 40 minutes on the most pressing problems.

Six weeks later, Lobov gave an interview in which he revealed that during that time ten interdepartmental commissions had been formed, twice their original number. The purpose was "to ensure that strategic problems [be] considered and resolved in the sphere of military, economic, environmental, and information security, health protection, the fight against crime and corruption, and public security."[34] He has recruited a large number of lawyers. (See Chart 2.3.)

On 6 January 1994, an assistant (*pomoshchnik*) for national security affairs was appointed by President Yeltsin. He is Iurii M. Baturin, who had served as presidential aide for legal questions over the preceding seven months. In the course of an interview, he explained that his responsibility would be to provide oversight vis-à-vis the power ministries (defense, interior, security, and counterintelligence).[35] Baturin, a lawyer who had considerable influence on the wording of the Russian constitution, is not invited to Security Council meetings unless requested to give a special report.

On 12 March 1994, Yeltsin issued an executive order that established a commission on senior military and special ranks. It will report directly to the president. Baturin was appointed chairman,[36] which means that he should be spending more time with the armed forces' high command as well as with leading officials in the other power ministries who hold military rank.

In an interview with a German magazine correspondent, Baturin explained the value of a security advisor as being able to predict what kind of developments would result in danger for Russia.[37] He stated that decisions were made by the Security Council. If the latter had any doubts, then Yeltsin decided the issue. It is not clear, however, that Baturin's office or individual council members receive the most accurate information, as suggested in chapter 1 regarding Chechnya.

Where bureaucratic matters are concerned, Baturin insisted that while the presidential administration had become too large, which hindered effective operations, the five-member team of principal advisors remained manageable.[38] He also contended that the new office of security advisor meant the beginning of civilian control over interior, defense, and security ministries, as well as the counterintelligence service. Presumably, these "power" agencies as a bloc are better represented than any other constituencies.

The Security Council gave Yeltsin its unanimous support on 28 November 1994, thirteen days before the initial 40,000 interior ministry and army troops invaded the Republic of Chechnya.[39] Carpet bombing transformed much of the defenseless capital city of Groznyi into rubble, with tens of thousands of former inhabitants fleeing into the mountains as refugees. Yeltsin's televised address on 27 December 1994 offered Chechen-elected president Maj. Gen. Djokar M. Dudayev the opportunity to resign. Direct negotiations were never offered, however. Dudayev's chosen replacement would be a 53-year-old former oil executive, Salambek Khadzhiev, a quisling waiting in Moscow. About 58,000 armed Russian police and military units were assigned responsibility for disarming Dudayev's army of 3,000 men.

All of these activities were based on a secret directive, "Measures for Reestablishment of Constitutional Legality and Enforcement of Laws on the Territory of the Chechen Republic," signed by President Yeltsin on 30 November 1994. Taking effect the next morning, this document lists the names of twelve individuals (see Table 2.2), assigned to implement the presidential decree. It represented the basis for an appeal by the State *Duma* to the Constitutional Court which was requested to declare the war in Chechnya illegal.

The document gave General Grachëv plenipotentiary authority to coordinate federal agencies and troop movements. He reported directly to Yeltsin. The secret directive assigned the following basic tasks to the group of twelve:[40]

- Disarm and liquidate armed formations in Chechnya.
- Free prisoners and citizens held by force.

CHART 2.3
Security Council Apparatus

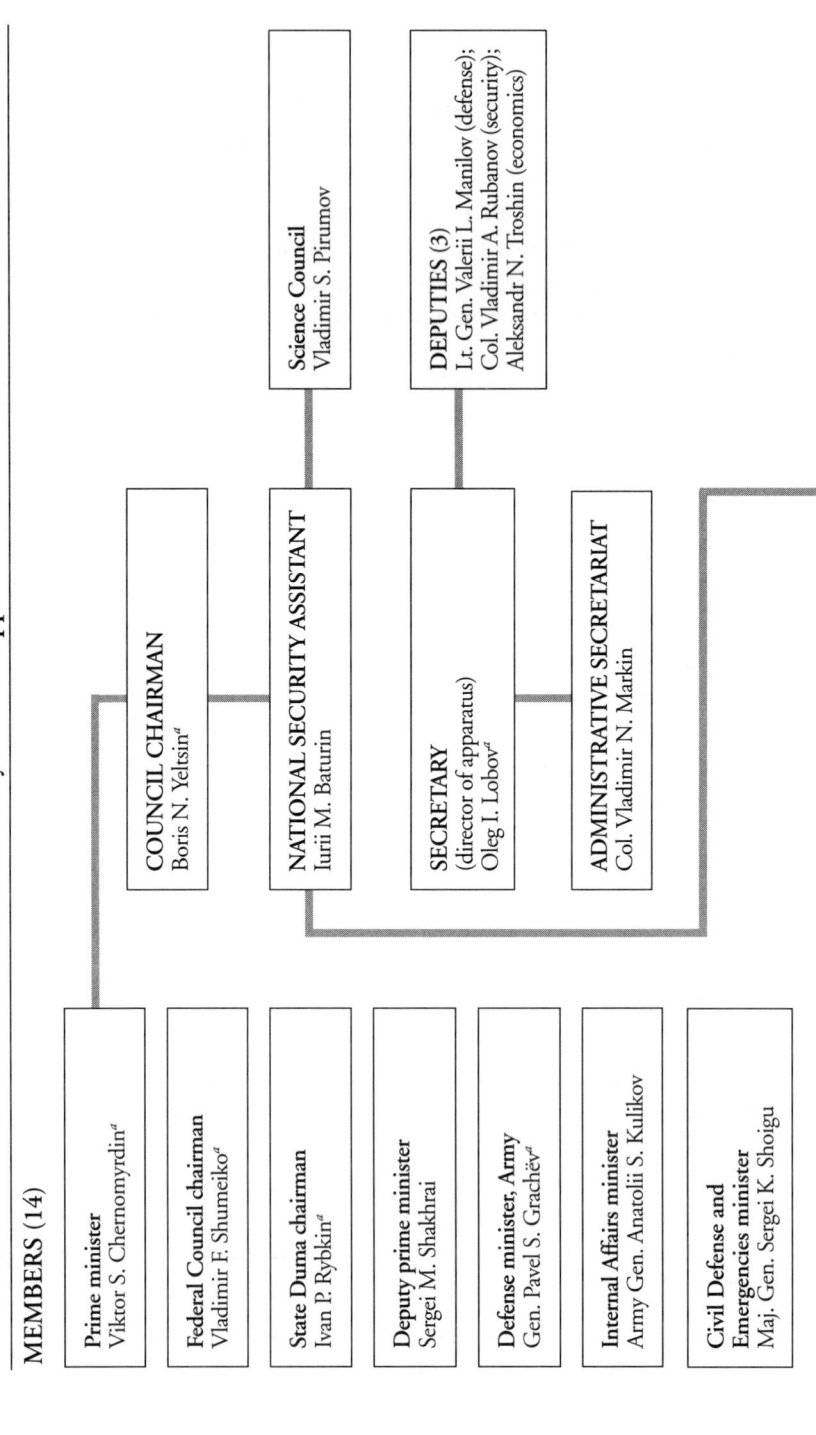

COUNCIL CHAIRMAN
Boris N. Yeltsin[a]

NATIONAL SECURITY ASSISTANT
Iurii M. Baturin

Science Council
Vladimir S. Pirumov

DEPUTIES (3)
Lt. Gen. Valerii L. Manilow (defense);
Col. Vladimir A. Rubanov (security);
Aleksandr N. Troshin (economics)

SECRETARY
(director of apparatus)
Oleg I. Lobov[a]

ADMINISTRATIVE SECRETARIAT
Col. Vladimir N. Markin

MEMBERS (14)

Prime minister
Viktor S. Chernomyrdin[a]

Federal Council chairman
Vladimir F. Shumeiko[a]

State Duma chairman
Ivan P. Rybkin[a]

Deputy prime minister
Sergei M. Shakhrai

Defense minister, Army
Gen. Pavel S. Grachëv[a]

Internal Affairs minister
Army Gen. Anatolii S. Kulikov

Civil Defense and Emergencies minister
Maj. Gen. Sergei K. Shoigu

INTERDEPARTMENTAL COMMISSIONS (10)

Foreign Affairs minister
Andrei V. Kozyrev

Federal Secretary director
Army Gen. Mikhail V. Barsukov

Border Troops CO
Col. Gen. Aleksandr I. Nikolaev

Foreign Intelligence director
Evgenii M. Primakov

Finance minister
Vladimir G. Panskov

Justice minister
Valentin A. Kovalëv

Atomic Energy minister
Viktor N. Mikhailov

FOREIGN POLICY
Anatolii L. Adamishin

DEFENSE SECURITY
Andrei A. Kokoshin

INTERREGIONAL AFFAIRS
Sergei M. Shakhrai

ECONOMIC SECURITY
Andrei V. Zverev

SCIENTIFIC AND TECHNICAL QUESTIONS IN THE DEFENSE INDUSTRIES
Mikhail D. Malei

ENVIRONMENTAL SECURITY
Aleksei V. Iablokov

PUBLIC SECURITY, CRIME AND CORRUPTION
Valentin A. Kovalëv

INFORMATION SECURITY
Arkadii Zheludkov

PUBLIC HEALTH
Aleksandr Opatov

SENIOR MILITARY AND SPECIAL RANKS
Iurii M. Baturin

Sources: ITAR-TASS, "Peresmotren sostav soveta bezopasnosti Rossii," *Izvestiia*, 22 October 1993, p. 1; INTERFAX, "Obnovlen Sovet bezopasnosti," *Izvestiia*, 2 February 1994, p. 1; Aleksandr Shal'nev, "Glavnee generalov," *Izvestiia*, 8 June 1994, p. 4 (interview with Baturin); Lyudmila Telen, "The Security Council," *Moscow News*, no. 23 (10–16 June 1994), p. 2; Valerii L. Manilov, "Soviet bezopasnosti . . . ," *Krasnaia zvezda*, 29 October 1994, p. 4; Iurii M. Baturin, "S korablia ne begu," *Izvestiia*, 6 January 1995; "Ukaz ob utverzhdenii Kovalëva V. A. chlenom Soveta Bezopasnosti . . . ," *Rossiiskaia gazeta*, 26 April 1995, p. 3; and Roman Ukolov, "V mesto trekh komissii . . . ," *Segodnia*, 15 June 1995, p. 2.

Note: Kulikov and Mikhailov were appointed on 7 July 1995, while Barsukov was appointed on 24 July 1995. Kulikov and Barsukov were promoted to the rank of army general on 9 November 1995.

[a] Permanent member of the Security Council.

TABLE 2.2
Group to Implement Decree of 30 November 1994

Name	Position
Pavel S. Grachëv (head)	Minister of Defense
Nikolai D. Egorov[a]	Minister of Nationality and Regional Affairs
Viktor F. Erin[a]	Minister of Internal Affairs
Anatolii S. Kruglov	Chairman, State Customs Committee
Anatolii S. Kulikov	Deputy Minister of Internal Affairs
Valentin N. Panichev	Deputy Prosecutor General
Boris N. Pastukhov	Deputy Minister of Foreign Affairs
Aleksandr V. Starovoitov	Director-General, Federal Communications and Information Service
Sergei V. Stepashin[a]	Director, Counter Intelligence Service
Pëtr P. Shirshov	Chairman, Security and Defense Committee of Federation Council
Sergei N. Iushenkov	Chairman, Defense Committee of State *Duma*

Source: "Ukaz Prezidenta Rossiiskoi Federatsii," *Novoe vremia*, no. 14 (April 1995), 7.

[a] Dismissed by Yeltsin on 30 June 1995.

- Establish control over entry into and exit from Chechnya, together with all movement within that country.
- Secure a new administration of Chechnya.
- Create conditions to restore legality.
- Conduct negotiations to end armed conflict.

These objectives were inadequately implemented and, hence, the removal of three high-ranking cabinet members from their positions as well as from the group. Since publication of the names, it has become common knowledge who bears responsibility for the conduct of the war, handling of the hostage crisis at Budennovsk, and of the subsequent peace talks at Groznyi.

The adventure in Chechnya triggered a breakdown of discipline in the Russian armed forces. About ten generals were dismissed, transferred to reserve status, or retired because of insubordination. This will be discussed in the next chapter, which also covers a military reform that had become still-born.

Notes

1. Major General Egorov, interview with Lobov, "Politika, doktrina i strategiia…," *Krasnaia zvezda,* 23 October 1991, 2. The author is grateful to Mary C. FitzGerald for calling his attention to this source.

2. "O voennoi doktrine SSSR (proekt)," *Voennaia mysl',* spetsial'nyi vypusk,

"Victory" with flower and headless soldier, a poster in Moscow at the time of the Chechnya ceasefire. *(Photograph courtesy of Prof. Roman Laba, Naval Postgraduate School, Monterey, California.)*

24–28; signed to press on 30 November 1990. For a solid and perceptive background, see Harriet Fast Scott and William F. Scott, *Soviet Military Doctrine: Continuity, Formulation, and Dissemination* (Boulder, Colo.: Westview Press, 1988), 315 pp.

3. Sergei M. Rogov, "The Debates on the Future Military Doctrine of Russia," *CNA Occasional Paper* (Alexandria, Va.: Center for Naval Analyses, December 1992), 13–28. See also Col. David M. Glantz, "Soviet and Commonwealth Military Doctrine in Revolutionary Times" (Fort Leavenworth, Kans.: Foreign Military Studies Office, March 1992), esp. 24–30.

4. "Osnovy voennoi doktriny Rossii (proekt)," *Voennaia mysl'* (May 1992), spetsial'nyi vypusk, 2–9; signed to press on 19 May 1992; preface on 2.

5. Ibid., 3–4.

6. Ibid., 8–9. For an excellent comparison between the 1990 and 1992 drafts, see Mary C. FitzGerald, "Russia's New Military Doctrine," *Naval War College Review* 46, no. 2 (Spring 1993): 24–44.

7. Col. Gen. Igor' N. Rodionov, "Nekotorye podkhody k razrabotke voennoi doktriny Rossii," *Voennaia mysl'* (July 1992), spetsial'nyi vypusk, 6–13; see also Jacob W. Kipp, "Russian Military Doctrine and Military Technical Policy," *Comparative Strategy* 13, no. 1 (January-March 1994): 25–41.

8. Rodionov, "Nekotorye podkhody k razrabotke voennoi doktriny Rossii," 10–11.

9. Iurii V. Skokov, "My povernuli reformu ne v tu storonu...," *Pravda*, 22 July 1993, 1. For his biographic sketch, see Anastasiia Zhukovskaia, "9 krugov Iuriia Skokova," *Ogonëk*, no. 18 (May 1995): 20.

10. Sergei V. Stepashin, "Strane nuzhna kontseptsiia bezopasnosti," *Krasnaia zvezda*, 11 August 1993, 2.

11. Grachëv over Moscow Radio, 3 November 1993, in FBIS-SOV-93-212 (4 November 1993), 34–36.

12. Ol'ga Glezer et al., "Samaia politicheskaia karta byvshego SSSR," *Moskovskie novosti*, no. 13 (29 March 1992): 9.

13. See interview with Security Council Secretary, Oleg I. Lobov, "O voennoi doktrine Rossii...," *Izvestiia*, 4 November 1993, 1.

14. Chapter 4, paragraph 13, "Zakon Rossiiskoi Federatsii ob oborone," *Armiia*, no. 20 (October 1992): 3–10, at 7.

15. Grachëv over Moscow Radio, 3 November 1993.

16. "Osnovnye polozheniia voennoi doktriny Rossiiskoi Federatsii," *Izvestiia*, 18 November 1993, 1, 4; *Rossiiskie vesti*, 18 November 1993, 1–2; *Krasnaia zvezda*, 19 November 1993, 3–4.

17. Moscow Mayak Radio network, 8 December 1993, in FBIS-SOV-93-235 (9 December 1993), 40. See also James F. Holcomb and Michael M. Boll, "Russia's New Doctrine: Two Views" (Carlisle Barracks, Pa.: U.S. Army War College, 20 July 1994), 37 pp.

18. "Konstitutsiia Rossiiskoi Federatsii," *Izvestiia*, 28 December 1993, 4 and 5.

19. "Osnovnye polozheniia voennoi doktriny." These identical summaries do not identify articles by number.

20. Interview by Kim Gerasimov with Kokoshin over Moscow Ostankino Television, 23 November 1993, in FBIS-SOV-93-225 (24 November 1993), 40.

21. Quoted by Aleksandr Mnatsakanian, "Vnov' ot taigi do britanskikh morei...," *Rossiia,* no. 48 (24–30 November 1993): 1.

22. Aleksei G. Arbatov, "Iadernaia dilemma voennoi doktriny," *Nezavisimaia gazeta,* 3 December 1993, 3.

23. Ibid.

24. Alexander Zhilin, "Military Policy and a War of Politicians," *Moscow News,* no. 48 (26 November 1993): 3.

25. "Rasporiazhenie Prezidenta RF - no. 129-pn," *Rossiiskaia gazeta,* 18 March 1994, 2 (signed on 11 March 1994).

26. Zhilin, "Military Policy and a War of Politicians."

27. Ibid.

28. Charles J. Dick, "The Military Doctrine of the Russian Federation," *Occasional Brief 25* (25 November 1993), 21 pp.

29. Vasilii Fatigarov, "Ob'iavlen novyi sostav Soveta bezopasnosti," *Krasnaia zvezda,* 2 February 1994, 1. Article 83 of the constitution only states that the president "forms and leads the Security Council of the Russian Federation."

30. Viktor Litovkin, "Marshal Shaposhnikov vykhodit na rabotu v grazhdanskoi odezhde," *Izvestiia,* 17 June 1993, 2.

31. Mikhail Lashch, "Sovet bezopasnosti pomenial politicheskoe litso," *Kommersant-Daily,* 10 August 1993, 17–18. Dmitrii Trenin, "Bez 'kukhonnogo kabineta'?" *Novoe vremia,* no. 7 (February 1995): 10, compares the Security Council with the CPSU political bureau.

32. Viktor Litovkin, "Marshal Shaposhnikov tozhe ukhodit v otstavku," *Izvestiia,* 12 August 1993, 1–2.

33. This new commission is headed by Mikhail D. Malei, who had previously resigned as advisor to President Yeltsin on matters of the military-industrial complex. See his interview with Andrei Vaganov, "Ia samyi osvedomlënnyi chelovek v Rossii," *Nezavisimaia gazeta,* 2 October 1993, 1–2.

34. Vasilii Kononenko, "V voennoi doktrine Rossii net obiazatel'stva ne primeniat' iadernogo oruzhiia pervoi," *Izvestiia,* 4 November 1993, 1.

35. Andrei Poleshchuk, "Menia uchili ne boiatsia trudnykh zadach," *Nezavisimaia gazeta,* 11 January 1994, 1, 3.

36. Moscow Radio, ITAR-TASS, 12 March 1994, in FBIS-SOV-94-049 (14 March 1994), 25. On the secretive nature of Security Council proceedings, see Tamara Zamiatina, "Dostich' balansa interesov...," *Rossiiskie vesti,* 7 March 1995, 2.

37. "Wir bleiben Grossmacht," *Der Spiegel* 48, no. 6 (7 February 1994): 123–25, at 124; interview conducted by unidentified correspondent. On the inner workings, see also Roman Podoprigora's interview with Lobov, "Soviet bezopasnosti...," *Komsomol'skaia pravda,* 17 February 1995, 5.

38. Yeltsin finally ordered his administrative staff cut by one-third, although part of it will be transferred to other government agencies. Yelena Pestrukhina, "Administration Cuts Announced," *Moscow News,* no. 45 (11–17 November 1994): 2.

39. Those who hesitated and voiced reservations, *after* the vote had been taken to invade Chechnya, included Justice Minister Iurii Kh. Kalmykov (who was asked to resign soon thereafter), SVR Director Evgenii M. Primakov, and Foreign Minister Andrei V. Kozyrev. See Valerii Vyzhutovich, "Mezhdu SB i politbiuro…," *Izvestiia*, 16 February 1995, 4. Decisions are made by consensus, according to Deputy Secretary Manilov, who had been interviewed for this article.

40. "Skandal: Tainoe stanovitsia iavnym," *Novoe vremia*, no. 14 (April 1995): 7.

Myth No. 3
Reform Remains on Course

> Can the son of a colonel become a general? No, replies
> the old soldier, because generals have their own sons.
> *Krasnaia zvezda* (1 February 1995)

The eleven-member Commonwealth of Independent States (SNG) came into being during December 1991, as the USSR began to disintegrate. SNG members agreed that Russia would control strategic nuclear weapons. Conventional armed forces, on the other hand, would remain under the SNG for a five-year period.[1] After several former Soviet republics subsequently announced the intention to organize their own armies, President Yeltsin issued a decree entitled "Establishment of Russian Federation Armed Forces" on 7 May 1992 and called upon other SNG member states to sign a collective security treaty.[2]

The Services

Even before this presidential decree Russia had claimed all troops and facilities outside the borders of the former USSR, that is, those located in the Baltic States, East-Central Europe, Mongolia, and Cuba. On 18 May, Yeltsin promoted Pavel S. Grachëv to general of the army and appointed him defense minister of Russia. During his first interview, the latter stated that the new military establishment would be based on the old Soviet armed forces.[3]

A separate law on defense, signed by Yeltsin after approval of parliament, appeared to represent the high point of cooperation between legislative and executive branches of government.[4] Grachëv left a hospital, where he had been visiting his dying father, to appear before the 8th

Congress of People's Deputies in December 1992. He pledged personally to refrain from political involvement and that the army "would not...turn into a force threatening the country with a dictatorship."[5] These words represented a commitment broken less than a year later, during the 3–4 October 1993 military assault on the parliament building.

In the meantime, appointments to the high command were completed by mid-1993. No longer did commanders of type-forces hold the rank of deputy minister. Several of the new deputies had experience with airborne assault forces, and an even larger number had served one or more tours of duty in Afghanistan.[6] Such generals also are linked by a common bond as "soldier-internationalists" with others who had been stationed at various times in Angola, Nicaragua, Ethiopia, and elsewhere overseas. Russian military advisors and specialists reportedly served in almost fifty countries throughout the world.[7]

Among the five traditional services (see Chart 3.1 for organizational structure), preeminence continues to be accorded the Strategic Missile Forces. RVSN or *Raketnye voiska strategicheskogo naznacheniia* have been commanded since August 1992 by Col. Gen. Igor' D. Sergeev. Operational control over nuclear weapons remains in the hands of the Russian president, who is supreme commander-in-chief of the armed forces. The defense minister and chief of the General Staff also maintain sets of launch codes. Presumably all three would act in concert to activate the missiles. Large numbers of ICBMs had been located in silos throughout Belarus, Kazakhstan, and Ukraine, apart from Russia.

Control over ICBMs, SLBMs, and strategic bombers has always been in the hands of Russians. At one time, the "button" or launch codes also were held by the SNG commander-in-chief, who lost this prerogative when he changed positions to become secretary of the Security Council for Russia. The keys to the black briefcase were then transferred to Defense Minister Grachëv and later also to the chief of the General Staff.[8] The fiction of an SNG military organization became apparent when Air Marshal Shaposhnikov was not replaced as commander-in-chief, the position being abolished shortly thereafter.

Command posts for strategic weapons continue to be protected in deep underground shelters. Yet an additional such battle station reportedly is being built in the Ural Mountains area near Ufa. An improved intercontinental ballistic missile, the *Topol* M-2, will replace the mobile SS-25, which has a single warhead. Compared with other services that suffer from being undermanned, the RVSN has been able to report that almost all of its billets are filled although they claim to receive only 5 to 6 percent of the defense budget.[9]

Ground Troops (SV—*Sukhoputnye voiska*), numerically the largest military branch, have been commanded since August 1992 by Col. Gen. Vladimir M. Semënov. In the future, this service will be divided into corps and brigades rather than armies and divisions. Today, some of the ground troops are being used for peacemaking missions within the borders of the Russian Federation and in the "near abroad" or former Soviet republics. Token units also remain subordinate to UN command, like the two battalions in former Yugoslavia.

SV consists of motorized rifle, armored, airborne, tactical rocket or artillery, and air defense formations. Airborne troops may become the largest part of these ground forces, especially in view of plans for lighter immediate-reaction and rapid-deployment units. They have six divisions, four brigades, and four regiments at an 85 percent manning level and total 90,000 men. Thirteen paratroop battalions fought to take Groznyi during January–February 1995. Manning of other ground force units had dropped to 40 percent at this time, and they performed poorly in Chechnya.[10]

The Air Forces (VVS—*Voenno-vozdushnye sily*), under the command of Col. Gen. Pëtr S. Deinekin since October 1992, include strategic (long-range), tactical, and transport elements. Frontal or tactical aviation is being reorganized to provide air support for the new mobile forces. Aircraft stationed in Ukraine were claimed by that government after independence. They initially included the latest MiG-29 and Su-27 fighters, as well as long-range Tu-160 "Blackjack" and Tu-95MS heavy bombers.

Russia does not have sufficient airlift capability and will be forced to augment its Il-76 and An-124 military transport aircraft in order to meet future requirements for rapid-deployment forces. The medium An-70 will carry twenty tons of freight and the new Il-96M airbus a total of 380 troops. Russian design bureaus are developing a "super fighter for the twenty-first century, the Su-27IB." R&D work is also concentrating on a fourth-generation Su-34 tactical bomber, with a range of about 2,500 miles (and considerably more after in-flight refueling).[11]

Troops for Air Defense (PVO—*Voiska protivo-vozdushnoi oborony*) are second in strategic importance, even though at first they appeared to have lost many early warning sites and air bases located throughout former Soviet republics. However, bilateral agreements have restored access to most of these facilities. PVO have been commanded by Col. Gen. Viktor A. Prudnikov since August 1992. The Moscow air defense district is still the most heavily fortified, with some thirty regiments of S-300V surface-to-air missiles, similar to the U.S. Patriot weapons system.[12]

CHART 3.1
Structure of the Russian Armed Forces

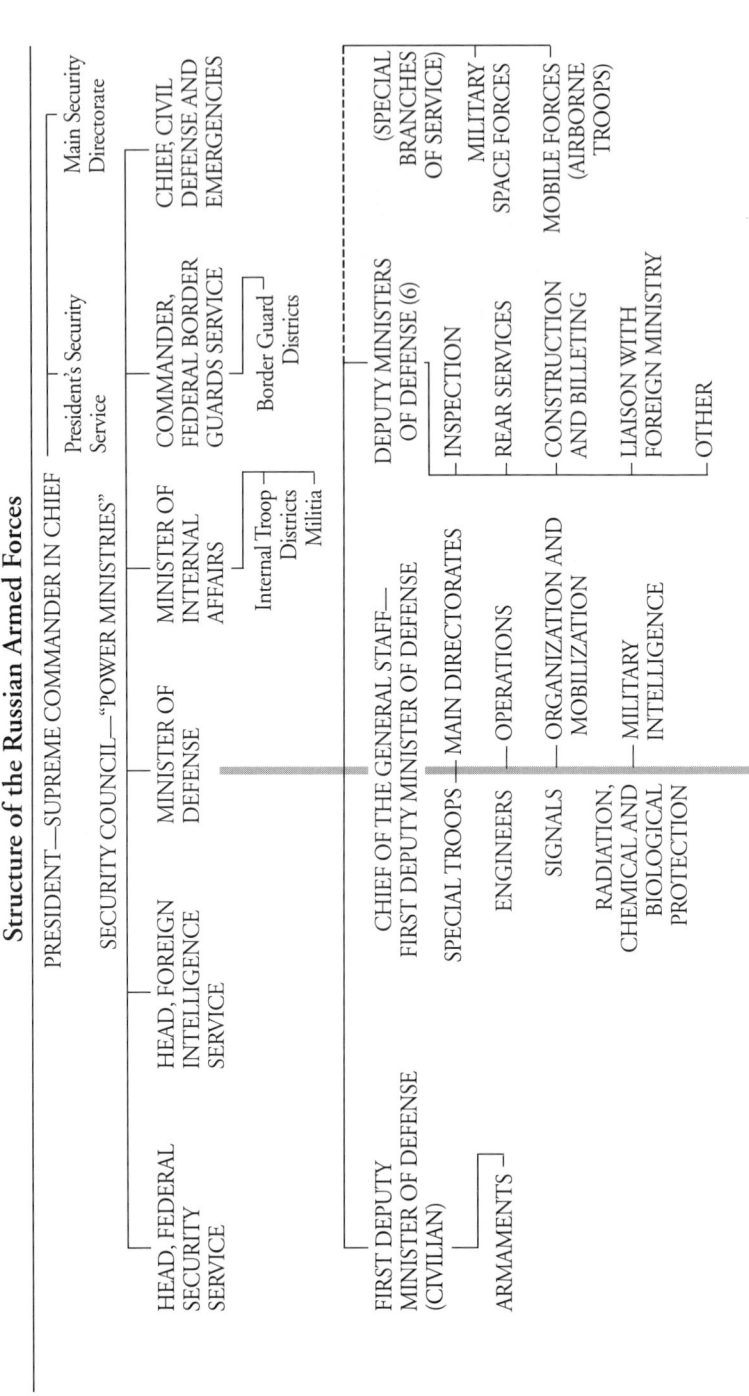

PRESIDENT—SUPREME COMMANDER IN CHIEF

SECURITY COUNCIL—"POWER MINISTRIES"

- HEAD, FEDERAL SECURITY SERVICE
- HEAD, FOREIGN INTELLIGENCE SERVICE
- MINISTER OF DEFENSE
- MINISTER OF INTERNAL AFFAIRS
  - Internal Troop Districts
  - Militia
- President's Security Service
- COMMANDER, FEDERAL BORDER GUARDS SERVICE
  - Border Guard Districts
- CHIEF, CIVIL DEFENSE AND EMERGENCIES
- Main Security Directorate

FIRST DEPUTY MINISTER OF DEFENSE (CIVILIAN)
- ARMAMENTS

CHIEF OF THE GENERAL STAFF—FIRST DEPUTY MINISTER OF DEFENSE
- MAIN DIRECTORATES
  - OPERATIONS
  - ORGANIZATION AND MOBILIZATION
  - MILITARY INTELLIGENCE
- SPECIAL TROOPS
  - ENGINEERS
  - SIGNALS
  - RADIATION, CHEMICAL AND BIOLOGICAL PROTECTION

DEPUTY MINISTERS OF DEFENSE (6)
- INSPECTION
- REAR SERVICES
- CONSTRUCTION AND BILLETING
- LIAISON WITH FOREIGN MINISTRY
- OTHER

(SPECIAL BRANCHES OF SERVICE)
- MILITARY SPACE FORCES
- MOBILE FORCES (AIRBORNE TROOPS)

SERVICES OF THE ARMED FORCES

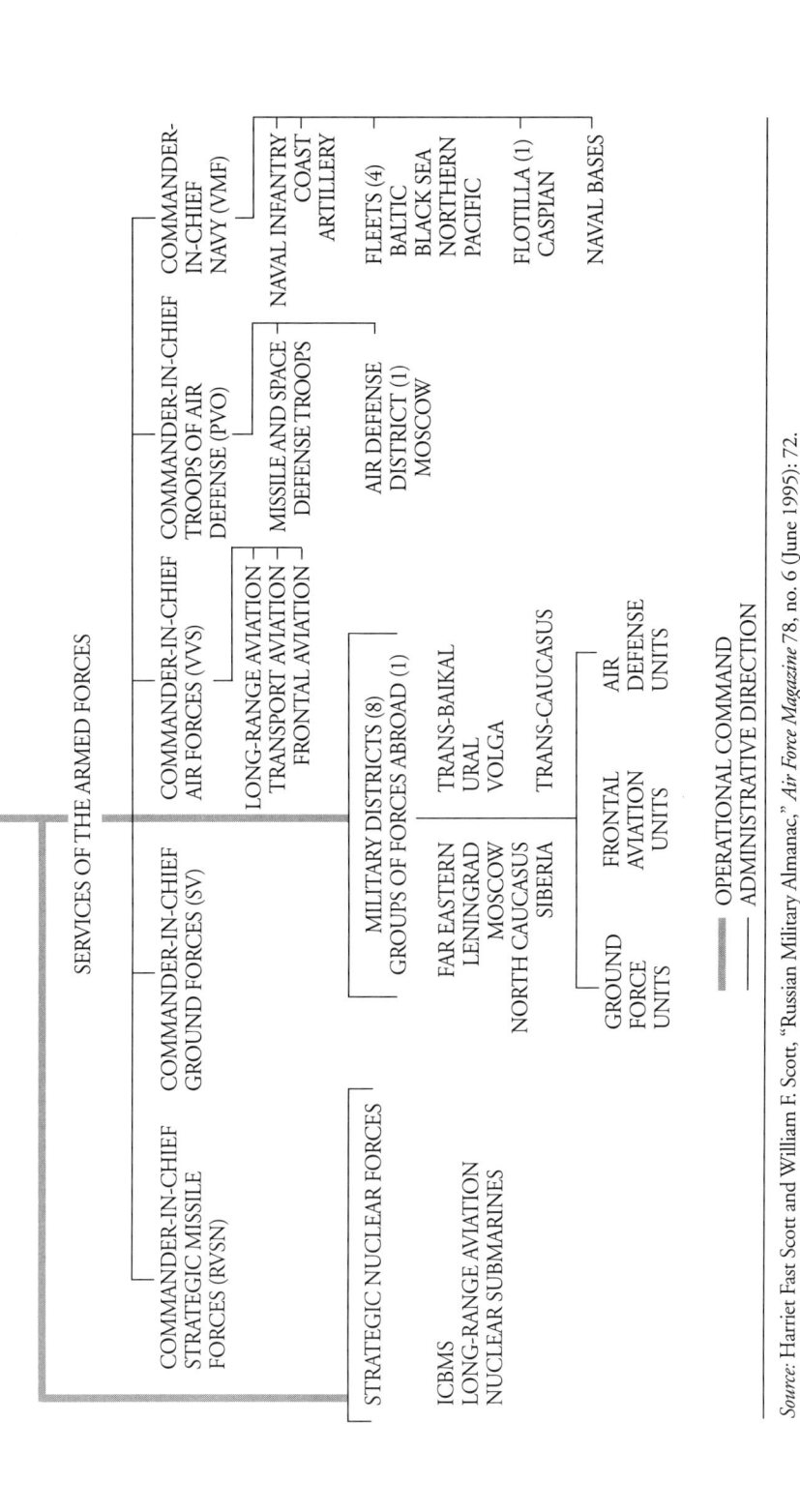

```
COMMANDER-IN-CHIEF        COMMANDER-IN-CHIEF    COMMANDER-IN-CHIEF    COMMANDER-IN-CHIEF        COMMANDER-
STRATEGIC MISSILE         GROUND FORCES (SV)    AIR FORCES (VVS)      TROOPS OF AIR             IN-CHIEF
FORCES (RVSN)                                                         DEFENSE (PVO)             NAVY (VMF)
```

COMMANDER-IN-CHIEF STRATEGIC MISSILE FORCES (RVSN)
- STRATEGIC NUCLEAR FORCES
  - ICBMS
  - LONG-RANGE AVIATION
  - NUCLEAR SUBMARINES

COMMANDER-IN-CHIEF GROUND FORCES (SV)
- MILITARY DISTRICTS (8)
- GROUPS OF FORCES ABROAD (1)
  - FAR EASTERN
  - LENINGRAD
  - MOSCOW
  - NORTH CAUCASUS
  - SIBERIA
  - TRANS-BAIKAL
  - URAL
  - VOLGA
  - TRANS-CAUCASUS
- GROUND FORCE UNITS
- FRONTAL AVIATION UNITS
- AIR DEFENSE UNITS

COMMANDER-IN-CHIEF AIR FORCES (VVS)
- LONG-RANGE AVIATION
- TRANSPORT AVIATION
- FRONTAL AVIATION

COMMANDER-IN-CHIEF TROOPS OF AIR DEFENSE (PVO)
- MISSILE AND SPACE DEFENSE TROOPS
- AIR DEFENSE DISTRICT (1) MOSCOW

COMMANDER-IN-CHIEF NAVY (VMF)
- NAVAL INFANTRY
- COAST ARTILLERY
- FLEETS (4)
  - BALTIC
  - BLACK SEA
  - NORTHERN
  - PACIFIC
- FLOTILLA (1) CASPIAN
- NAVAL BASES

━━━ OPERATIONAL COMMAND
─── ADMINISTRATIVE DIRECTION

Source: Harriet Fast Scott and William F. Scott, "Russian Military Almanac," *Air Force Magazine* 78, no. 6 (June 1995): 72.

Air defense claims to have 92 percent of authorized officer and 85 percent of enlisted billets filled. PVO disposes of fighter interceptors, radar, and surface-to-air missiles. It has a separate branch for rockets and space, comprising (1) missile, space, and air-attack early warning units; and (2) direct missile and space defense that includes a space control system. The Central Command Post is located tens of meters underground, near Moscow. Defense Minister Grachëv announced over Radio Mayak on 19 August 1994 that PVO would lose its status as one of the five independent military services.

The Navy (VMF—*Voenno-morskoi flot*) has been under the command of Adm. Feliks N. Gromov since August 1992. It sustained several setbacks during forced reorganization, with loss of ports and shipbuilding

TABLE 3.1
Fleets and Flotillas

Designation	Headquarters	Responsibilities	Commander	Appointed
Baltic Fleet	St. Petersburg	Baltic and Central Atlantic	Adm. V. G. Egorov	Sept. 1991
Northern Fleet	Murmansk	Northern Arctic Ocean	Adm. O. A. Erofeev	March 1992
Pacific Fleet	Vladivostok	Pacific and Indian Oceans	Adm. I. N. Khmel'nov	May 1994
Black Sea Fleet	Sevastopol	Black Sea, Mediterranean, Central Atlantic, N.E. Indian Oceans	V. Adm. E. D. Baltin	Dec. 1992
Amur River Flotilla	operational subordination to Far East MD, Khabarovsk			
Kamchatka Flotilla	operational subordination to Pacific Fleet, Vladivostok		R. Adm. V. T. Kharnikov	August 1993
Caspian Sea Flotilla			V. Adm. B. N. Zinin	1991
White Sea Flotilla			Adm. N. P. Parmokhov	Oct. 1991

Source: Joint Publications Research Service, *Directory of Russian Military Organizations and Personnel* (Washington, D.C., 5 April 1995), 95–137.

facilities along the Black Sea littorals of Ukraine and Georgia. The same kind of withdrawal has taken place from the Baltic Sea coastal areas of Lithuania, Latvia, and Estonia. Many ships have been transferred to the port of Baltiisk in Kaliningrad *oblast'* or to the Northern Fleet in the Kola Peninsula area. (See Table 3.1.)

The VMF is reported to have a large number of warships moored and rusting at various naval bases in the Pacific, Black Sea, Arctic, and Baltic. A total of 127 nuclear-powered submarines had been phased out by 1995, although fuel cores were removed from only one-third of them. Another 154 have nowhere to unload their spent fuel.[13] None of the active duty units can boast a full personnel complement. However, a new SLBM and a multipurpose attack submarine are being readied for production. A total of seventy warships were 90–95 percent completed by early 1995, including the "world's most powerful missile cruiser named *Pëtr Velikii*" (Peter the Great). The navy's 25 percent of total strategic nuclear military power will increase to 45 percent in the future, and two overseas naval bases are maintained at Cienfuegos in Cuba and Cam Ranh Bay in Vietnam. With Russian personnel reduced to one-fourth of the 1980 strength already by mid-1994, the latter agreement will expire in 2004.[14]

The VMF also includes naval infantry as components of all fleets. The Pacific has a marine division, whereas the other three fleets (Northern, Baltic, and Black Sea) have one brigade each. According to coastal troop (*beregovye voiska*) commander Col. Gen. Ivan S. Skuratov, their combat training has been cut to a minimum. Catastrophic underfunding allegedly is causing delays with repair of old and construction of new landing craft.

In addition to the above services, the interior and security ministries traditionally include substantial numbers of troops. The ministry of interior OMON detachments are part of some 300,000 militarized police who maintain public order and exercise riot control. Border troops also serve outside Russia proper, for example, in Central Asia and the Trans-Caucasus. They number 250,000 on paper and organizationally had belonged to the security (former KGB) ministry. In view of the latter's division into a Foreign Intelligence Service and a Federal Security Service (130,000 troops), border guards were subordinated on 30 December 1993 directly to the president of Russia and renamed the Federal Border Service.[15]

Almost one-half of all heavy armaments were situated outside the Russian republic at the time the USSR fell apart. (See Table 3.2.) In addition, fewer than half of the military personnel west of the Ural Mountains

TABLE 3.2
Estimated Deployment of Military Equipment and Personnel (1992)

Country	Tanks		ACVs[a]		Artillery		Helicopters		Aircraft		Personnel
Armenia	258	(220)	641	(220)	357	(285)	7	(50)	0	(100)	20,000
Azerbaijan	391	(220)	1,285	(220)	463	(285)	24	(50)	124	(100)	66,000
Georgia	850	(220)	1,054	(220)	363	(285)	48	(50)	245	(100)	30,000
Central Asia[b]	4,000		10,000		3,200		170		220		150,000
Estonia	184		201		29		10		153		⎫
Latvia	138		100		81		23		183		⎬ 170,000
Lithuania	184		1,591		253		0		46		⎭
Belarus	5,100		5,000	(2,600)	2,500	(1,615)	84	(80)	650	(260)	170,000
Moldova	135	(210)	102	(210)	243	(250)	0	(50)	0	(50)	100,000
Ukraine	6,404	(4,080)	6,394	(5,050)	3,052	(4,040)	285	(330)	2,431	(1,090)	
Russia (European)	21,500	(6,400)	33,500	(11,450)	15,500	(6,415)	1,215	(890)	2,750	(3,450)	2,000,000
Outside former USSR	5,081	(4,050)	9,167	(5,050)	4,228	(4,040)	432	(330)	2,029	(1,090)	240,000
Total	*44,245*		*69,135*		*30,269*		*2,298*		*8,831*		*2,946,000*

Sources: Academician E. Pozdniakov, "Rossiia v novom mire," *Armiia*, no. 22 (1993): 40; Sergei M. Rogov, ed., "Russian Defense Policy," *CNA Occasional Paper* (Alexandria, Va.: Center for Naval Analyses, 1993), Table 3, p. 6 for Tashkent allocations in parentheses.

[a] Armored Combat Vehicles
[b] Includes Kazakhstan, Kyrgyzstan, Tajikistan, Turkmenistan, and Uzbekistan

The aircraft carrier *Admiral Kuznetsov* en route to Murmansk. *(U.S. Naval Institute photo collection)*

held assignments inside Russia, the remainder being stationed throughout other former Soviet republics or in foreign countries. Several of the newly independent states began to nationalize armed forces personnel and armaments located on their sovereign territories. If all had done so, the allocation portrayed in Table 3.3 would have resulted. Approximately one-half of all

TABLE 3.3
Russian Forces Previously Deployed Abroad

Country	Servicemen	Operational Tactical Missile Launchers	Tactical Missile Launchers	Tanks	Armored Fighting Vehicles	Artillery	Airplanes	Helicopters
Germany	351,274	62	90	7,900	7,537	4,414	940	785
Poland	44,088	12	8	685	963	449	300	134
Czechoslovakia	75,000	12	18	1,412	2,563	1,240	127	189
Hungary	60,500	12	24	1,292	1,679	789	270	160
Mongolia	75,500		22	1,816	2,531	1,416	192	123
Cuba	560							
Moldavia					54	26	8	
Lithuania	35,054							
Latvia	50,357			682	2,504	1,265	588	141
Estonia	30,724							
Trans-Caucasus	36,000			44	474	60	297	312
Total: *(figures as published)*	*759,057*	*98*	*162*	*13,831*	*18,305*	*9,668*	*2,722*	*1,844*

Source: Viktor Litovkin, "Kak mnogo nas tam bylo," *Izvestiia*, 31 August 1994, 1.

conventional weapons systems, except for combat aircraft, would have been retained by Russia. However, those republics that had refused to join the Commonwealth of Independent States (e.g., Lithuania, Latvia, and Estonia), received nothing.

An agreement signed by SNG heads of state at Tashkent on 15 May 1992 allocated equipment in accordance with the Conventional Armed Forces in Europe treaty, which had been signed in November 1990 at Paris. Soon thereafter, Russia assumed command over all former Soviet armed forces with the exception of those in Belarus and Ukraine, both of which had more substantial troop concentrations than any of the other non-Russian republics.[16] Since their populations were Slavic, Yeltsin probably hoped to keep them in a tight military alliance. This, of course, did not work out with Ukraine.

The republics of Belarus, Kazakhstan, and Ukraine were the first to nationalize former Soviet troops stationed on their respective territories. As an exception, Armenia welcomed the Russians since their presence deterred potential aggression by neighboring countries. In most other cases, however, the situation that evolved would appear to have been based on duress.

Despite earlier pledges to continue withdrawal of Russian troops from the sovereign Baltic States, Yeltsin briefly suspended these activities in October 1992. The reasons given included lack of housing for those to be redeployed and alleged discrimination against ethnic Russians who had settled in these countries as colonists during and after World War II. Yet another concern involved Kaliningrad (former Königsberg) *oblast'*, which depends on Lithuania for electric power and land access to Russia.

Since that time, all occupation troops have been removed from Lithuania. There were still some Russian military personnel in Latvia until 1994. The principal obstacle to their departure appears to be retention of the missile-attack early warning radar at Skrunda. An agreement reached in early 1994 allowed Russians to operate the installation over the next four years, with an additional eighteen months for dismantling the equipment.[17] The last troops withdrew on 31 August 1994, with the exception of 600 specialists who remained at the Skrunda radar station.

In Estonia, on the other hand, Russian deployment continued near the cities of Tallin (144th Motorized Rifle Division), Paldiski (submarine base), Parnu and Tartu (strategic bomber airfields). These installations were operated by some 2,400 servicemen. Here, also, Russian negotiators attempted to link withdrawal with residence permits for 8,000 of their

TABLE 3.4
Armed Forces High Command

Position (12)	Incumbent	Appointed
Minister of Defense	Army Gen. P. S. Grachëv	18 May 1992
First Deputy Minister (chief of General Staff)	Army Gen. M. P. Kolesnikov	23 December 1992
First Deputy Minister	(civilian) A. A. Kokoshin	3 April 1992
Deputy Minister (Inspector General)	Army Gen. K. I. Kobets	3 June 1993
Deputy Minister (physical fitness)	Col. Gen. V. M. Toporov	9 June 1992
Deputy Minister (construction and billeting)	Col. Gen. A. V. Solomatin	20 January 1995
Deputy Minister (logistic support)	Col. Gen. V. T. Churanov	20 January 1995
CO, Strategic Missile Troops	Col. Gen. I. D. Sergeev	1 September 1992
CO, Ground Troops	Col. Gen. V. M. Semënov	11 September 1992
CO, Anti-Air Defense Forces	Col. Gen. V. A. Prudnikov	31 August 1991
CO, Air Forces	Col. Gen. P. S. Deinekin	3 September 1992
CO, Navy	Fleet Adm. F. N. Gromov	19 August 1992

Source: Joint Publications Research Service, *Directory of Russian Federation Military Organizations and Personnel* (Washington, D.C., 5 April 1995), 95–137.

military pensioners. Moscow complained at the United Nations that Estonia and Latvia planned to expel thousands of Russian families, in effect, to engage in a form of "ethnic cleansing."[18] As of this writing, no such activity has taken place. By the end of August 1994, all foreign troops had left Estonia except for 200 specialists involved with dismantling the two nuclear reactors at the Paldiski submarine base. See Table 3.3 for other former deployments abroad.

Reform of the Armed Forces

At the beginning of 1993, General of the Army Vladimir N. Lobov gave an interview in which he discussed his conclusions about reforming the Russian military establishment. He joined the General Staff in February 1987 as first deputy chief and received promotion to chief on 23 August 1991, that is, two days after the attempted coup collapsed. Lobov lasted only until 7 December 1991, when he was retired at age 56.[19]

More than a year after his premature retirement, Lobov met with the press and stated that the "army...administrative structures remain redundant or overstaffed." Recreating a military establishment requires a new policy and a new doctrine (the latter appeared only in November 1993). Lobov warned against the danger of making the economy dependent on military orders for equipment, which had been the case even under Gorbachëv.[20] Unfortunately, the idea of dividing the high command into two parts disappeared with Lobov's departure. He had envisaged a civilian defense minister for policy and administration, with a uniformed military chief of the General Staff for operational control over the armed forces.

Detailed support for Lobov's criticism appeared almost simultaneously with the above-cited article in a monthly journal published by the Institute of the World Economy and International Relations (IMEMO) at Moscow.[21] The author contended that the struggle for political control over the high command resulted in appointment of only a single high-ranking civilian, that is, Andrei A. Kokoshin, as one of two first deputy ministers (see Table 3.4). Other civilian experts were not brought into the ministerial apparatus. The General Staff retained full authority over the armed forces, whereas the defense ministry carried out only administrative responsibilities. In effect, no civilian oversight over the military has been introduced.

The military establishment looked rather impressive on Russian territory: strategic, offensive, and defensive forces; eight military districts (see Table 3.5); the Northern, Pacific, Black Sea, and Baltic fleets; the Trans-Caucasus group

TABLE 3.5
Military Districts

Designation	Headquarters	Commander	Appointed
Far East	Khabarovsk	Col. Gen. V. S. Chechevatov	September 1992
Trans-Baikal	Chita	Col. Gen. V. S. Tret'iakov	September 1991
Leningrad	St. Petersburg	Col. Gen. S. P. Seleznëv	December 1991
Moscow	Moscow	Col. Gen. L. V. Kuznetsov	July 1992
Volga	Samara	Col. Gen. A. I. Sergeev	July 1992
North Caucasus	Rostov/Don	Col. Gen. A. N. Mitiukhin	June 1993
Siberia	Novosibirsk	Col. Gen. V. A. Kopylov	August 1991
Ural	Ekaterinburg	Col. Gen. I. P. Grekov	July 1992

Source: U.S. Government, Joint Publications Research Service, *Directory of Russian Federation Military Organization and Personnel* (Washington, D.C., 5 April 1995), 95–137.

of forces; the 14th Army in Moldova; a naval base at the Caspian Sea; several ground units in Central Asia; detachments, primarily of a strategic nature, in other SNG countries; a listening post in Cuba; and even a naval base at Cam Ranh Bay, Vietnam.[22] The same IMEMO scholar cited above then complained that Russia had inherited obsolescent equipment from the rear areas facing Western Europe, whereas the latest and more advanced weapons remained in East-Central Europe or in Belarus and Ukraine.

Despite and to a certain extent perhaps because of their withdrawal from former Warsaw Pact countries, the Russian armed forces are being restructured.[23] Two military districts (along the Volga, and in the Urals) have been designated as areas for mobilization and training. In the future, these districts may be combined into a "Unified Command for Troops in Southern Russia," with staff headquarters at Krasnodar. Another such command would be located at Komsomol'sk on the Amur River and comprise the entire Far East.[24] The vast area from there to the Ural Mountains has been reserved for Siberian and Trans-Baikal troops, to be headquartered at Ulan-Ude. The remainder of European Russia (the Moscow and Leningrad [only the city was renamed St. Petersburg] Military Districts) might have its own unified command. (See Map 3.1.)

Toward the end of 1992 Maj. Gen. German V. Kirilenko, who had participated in a General Staff academy conference, was interviewed by a journalist for the armed forces daily newspaper. Kirilenko quoted Col. Gen. Evgenii N. Podkolzin, commander of airborne troops, as stating that the new mobile forces initially would include the following elements:[25]

Two airborne divisions ⟩ 60% of the total
Three airborne brigades ⟩
Several helicopter regiments from ground forces aviation
Three naval infantry (*morskaia pekhota*) battalions[26]
Some air defense and communications units
Fighter and bomber squadrons
Military transport aviation

for immediate response purposes. They would be based in the Volga and Ural Military Districts. Another joint structure, for subsequent deployment, would comprise three army corps and one division of armored troops with tanks plus other heavy equipment to be ready by the end of 1995. The war in Chechnya has caused slippage in this target date. These mobile forces would total approximately 200,000 men, when fully organized.[27] (See Chart 3.2.)

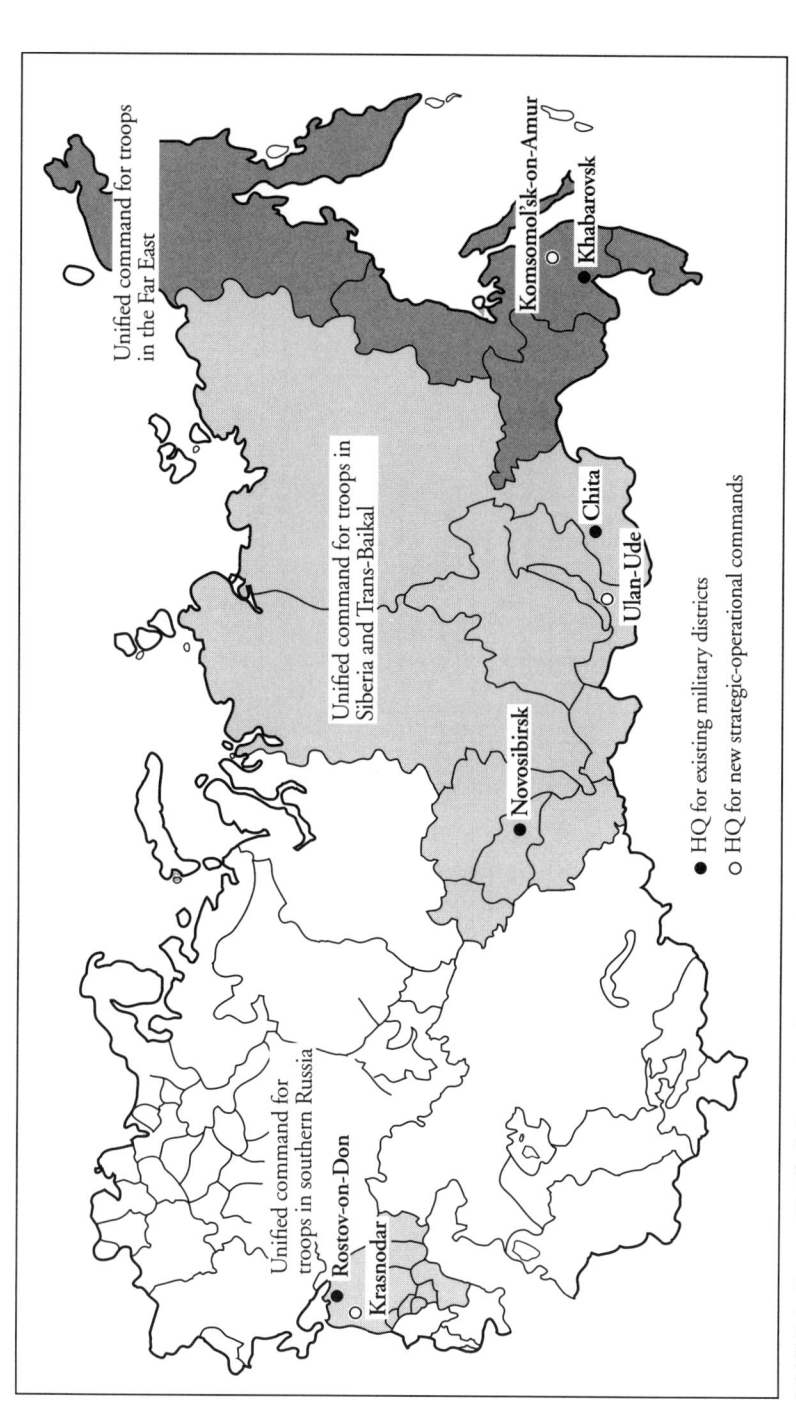

MAP 3.1: Future Unified Strategic-Operational Commands (*adapted from Kommersant-Daily, no. 76 [24 April 1993]: 11*)

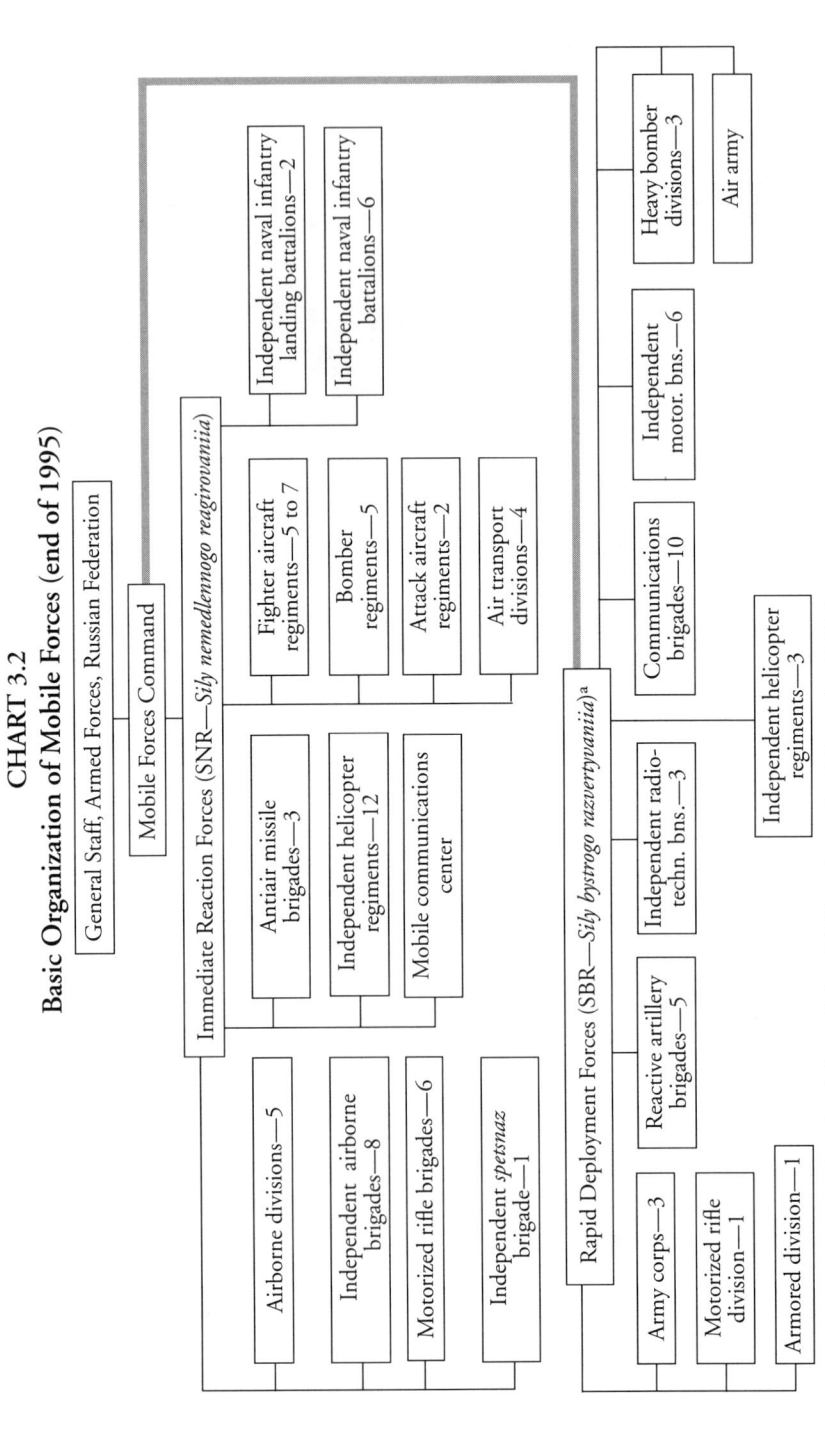

CHART 3.2.
Basic Organization of Mobile Forces (end of 1995)

General Staff, Armed Forces, Russian Federation

Mobile Forces Command

Immediate Reaction Forces (SNR—*Sily nemedlennogo reagirovaniia*)

- Airborne divisions—5
- Independent airborne brigades—8
- Motorized rifle brigades—6
- Independent *spetsnaz* brigade—1
- Antiair missile brigades—3
- Independent helicopter regiments—12
- Mobile communications center
- Fighter aircraft regiments—5 to 7
- Bomber regiments—5
- Attack aircraft regiments—2
- Air transport divisions—4
- Independent naval infantry landing battalions—2
- Independent naval infantry battalions—6

Rapid Deployment Forces (SBR—*Sily bystrogo razvertyvaniia*)[a]

- Army corps—3
- Motorized rifle division—1
- Armored division—1
- Reactive artillery brigades—5
- Independent radio-techn. bns.—3
- Communications brigades—10
- Independent helicopter regiments—3
- Independent motor. bns.—6
- Heavy bomber divisions—3
- Air army

Source: Lt. Col. Oleg Vladykin, "Mobil'nye sily Rossii," *Krasnaia zvezda*, 19 December 1992, 2.
[a] SBR is operationally subordinate to the Mobile Forces Command.

Two airborne divisions, stationed at Vitebsk and Fergana, were allocated to the new governments of Belarus and Uzbekistan, respectively. The airborne brigade at Kapchagay has been taken over by Kazakhstan, although one remains in Belarus, and two others have been acquired by Ukraine. The remaining five airborne divisions were deployed as follows: two in the western part of European Russia, the third to be transferred to the Black Sea area, the fourth moved from the Trans-Caucasus to the Volga Military District, and the fifth from Ukraine to either the Volga or the Ural Military District.[28] Presumably, two of the five divisions and individual brigades from the other three are destined to become part of the new Mobile Forces Command.

When asked about basic tasks for these future military formations, the chief of operations at the airborne assault troops main staff explained that mobile forces would

- defend the territorial integrity of Russia;
- preempt and decide regional conflicts;
- render assistance after a technological or ecological catastrophe;
- provide military aid to allied states;
- participate in armed UN peacekeeping operations; and
- move rapidly in any direction to counter a threat of aggression.[29]

The commander of all Russian airborne divisions, the above-cited Colonel General Podkolzin, boasted that his troops could transport seventeen tons of cargo in one aircraft, including tracked armored personnel carriers, and that (light) fighting vehicles are routinely air-dropped by parachute with crews sitting inside. The men are trained in special combat techniques, which allegedly makes them superior to any other soldiers in the world, according to their commanding officer.[30]

Recruitment and the Draft

Until a presidential decree abolished the Supreme Soviet on 21 September 1993, that body had included an effective legislative committee on defense and security headed by Sergei V. Stepashin. This man gave an interview concerning his official activities.[31] He claimed to have had a good working relationship with the defense ministry, even though the latter remained dissatisfied with Article 21 of the law on military conscription and service. Deferment represents the main official cause for insufficient draftee numbers, with some divisions at only 30 or 40 percent of normal strength. The average for the entire army and navy dropped below 50 percent.[32] (See Table 3.6.)

TABLE 3.6
Active Duty Military Personnel

Component	Authorized	Actual[a]
Ground troops (SV)	1,100,000	790,000
Air forces (VVS)	170,000	90,000
Navy (VMF)	295,000	165,000
Strategic defense (PVO)	205,000	135,000
Strategic offense (RVSN)[b]	144,000	110,000
Command and Rear Service	150,000	105,000
Total	*2,064,000*	*1,395,000*

Source: Harriet Fast Scott and William F. Scott, "Russian Military Almanac," *Air Force Magazine* 78, no. 6 (June 1995): 73.

[a] Figures in this column represent estimates.
[b] Includes strategic missile troops as well as strategic nuclear elements of the navy and the air force.

During the October–December 1993 draft period, the second of that year, recruiters could not possibly fill the gap created by 580,000 young men being released after having served either eighteen months (new system) or two years (old system), the end periods of which coincided. Among the 1.8 million draft-age youth, about 1.5 million had the right under law to request deferment. Also, only a little over half of the men who were expected to be drafted (130,000) would go to army combat units, with the others taken by border troops, interior forces, railroad guards, and construction battalions. The navy is favored by draftees because of the perception that no one is shot at while on a ship. During the October–December 1994 draft, a total of 251,600 were to be conscripted, again only half allocated for the army.[33]

In early December 1993, the city police undertook a series of sweeps throughout Moscow in order to find 70 percent of the city's 18,697 personnel quota, which had to be filled by the end of the year. Draft dodgers do not spend the night at home; they stay in friends' apartments, at other people's country dachas, or rent rooms in different city districts to avoid military service. A total of 70,000 young men escaped conscription during 1993 and, hence, the recruitment year had to be extended into the spring of 1994. During April–June 1995, only 23.8 percent of the draft pool was expected to become available for conscription, or about 210,000 18- to 27-year-olds.[34]

Several of the twenty-one republics comprising the Russian Federation placed restrictions on where a draftee may serve and also took advantage of deferments legislated by the former Supreme Soviet. Thus, until recently some 15,000 recruits had been available annually from Tatarstan; during the spring draft of 1993, this number dropped to 1,530. None of these men could be sent to a "trouble spot" without written consent of the conscriptee and his parents. It is anticipated that the draft will continue at least through the year 2000, if not longer. On 30 April 1995 the State *Duma* adopted legislation that would extend obligatory service from eighteen to twenty-four months. The new law also should increase the percentage of those not exempt from the draft as follows:[35]

1990	42.0
1991	33.6
1992	28.5
1994	19.0
1995	23.8

One reason for reluctance to join the armed forces is that an estimated 40,000 conscripts died from brutal bullying (*dedovshchina*), ethnic gang warfare, and "suicide" between 1985 and 1990, more than had been killed during the ten-year war in Afghanistan.[36] The spring 1993 draft was avoided by 95 percent of those in the eligible age group throughout the Moscow Military District alone. A law adopted by the Supreme Soviet on 19 May 1993 deferred 84 percent of the 1.8 million youths within the nationwide draft pool. Sergei V. Stepashin predicted that by early 1994 the Russian army would have 630,000 officers and only 544,000 enlisted men. This represents a top-heavy ratio, probably unmatched anywhere else in the world. The U.S. Army in early 1995 had one officer for an average of 6.2 enlisted personnel.

The number of generals and admirals, totaling some 4,343 in the USSR during 1989, dropped to 1,793 for Russia alone by mid-1995. The United States, with about the same number of troops (1.6 million), could claim only 1,008 such high-ranking officers during the same time.[37] After the planned restructuring that will bring the military's size down to about 1.5 million or fewer men and women by the year 2000, the number of Russian generals and admirals should also decline, as long as the commander-in-chief has no political reason for promoting them. See Table 3.7 for officer ranks.

At the same time, the percentage of enlisted men as well as officers who reenlist voluntarily under contract should increase throughout the Russian armed forces. About 125,000 were recruited in this manner during 1993. Such volunteers were anticipated to comprise 30 percent of the

TABLE 3.7
Ranks of Army and Navy Officers, Russia and the United States

Army/AirForce		Navy	
Russian	**U.S.**	**Russian**	**U.S.**
Mladshii leitenant	2nd lieutenant	Mladshii leitenant	Ensign
Leitenant	Lieutenant	Leitenant	Lieutenant, j.g.
Starshii leitenant	(Sr. lieutenant)	Starshii leitenant	(Sr. Lieutenant)
Kapitan	Captain	Kapitan-leitenant	Lieutenant
Maior	Major	Kapitan 3-go ranga	Lieutenant commander
Podpolkovnik	Lieutenant colonel	Kapitan 2-go ranga	Commander
Polkovnik	Colonel	Kapitan 1-go ranga	Captain
General-maior	Brigadier general	Kontr-admiral	Rear admiral (lower half)
General-leitenant	Major general	Vitse-admiral	Rear Admiral (upper half)
General-polkovnik	Lieutenant general	Admiral	Vice admiral
General armii	General (4 stars)	Admiral flota	Admiral (4 stars)
Marshal Rossiiskoi Federatsii	General of the army (wartime only)	Admiral Rossiiskoi Federatsii	Admiral of the fleet (wartime only)

Source: "Zakon o voinskoi obiazannosti i voennoi sluzhbe," *Krasnaia zvezda*, 27 February 1993, 3; courtesy of Harriet F. Scott.

Note: The highest rank in the USSR had been Marshal of the Soviet Union, whose recipients remain on active duty as consultants for life. Only Sergei L. Sokolov, Viktor G. Kulikov, and Vasilii I. Petrov were in this category as of mid-1995. Dmitrii T. Iazov presumably lost that privilege when indicted for high treason after the abortive coup in August 1991. See "Poslednim marshalam prodlili raiskuiu zhizn'," *Moskovskii komsomolets*, 19 February 1994, 1.

total force by the end of 1995, and half of the military by the year 2000. However, during 1993 the following percentages of allocated contract personnel were taken in: airborne (60), army (75), navy (142), strategic missile forces (156), air forces (169). Only 161,000 women are in uniform, for 8.5 percent of the military. Four of them attained the rank of colonel (0.002%), none general or admiral.[38]

According to the then–first deputy commanding officer for Russian ground forces, Col. Gen. Ed'uard A. Vorob'ëv, the 201st Motorized Rifle (Guards) Division stationed in Tajikistan had been selected to become the initial all-volunteer unit. Enlisted personnel and officers sign contracts to serve three, five, or ten years. Some 150,000 such contracts represented the projected goal for 1994, which would have required additional funding from the government.[39]

Allocations for Defense

The defense budget, due to inflation, has increased from 985 billion (1992) to 10.8 trillion (1993), 40.6 trillion (1994), 48.5 trillion (1995), and a projected 69.8 trillion rubles (1996). The slight increase adopted for 1995 represented only one-third of the army's minimum requirement, according to General Grachëv's testimony before the State *Duma* on 18 November 1994. He warned that the military had incurred 6 trillion rubles in debt and that 90 percent of the equipment would become obsolete by the year 2000.

However, an enterprising reporter was able to examine the 1994 draft legislative document submitted for approval to parliament. He found that the ostensible total of R 55 trillion, requested by the military, did not include at least fourteen items hidden under other chapters of the law. (See Table 3.8.) In fact, these other proposed expenditures bring the total to over R 84 trillion, which represented 65 percent of the entire government budget for calendar year 1994. The same may be true of official defense allocations for 1995, which envisaged only 48.5 trillion rubles or just under 20 percent of the state budget.[40] By comparison, the U.S. Department of Defense budget for 1995 comprised 20 percent of all federal outlays, without any hidden items. Could these almost identical percentages be a coincidence?

Lessons from "Desert Storm"

Russian military experts appear to have become mesmerized by the Persian Gulf War. The theoretical journal of the armed forces carried several articles on the subject. One of these stressed that technological superiority had overpowered the Iraqi quantitative troop advantage in the following manner:[41]

1. Air operations lasted thirty-eight days, compared with only four on the ground, giving a ratio of 9 to 1.
2. Use of the latest electronic warfare (EW) equipment, including AWACS and JSTARS, added to the element of surprise.
3. Enemy communications were attacked simultaneously at all levels, from tactical to strategic.

TABLE 3.8
Defense Budget for 1994

	Rubles (trillions)
Chapter V	
Maintenance of Armed Forces (2.1 million men)	26.3
Development and Purchase of Weapons	17.4
Major Construction and Nuclear Energy	8.8
Pensions for Retirees	2.5
Official total	*55.0*
Defense Expenditures Hidden in Other Parts of Budget	
Chapter VII: Law Enforcement and Security	
Interior, border and counterintelligence forces (680,000)	12.000
Chapter XI	
Replenishment of government supplies (so-called untouchable military food stocks)	5.900
Reserve Funds	0.500
Chapter XII	
Civil defense and emergency situations (including R 344 billion for mobilization preparedness)	2.000
Chapter XIV	
Financial assistance to "closed cities"[a]	0.583
Dependents and children of servicemen	0.150
Russian Defense, Sports and Technical Society	0.009
Lease of Baikonur Space Center, Kazakhstan	0.135
Federal directorate of railroad troops	0.282
Federal directorate of road construction	0.171
Federal directorate for special military construction (97,000 military workers)	1.500
Other	
Defense industry conversion	0.755
Implementation of arms reduction treaties	0.836
Basic R&D for scientific and technical projects	4.200
Total	*29.021*
Grand Total (65% of state budget)	*84.0*

Source: Anatolii Zhuravlëv, "Vse my zalozhniki VPK," *Rossiiskaia gazeta*, 7 June 1994, 1, 3.

[a]See chapter 4.

4. EW and fire strikes reinforced one another through careful coordination regarding target, location, and time.
5. Intensity of air strikes (at certain stages from 2,000 to 3,000 sorties per day) had no precedent in any previous war.

The author's conclusion is that such high-tech military operations are capable of achieving their objective, that is, defeat of the enemy, essentially without the use of ground troops.

In another article, published by the same journal a few months earlier, three Russian officers expressed their disbelief that air power alone could have destroyed the Iraqi army. Saddam Hussein surrendered unconditionally, after the 100-hour ground offensive had smashed his main grouping of forces.[42] Do the Russians need to achieve such an advantage? The answer is that they cannot afford it. However, a higher degree of mobility remains an absolute priority in order to move Russian units as rapidly as possible.

Based on the foregoing, it is likely that the Russian army of the future will consist of two parts. Basic Forces would be positioned in the forward areas, reinforced by reservists. They should cost less to maintain and have more limited tasks. Mobile Forces would dispose of a full complement of personnel during peacetime so as to undertake deep strikes in their assigned configuration, when ordered to do so.

The battalion will make up the basic combined arms unit, commanded by an experienced officer. Brigades will receive more maneuver power. An army corps of five brigades should have the strength of three former divisions. Its equipment would include "surface to surface missiles, multi-barreled rocket launchers, attack helicopters, air assault and air mobile forces (a strong special forces element), and appropriately matched reconnaissance and C^3 [command, control, and communications] capabilities."[43]

Such an army might defend itself well against an adversary like Turkey or Iran, although less well vis-à-vis China, where the border is incomparably longer. These future Russian troops might be more than sufficient to handle unruly Commonwealth members throughout the "near abroad," not to mention domestic insurgencies on Federation of Russia territory. During the initial four months of war in Chechnya, a total of 557 Russian officers were dismissed for refusal to serve in that republic according to the chief of the General Staff's personnel administration, Lt. Gen. Evgenii V. Vysotskii, in a statement to the ITAR-TASS news agency on 7 April 1995. The most common reason given was lack of confidence in the soldiers under their command.

Discipline and Morale

When one examines the educational background and health of new draftees, according to the commander of ground forces,[44] one finds that 3 percent received only a fourth-grade education, about 27 percent did not complete secondary school, and 11 percent failed the physical fitness test. These deficiencies did not prevent them from being drafted.

Pay of enlisted personnel averages $20 per month and is rarely received. Most of the teenagers probably never enjoyed destroying villages and towns in Chechnya, although drinking reportedly began each day at 1600 and this presumably helped to dull the pervasive fear of combat.[45] However, one must distinguish army recruits from elite airborne and naval infantry troops, both of which fought well.

Northern and Baltic Fleet personnel were mobilized from more than fifty units, whereas the Pacific Fleet called upon over 100 coastal units and ships to augment personnel for military operations in Chechnya. They were ordered into combat without adequate training. Colonel General Skuratov, their commander, revealed that 110 marines had been killed over a period of four months in Chechnya. He also criticized obsolete equipment, like bulletproof vests weighing thirteen kilograms (almost thirty pounds), and helmets manufactured during the 1940s.[46] Interior ministry troops, by contrast, received the latest weapons and gear.

The same conditions apply to the navy as a whole. The commander-in-chief, Fleet Admiral Feliks N. Gromov, told a reporter that his 1995 budget included 1.5 trillion rubles less than the minimum requirement. He gave as an example the presence of foreign submarines in the Northern Fleet's zone of responsibility. They were detected over fifty separate times during the first 4 1/2 months of the year. The admiral warned that, without more financial support, naval ships will become piles of scrap metal.[47]

The navy, long considered the most prestigious among the five services, conducted a survey of its contract personnel. Nine out of ten had been recruited from among draftees at the end of their conscription. Only 9 percent had signed contracts because of patriotism. Incentives for the rest centered upon being paid well and becoming independent. Complaints among these same individuals were directed at unsettled conditions (32%), restrictions on personal freedom (61%), separation from relatives (15%), and insufficient attention from commanders (37%).

The same study[48] also dealt with discipline. Gross infractions included being absent-without-leave (AWOL), late return from leave, and drunkenness in public, which affected every sixth seaman. Thus the conclusion that navy contract personnel require no less, and frequently more, attention than draftees. The foregoing applies to those who remain in the service. Thousands desert and tens of thousands dodge the draft, as already mentioned. One should also remember the Committee of Soldiers' Mothers, whose members have repeatedly demonstrated against *dedovshchina* and the war in Chechnya.

There also exist organizations like the Union of Russia's Veterans-Internationalists, which includes nine regional groups. Organized by Col. Gen. Boris V. Gromov, it claims to have 60,000 members and supports military reform. The Russian Military Brotherhood unites more than thirty veterans' and public organizations. It is headed by (reserve) Col. Gen. Vitalii Ia. Kremlev and also supports reform as well as the patriotic spirit. Finally, the right-wing Russian Officers' Union, led by former Lt. Col. Stanislav N. Terekhov, claims to have chapters in seventy-eight major military units throughout the country.[49]

Many officers supposedly agree with the antidemocratic philosophy of Terekhov's organization, although they hesitate to join it. The Russian Officers' Union is prone to violence, hoping to attain power without a military struggle and yet willing to use force if necessary. The officers' corps is more than 95 percent Slavic (see Table 10.2), which makes it a homogeneous entity and perhaps receptive to Terekhov's propaganda.

It would seem obvious that the Russian military as an institution must accept

> oversight by the civilian government, including parliament;
> depolitization, where regular active-duty officers are prohibited from engaging in political activities; and
> military promotions based upon merit and not politics.[50]

At present, these objectives appear to be far from attainment. A future reform could possibly succeed, although what currently is being done involves only structure and none of the above.

The next chapter deals with the military-industrial complex and acquisition of weapons systems by the armed forces. After all of the military equipment destroyed in Chechnya, the Russian Armed Forces will require replacements from their defense industry.

Notes

1. Evgenii I. Shaposhnikov, *Vybor: zapiski glavnokomanduiushchego* (Moscow: PIK, 1993), 128, 134.

2. Ukaz Prezidenta Rossiiskoi Federatsii, "O sozdanii Vooruzhënnykh Sil Rossiiskoi Federatsii," *Krasnaia zvezda,* 9 May 1992, 1. See also Sergei M. Rogov, ed., "Russian Defense Policy," *CNA Occasional Paper* (Alexandria, Va.: Center for Naval Analyses, February 1993), 35–36.

3. See, e.g., "Ukaz o perekhode pod iurisdiktsiiu R. F. voinskikh chastei... na territorii Respubliki Moldova," *Rossiiskaia gazeta,* 3 April 1992, 4. A. Krainin, "Liudi - ne kartoshka," *Komsomol'skaia pravda,* 20 May 1992, 1, for interview with Grachëv.

4. "Zakon Rossiiskoi Federatsii ob Oborone, priniat Verkhovnym Sovetom Rossiiskoi Federatsii 26 iiunia 1992 goda," *Voennyi vestnik,* no. 11 (November 1992): 1–2. For a summary of other military legislation, see "Kratkoe soderzhanie osnovnykh voennykh zakonov Rossii," *Voennyi vestnik,* no. 3 (March 1994): 92–95.

5. Interview with Vladimir Urban, "Lish' v usloviiakh grazhdanskogo soglasiia," *Krasnaia zvezda,* 11 December 1992, 1; see also Rogov, ed., *Russian Defense Policy,* 41.

6. Harriet Fast Scott, "Rise of the Afghantsi," *Air Force Magazine* 76, no. 8 (August 1993): 33–36. Afghan veterans number 545,000, according to General Grachëv, "Afganskoe bratstvo...," *Krasnaia zvezda,* 17 February 1995, 1.

7. Aleksandr Oleinik, "Voin-internatsionalist," *Krasnaia zvezda,* 5 May 1993, 1, 3. See also Maj. Gen. P. A. Golitsyn (ret.), "Trem'ia moia voina...," *Voenno-istoricheskii zhurnal,* no. 3 (March 1994): 54–60, on his service in Ethiopia during 1977–78.

8. Editorial, "Grachëv: The New 'Master' of Russian Nuclear Weapons," *Moscow News,* no. 30 (23 May 1993): 1.

9. See interviews with RVSN Commander and First Deputy CO by Aleksandr Dolinin, "Kliuchi na start u raketchikov...," *Krasnaia zvezda,* 8 February 1995, 2; and Tamara Semënova, "Samye silnye voiska...," *Rossiiskie vesti,* 20 May 1995, 3.

10. Pavel Fel'gengauer's interview with paratroop commander Col. Gen. Evgenii N. Podkolzin, "Desantnye voiska ne sokratiat...," *Segodnia,* 21 February 1995, 2. See also "Defense Ministry Begins Forming Mobile Forces," Moscow Radio INTER-FAX, 22 May 1995, in FBIS-SOV-95-099 (23 May 1995), 29–30.

11. On air force problems, see interview with Maj. Gen. Nikolai I. Chaga, chief of the front-line center for combat, in *Pravda,* 25 January 1995, 8. The super fighter is discussed by Irina Shkarnikova, "Samolët XXI veka," *Voennoe obozrenie* insert, p. 1 of *Nezavisimaia gazeta,* 22 April 1995.

12. See interview with Moscow Air Defense District commander Col. Gen. Anatolii M. Kornukov, who stated that his command has been reequipped with the latest S-300 air defense systems and the most modern fighter interceptors. Aleksandr Ivanov, "Voiska postoiannoi gotovnosti," *Krasnaia zvezda,* 8 April 1995, 1.

13. Radii Zubkov and Mikhail Vinogradov, "Kakoi VMF neobkhodim Rossii?" *Voennoe obozrenie,* insert to *Nezavisimaia gazeta,* 11 February 1995, 3; "Getting Rid of the Atomic Fleet's Nuclear Fuel," *Moscow News,* no. 14 (14–20 April 1995): 14.

14. Andrei Bychkov, "Camranh Naval Base to Be Resolved on 'New Principles,'" Moscow Radio, ITAR-TASS, 16 June 1994, in FBIS-SOV-94-117 (17 June 1994), 7; "V 1995 godu korabli VMF Rossii...," *Izvestiia,* 21 February 1995, 1.

15. In July 1994 Defense Minister Grachëv included railroad, construction, and civil defense troops in this "second army" whose total in numbers equals the regular armed forces; listed as 1.9 million each by Vladimir Lopatin, "Manevry generalov," *Izvestiia*, 27 April 1995, 4. See Table 10.1.

16. Rogov, ed., *Russian Defense Policy*, 8.

17. Moscow Radio, ITAR-TASS, 8 February 1994, in FBIS-SOV-94-027 (9 February 1994), 53.

18. Gennadii Charodeev, "Estoniia i Latviia khotiat vyselit' tysiachi russkikh semei," *Izvestiia*, 3 December 1993, 3.

19. For an earlier biography, see Vladimir N. Lobov, *Kommunist vooruzhënnykh sil*, no. 10 (May 1989): 14; announcement of appointment as chief of the General Staff by decree of President Gorbachëv appeared in *Krasnaia zvezda*, 24 August 1991, 1.

20. Vladimir Dudnik, "General Lobov: Army Needs to Be Recreated, Not Reformed," *Moscow News*, no. 5 (28 January 1993): 4.

21. Konstantin E. Sorokin, "Vozrozhdenie rossiiskoi armii," *Mirovaia ekonomika i mezhdunarodnye otnoshenia*, no. 1 (January 1993): 4–8.

22. Sergei Blagoev, "Delegation Visits Military Installation in Vietnam," Moscow Radio, ITAR-TASS, 16 April 1994, in FBIS-SOV-94-074 (18 April 1994), 25.

23. Interview with chief of the General Staff, Col. Gen. Mikhail P. Kolesnikov, "Ostanovit' voennye reformy nikomu ne pod silu," *Armiia*, no. 9 (1993): 26–27.

24. See "The New Russian Far Eastern Command," *Jane's Intelligence Review* 6, no. 1 (November 1993): 1–2.

25. Lt. Col. Oleg Vladykin, "Mobil'nye sily Rossii," *Krasnaia zvezda*, 18 December 1992, 2. See also Capt. A. V. Bobrakov, "Sily bystrogo reagirovaniia," *Voennyi vestnik*, no. 2 (February 1993): 24–26.

26. For an interview with Lt. Gen. Ivan S. Skuratov, naval infantry commander, see Vladimir Mariukha, "Beregushchie more i bereg," *Krasnaia zvezda*, 18 February 1994, 2.

27. Nikolai Astashkin and Vladimir Ermolin, "Mobil'nye sily na iuge Rossii," *Krasnaia zvezda*, 5 July 1994, 1.

28. Robert Hall, "Russia's Mobile Forces," *Jane's Intelligence Review* 5, no. 4 (April 1993): 154–55.

29. Maj. Gen. Evgenii A. Belianin, "Zachem Rossii mobil'nye sily?" *Armiia*, no. 12 (1993): 19.

30. "Airborne Troops Commander on Mobile Forces," Moscow Central Television, 1 August 1993, in FBIS-SOV-93-163 (25 August 1993): 28–29.

31. Discussed by Pavel Fel'gengauer in the opinion column of *Segodnia*, no. 17 (18 May 1993): 11.

32. Oleg Falichev, "Komplektovat' Vooruzhënnye Sily...," *Krasnaia zvezda*, 23 March 1995, 1. See also Benjamin S. Lambeth, "Russia's Wounded Military," *Foreign Affairs* 74, no. 2 (March-April 1995): 86–98.

33. Viktor Litovkin, "Moskvichi khotiat sluzhit' na flote," *Izvestiia*, 23 November 1993, 1. "Voennuiu formu nadenut 251,600 chelovek," *Krasnaia zvezda*, 5 October 1994, 1. Of the 22,000 draft dodgers during fall 1994, only 1,327 were prosecuted

and 127 convicted, according to Nikolai Poroskov, "Na voinskom uchete ne sostoit…," *Krasnaia zvezda,* 23 June 1995, 2.

34. V. Litovkin, "Militseiskaia set' dlia prizyvnika," *Izvestiia,* 4 December 1993, 8; Lt. Col. Nikolai Chebotarev, "A Lëkha slushaet…," *Krasnaia zvezda,* 23 March 1994, 3; Falichev, "Komplektovat' Vooruzhënnye Sily."; Andrei Kirillov, "Vesna: prizyv i uklonisty," *Rossiiskaia gazeta,* 29 April 1995, 13.

35. See interview with Lt. Gen. Vasilii Smirnov, head of the General Staff mobilization directorate, "Voennye trebuiut…," *Izvestiia,* 18 February 1995, 1–2. Source for percentages is Aleksandr Kasatov, "Vo soldaty…," *Ogonëk,* no. 26 (June 1995): 21, who does not provide 1993 figures.

36. Quoted in "Russia's Armed Forces," *The Economist,* London (28 August–3 September 1993): 18–19. See also Stanislav Telegin, "Umerla li v armii Dedovshchina?" *Krasnaia zvezda,* 4 July 1995, 3; interview with Lt. Gen. Stanislav E. Gaveto, deputy chief military prosecutor.

37. Interview with Col. Gen. Kolesnikov, chief of the General Staff, by Nikolai Burbyga, "Tak skol'ko zhe v Rossii voennykh?" *Izvestiia,* 17 July 1994, 2; number of flag officers from Col. Gen. E. V. Vysotskii, director for cadres at defense ministry, in "Marshal'skii zhezl v karmanie?" *Argumenty i fakty,* no. 22 (May 1995): 7.

38. Interview with Lt. Gen. Gennadii N. Bochaev, "Nabor po kontraktu budet prodolzhen," *Krasnaia zvezda,* 17 August 1993, 2; Col. Gen. Vladimir Zhurbenko, first deputy chief of the General Staff, "V armii zhenshchin - generalov net," *Krasnaia zvezda,* 10 March 1995, 3.

39. Maj. A. E. Ostankevich, "O kontraktnom sposobe komplektovania VS," *Voennaia mysl',* no. 4 (April 1994): 70–75; Maj. Gen. (Justice) V. Ivakhniuk, "Osobennosti sluzhby po kontraktu," *Armeiskii sbornik* 1, no. 1 (July 1994): 90–93.

40. Valerii Konovalov, "Biudzhet odobren…," *Izvestiia,* 24 March 1995, 2. The Federation Council subsequently also approved the budget. The 1996 figure assumes that the military officially will receive again only 21 percent from the 349 trillion rubles for total expenditures, according to *Rossiiskaia gazeta,* 2 June 1995, 9.

41. Maj. Gen. I. N. Vorob'ëv, "Uroki voiny v zone Persidskogo zaliva," *Voennaia mysl',* nos. 4–5 (April-May 1992): 70. See also Jacob W. Kipp, "The Soviet General Staff Looks at 'Desert Storm': Through the Prism of Contemporary Politics," in Stephen J. Blank and Jacob W. Kipp, eds., *The Soviet Military and the Future* (Westport, Conn.: Greenwood Press, 1992), 115–44.

42. Maj. Gen. Iu. V. Lebedev, Lt. Gen. I. S. Liutov, and Col. V. A. Nazarenko, "Voina v zone Persidskogo zaliva," *Voennaia mysl',* nos. 11–12 (November-December 1991): 116–17. See also Mary C. FitzGerald, "The Soviet Image of Future War: Through the Prism of the Persian Gulf," *Comparative Strategy* 10, no. 4 (October-December 1991): 393–435.

43. Charles Dick, "Russian Views on Future War—Part 3," *Jane's Intelligence Review* 5, no. 11 (November 1993): 488–95; quotation at 493. See also Mary C. FitzGerald, "The Russian Military's Strategy for 'Sixth Generation' Warfare," *Orbis* 38, no. 3 (Summer 1994): 457–76.

44. [Col. Gen.] Vladimir [M.] Semyonov, "Army Exists Mainly Owing to the

Selflessness of Personnel," *Moscow News,* no. 9 (3–9 March 1995), 4.

45. Michael Specter, "Killed in Chechnya: An Army's Pride," *New York Times,* 21 May 1995, sec. 4, p. 3.

46. Andrei Gavrilenko, "Morskaia pekhota v chechenskom konflikte," *Krasnaia zvezda,* 17 May 1995, 2; interview with Col. Gen. Ivan S. Skuratov.

47. Vladimir Gundarov, "Proboina razmerom v poltora trilliona rublei," *Krasnaia zvezda,* 20 May 1995, 1.

48. Capt. (1st rank) V. Masiagin, "Povoda dlia samouspokoennosti net," *Morskoi sbornik,* no. 2 (February 1995): 58–61.

49. Laura Belin, "Gromov Forms Veterans' Group," OMRI *Daily Digest,* no. 105 (31 May 1995): 2.

50. Robert Arnett, "Russia after the Crisis," *Orbis* 38, no. 1 (Winter 1994): 41–57, at 41.

Myth No. 4
Military-Industrial Complex Is Dead

> At present, this complex is the largest consumer of financial, raw materials, labor, and intellectual resources in Russia.
> *Armeiskii sbornik* (September 1994)

Russia retained 70 percent of the USSR's military-industrial complex (*Voenno-promyshlennyi kompleks*, or VPK), with between 2,000 and 4,000 industrial plants that employ from 5 to 8 million highly skilled workers. Three-quarters of all research and development in 500 scientific centers as well as weapons-testing facilities that belonged to this complex are located in the Russian Republic, according to a Central Intelligence Agency study. Among the former Soviet republics, only six have been able to produce and assemble major weapons systems: Russia, Ukraine, Belarus, Georgia, Uzbekistan, and Kazakhstan. Some of the VPK plants were geographically dispersed for strategic reasons. Other plants were developed to take advantage of local resources, and some plants were set up to provide high-tech industry for local labor or colonizing Russians.[1]

Because of its size and diversity, Russia retains the capability to operate an autonomous defense industry base, commonly known as *oboronka*. At present, the VPK will continue to function under a program that covers the period through the year 2005. Priorities include communications, reconnaissance, electronic warfare, battlefield equipment, and so on. Ukraine, Kazakhstan, Belarus, and other SNG member states presumably will cooperate on joint projects in these fields. One such agreement was signed on 10 March 1995 in Moscow by the Kazakh and Russian defense industry committees.

Oboronka had exerted enormous influence on the stability of the USSR as a whole. One source claims that "the economic and social life of 30, 35, or according to some calculations, 40 million people" (including those who supported them) had been involved with the defense sector.[2] That figure certainly includes families of VPK employees. Academician Iurii V. Iaremenko, a senior economist and director of the Russian Institute for Forecasting, expressed his view at a conference in Washington, D.C., that about half of the Soviet economy (22% for production of weapons plus up to an additional 28% for investments in plant and machinery) had worked for the military-industrial complex.[3]

One of the problems faced by the VPK in the Russian Federation has been nonpayment by the ministry of defense for delivered equipment. An example includes some 400 billion rubles' worth of tanks, aircraft, guns, and so on, that had been manufactured on the basis of government orders, with some bills dating back to 1992. The 67 percent drop in procurement that year and the official 10 percent increase during 1993 were followed with a defense budget request for a 50 percent funding increase (not approved) during 1994. Almost two-thirds of all Russian enterprises work for VPK, yet in 1993 the ministry of defense could pay only half of the 2.2 trillion rubles it owed. In the fall of 1994, accumulated debts again totaled 3.1 trillion rubles. This figure had dropped to 1.75 trillion by the following May.[4]

One of the first deputy defense ministers warned that same year that one-third of the 15 million people (obviously including families and support personnel) employed by the VPK could lose their jobs, if the majority of VPK enterprises were to stop production.[5] The defense-industry complex traditionally had absorbed the lion's share of USSR industrial resources, with reportedly 80 percent allocated for the military and the remainder for civilian production of consumer goods. In Russia alone, about seventy-four "city-factories" had four-fifths or more of their populations working for the VPK in 1991, according to information disseminated at a Moscow news conference organized by the League of Defense Enterprises.[6]

Hidden Cities

In addition to regular military-industrial facilities, there exist at least ten major "secret cities" where nuclear weapons have been designed and tested and warheads manufactured. Some of them continue to produce enriched uranium and weapons-grade plutonium. These cities, which do not appear on any maps available to the public, house approximately 700,000 employees and families. This total may include those who made the cities viable. Only a few thousand of the workers are actually scientists. (See Table 4.1.) Western sources estimate that the former USSR had a total of 100,000 VPK employees with nuclear expertise.[7]

TABLE 4.1
Russia's Hidden Cities

Designation	Location	Activities	Population
Arzamas-16 on Volga River[a]	Kremlev, Nizhegorodskaia oblast (60 km S.W. of Arzamas)	Scientific Research Institute of Experimental Physics; warhead design and assembly; Iskra (Spark)-5 laser technology	80,300
Cheliabinsk-65 on Techa River	Ozersk, South Urals (80 km S. of Ekaterinburg)	Mayak (Beacon) Chemical Combine; tritium; plutonium; waste vitrification	83,500
Cheliabinsk-70[a]	Snezhinsk, South Urals	Research Institute of Technology and Physics; design of experimental and prototype warheads	46,300
Krasnoiarsk-26 on Enisei River	Zheleznogorsk, West Siberia (50 km N.W. of Krasnoiarsk)	Nuclear warheads; weapons-grade plutonium; spent-fuel reprocessing (all underground)	90,300
Krasnoiarsk-45 on Kan River	Sosnovoborsk, West Siberia (60 km from Krasnoiarsk)	Electrochemical plant; uranium enrichment	63,400
Penza-19 on Sura River	Zarechnyi, Central Russia (40 km from Penza)	Warhead assembly; warhead storage; series-produced nuclear weapons	61,400
Sverdlovsk-44 on Neva River	Novoural'sk, Central Urals (320 km S.E. of Perm)	Urals electrochemical combine; uranium enrichment	88,500
Sverdlovsk-45	Lesnoi, Central Urals (200 km N. of Ekaterinburg)	Warhead assembly; series-produced nuclear weapons	54,700
Tomsk-7 on Tom River	Seversk, West Siberia (2,900 km E. of Moscow)	Siberian Group Chemical Works; plutonium and enriched uranium; warhead components	107,700
Zlatoust-36 on Tobol River	Trekhgornyi, South Urals (145 km E. of Cheliabinsk)	Warhead assembly; series-produced nuclear weapons	29,800
Total			703,900

Sources: Listing only of above designations appeared in *Izvestiia*, 19 March 1993, 6; Central Intelligence Agency, *Defense Industries of Newly Independent States of Eurasia*, (Washington, D.C.: Directorate of Intelligence, 1993), Figure 13, for map with locations of secret cities. See also Alexander Bolsunovsky and Valery Menshchikov, "Nuclear Security Is Inadequate and Outdated," *Moscow News*, no. 49 (9–15 December 1994): 14; and Kimberly Marren Zisk, "Arzamas-16," *Post-Soviet Affairs* 11, no. 1 (January–March 1995): 57–79.

[a] Named by presidential decree in February 1993 as the two Federal Nuclear Science Centers, according to *Krasnaia zvezda*, 26 June 1993, 4. By comparison, the ten premier physics labs in the U.S. employ about 50,000 personnel, according to Philip J. Hilts, "Panel Seeks to Streamline ...," *New York Times*, 2 February 1995, A-8.

Many of the hidden VPK centers were built around a single defense enterprise and, hence, became totally dependent upon military procurement. Apart from the ten officially identified secret cities, there are many others (such as Eniseisk-15 near Krasnoiarsk; Kazan-34 and -103; Perm-7; Petropavlovsk-50 on Kamchatka peninsula; Semipalatinsk-21 in Kazakhstan; Shkatovo-17 in the Maritime Territory; Ufa-78; and Volsk-17, about 100 kilometers from Saratov).[8] All are located on rivers.

Although most of the closed regions initially had been opened by President Yeltsin, the Russian government announced on 9 July 1992 that sixteen areas would again be off-limits to foreigners: Kamchatka peninsula, Komsomol'sk on the Amur River, Russkii Island in the Far East, several *raion*s in Moscow and St. Petersburg; the *oblast*'s of Orenburg, Nizhnyi Novgorod, Arkhangel'sk, Murmansk, Sverdlovsk, Cheliabinsk, and Kaliningrad; and the Mordovia republic. Special permission from the ministry of security (former KGB) was required for entry.[9] The atomic energy ministry has jurisdiction over the closed nuclear cities. (See Map 4.1.)

On 25 September 1992, restrictions applied to American journalists and business people were supposedly removed as a result of a bilateral agreement between Russia and the United States. Nonetheless, special permission is still required to enter "all regions of Russia involved in developing, producing, storing, or utilizing weapons of mass destruction; processing radioactive materials; and accommodating military or other facilities which require a special security regime," based on legislation signed 10 August 1992 by President Yeltsin.[10]

Brain Drain

Despite travel restrictions, several thousand Russian scientists and technicians have been recruited by foreign governments. In response to a written question from a member of the U.S. Senate Committee on Governmental Affairs, Vice Adm. William O. Studeman (at the time acting CIA director) is reported to have asserted that "a centralized automated data system containing information on [Russian] citizens who possess state secrets does not exist." The chief of the passport and visa service in Moscow was cited as the source for this information. Missile experts reportedly were able to leave Russia for North Korea.[11] An immensely greater threat derives from such recruitment by Beijing.

According to U.S. government officials, up to 1,000 technicians, scientists, and engineers from Russia's military-industrial complex have moved to China. Others remain at their weapons laboratories, from

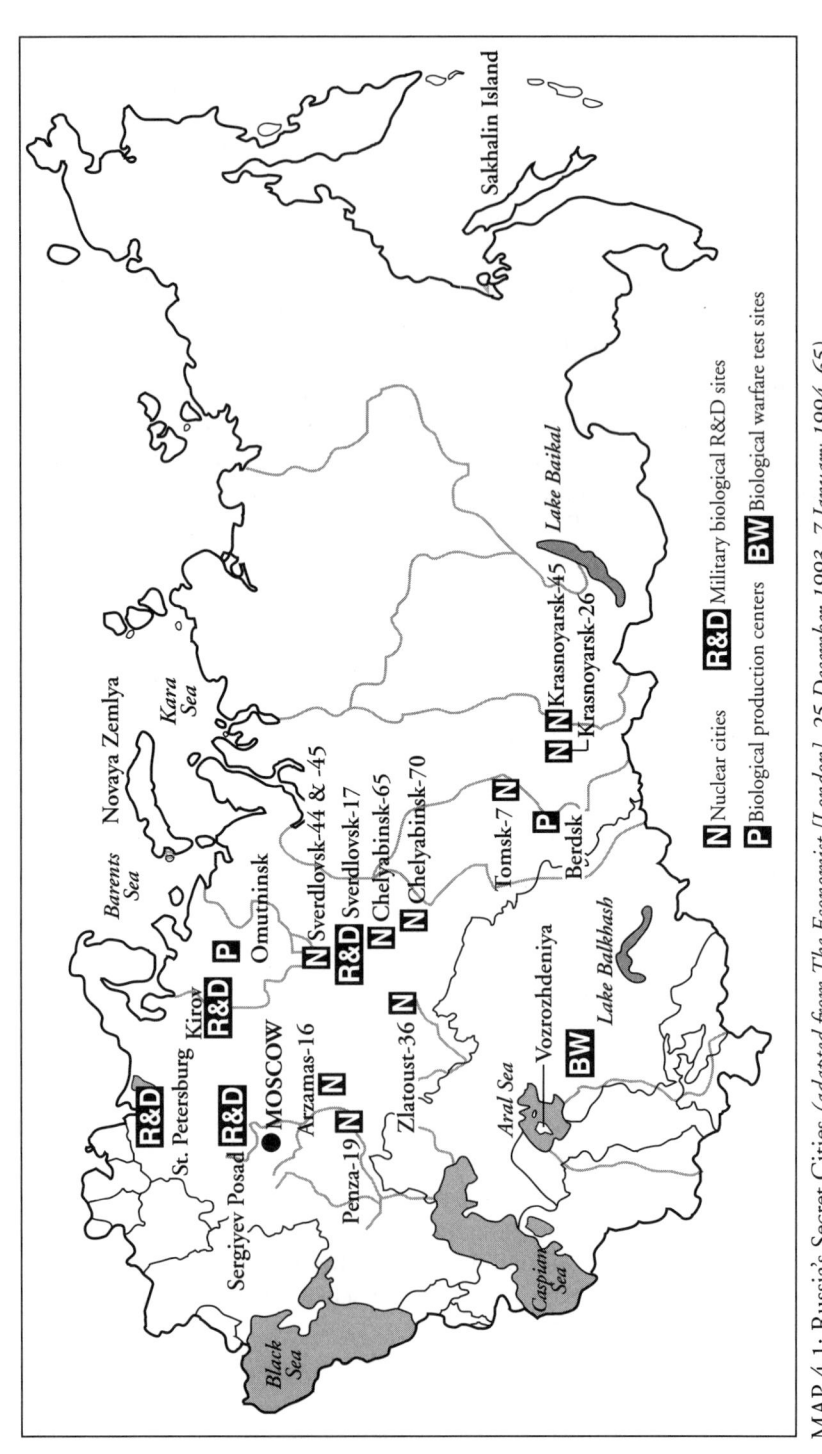

MAP 4.1: Russia's Secret Cities *(adapted from The Economist [London], 25 December 1993–7 January 1994, 65)*

which they reportedly send designs and mathematical models to their Chinese colleagues by electronic mail. A former American ambassador, James R. Lilley, cites the Chinese press on Taiwan as reporting that many Russian experts have been recruited at salaries of up to $24,000 a year, with housing, an automobile, and per diem for living expenses included gratis.[12] In contrast, most experts in Russia could expect to earn, under the best of conditions, less than $5,000 a year without similar amenities. See Table 4.2 for attitudes in two key defense industries toward employment in foreign countries. It is interesting to note that the widest differences exist in the age group between 50 and 59.

Furthermore, a considerable number of younger scientists, between 30 and 40 years of age, have accepted positions in the West. As of December 1993, it was difficult for a university graduate to spend three to five years working toward an advanced degree and then receive an annual salary of 20,000 rubles (U.S. $1,500). In the meanwhile, corresponding members and full members in the Russian Academy of Sciences at that time were awarded 75,000 or 150,000 rubles, respectively, as supplements to their salaries because of membership in this prestigious organization.[13]

A leading research associate at the Institute for National Economic Forecasting in Moscow has calculated that between 1985 and 1993 employment in science dropped from just over 3,420,000 to 1.9 million. During 1992 alone 5,300 scientists emigrated. For every one who left the country, at least ten or fifteen others changed their professions by becoming administrators or businessmen in various government and financial organizations.[14]

TABLE 4.2
Attitudes toward Work Abroad by Age Group (percentages)

Age Group	Aerospace (Nuclear) Industries	
	Positive	Negative
Below 30	100.0 (100)	0 (0)
30–39	84.5 (83.5)	15.5 (16.7)
40–49	86.8 (73.2)	14.2 (26.8)
50–59	75.7 (46.3)	24.8 (53.7)
60 plus	35.7 (23.1)	64.3 (76.9)
Averages	*76.6 (65.2)*	*23.8 (34.8)*

Source: Sergei Babusenko and Andrei Vaganov, "Bolevaia tochka," *Nezavisimaia gazeta,* 28 July 1994, 7.

Note: Figures in parentheses indicate attitudes of employees in nuclear industries.

This same source lists five Latin American countries, China, and South Korea as having expressed an interest in obtaining the services of Russian missile specialists. Iran and Iraq are said to want nuclear physicists who would be paid almost as much as their counterparts in the United States. This last country, together with Germany and Japan, have taken the vast majority of Russian-emigré scientists.

Academy of Science members in Moscow cite statistics to the effect that about 80 percent of students at higher technical schools intend to go abroad or work in business at home. They assert that the $100 million per year that may be allocated by the Russian government for its Basic Research Fund is inadequate. They suggest that the G-7 countries (Western Europe, United States, Japan) provide $1 billion for this purpose over a five-year period.[15]

Conversion

Two Russian writers claimed in the summer of 1992 that only about a dozen of the 2,000 defense plants had stopped producing weapons. One year later, presidential decree no. 1267 suspended privatization of approximately 500 targeted defense factories, research institutes, and design bureaus. It ordered preparation within three months of a list of VPK organizations not to be privatized.[16]

Another presidential decree, in November 1993, paved the way for payment to the defense ministry of 600 to 700 billion rubles owed for weapons deliveries. Salaries of VPK workers were increased to eight times the minimum wage. The decree also mandated preparation by year's end of a long-term armaments program through the year 2000. Henceforth, advance payments of up to 20 percent of the total cost would be provided to VPK by the government—at least that appeared to be the intention.[17] The total estimated cost of conversion reached $150 billion in 1992 prices.

A full-day session of the Security Council chaired by President Yeltsin in November 1993 concentrated on defense industry matters. The discussion stressed that VPK enterprises involve "critical technologies" that must be preserved at all cost. One way of saving such capabilities appeared to be establishment of dual-purpose production lines for both military and civilian items at the same plant (fighter aircraft and civilian airliners, warships and passenger or cargo ships, military electronics and electronic consumer goods).[18] Yeltsin had previously demanded that research and development receive 10 percent of overall defense procurement expenditures in order to maintain a "surge" potential for military production.

Not much progress has been made since the presidential decree of 20 March 1992, which had provided a schedule for submission of the following documents to parliament: basic principles of a new military doctrine; a list of conversion priorities; and a set of approved procedures for joint production of arms and VPK conversion.[19]

A strategic production base for future Russian weapons systems will be maintained as a top priority. Hence, the VPK should continue to receive subsidies, without which most of it would soon collapse. An article appearing in September 1994 ran the title, "Military Industrial Complex Is Dead,"[20] which appears to be an exaggeration.

An important step in promoting stability during conversion should have been the release by Russian leaders to the civilian economy of vast military-related stockpiles, the so-called untouchable state strategic reserves (*neprikosnovennye zapasy*), and mobilization stockpiles. The most recent Russian military encyclopedia defined the former as including fuel, matériel, capital equipment, spare parts, and so on, apart from food.[21] They were maintained to prepare for, fight, and finally recover from a war. Only the supreme commander-in-chief had the authority to open these reserves.

Some stockpiles have been tapped, according to Defense Minister Grachëv. At a press conference in Nizhnii Novgorod, he announced in September 1994 that "we have already entered the country's untouchable strategic reserve."[22] About three weeks later, the defense minister told the government cabinet that the army had consumed one-third of the fuel and food from the strategic reserve. At that time, the defense ministry owed the equivalent of $1.1 billion for weapons, food, and other supplies. Grachëv also complained that the finance ministry had actually paid out only 38 percent of the defense budget allocated to him, although more than nine months of the calendar year already had passed.

Mobilization stockpiles, on the other hand, are decentralized and located adjacent to VPK factories. Their size had been determined in the former Soviet Union on the basis of sustaining wartime defense production from four to six months (four in Europe and six in Asia), until total mobilization could be achieved. The value of these stockpiles was estimated[23] at several hundred billion rubles' worth in 1991, or almost the equivalent of that year's total GNP. These stockpiles remained intact until an edict signed by President Yeltsin on 8 July 1994 ordered their reduction "by a multiple factor."[24] The objectives appeared to include cost-cutting and making defense enterprises more competitive. It probably will save defense plants and "factory towns" from being abandoned en masse.

Past Experience with Conversion

There have been three efforts at defense conversion during the past half century. The first began even before World War II had ended, when the USSR's military expenditures were cut from 33 percent in 1945 to 18 percent of the total budget for 1946. However, funds allocated toward research and development as well as design bureaus were increased. Efforts concentrated on developing new types of military equipment. Defense plants were reoriented toward the future rather than converted to production of goods for the civilian population.[25]

The second effort at conversion had more in common with the current one. Obviously not intended to transform even most of the military-industrial complex, the 1955–65 decade of experimentation did achieve significant gains in the percentage of civilian-oriented output by the following industrial branches: aviation (24%), defense (63%), general machine-building (70%), radio/electronics (73%), and ship construction (44%). No other figures were provided by this source.

The most recent plan envisaged the following nine stages in the conversion process:[26]

1. A political decision to implement conversion
2. Development of a new military doctrine
3. Cutting the armed forces and improving their structure as well as equipment
4. Limiting production of weapons, as required by the defense ministry
5. Preparation of a general concept with objectives, specific tasks, and deadlines for implementation
6. Development of a government program for conversion
7. Establishment of appropriate legal, organizational, financial, and social foundations and institutions
8. Implementation of the adopted program at national, regional, and local levels
9. Analysis of conversion results at each level, in order to adjust as necessary.

According to this source, after the first step (in 1988), the government almost immediately moved to the eighth step or the implementation stage (in 1989). The overall concept was approved during the following year, although control over the process could not be introduced until 1991. The new military doctrine (step 2) was adopted two years later, whereas through early 1992 a specific program as well as implementation had been avoided altogether.

Conversion during the 1990s

Apparent success has been achieved in cases where relatively little modification is required to use the same assembly line for production of military and civilian goods, even though modified. For example, the Saratov Aircraft Plant by 1992 had won in competition against Boeing for the sale of civilian airliners to China. Additionally, several factories that used to build tanks developed sixteen vehicles for civilian use by detaching the armor plates and converting the chassis into prime movers for the lumber, gas, and oil industries, firefighting, and other uses.[27]

By spring 1993, navy orders for warships had dropped from 85 to 25 percent of production capacity at the Iantar Shipbuilding Enterprise. The shipyard, located near Kaliningrad, is now concentrating on foreign customers such as Germany and Estonia. The latter ordered five large dry-cargo vessels. Ten river/sea ships also were being built for Baltic Sea Lines and another ten for the Western Steamship Company.[28]

Another type of conversion, due to necessity based on the strategic arms reduction treaties, is the use of SS-25 missiles (minus warheads) for launching satellites into orbit. Since the rockets were not initially powerful enough

Delta IV ballistic-missile submarine *(U.S. Naval Institute photo collection)*

to lift the payload, additional stages had to be added. The first successful attempt took place in the spring of 1993 from the Plesetsk launch center. During the summer, contracts were being offered to foreign companies interested in paying $10,000 per kilogram (2.2 lbs.) to send their payloads into orbit.

The above-mentioned aviation plant at Saratov has designed a flying saucer that will weigh 120 tons and measure 25 meters in diameter. Foreign companies are being invited to participate in this $70-million project. The vehicle should be able to carry half of its weight in cargo over 8,500 kilometers at speeds of between 650 and 700 km per hour. If successful, this vehicle could revolutionize freight transportation. In addition, as of May 1995 the Tu-334 commercial airliner's fuselage had been assembled for the prototype at the Kiev state aircraft works. It should replace the Tu-134, which is more than three decades old.[29]

Obstacles to Conversion

Larger-scale attempts at conversion from military to civilian production would appear bound to fail, if only because some 85 percent of management-level personnel throughout the VPK and civilian industry have had no training in Western finance and marketing.[30] Most of these veterans belonged to the former communist party apparatus and received promotion in their careers because of unquestioning implementation of orders received from Moscow.

Nonetheless, many defense plant directors have taken advantage of privatization not only to retain their executive positions but even to control the shares that have been distributed to workers and managers alike. Such industrial enterprises are no longer owned by the Federation of Russia government. Many of these corrupt directors consider the plants their personal property, reducing the number of workers, delaying payment of wages, and transferring overhead expenses into foreign currency for themselves.[31]

Major difficulties in the conversion process include the huge size of the VPK, the rapid drop of orders for military equipment, the unpredictable rate of inflation and huge debts accumulated by the defense ministry, and finally the pressure on managers to operate within a semi-market economy. Ninety-seven percent of the VPK remains in government monopoly ownership.[32]

However, the State Committee for Defense Industry (*Goskomoboronprom*) is required to maintain a mobilization base for Russia's military-industrial complex. Its first deputy chairman, Iurii A. Glybin, complained that fewer than one-third of all VPK enterprises were solvent during the 1993 calendar year. Reasons for this included the need to repay commercial bank credits from profits on defense orders and mounting debts owed by the defense ministry for weapons systems delivered without payment to the VPK. Elena Novikova, a directorate chief in *Goskomoboronprom*, suggested that the only realistic solution would be to close down nearly one-third of all military-industrial installations. This would mean unemployment for an estimated 1.4 million workers, not counting their dependents.[33] That solution, of course, would be fought by the VPK and its powerful supporters in government. In addition, no "safety net" assistance is yet in place to provide help for the unemployed.

Other Possible Solutions

Eleven conversion experiences in Russia were summarized in a recent American study. The sites included an electronics firm near the border of Finland, a complex of twenty large defense plants at Nizhnii Novgorod, another thirty in Perm, the former SS-20 intermediate-range ballistic missile factory at Votkinsk, the aircraft plant in Saratov, radio-electronics production at Tambov and Orël, the *Krasnyi proletariat* nuclear warhead manufacturing enterprise in Moscow, the *Svetlana* electronic instruments factory at St. Petersburg, the aerospace technology institute in Kaliningrad, and even the closed city of Cheliabinsk-70, whose research and development facility is accepting foreign investments.[34]

All of these case studies of conversion have several characteristics in common. The enterprises are among the strongest throughout the military-industrial complex. As such, many had been privatized in advance of the comprehensive program that will be pursued over the next several years. Farsighted managers introduced new machinery and supply lines as well as financing, often from abroad. Most are attempting to export their products for hard currency.

William J. Perry, prior to becoming U.S. secretary of defense, addressed a 1993 conference on conversion at Stanford University in which he described the magnitude of the problem inherited by Russia from the former USSR: 11 million workers in the military-industrial complex, 5 million soldiers in the Soviet army, and 3 to 4 million employed by the civilian sector of the military, for a total of 20 million in the VPK, or 60 to 80 million including dependents. This number comprised one-fourth of the population of Russia, or ten times the problem faced by similar conversion efforts in the United States, according to Dr. Perry.[35]

Attempting to reduce the share of defense spending from 6 to 3 percent of America's GNP over ten years was contrasted with Russia's effort to cut 25 percent down to 5 percent over a much shorter period of time. Russian defense industry managers are not told how to accomplish this objective; lack of planning or adequate preparation at the highest levels of government virtually dooms such efforts from the outset.

It was recommended to Russian participants at the above-mentioned conference that their government support the VPK until a phased reduction could be introduced at the rate of a few percent each year. As employees are released, they could be transferred to work at rebuilding communications, transportation, energy, and food systems, in order to prevent massive unemployment. It was also suggested that this new reconstruction effort be separated from the VPK, in the form of new joint-venture stock companies that would attempt to attract Western partners.[36]

Instead of following such advice, the Russian government apparently has opted for the "quick fix" of paying some but not all of the debts incurred by the ministry of defense with the VPK for delivery of weapons and equipment. This decision ultimately cannot solve the problem. Given a lack of specific guidelines from the center and a declining defense budget, the VPK will continue to deteriorate.[37] It faces only a slight chance to achieve massive conversion and survival in any form.

As one Russian military observer has pointed out, however, current approaches to conversion have neither strong theoretical foundations nor rational plans and programs that could be implemented. He predicts that the government's extremely optimistic program will register few concrete results through 1996, despite the fact that the law on conversion will have been in effect for almost five years by that time.[38] The general approach has been to concentrate on high technologies that would produce consumer goods competitive on the world market.

Although the proposed defense budget for 1995 had been promoted as being more or less the same as the previous year's in purchasing power, the armed forces daily newspaper claimed that only 300,000 workers would remain in the military-industrial complex. "The other 15 million would become unemployed or work only part-time."[39] Such figures, especially the latter, should be taken with the traditional grain of salt.

The U.S. government has launched a modest rescue effort by selecting four VPK companies to receive a total of $20 million, in support of joint ventures with Western partners. As signed by U.S. and Russian officials, the new program will encourage implementation of certain ideas suggested at the 1993 Stanford conference.[40] Obstacles to success include the absence of Russian commercial and contract law, the lack of investment insurance, and the proclivity of bureaucrats in Moscow to introduce new taxation, which discourages foreign business.

Examples of the latter are the 20 percent value-added tax (VAT), a related 3 percent special tax, and taxes on transportation as well as by the customs service on foreign equipment for the ailing oil industry in Russia. Such purchases were to be made through loans from the World Bank and the European Bank for Reconstruction and Development.[41] The VAT would apply to the loans themselves as well as to the equipment imported from abroad which, in effect, represents double taxation. An earlier tax already levied six dollars on each barrel of exported oil.

The Defense Order

VPK arms production depends upon what the military decides are its weapons' requirements. This process culminates in a document, called the defense order (*oboronnyi zakaz*). According to the director of the General Staff Academy, the situation remains abnormal, because there exist large numbers of systems in production that perform essentially the same combat missions: sixty-two missile and artillery models (thirty seven, U.S.); sixty-two different types of armored equipment (sixteen, U.S.); and twenty-six surface-to-air missiles (four, U.S.).[42]

This situation may or may not be remedied when the multiyear plan for armaments appears in October 1995. It should include the National Technological Base program, which will concentrate on the implementation of a comprehensive R&D and testing effort, especially for

- Information technology
- Advanced engines
- New materials
- High productivity industrial equipment
- Micro- and nano-electronics
- Optics
- Special chemicals
- Laser and radio-electronics
- Energy-intensive materials
- Power generation
- Unique nuclear technologies
- Biotechnology

with finances projected at 7.3 trillion (1996–97) and 18.9 trillion rubles through the year 2005.[43]

About the same time that the above information was released, a deputy secretary at the Russian Academy of Sciences presented an optimistic assessment of the future. He claimed that science is not in a state of collapse, that the exodus of scientists has slowed down, and that the number of graduate students had increased. Furthermore, the envisaged appropriation of 3 percent from the 1996 federal budget would assure continuation of the scientific community. Import duties on foreign instruments and equipment have been removed, and funds from abroad are tax exempt. He then issued a caveat that only 55 percent of the budget allocated for 1995 had actually been received.[44]

On the other hand, the VPK is developing major weapons systems for the twenty-first century, such as the Su-34 frontal aviation bomber, the new MiG-31 interceptor, and a super-modern multipurpose submarine, as well as new generations of silo-based, mobile, and submarine-launched intercontinental ballistic missiles, which will all be produced within the next decade.[45]

Paradoxically, the debts incurred because of conversion have led the VPK to increase production of weapons systems, which are the only items currently suitable for hard-currency sales.[46] However, the demand for arms has dropped throughout the world. They are becoming more difficult to sell also due to the VPK's outdated technology. The state of arms sales is discussed in the next chapter.

Notes

1. Central Intelligence Agency, *The Defense Industries of the Newly Independent States of Eurasia* (Washington, D.C.: U.S. Government Printing Office [hereafter GPO], 1993), 1.

2. Interview with First Deputy Defense Minister Andrei A. Kokoshin by Valentin Rudenko, "Oboronnyi zakaz," *Krasnaia zvezda*, 6 October 1993, 2.

3. J. D. Crouch and William R. Van Cleave, "The Politics of Reform in Russia," *American-Russian Meeting* (Washington, D.C.: 15–16 April 1993), 23–24, summary in typescript form.

4. Igor' Cherniak, "Skoro VPK voz'mëtsia za metlu?" *Komsomol'skaia pravda*, 16 September 1993, 2. See also the interview with Minister of Defense Pavel Grachëv by Aleksandr Khokhlov, "Pavel sh'ët zheleznye zanaveski," *Komsomol'skaia pravda*, 22 March 1994, 2; Upravlenie informatsii i pechati MO RF, "Oboronke vozvrashchaiut dolgi," *Krasnaia zvezda*, 16 September 1994, 1; Moscow Radio INTERFAX, 8 May 1995, in FBIS-SOV-95-089 (9 May 1995), 40.

5. Andrei A. Kokoshin over Moscow Russian Television, 6 March 1994, in

FBIS-SOV-94-044 (7 March 1994), 26–27. See also Iu. Konorov, "Oboronka ostanovilas'...," *Rossiiskaia gazeta,* 16 March 1994, 1.

6. Interview with Gennadii E. Burbulis, then third-ranking member of President Yeltsin's government, by Andrei Karaulov, "Segodnia ia zhivu," *Nezavisimaia gazeta,* 4 April 1992, 8.

7. Iurii K. Nazarkin, "Konversiia: nekotorye mezhdunarodnye aspekty," *Mezhdunarodnaia zhizn',* no. 5 (May 1992): 26. It may be significant that Ambassador Nazarkin cites this figure and provides no Russian source for comparison.

8. Sergei Kulik, "Russian Arms Exports," *CNA Occasional Paper* (Alexandria, Va.: Center for Naval Analyses, February 1993), 37; Sergei Smirnov, "Takoi vot biznes," *Literaturnaia gazeta,* no. 16 (19 April 1995): 13.

9. Moscow Radio, ITAR-TASS (9 July 1992), in FBIS-SOV-92-133 (10 July 1992), 33. One such closed area, Krasnoiarsk-26, has been recently ordered by Yeltsin to construct facilities for recovering spent fuel from domestic nuclear power plants and to accept the same from installations in foreign countries. Moscow Radio, ITAR-TASS, 25 January 1995, in FBIS-SOV-95-017 (26 January 1995), 38. See also A. Mikushin, "Iadernyi poezd," *Gudok,* 9 February 1995, 4, about spent nuclear fuel from Hungary.

10. Stephen Foye, "Yeltsin Signs Law," RFE/RL *Daily Report,* no. 152 (11 August 1992): 1.

11. U.S. Senate, Committee on Governmental Affairs, "Proliferation Threats of the 1990s," *Hearing* (Washington, D.C.: GPO, 1993), 172. The ministry of security frustrated a subsequent attempt by North Korea to recruit a large group of Russian missile and space experts, according to Moscow Radio, 15 November 1993, in FBIS-SOV-93-219 (16 November 1993), 5.

12. "Moscow Offers India Weapons Joint Ventures," *Financial Times* (London), 17 June 1992, 3. Seventy percent of India's weapons systems were produced in the former USSR or in today's Russia, according to Iurii Kozmin over Moscow Radio, 30 March 1995, in FBIS-SOV-95-065, *Daily Report* (5 April 1994): 14.

13. Col. Gen. N. Dimidiuk, "K rynku oruzhiia...," *Voennyi vestnik,* no. 11 (November 1993): 2–5; Aleksandr Ivanov, "Politicheskii tovar," *Voennoe obozrenie,* no. 1 supplement to *Nezavisimaia gazeta,* 11 February 1995, 1.

14. Vladimir Kosarev, "Rossiia dolzhna zaniat' mesto...," *Krasnaia zvezda,* 6 January 1994.

15. Vladimir Zakharov and Vladimir Fortov, "Nauka uzhe v kome," *Izvestiia,* 2 November 1994, 4. For a less pessimistic assessment, see Viacheslav Tikhonov, "Segodnia utechka umov," *Kuranty,* 5 May 1995, 10.

16. E. Aleksandrov and V. Kolbin, "Ekonomika strany pogrebena pod grudami oruzhiia," *Izvestiia,* 16 June 1992, 3.

17. Ukaz no. 1850, "O stabilizatsii ekonomicheskogo polozheniia," *Rossiiskaia gazeta,* 13 November 1993, 4.

18. Aleksandr Egorov, "Problemy VPK trebuiut resheniia," *Krasnaia zvezda,* 27 November 1993, 2.

19. "Zakon o konversii oboronnoi promyshlennosti v Rossiiskoi Federatsii," *Rossiiskaia gazeta,* 27 April 1992, 6.

20. Oleg Antonov, "VPK mërtv," *Nezavisimaia gazeta,* 1 September 1994, 4.

21. Marshal of the Soviet Union Nikolai V. Ogarkov, chief editor, *Sovetskaia voennaia entsiklopediia* (Moscow: Voenizdat, 1978), 5:578. See also Richard F. Staar, "Byvshii Sovetskii Soiuz imeet izbytok zerna," *Izvestiia,* no. 18 (22 January 1992): 5; translated from R. F. Staar, "The Former USSR Has Grain in Abundance," *Wall Street Journal Europe,* 17–18 January 1992, 6.

22. Nikolai Efimovich, "Zatianite remni generaly!" *Komsomol'skaia pravda,* 15 September 1994, 2.

23. Estimates are from Col. Vitalii V. Shlykov, interviewed by the author on 16 November 1993.

24. "O sokrashchenii mobilizatsionnykh moshchnostei i mobilizatsionnogo rezerva," *Rossiiskaia gazeta,* 13 July 1994, 4.

25. A. Kotov and V. Artiukhov, "Problemy konversii," *Tekhnika i vooruzhenie,* no. 1–2 (January–February 1992): 32.

26. Ibid., 34.

27. Ruslan Lynev, "Tanki: konversiia i problemy," *Delovoi mir,* 9 May 1992, 3; interview with Col. Gen. A. A. Galkin, at that time chief of the main directorate for armor in the Commonwealth of Independent States military headquarters.

28. Valerii Gromak, "Na Baltiiskom flote popolnenie," *Krasnaia zvezda,* 17 March 1993, 5.

29. Viktor Litovkin, "Letaiushchie tarelki," *Izvestiia,* 14 July 1993, 8; Moscow Radio, 4 May 1995, in FBIS-SOV-95-087 (5 May 1995), 63–64.

30. L. Efanov, "Konversiia i menedzhment," *Voenno-ekonomicheskii zhurnal,* no. 1 (January 1994): 7.

31. John R. Thomas, "Russian Conversion Under Old Management," in U.S. Congress, Joint Economic Committee, *The Former Soviet Union in Transition* (Washington, D.C.: GPO, 1993), 760; Oleg Antonov, op. cit. See also Valerii Kornev, "Gigant oboronki zaplaty ne platil," *Izvestiia,* 15 February 1995, 2, for corruption at the *Barrikada* defense plant in Volgograd.

32. James H. Noren, "The Russian Military-Industrial Sector and Conversion," *Post Soviet Geography* 35, no. 9 (November 1994): 495–521, at 505–11. See also L. Efanov, "Strategiia konversii," *Armeiskii sbornik,* no. 3 (September 1994): 11, for ownership.

33. Evgenii Spiridonov, "Goskomoboronprom preduprezhdaet," *Segodnia,* 6 April 1994, 2. Note discrepancies in figures for VPK employment which are given by different Russian sources.

34. Dominick Bertelli, *Defense Conversion in Russia* (New York: Council on Economic Priorities, April 1994), 15–24.

35. Michael McFaul and David Bernstein, *Industrial Demilitarization, Privatization, Economic Reform, and Investment in Russia* (Stanford, Calif.: Center for International Security and Arms Control, Stanford University, 1993), 35–38.

36. For case studies of six VPK enterprises, see David Bernstein, ed., *Defense*

Industry Restructuring in Russia (Stanford, Calif.: Center for International Security and Arms Control, Stanford University, December 1994), chaps. 2–6, pp. 9–107.

37. The chairman of *Goskomoboronprom,* Viktor K. Glukhikh, envisages a future nucleus of slightly more than 400 VPK defense plants, completely financed by the government. See interview with Igor' Cherniak, "Budet li VPK shturmovat' Belyi dom?" *Komsomol'skaia pravda,* 27 April 1994, 6.

38. Col. A. V. Priskunov, "Konversiia i ekonomicheskaia bezopasnost' Rossii," *Voennaia mysl',* no. 12 (December 1993): 8–11; "Zakon o konversii oboronnoi promyshlennosti v R.F.," 6. This legislation had been signed by President Yeltsin on 20 March 1992.

39. Valerii Baberdin and Aleksandr Egorov, "Rekviem po 'oboronke'," *Krasnaia zvezda,* 15 March 1994, 3. See also Noren, "The Russian Military-Industrial Sector and Conversion," 517–21.

40. Richard W. Stevenson, "Russia's Arms Makers Try Change," *New York Times,* 2 May 1994, C-1, C-3.

41. "Russia's Aid Is Put at Risk Over New Taxes on Loans," *New York Times,* 2 May 1994, C-2.

42. Col. Gen. Igor' N. Rodionov, "V Rossii i dlia Rossii…," *Voennoe obozrenie,* no. 2, pp. 1–2; insert from *Nezavisimaia gazeta,* 22 April 1995.

43. Aleksandr Egorov, "Natsional'naia tekhnologicheskaia baza," *Krasnaia zvezda,* 29 April 1995, 4.

44. Vsevolod Medvedev, "Neotlozhnaia pomoshch' nauke," *Rossiiskaia gazeta,* 26 April 1995, 5; commentary to published government decision.

45. See, for example, Major Sergei Babichev, "Su-34: start v budushchee," *Krasnaia zvezda,* 29 April 1995, 5; "Northern Fleet Feature Shown," Russian Public TV, 16 April 1995, in FBIS-SOV-95-082 (28 April 1995), 32–33.

46. Vadim Mikhnevich, "Investorov v poiskakh," *Delovoi mir,* 21 January 1995, 8. VPK enterprises producing for the military will not be privatized, according to the chairman of the State Committee for Property, over Moscow Radio, 12 May 1995, in FBIS-SOV-95-093 (13 May 1995), 41.

―――――― *Myth No. 5* ――――――
Export of Defensive Weapons Only

> Russia strictly adheres to [the] principle of selling only defensive arms.
> *Aleksandr N. Panov, deputy foreign minister*

During the 1980s, the Soviet Union exported weapons valued at $121 billion to fifty-five countries. Only about one-tenth of that total could be collected. The balance, in the form of long-term credits, most probably will never be repaid. The current Russian decisionmakers are selling incomparably less, although the return comes in the form of hard currency or commodities that can be resold on the international market.

One estimate for 1992 cited about 40 percent of all defense production as the amount of weaponry that had to be exported to maintain the military-industrial complex operational.[1] That same year the total for Russian arms sales dropped to $2.4 billion (5.9% of the world total) from $6.6 billion (20.7%) during 1991. This represented a considerable decline from the high of $21.5 billion (34%) in 1986. The range of weapons being sold varies from basic to advanced and is accompanied by large quantities of munitions.[2]

During 1993, with sales totaling $2.6 billion, the following countries appear to have been the three largest recipients of Russian arms:

Iran: $1.5 billion for three diesel-powered submarines, 24 each of Su-24 bombers, MiG-29 and MiG-31 fighters, Su-27 fighter bombers, 200 T-72 tanks, and several S-300V air defense systems.
China: $1.8 billion for 26 top-of-the-line Su-27s, a number of S-300V air defense systems, and SA-10 surface-to-air missiles.

Syria: $2 billion for two dozen MiG-29s, one dozen Su-27s, exactly 200 T-72 tanks, several S-300V air defense systems, and SA-14 shoulder-fired surface-to-air missiles.[3]

Some of these items had been contracted for delivery over more than one year.

Apart from the above customers, Russia signed an agreement with India to deliver $400 million worth of dual-use missile technology, which included two large cryogenic rocket engines. In late June 1993, a shipment of Russian rocket fuel chemical ingredients for Libya (under UN embargo) was detained while being trans-shipped across Ukraine. The U.S. government registered strong protests against such proliferation of missile technology and threatened to invoke sanctions against Russia. The latter responded by canceling certain parts of the agreement with India in return for a share in launching American commercial satellites. However, toward the end of July 1994, Moscow agreed to sell Delhi seven smaller cryogenic rocket engines in place of the larger models,[4] to be delivered during the following year.

Despite such problems with supplying sophisticated equipment, Russia is attempting to become highly competitive in the international arms market for conventional weapons. See Table 5.1 for the prices (in U.S. dollars) for conventional weapons as listed in a Moscow weekly magazine.

The war in Chechnya demonstrated that most of the Russian weapons systems were incapable of operating under conditions of fog or in darkness. This has been due to the "permanent lag behind developed countries with regard to infra-red target acquisition equipment."[5]

MiG-31 "Foxhound" interceptor *(U.S. Naval Institute photo collection)*

TABLE 5.1
Prices for Conventional Weapons

Weapon	Price (US$)
Armored personnel carriers	
BMP-2	$ 400,000
BMP-3	800,000
Main battle tanks	
T-72 S	1,200,000
T-80 UP	2,200,000
152mm self-propelled howitzer	
2S19	1,600,000
Self-propelled antiaircraft complex	
2S6M	12,000,000
Fighter aircraft	
MiG-29	12,000,000
MiG-31	45,000,000–50,000,000
Kalashnikov automatic rifle	
AK-47	150–200

Source: Pëtr Vasil'ev, "Kupite avianosets!" *Novoe vremia*, no. 17 (April 1993): 21.

The current system through which arms sales are effected differs from the pre-coup (19–21 August 1991) monopoly situation, when the Soviet Union still existed and decisions were made by the ruling communist party's political bureau. A new ministry of foreign economic relations currently oversees these activities through an intermediary state company called *Rosvooruzhenie*, which absorbed three earlier commercial structures on 18 November 1993: *Oboroneksport, Spetsvneshtekhnika,* and *Russkoe oruzhie*. Air Marshal Evgenii I. Shaposhnikov was appointed two months later as President Yeltsin's personal representative to *Rosvooruzhenie* and as a watchdog against corruption.[6] (See Chart 5.1.)

Previous Experiences

In 1992, President Yeltsin issued a decree allowing the region of Tula to sell defense products directly to foreign buyers. Although such independent transactions still adhered to arms-export lists, that precedent in theory broke the long-standing monopoly of the center. In practice, however, the Moscow bureaucracy still retains power to block any initiative by a local enterprise. Competition with the official trading system, described above, is provided by an active black market, which has been estimated to comprise between 15 and 20 percent of the overt annual arms-export flow.[7]

CHART 5.1
Restructured Arms-Export Mechanism

PRESIDENT OF RUSSIA
(Boris N. Kuzyk, special assistant)

INTERDEPARTMENTAL COORDINATING COUNCIL ON MILITARY-TECHNICAL POLICY
Oleg N. Soskovets, chairman
(Sergei I. Svechnikov, deputy chairman)

Working Group of the Council (Vladimir I. Sukhanov, executive secretary)

MINISTRY OF FOREIGN ECONOMIC RELATIONS
(Deputy Minister Vladimir D. Shibaev, supervisor)

Main Directorate for Military-Technical Cooperation
(Col. Valerii S. Mironov, head)

COMMERCIAL STRUCTURE FOR ARMS TRADE

Rosvooruzhenie
(Aleksandr I. Kotelkin, director general)
(Valerii D. Tret'iak, first deputy director general)

Oboroneksport	**Spetsvneshtekhnika**	**Russkoe oruzhie**
(Maj. Gen. Valentin F. Trofimov, director)	(Maj. Gen. Valerii G. Brailovskii, director)	(Stanislav P. Chernov, director)

Sources: Pavel Fel'gengauer, "Sozdana spetskorporatsiia 'Russkoe oruzhie,'" *Segodnia*, no. 31 (6 July 1993): 2; Valentin Rudenko, "Firma, gde znaiut tolk," *Krasnaia zvezda*, 1 October 1993, p. 3; Igor' Cherniak, "Kogda verstalsia nomer," *Komsomol'skaia pravda*, 23 December 1993, p. 2; Viktor Badurkin, "Dollar pishet. Chto v ume?" *Trud*, 8 February 1994, p. 5; Aleksandr Sychëv, "Rukovodit' torgovlei oruzhiem . . . ," *Izvestiia*, 30 November 1994, p. 3 (interview with Kotelkin); Ukaz Prezidenta, no. 2251, "O gosudarstvennom komitete po voenno-tekhnicheskoi politike," *Rossiiskaia gazeta*, 10 January 1995, p. 1; "Oruzheiniki i prodavtsy budut rabotat' druzhno," *Rossiiskie vesti*, 16 June 1995, p. 1, for presidential decree on interdepartmental council.

Part of this illicit trade occurs through former republics of the now-defunct USSR. The case of the state arms company Beltekheksport in Minsk selling the S-300 PMU antimissile system to an American company is instructive. This equipment had been left to Belarus by Russia, which markets the same model to foreign customers, having displayed it at the arms fair in Abu Dhabi during 1993. After charges and countercharges, a Russian An-124 transport aircraft landed toward the end of the following year in Huntsville, Alabama, with the system's components—presumably destined for Redstone Arsenal. Subsequent reports claimed that Russian military intelligence (GRU) had replaced the command and control subsystems, which integrated radar information and missile flight, with obsolete equipment.[8]

Yet much of the arms trade originates with the ministry of defense itself. This government agency had been permitted through its own organization called *Voentekh* to redistribute excess weapons stockpiles to Commonwealth of Independent States members and use the proceeds for construction of housing and for other social needs of the new Russian armed forces. It was also allowed to sell decommissioned weapons systems.

Some of the older equipment and armaments were being marketed by individual military commands. For example, Black Sea fleet naval officers identified forty-nine ships to be auctioned off, including fifteen submarines that had already been sold. The cruiser *Zhdanov* was purchased by India, reportedly for less than would have been received if offered as scrap metal. These sales were being managed through a joint stock company in Moscow called *Nevikon-ziuid*, headed by a retired Russian admiral.[9]

Just before he signed the decree concerning Tula's defense complex, Yeltsin issued one permitting the Russian air force to market 1,600 surplus military aircraft. Two months later, Omsk province authorities offered about 1,000 old tanks for sale at scrap-metal prices. The more recent T-72 and T-80 models reportedly can be purchased for $350,000 each on the black market, compared with official prices of $1.2 and $2.2 million respectively. Mikhail N. Bazhanov, at the time chairman of the State Committee on Conversion, had predicted optimistically an income of at least $10 billion during 1992 from such arms exports.[10] As noted at the beginning of this chapter, the above-estimated figure was four times greater than could be achieved.

Apart from the sale of cryogenic rocket engines, Russia has continued to provide other weapons to India, which received $830 million in defense credits from Moscow. Tanks as well as MiG-21, MiG-23, and MiG-27 military jets are being produced under license by Delhi. The latter has been offered a joint venture by Moscow to market these weapons systems throughout the Third World.[11] Russia thus continues escalating the arms race between India and Pakistan, neither of which has signed the nuclear nonproliferation treaty. It would appear that President Yeltsin has decided to sell arms almost wherever there is a customer, with the exception of actual belligerents. A special nine-page advertisement section in an American trade journal provided descriptions, diagrams, and photographs of eighteen weapons systems, ranging from pistols to submarines, for sale through the former *Oboroneksport* commercial enterprise.[12] (See Table 5.2.)

Arms Bazaars

Russia is also participating in trade fairs, such as the one held during 7–11 November 1993 at Abu Dhabi in the United Arab Emirates (UAE), which resulted in a $760-million contract with Kuwait. An earlier fair at the same place, where 370 weapons systems were displayed, had cost Moscow $3 million for transportation, rental space, and delegation expenses. The IDEKS-93 air show included Russian fighter planes, attack helicopters, passenger and freight airliners, as well as stunt aircraft. For some unexplained reason, neither the MiG-29 nor the new Ka-50 combat helicopter made an appearance. Countries throughout the Persian Gulf reportedly have purchased about fifty Russian Il-76 cargo planes. The Russians hope to enter the arms markets of Saudi Arabia, Kuwait, UAE, Oman, Qatar, and Bahrain—the six oil-producing states in this region. Moscow expects the Saudis to spend $20 billion on the purchase of weapons during the next few years.[13]

Dubai was followed by the LIMA-93 exposition in Malaysia late the following month. Equipment on display included the S-300PMU-1 and S-300V antimissile complexes; the *Igla* and *Tor*-M1 antiaircraft missile systems; the *Piran'ia* and *Triton* midget submarines; the Ka-50 combat helicopter; and MiG-29, Su-27, and MiG-31 fighter aircraft. Independent experts reportedly estimated that sales could total $1 billion. During 1995, Russia was delivering MiG-29s to Malaysia and training its pilots.[14]

Another arms exhibit, this time in Latin America (FIDAE-94), took place at Santiago de Chile toward the end of March 1994, with more than 100 models of Russian weaponry and military equipment on display. Apart from the above-listed products, Moscow showed weapons for underwater combat against terrorists: a 4.5mm SPP-1M pistol that hits targets at 30 feet and a lightweight APS submachine gun with a range of up to 100 feet. Guns equipped with silencers included the 7.62mm PSS pistol, the 9mm AS submachine gun, and the 9mm VSS sniper rifle. During the second half

TABLE 5.2
Selected Weapons for Sale

Category	Description
Air Defense Systems	
S-300V (Type I and II missiles, target station, radar vehicles, command vehicle, guidance stations)	Complete battle unit, five-minute operational-status conversion time; tactical and ballistic intercept, engages up to 24 targets at once (range = 100 km; speed = 8,640 km/hr)
S-300PMU1 (mobile, single-stage multichannel missile tracking, transportation device; flexible interface)	Similar to U.S. Patriot, can engage 32 missiles and 6 targets at once; 5 min. deployment (range = 150 km)
Strela–10M3 (light surface-to-air missile device; locks out friendly targets; operational under all temperature conditions)	Three-man vehicle with eight 9M333 missiles; radar (range = 500–5,000 m; elevation = 25–3,500 m)
2K22M *Tunguska* SP (gun and missile in one vehicle; antiaircraft escort for armored and motorized infantry; radar; 30mm guns; repair, maintenance, ammunition trucks, etc.)	5,000 rounds/min.; 8 launchers for 9M311 surface-to-air missiles (guns: up to 3,000 m altitude and 200–4,000 m range; missiles: 15–3,500 m altitude and 2,500–8,000 m range)
Artillery Systems	
2S19 *Msta*-S SP (diesel-powered 152mm SP artillery vehicle; also fires *Krasnopol* laser-guided rounds; can sustain 100 rounds fired in first hour)	Five-man crew; controls 70 projectiles in flight (range = 24,700 m/standard HE round; speed = 60 km/hr with 500-km road range)
9P140 *Uragan* (220mm multiple-launch rockets with two vehicles; fires variety of single warheads or salvoes; 16 launch tubes)	Four-man crew; 16-rocket salvo, saturates 426,000 square meters
2S5 *Giatsint* (152mm self-propelled howitzer; easy construction of self-protection trench)	Five-man crew; carries 30 complete rounds; fires 5 to 6 rounds/min. (max. range = 28,400 m; max. road speed = 60 km/hr)
Antitank Systems	
Konkurs (medium-range antitank missile; multipurpose; thermal imaging camera)	Missiles pierce 750 to 800mm homogeneous steel armor (missile speed = 250 m/sec; max. day range = 4,000 m; max. night range = 2,500 m)

Category	Description
Antitank Systems *(cont.)*	
Sturm-S Tank Destroyer (amphibious; carries 12 missiles; fires up to four missiles/min.)	Two-man crew; vehicle is inconspicuous; engages armed helicopters
Armored Vehicles	
T-72S *Shilden* (T–72 MBT, plus protective armor and laser-guided antitank missiles)	Three-man crew (max. speed = 60 km/hr)
BMP-3 MICV (two-man turret for 100mm pressure gun and 30mm automatic cannon; amphibious; significant ammunition reserves)	Three-man crew, plus nine other infantry men; can fire 10 rounds/min. (range = 4,000 m; max. speed = 70 km/hr on land, 10 km/hr in water)
2S23 *Nona* SP (two-man turret for 120/24mm rifled gun/mortar; uses all standard Russian ammunition; variety of projectiles, including foreign designs; amphibious, like APC version)	Fires 8 to 10 rounds/min.; turret compatible with Russian and foreign-designed chassis
Landing Craft	
Type 12061 Air Cushion (amphibious ferry for troops and vehicles)	(Speed = 55 km/hr; range = 200 miles; full-load wt. = 150 ton)
Submarines	
Type 877EKM (diesel-electric powered; antisurface and ASW roles)	51-man crew; max. operating depth = 240 m (range = 3,600 km)
Fighter Aircraft	
Su-27 (comes also as trainer; variety of missiles; 30mm gun; etc.)	Holds 27 rate-of-climb records (max. speed = Mach 2.35; ceiling over 18,000 m; range = 4,000 km)
MiG-29 (excels in both BVR and close-range combat; 30mm cannon; 6 to 8 missiles; can carry gravity bombs and rocket pods)	(Max. speed = Mach 2.3; 240 m takeoff run; ceiling = 17,000 m)
Guns	
AKR-74U SMG (submachine gun of Kalashnikov AK-47; compact)	Fires 600 rounds/min.; bullet muzzle velocity = 700 m/sec; empty wt. = 3.2 kg)
Makarov (pistols for armed forces; compact models for security and police forces; civilian use)	Lightweight; PM and PSM magazine capacity of eight rounds

Source: "Defense Products from Russia," *Military Technology* (February 1993), special advertising section.

TABLE 5.3
Costs for Modernizing Equipment

Weapons System	Modernization Prices (US$)
Armored personnel carrier, BMP–1 (10,000 sold abroad)	$ 250,000
Fighter aircraft, MiG–21 (3,000 exported)	400,000
Multiple rocket launcher, *Grad*	200,000
Main battle tank, T–72	200,000
Self-propelled antiaircraft artillery, *Shilka*	100,000

Source: Leonid Zavarskii, "Sluzhenie Marsu ne terpit nishchëty," *Kommersant-Daily*, 15 October 1994, 10.

of April 1994, Russians exhibited their Tu-204 civilian passenger aircraft at the "Aviation Africa—1994" fair in Johannesburg.[15]

During 1994, Russian military hardware was shown in a total of eighteen foreign countries, including the ILA-94 aerospace exhibition in Berlin (May and June) and the air show at Farnborough in early September. The following month, Russia displayed its weapons at the DEFENDORY-94 exhibit in Greece. It also planned to participate at IDEX-95 in Abu Dhabi, UAE, during March of 1995 with 200 samples of fast attack boats, antiaircraft missile systems, tanks, armored vehicles, and firearms.[16]

Some eighty countries throughout the world now have Russian weapons, although the latest systems comprise only 5 percent of the total. Because of the relatively high prices for the new models, many foreign armies have opted to modernize their older equipment. See Table 5.3 for the cost of this process.

Any number of these countries may decide to have Russia upgrade their arsenals rather than purchase newer models, which may be up to ten times more expensive (e.g., the T-80 main battle tank).

The Record

Under UN General Assembly resolution No. 46/366, Russia has been reporting its annual arms sales to the United Nations since 1992. The figures on Table 5.4 (for 1993) are obviously incomplete. For instance, neither China nor Syria is listed. Foreign Minister Andrei V. Kozyrev is reported to have revealed that Russia sold $1.2 billion in military hardware during calendar year 1992 to China alone. On the other hand, Moscow has refused to provide Washington, D.C., with a detailed accounting of its arms sales to Iran.[17]

The chairman of the State Committee for Defense Industry, Viktor K. Glukhikh, predicted that arms sales during 1993 might reach $3.5 billion. However, during the first five months of that year, the total amounted to just over half a billion dollars.[18] It would seem that, at such a rate, Russian exports of weapons should have dropped even lower for 1993 than they were during the preceding year. Much would depend upon sales to China, estimated as high as $1.2 billion for the 1993 calendar year.[19]

On 11 November 1993, a five-year agreement was signed at Beijing by the Chinese and Russian defense ministers. This was a follow-on to President Yeltsin's visit to China in December 1992. The pact envisages an "exchange of experiences in various [military] areas" between the two high commands. During 1994, Russia obligated itself to dispatch seven military delegations of different types, whereas China would reciprocate

TABLE 5.4
Russian Arms Sales in 1993

Category	Number	Purchaser
Main battle tanks (120)	100	Iran
	20	Angola
Armored combat vehicles (357)	115	Turkey
	95	United Arab Emirates
	35	Angola
	20	Uzbekistan
	12	Bangladesh
	80	Iran
Large-caliber artillery systems	14	Angola
Combat aircraft (33)[a]	28	Hungary
	5	Slovakia
Attack helicopters	—	—
Warships		
(submarines)	(1)	Iran
Missiles and missile launchers	—	—

Source: Report of the Secretary General, *United Nations Register of Conventional Arms* (New York: UN General Assembly, 13 October 1994). See also Edward J. Laurance and Christine K. Woodward, "An Evaluation of the Second Year of Reporting to the United Nations Register of Conventional Arms," *Research Report* (Monterey, Calif.: Monterey Institute of International Studies, 13 October 1994), 19 pp.

[a] Although not identified regarding models, it is significant that both recipients are former Warsaw Pact members (Slovakia, as part of then-Czechoslovakia). It is difficult for Russia to sell the Il-96 m, MiG-29, and Su-27 to hard-currency customers, because there are no simulators for these aircraft. Aleksandr Dymkovets, "Konversiia," *Rossiiskie vesti*, 21 February 1995, 2.

with six. Defense Minister Grachëv refused to provide any answer to questions dealing with arms sales when he visited Beijing. However, the first of four Russian "Kilo"-class diesel-powered submarines was delivered in February 1995 on a Chinese freighter. China agreed to purchase six more of these subs during the following months and was negotiating an additional twelve over the next five years.[20]

Two heavy Kiev-class aircraft carriers from the Russian navy were sold for scrap to Young Distribution, Inc., in South Korea. The *Minsk* and *Novorossiisk* were to be moved from Vladivostok to a special worksite near Pusan by mid-1995. The scrap-market price for such a 40,000-ton vessel is $100 per ton. Adm. Igor' N. Khmel'nov, commander of the Pacific Fleet, stated in an interview that thirty-two other warships would be sent to the same place later in the year.[21] During 1994, North Korea purchased a fleet of Russian submarines, ostensibly for scrap.

These results were indeed minuscule in comparison with sales throughout the 1980s and into 1990–91 as mentioned earlier, when the Soviet Union exported in excess of $121 billion worth of arms to fifty-five countries. The largest buyers, in billions of U.S. dollars, included the following: India (18.5), Iraq (13.7), Syria (12.6), Czechoslovakia (10.1), Poland (6.7), Afghanistan (6.6), Angola (6.3), North Korea (6.1), Libya (6.1), and East Germany (6.1).

However, only about 10 percent of these vast sums could ever be collected. Much of the rest amounted to "fraternal aid," that is, free to the recipient or offered on long-term credit that will never be paid. Total accumulated debts are estimated at $142 billion, including interest. USSR allies received about one-fourth of the total deliveries, with the remainder going to Third World countries.[22] (See Table 5.5.)

During mid-1994, Russia had military-technical agreements with forty-four countries. Such cooperation, apart from arms sales, included training of foreign specialists, delivery of spare parts, exchange of military delegations, servicing of equipment, maintenance, and modernization. The first deputy chief of the General Staff, charged with this work, claimed that only five countries in the world seriously develop weapons systems (Russia being one of them), whereas 195 countries purchase such arms.[23]

New Sales Structure

On the basis of secret presidential edict No. 1932 s, dated 18 November 1993, a single commercial enterprise, *Rosvooruzhenie* (acronym means State Company for Export and Import of Arms and Military Equipment), absorbed three former entities. The first head of this new organization was Lt. Gen. Viktor A. Samoilov, a former colonel in the main administration

TABLE 5.5
Soviet/Russian Arms Exports, 1986–1995
(billions of current U.S. dollars)

Year	Total
1986	21.5
1987	23.0
1988	22.5
1989	19.7
1990	15.4
Total	*102.1*
1991	6.6
1992	2.4
1993	2.6
1994	1.7
1995	est. 2.5
Total	*15.8*
10-year total	*117.9*

Sources: Richard F. Grimmett, "Conventional Arms Transfers to the Third World, 1986–1993," *CRS Report for Congress* (Washington, D.C.: Legislative Reference Service, 29 July 1994), Table 9, p. 86; Aleksandr I. Kotelkin, *Rosvooruzhenie* director general, over Moscow Russian TV, 9 March 1995; FBIS-SOV-95-050 (15 March 1995), 13–14, for the 1994 figure and the 1995 estimate.

for personnel at the defense ministry. After the unsuccessful coup in 1991, he received promotion to major general and again only two months later to his present rank.[24]

Director General Samoilov was graduated from the polytechnic institute at Tula. In 1991, he forfeited membership in the communist party because of "support for Boris Yeltsin and his democratic views." At that time, Samoilov served as chief of staff to the (Russian) State Committee on Defense and Security. The following year, on recommendation of General Grachëv, he became military advisor to then–Deputy Prime Minister Vladimir F. Shumeiko, currently chairman of the Federation Council or upper chamber of parliament.[25]

Simultaneously, a presidential representative received appointment to oversee *Rosvooruzhenie*. As mentioned above, he was Air Marshal Evgenii I. Shaposhnikov, who had served successively as USSR defense minister (after August 1991), commander-in-chief of Commonwealth armed forces (1992), and secretary of the Russian Security Council (1993). In an interview, Shaposhnikov revealed that he would analyze each arms-export agreement and make sure that profits went into the state treasury and not "Western bank accounts of dubious economic organizations."[26] In other words, the air marshal was there to prevent some of the rampant corruption that had siphoned off between $10 and $15 billion per year from all of Russia's foreign trade transactions.

Rosvooruzhenie has been given a new objective, namely to invest private as well as government funds for the purpose of producing weapons that will compete on the world market. Russia's largest defense plants in the military-industrial complex (VPK) will sign contracts with *Rosvooruzhenie* for delivery of their arms for export. Money received from foreign purchasers will be transferred to VPK producers (and not the government as heretofore), minus commission fees of 3 to 5 percent for *Rosvooruzhenie*. Taxes on sales will be collected by the federal government.[27] Initially, the foreign economic relations ministry will license all exports.

This new organization *Rosvooruzhenie* already has representatives in forty countries and, apparently, the expertise to market weapons. Samoilov had taken three of his deputies from *Oboroneksport,* the foreign trade company previously responsible for 90 percent of all former arms exports, and one deputy from *Spetsvneshtekhnika*, which had been charged with delivery of spare parts and establishing defense infrastructures in foreign countries.[28] On 25 November 1994, the former chairman from the board for foreign cooperation at the ministry of foreign economic relations, Aleksandr I. Kotelkin, replaced Samoilov. (See Chart 5.1.)

The 40-year-old Kotelkin has a military/technical as well as diplomatic background. He began his service in the Kiev Military District and ended up as chief of engineering for an air force army. Subsequently, Kotelkin worked at the diplomatic mission to the United Nations in New York. From there, he transferred to the ministry of foreign economic relations in Moscow, where he headed the chief administration for military/technical cooperation. That work brought in more than $2 billion. So, this man is reportedly a true professional.[29]

Kotelkin inherited a situation where some 500 special export organizations dealt with strategic raw materials, weapons, and technology that potentially could be utilized for the production of arms. All had been registered with the ministry of foreign economic relations and received licenses for the above purpose. Reregistration for calendar year 1995 should reduce the number of exporters and establish stricter controls. However, a new military and technical policy committee has been created, and the producers of MiG aircraft received official permission to enter foreign markets, which would seem to undercut the monopoly of *Rosvooruzhenie*.[30]

Future Sales Prospects

Not only has Russia been selling its most advanced weapons systems to countries that can afford to pay in hard currency, it is also doing so in order to reduce debts owed abroad. The results have been less than successful in maintaining a robust military-industrial complex (VPK), and they have not brought in substantial funds for conversion. This situation has not discouraged domestic supporters of expanded arms sales who saw a potential for reaching $20 billion during 1994 or eight times more than two years earlier, in the words of former *Rosvooruzhenie* General Director Samoilov.[31] This potential, of course, could not be fulfilled.

For several years, the VPK produced approximately three times less for government exports than for the ministry of defense. It may have been dealing directly with foreign customers to make up the difference in costs. Col. Vitalii V. Shlykov, the already mentioned former deputy chairman of the State Defense and Security Committee (precursor to the current ministry of defense) for the Russian Federation, has charged that the VPK was using mobilization reserves to maintain production levels. Even those "untouchable" supplies cannot last forever.

One would think that decisionmakers in Moscow realize the danger of such policies, and that may be one reason for the appointment of Air Marshal Shaposhnikov as presidential representative to oversee arms sales and root out the corruption that seems to have become pervasive. His report on this subject is said to have impressed President Yeltsin,[32] although it remains doubtful whether any new reorganization can eliminate graft.

One example of such corruption involved Sergei N. Oslikovskii, deputy director of *Rosvooruzhenie,* who had been paid a personal commission of 20 percent for delivery of "special goods" as well as negotiation of contracts with the Terimon Company in Zurich. Documents seized by the Russian procurator general's office proved that Oslikovskii had visited Libya with a proposal to supply $50 million worth of "special materials,"[33] which would have violated the UN embargo.

This ban remains in effect vis-à-vis Libya, Somalia, Iraq, and the countries of former Yugoslavia. In November 1994, Russia's foreign minister, Andrei V. Kozyrev, reportedly signed an agreement with Iraq's deputy prime minister Tariq 'Aziz to replace the tanks, defense systems, and radar installations destroyed during the Gulf War. Russia also undertook to modernize Iraq's armed forces and rebuild air bases as soon as UN sanctions have been lifted.[34]

Serbia reportedly received ninety-two of Russia's T-72 tanks during

May and eighty-three of its 122mm howitzers at the end of December 1993, some shipped via Ukraine. During the final withdrawal of Russian troops from Germany, air defense missiles were "lost" by the Western Group of Forces. A total of 400 freightcar loads of such military hardware found their way into the Balkans. Croatia received many of those weapons, disguised as "humanitarian aid." The current executives at *Rosvooruzhenie* (Svechnikov, Kuzyk, Kotelkin) received annual bonuses of between $20,000 and $58,000 (in U.S. dollars).[35]

It is obvious from the foregoing that Russia has been and will continue to trade primarily in offensive weapons, even for the arsenals of potential enemies. Thus, when a deputy foreign minister named Aleksandr N. Panov announced publicly at a meeting held in his Moscow office building, "Russia strictly adheres to the principle of selling only *defensive* arms. Moreover, Russia sells these armaments in the amount that would not upset the existing balance of forces in some or other region. *Every deal* is reported to the U.N. register which ensures the transparency of trade operations,"[36] one wonders whether those who make such claims actually believe them.

Will Order Prevail?

As suggested in the foregoing, the military had its own export company called *Voentekh* for the sale of arms since 15 October 1992. That same year, it delivered a state-of-the-art T-80U main battle tank and the *Tunguska* anti-aircraft missile complex to Britain, at a time when the export of such weapons systems had been banned. Other such transgressions led to a decision by the State Committee for Military-Technical Policy to forbid *Voentekh* from any contact with the world arms market in which it already controlled about one-third of such Russian exports. This ban was ignored.[37]

Maj. Gen. Aleksandr V. Korzhakov, commander of presidential security, undertook an investigation of arms sales. He reported to Yeltsin that *Voentekh* had delivered T-72 tanks to Croatia in October 1992 and one year later attempted to send artillery pieces plus 2,000 machine guns with ammunition to Serbia, despite the UN embargo. Russian foreign intelligence supposedly blocked these latter shipments. The seven-page report by Korzhakov described "falsified documents and audits, disregard for international and domestic laws, bypassing of contracts, and illegal agreements."[38]

Repercussions from the above as well as from Air Marshal Shaposhnikov's earlier investigation of corrupt practices at *Rosvooruzhenie* apparently convinced Yeltsin to remove active-duty officers from weapons sales. The defense ministry issued a May 1995 directive, ordering experts and advisors in uniform recalled back to their military units.[39] All key positions at *Rosvooruzhenie* are now held by officers from the former KGB or army intelligence (GRU). The de facto chain of command runs from Korzhakov to Kuzyk, to Svechnikov, to Kotelkin. (See Chart 5.1.) Of the 243 permanent positions allocated to the State Committee for Military-Technical Policy, about 95 vacancies or almost 40 percent were filled by military intelligence and federal security officers.[40]

Army General Grachëv reportedly submitted in early May 1995 a draft document which, if approved by Yeltsin, would transfer control over all weapons sales to the defense ministry. The reason? *Rosvooruzhenie* had been compromised and should be disbanded. However, that organization was controlled by army officers who demonstrated their inefficiency and susceptibility to corruption, not the least of which related to clandestine sales through *Voentekh* to both sides in civil and other wars. After all, Grachëv himself had set up that company.[41]

Which side will receive the support of Yeltsin is not known, although *Rosvooruzhenie* appears to be in business. Its director-general announced that, in the near future, a number of large Russian weapons' producers would be authorized to trade independently on foreign markets. Ten such enterprises were being considered as prime candidates for such operations.[42]

Only a few years ago, the sharing and distribution of surplus "defensive" weapons among newly sovereign countries that had joined the Commonwealth of Independent States contributed to the proliferation of regional conflicts. These and other developments are discussed in the next chapter.

Notes

1. Aleksei V. Iablokov, "Smozhet li 'oboronka' nas nakormit?" *Izvestiia*, 23 April 1992, 2; the author was an advisor to the Russian Federation government at that time.

2. Richard F. Grimmett, "Conventional Arms Transfers to the Third World, 1985–1993," *CRS Report for Congress* (Washington, D.C.: Congressional Research Service, Library of Congress, 29 July 1994), 7–8.

3. The forecast of $3.5 to $4 billion during 1993 comes from Viktor K. Glukhikh, chairman of the State Committee for Defense Industries, over Moscow Television, 30 November 1993, in FBIS-SOV-93-228 (30 November 1993), 49. Other data are in Steven Erlanger, "Russia Sells War Machines," *New York Times*, 3 February 1993, A-1, 7.

4. "Rossiia soglasilas' prodat' Indii raketnye dvigateli," *Izvestiia*, 27 July 1994, 1. India has a small arsenal of nuclear warheads and is developing longer-range ballistic missiles to carry them, according to the U.S. government.

5. Pavel Fel'gengauer, "Torgovlia oruzhiem ne tak vygodna…," *Segodnia*, 10 March 1995, 2.

6. Kulik, "Russian Arms Exports," 32–35; official press release, "GK 'Rosvooruzhenie:' zadachi i vozmozhnosti," *Krasnaia zvezda,* 27 January 1994, 1, 3.

7. Kulik, "Russian Arms Exports," 37; Sergei Smirnov, "Takoi vot biznes," *Literaturnaia gazeta,* no. 16 (19 April 1995): 13.

8. Viktor Litovkin, "Taina polëta AN-124 v Alabamu raskryta," *Izvestiia,* 24 December 1994, 2; Aleksandr Koretskii and Aleksandr Safronov, "'Kukla' po-armeiskii...," *Kommersant-Daily,* 9 March 1995, 1, 4.

9. Sergei Tsykora, "Nachalas' rasprodazha Chernomorskogo flota," *Izvestiia,* 18 February 1992, 2.

10. M. Poliakov, "Plus 11" program on Moscow Television, 2 May 1992, in FBIS-SOV-92-086 (4 May 1992), 6–7.

11. "Moscow Offers India Weapons Joint Ventures," *Financial Times* (London), 17 June 1992, 3. Seventy percent of India's weapons systems were produced in the former USSR or in today's Russia, according to Iurii Kozmin over Moscow Radio, 30 March 1995, in FBIS-SOV-95-065 (5 April 1995), 14.

12. Col. Gen. N. Dimidiuk, "K rynku oruzhiia...," *Voennyi vestnik,* no. 11 (November 1993): 2–5; Aleksandr Ivanov, "Politicheskii tovar," *NG Voennoe obozrenie,* no. 1 (11 February 1995): 1.

13. Vladimir Kosarev, "Rossiia dolzhna zaniat' mesto...," *Krasnaia zvezda,* 6 January 1994, 3; Stanislav Bychkov over Moscow Radio, 30 March 1995, in FBIS-SOV-95-065 (5 April 1995), 14.

14. Sergei Akshintsev, "Boevye samolëty Rossii," *Krasnaia zvezda,* 1 June 1995, 4.

15. "...A dukh v kazarmakh vsë krepchaet," *Komsomol'skaia pravda,* 19 April 1994, 2; Valentin Rudenko, "U aviastroitelei poiavilsia shans...," *Krasnaia zvezda,* 30 April 1994, 6.

16. Evgenii Ruzhitskii, "Rossiia na vzlëte," *Armeiskii sbornik,* no. 5 (November 1994): 66–69; Viktor Litovkin, "Na vystavke v Abu-Dabi," *Ogonëk,* no. 18 (May 1995): 76–77; "Kolumbia otkryvaet Ekspomilitar-95," *Krasnaia zvezda,* 17 June 1995, 3.

17. Cited by Patrick E. Tyler, "Russia and China in Military Pact," *New York Times,* 10 November 1993, A-4; Elaine Sciolino, "U.S. and Russia at Odds...," *New York Times,* 19 January 1995, A-9.

18. "Goskomstat Rossii ob eksporte vooruzhenii," *Segodnia,* no. 29 (29 June 1993): 3.

19. Stephen Foye, "Grachëv in China," *RFE/RL Daily Report* (9 November 1993), 1.

20. Vladimir Skosyrev, "Kitaitsy govoriat dobrye slova Grachëvu," *Izvestiia,* 11 November 1993, 3; *South Morning Post* (Hong Kong), 4 March 1995, cited by Doug Clarke, OMRI *Daily Digest,* pt. 1, no. 46 (6 March 1995): 3. See also "Recent Military Contracts with PRC," Moscow Radio, 15 May 1995, in FBIS-SOV-95-093 (15 May 1995), 14.

21. Moscow Radio, ITAR-TASS, 24 March 1995, in FBIS-SOV-95-057 (24 March 1995), 13. See also Steve Glain, "Korean Aircraft Carrier Deal Prompts Skepticism," *Wall Street Journal,* 5 April 1995, A-12.

22. Keith Bush, "Damascus Asked for Repayment," *RFE/RL Daily Report,* no. 81 (28 April 1994): 2; Vasil'ev, "Kupite avianosets!" 18.

23. Col. Gen. V. M. Zhurbenko, interviewed by Col. Valentin Rudenko, "Interesy gosudarstva prevyshe vsego," *Krasnaia zvezda*, 27 August 1994, 4.

24. Igor' Cherniak, "Kogda verstalsia nomer," *Komsomol'skaia pravda*, 23 December 1993, 2.

25. Nikolai Burbyga, "Rossiia budet torgovat' oruzhiem," *Izvestiia*, 1 February 1994, 3.

26. Aleksandr Zhilin, "Oruzhie v chistykh rukakh," *Moskovskie novosti*, no. 5 (30 January–6 February 1994): A-14.

27. Leonid Zavarskii, "Rosvooruzhenie," *Kommersant-Daily*, 15 March 1994, 1.

28. Aleksandr Sychev, "Torgovlia oruzhiem," *Novoe vremia*, no. 13 (March 1994): 13–14.

29. Aleksandr Sychev, "Rukovodit' torgovlei oruzhiem…," *Izvestiia*, 30 November 1994, 3.

30. Moscow Radio, 29 September 1994, in FBIS-SOV-94-190 (30 September 1994), 27. Interview with Director General Kotelkin over Moscow Ostankino TV, 7 February 1995, in FBIS-SOV-95-026 (8 February 1995), 17.

31. "Ob'ëmy prodazhi Rossiei vooruzheniia mogut byt' sokhraneny," *Segodnia*, no. 59 (31 March 1994): 2.

32. "Probe of Arms Company Carried Out Despite Threats," *Moscow News*, no. 51 (23–29 December 1994): 5.

33. Vasilii Kriukov, "Pushki k rynku edut zadom," *Rabochaia tribuna*, 19 January 1994, 2. For more on corruption at the highest levels, see "Borba za eksport oruzhiia," *Zavtra*, no. 16 (April 1994): 2; unattributed report.

34. Russia has lost more than $30 billion in trade with Iraq over the past four years because of the UN sanctions, according to Moscow Radio, ITAR-TASS, 13 March 1995, in FBIS-SOV-95-049 (14 March 1995), 14. For the alleged violations of these sanctions via third countries, see Konstantin Eggert, "Rossiia prodaet oruzhie Iraku?" *Izvestiia*, 7 April 1995, 3, citing the *Jerusalem Report*.

35. Evgenii Bovkun, "Tovarishcham generalam bylo vsë ravno," *Izvestiia*, 26 November 1994, 3; KP Investigative Service, "Strategi Rosvooruzheniia…," *Komsomol'skaia pravda*, 27 April 1995, 1–2.

36. Moscow Radio, ITAR-TASS, 15 November 1994, in FBIS-SOV-94-220 (15 November 1994), 4. Emphasis added.

37. Aleksei Fëdorov, "Ministr v oruzheinoi lavke," *Moskovskie novosti*, no. 32 (7–14 May 1995): 8.

38. Irina de Chikoff's interview with General Korzhakov, "Russie: ventes d'armes hors de contrôle," *Le Figaro*, Paris (7 April 1995), 3.

39. Pavel Fomin, "Genprokuratura vstala na zashchitu Rosvooruzheniia," *Segodnia*, 18 May 1995, 2.

40. Sergei Parkhomenko, "Merlin's Tower," *Moscow News*, no. 18 (12–18 May 1995): 6.

41. Aleksandr Zhilin, "Marshal vyshël iz okopa," *Moskovskie novosti*, no. 32 (7–14 May 1995): 8.

42. "Arms Producers May Trade Independently," Moscow Radio, 4 June 1995, in FBIS-SOV-95-107 (5 June 1995), 18.

Myth No. 6
Peacemaking Equals Peacekeeping

> Our peace-making operations comply with...the U.N. charter and are conducted at the request of both belligerents.
> *Andrei V. Kozyrev* (30 October 1994)

The agreement to establish a Commonwealth of Independent States (SNG—*Sodruzhestvo nezavisimykh gosudarstv*), which was signed on 8 December 1991, envisaged in Article 6 that most of the former USSR would be maintained as a "common strategic-military space under unified command, including a unitary control over nuclear weapons."[1] Three days later, President Yeltsin of the Russian Federation won over the armed forces generals to the new concept, which led to dissolution of the Soviet Union before the end of the year.

During that same month of December, at a summit meeting in Alma-Ata, heads of the three charter member states (Russia, Ukraine, Belarus) were convinced by eight other republics to sign an expanded treaty. Only Georgia and the three Baltic countries of Estonia, Latvia, and Lithuania initially remained outside the Commonwealth. Georgia finally joined the SNG in November 1993, although the agreement could not be ratified until 2 March 1994 by the legislature in Tbilisi. The Baltic States have never become members of the so-called Commonwealth.

At the Minsk summit on 14 February 1992, several military documents were signed by SNG members. One of these dealt with the status of strategic forces which would be subordinated to a Commonwealth commander-in-chief. The following month at Kiev, an agreement was reached to monitor peacemaking forces by SNG observers. Neither the former nor the latter became incorporated into the envisaged

Commonwealth unified armed forces, however. It was only at Tashkent on 15 May 1992 that a treaty on collective security could be signed by the presidents of Russia, Armenia, Belarus, and four of the states in Central Asia (Kazakhstan, Kyrgyzstan, Tajikistan, and Uzbekistan). Azerbaijan, Georgia, Moldova, Turkmenistan, and Ukraine did not join the others. Azerbaijan adhered to the treaty in late 1993.

Great power status also has been asserted by Russia through economic means in the "near abroad," that is, the former Soviet republics. An effort to maintain the ruble as Commonwealth currency did not succeed, as portrayed in Table 6.1, despite Moscow's original intention to use it as an instrument of control. A treaty for an economic union was signed on 24 September 1993 by ten members of the SNG, with Ukraine and Turkmenistan holding only associate status.[2] Earlier that month, six of those countries (Russia, Armenia, Belarus, Kazakhstan, Tajikistan, and Uzbekistan) agreed to establish a new ruble zone. The Central Bank of Russia was to unify credit, banking, tax, and customs policies. The economic union collapsed in November 1993, although it seems to have been revived in part on 9 September 1994 by the agreement for an SNG Interstate Economic Committee.

However, the Russian government has exercised "pipeline diplomacy" by stopping or at times reducing oil deliveries to Azerbaijan and Ukraine for nonpayment of energy debts. It has even claimed equity stakes in other SNG energy-producing companies, such as the one at Tengiz in Kazakhstan, in return for transporting petroleum to a Russian port on the Black Sea.[3] Belarus signed an economic union treaty with Moscow on 12 April 1994 in order to obtain oil and natural gas at subsidized prices. It can only be speculated why Russia's export of petroleum dropped during the first two months of 1995 to 42 percent of what it had been a year earlier.

Problems and Prospects

Although some Russians have done so, the SNG cannot be compared to the [West] European Union. The former represents an artificial creation which had been established to

- Divide the assets from a dismantled USSR.
- Solve problems of common interest.
- Maintain control over certain disputes.
- Keep nuclear weapons safe.
- Coordinate foreign policy issues.[4]

TABLE 6.1
Demise of the Ruble Zone

	Left Ruble Zone	
	Introduced own currency	Introduced parallel currency[a]
Russia	—	—
Ukraine	August 1992	—
Belarus	—	June 1992
Moldova	November 1993	—
Armenia	—	November 1993
Kazakhstan	November 1993	—
Uzbekistan[b]	June 1994	—
Kyrgyzstan	May 1993	—
Tajikistan	May 1995	—
Turkmenistan	November 1993	—

Sources: Erik Whitlock, "CIS Economies," RFE/RL *Research Report* 3, no. 1 (7 January 1994): 7; Boris Vinogradov, "Rossiiskie rubli s tadzhikskoi simbolikoi, "*Izvestiia*, 30 December 1994, 3; Lynda Maillet, "New States Initiate New Currencies," *Transition* 1, no. 9 (9 June 1995), table on p. 49.

[a] Circulates with pre-1992 rubles and/or new rubles.
[b] Banned use of the ruble on 15 April 1994 in order to support a national currency.

Numerous SNG agreements have been signed without any means to enforce them. During 1992, Azerbaijan left the Commonwealth, and the Moldovan parliament refused to ratify its country's membership (Moldova became a full member on 15 April 1994). President Islam Karimov revealed that 270 measures unacceptable to Uzbekistan were considered inapplicable and thus remain nonbinding.[5] The SNG charter states that the Commonwealth represents a voluntary association without any supranational powers.

The charter was adopted on 22 January 1993 by the Council of Heads of State meeting in Minsk.[6] It was signed by the seven presidents of Armenia, Belarus, Kazakhstan, Kyrgyzstan, Russia, Tajikistan, and Uzbekistan in cyrillic alphabetical order. Missing were five signatures from Azerbaijan, Georgia, Moldova, Turkmenistan, and Ukraine. Representatives of the latter explained that the SNG charter had to be ratified by their respective legislatures before it could be signed. (See Map 6.1.)

The document recognizes existing borders of member states (Article 3). It establishes a Defense Ministers' Council and a Council of Border Troop Commanders (Articles 30 and 31) through which military activities will be coordinated. Also mentioned is "support of security within

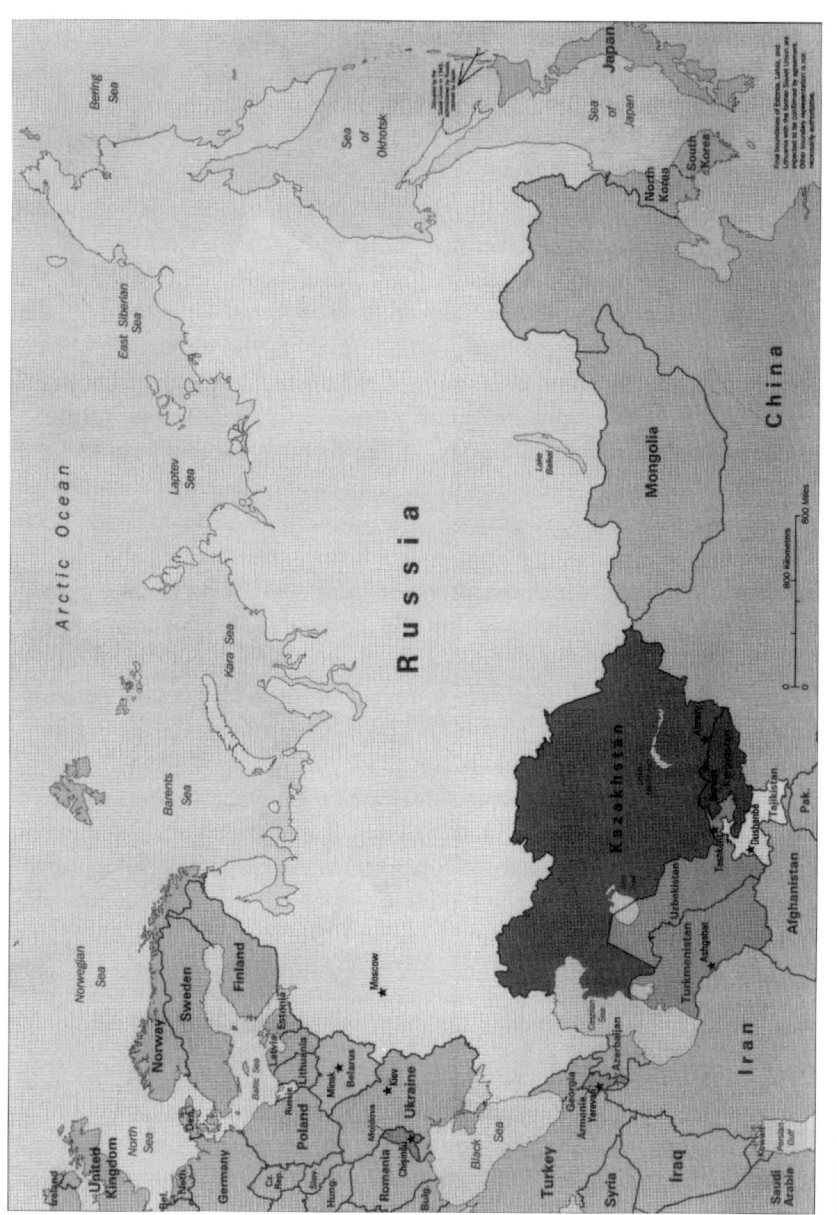

MAP 6.1: Commonwealth of Independent States *(Central Intelligence Agency)*

the Commonwealth" by means of military observers and collective forces to maintain peace (Article 11).

President Eduard Shevardnadze explained Georgia's subsequent adherence to the SNG charter as follows: "The only way this seemed possible [to be open toward all sides] was to join SNG; otherwise, we could not have improved relations with Russia. We would not be able to exist without Russia. The Georgian economy is disrupted."

He ignored completely the military role played by Russia in his country's civil war. The reasoning of other leaders who later joined the Commonwealth most probably was similar to the above. However, President Leonid Kuchma of Ukraine stated openly that "a shapeless organization like the Commonwealth of Independent States has no future."[7]

Many communist party leaders in the former Soviet republics have assumed positions of president or parliamentary chairman throughout the newly independent states. One notable exception had been Kyrgyzstan, where Askar A. Akaev is a former president of the Kyrgyz Academy of Sciences which meant, nevertheless, that he had been a trusted communist to hold such a position. By early 1995, his government was described as a "dictatorial regime camouflaging itself under democracy."[8] Despite such overwhelming predominance of former high-ranking communist functionaries, relations among SNG governments have been anything but fraternal. (See Table 6.2.)

A major casualty occurred in mid-June 1993, when the Joint Armed Forces Command was dissolved only eighteen months after establishment of the Commonwealth. Air Marshal Shaposhnikov's position as commander-in-chief was abolished by the Council of Defense Ministers before the end of August. The remaining 250 officers became part of a new Joint Staff for SNG Military Coordination.[9] Shaposhnikov went on to become secretary of the Security Council for Russia.

The new Joint Staff presumably remains occupied with preparations for the use of coalition forces during wartime. In the meanwhile, Russian border troops (subordinated to President Yeltsin on 30 December 1993) will attempt to patrol Commonwealth frontiers together with the host country and even recruit local citizens for service in Russian units when a bilateral agreement can be signed. Col. Gen. Andrei I. Nikolaev, commanding officer of federal border troops, stated that his forces will "guard SNG outer frontiers." They already do so for Armenia, Georgia, Tajikistan, and Kyrgyzstan "at their own request." Russia wants agreements also with Azerbaijan, Uzbekistan, and Turkmenistan to station its troops

TABLE 6.2
Commonwealth Leaders

Republic	Leader	Former Position(s)
Armenia	Levon H. Ter-Petrosyan	Chairman, Supreme Soviet (1992)
Azerbaijan	Heydar A. Aliyev	Member, CPSU Politburo (1982–87)
Belarus	Alyaksandr H. Lukashenka	State farm manager and parliamentary deputy (1987–94)
Georgia	Eduard A. Shevardnadze	Member, CPSU Politburo (1985–90)
Kazakhstan	Nursultan A. Nazarbaev	First Secretary, CP and member, CPSU Politburo (1990–91)
Kyrgyzstan	Askar A. Akaev	Vice-president and president, Kyrgyz Academy of Sciences (1987–90)
Moldova	Mircea I. Snegur	Secretary, CP (1985–89)
Russia	Boris N. Yeltsin	Candidate member, CPSU Politburo (1986–88)
Tajikistan	Imamali S. Rakhmonov	Chairman, Supreme Soviet (1992)
Turkmenistan	Saparmurad A. Niyazov	Member, CPSU Politburo (1990–91)
Ukraine	Leonid D. Kuchma	Director, Iuzhmash ICBM plant (1986–92); prime minister (1992–93)
Uzbekistan	Islam A. Karimov	First secretary, CP and member, CPSU Politburo (1992–93)

Sources: The Europa World Yearbook 1995 (London: Europa Publications Ltd., 1995), 2 vols.; Richard F. Staar and Margit N. Grigory, eds., *1991 Yearbook on International Communist Affairs* (Stanford, Calif.: Hoover Institution Press, 1991), 359–60, for the last column.

in those countries and share expenses. Ukraine, Belarus, and Kazakhstan have their own border guards, so Moscow has proposed integration of such forces on a bilateral basis, under SNG authority.[10]

One means of accomplishing the military part of this objective has been outlined by Lt. Gen. Leonid G. Ivashov, secretary to the Council of Defense Ministers. He suggested that the collective security treaty, signed in May 1992 at Tashkent, will not prevent military disintegration of the Commonwealth. In order to reverse this process, it will be necessary to establish regional collective security zones as follows:[11]

1. *Western* (Belarus, Kaliningrad, and western regions of Russia), with the center at Minsk and Belarus president as commander-in-chief.
2. *Caucasus* (Georgia, Armenia, Azerbaijan, and the northern Caucasus region of Russia), with the center at Rostov on the Don River and a local Russian commander.

3. *Central Asian* (Uzbekistan, Tajikistan, Turkmenistan), with a tentative center at Tashkent [and presumably a Russian commander].
4. *Eastern* (the Ural Military District and Kazakhstan), with the center at Almaty and Kazakhstan president as commander-in-chief.

Ivashov explained the rationale behind these subsystems as follows: to establish forces analogous to those of NATO, especially the German *Bundeswehr;* to maintain peace in the Caucasus; to create a military presence that would offset the Xinjiang Group of Forces in China; and to deter the opposition in Afghanistan. Implementation of this concept would commence with establishment of an SNG chiefs-of-staff committee and the above four regional collective security zones. After that, "Coalition Defense Forces" would train jointly and establish common standards. Proposals will be submitted to the SNG heads of state at the end of 1995, according to Ivashov.

The foregoing suggests that the Russian military recognizes full well who potential enemies may be in the future and, at least on paper, is thinking about preparing for such eventualities. It is noteworthy that the SNG heads of state reelected President Yeltsin as chairman of the organization and voted on 10 February 1995 to move headquarters from Minsk to Moscow.

Peacemaking

An article in a journal published by the General Staff placed the number of territorial-ethnic disputes in Russia (1992) at 164, of which 85 could result in armed conflict.[12] Not all of them have led to SNG or even unilateral Russian peacemaking efforts. The former USSR republics, now called the "near abroad" (*blizhnee zarubezh'e*), also encompass the three independent Baltic States even though they have never become members of the Commonwealth.

One should differentiate between the concept of "peacekeeping" as applied by the United Nations and the Russian term *mirotvorchestvo,* which literally means "peace-making."[13] For example, troops have been dispatched by Moscow prior to a ceasefire and frequently adopt a partisan stance that favors one side. Special peacemaking units include the 27th (Guards) Motorized Rifle Division in the Volga Military District (MD), the 45th in the Leningrad Military District, and the 201st in Tajikistan, plus parachute battalions.[14] A total of more than 36,000 Russian troops have been deployed as peacemakers. (See Table 6.3.)

TABLE 6.3
Russian Peacemaking Forces

Place of Deployment	Time of Initial Deployment	Number of Troops	Killed[a]	Wounded[a]
Dniester Region	August 1992	1,800	16	25
Tajikistan	October–November 1993	201st Motor. Rifle Division plus Border Guards, c. 26,000[b]	53	77
South Ossetia	July 1992	523	2	1
Abkhazia	October 1992	About 3,000	6	15
North Ossetia and Ingushetia	Peacekeeping fulfilled by interior ministry (MVD) troops of Russian Federation, November 1992	5,500	28	60
Nagorno-Karabakh	Offered in May 1994 (not accepted)	Two regiments and a rapid reaction group from 127th M.R. Division	—	—
Totals		36,823	105	178

Sources: "Rossiiskie sily podderzhivaniia mira," *Argumenty i fakty*, no. 14 (April 1994): 2; Capt. N. Chernyshëv, "Mirotvortsy iz Rossii," *Orientir*, no. 1 (June 1994): 16–18; Sergei Prokopenko's interview with Lt. Gen. Vasilii I. Iakushev, commander of Russian peacemakers in Abkhazia, "Ostaëtsia tol'ko gordit'sia . . . ," *Krasnaia zvezda*, 12 January 1995, 2, for the number of troops there.

[a] From date of deployment to the end of March 1994.

[b] Border troops alone number 16,000 according to Col. Gen. Andrei Nikolaev (director, Federal Border Service), "Natsional'nye interesy v pogranichnykh prostranstvakh," *Rossiiskie vesti*, 11 May 1995, 2, which is more than double the original contingent.

Russian military leaders are facing problems in establishing joint operations with other signatories to the Commonwealth charter. At a meeting of defense ministers to examine the Georgia-Abkhazia conflict, only nine appeared, with the other three (from Moldova, Turkmenistan, and Ukraine) sending observers. Attendees agreed that peacemaking within the SNG should be based on regional principles: Russian, Kazakh, Uzbek, and Kyrgyz troops in Tajikistan; Russian, Ukrainian, Armenian, and Azeri forces in Abkhazia. However, "the mechanism to enforce this principle will be very complicated," according to Col. Gen. Viktor N. Samsonov, chief of staff for SNG military coordination.[15] The following survey of

Moldova

In the case of the Trans-Dniester Republic, self-proclaimed in September 1990, which had been part of Soviet Moldavia (called Bessarabia before World War II as a province of Romania), only the Russians unofficially have supported the independence of that breakaway state since the cease-fire in July 1992. They also stationed the 14th (combined arms) Guards Army on the disputed territory. It consists of one division at 75 percent, two others at 50 percent, and one at only 25 percent strength, for a reported total of 3,500 combat troops with headquarters at Tiraspol.[16] These forces are allegedly neutral.

The 14th Army's former commanding officer, Lt. Gen. Aleksandr I. Lebed', won 88 percent of the popular vote when he ran for deputy to parliament of the so-called Dniester Republic against three local candidates in mid-September 1993, although he later resigned his seat. Lebed', a graduate of Russia's paratroop academy, had commanded an airborne assault battalion in Afghanistan during 1981–82. After Defense Minister Grachëv ordered the 14th Army downsized to one division (the 59th), Lebed' resigned from his position. Yeltsin accepted the resignation in mid-June 1995 after two weeks of deliberation.[17]

Despite the fact that almost three-fifths of the Trans-Dniester Republic population is Slavic, only 26 percent are Russians, most of the rest being Ukrainian. Three-quarters of the Russians live on the right bank of the Dniester River, in what is still independent Moldova. This group, however, does not have the equivalent of the 14th Army to protect it. Yeltsin's special mediator, Vladlen [Vladimir Lenin] Vasev, stated that "Russia has geostrategic interests in Moldova and also means to defend its *Russian-speaking* population."[18] Such a broad definition would include one-third of Moldova's citizens compared with only 13 percent for ethnic Russians. (See Map 6.2.)

Russian contributions to the tripartite peacemaking force included 1,800 men, all volunteers. The Moldovan armed forces (three battalions) and the Trans-Dniester national guard (two battalions) each allocated 1,200 men under a unified control commission that maintained a cease-fire throughout the region.[19] Russia began withdrawing its peacemakers in November 1994, claiming that it could not afford to pay costs and that the situation had become stable. However, the two undersized battalions

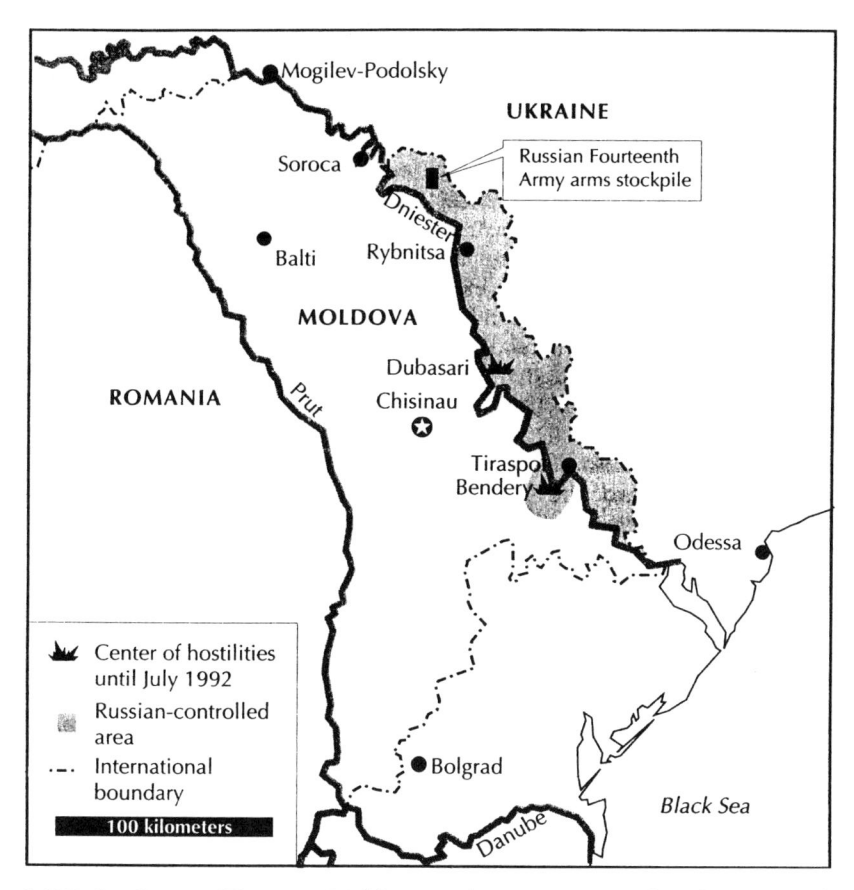

MAP 6.2: Russian Troops in Moldova *(Radio Free Europe/Radio Liberty, Research Report 2 (18 June 1993))*

(878 men) returned to their Volga Military District and were replaced in June 1995 with fresh troops.[20]

On 21 October 1994, an agreement on total withdrawal of the 14th Army was signed in Moscow by the prime ministers of Russia and Moldova. It provided for repatriation of these troops within three years *after* the treaty had been ratified by the two respective parliaments. Several more documents were added in early February 1995 on shipping equipment and property, cooperation with international inspection of Russian military forces arriving in Moldova, and pensions for servicemen and families.[21] The two presidents met on 28 June 1995 at Moscow, where

Mircea I. Snegur reaffirmed that his government would not accept foreign military bases on its territory.

Tajikistan

The civil war throughout this former Soviet republic began in late May 1992 and resulted at first in the ouster of a communist government by religious Muslims. The latter were in turn defeated, with support from Moscow, after only six months in power. Since July 1993, Russia's 201st Motorized Rifle Division has been defending the 800-mile-long frontier with Afghanistan, to which country some 60,000 Tajiks had fled. A group of Russian border guards, under Lt. Gen. Pavel Tarasenko (since May 1995), augments the 201st Division. Col. Gen. Valerii A. Patrikeev thus commanded a force of approximately 36,000 SNG peacemakers, including 31,000 Russians. The remaining 5,000 men were supposed to be comprised of Kazakhs, Uzbeks, and Kyrgyz.[22]

One official reason for such a relatively large engagement by Moscow is the alleged fear that, if not stopped, Muslim "fundamentalism" will spread north into Kazakhstan, which borders on the Russian Federation. A variation on that perceived danger was voiced by the chief of the General Staff, Col. Gen. Mikhail P. Kolesnikov, when he warned the Bulgarians that their country "lies within the scope of Turkey's ambitions." The announcement that Persian would replace the cyrillic script suggests alienation from Russia by the communist Tajik government.[23]

Whether the conflict over Tajikistan can be settled in the near future is questionable. It has already taken more than 100,000 lives. Of the half-million ethnic Russians and Russian speakers who had once lived mostly in the capital city of Dushanbe, only about 80,000 remained by early 1994, with official sources predicting that all who might wish to leave would do so by the end of that year. According to one of the then–deputy defense ministers, Col. Gen. Boris V. Gromov, the situation in Tajikistan had come to resemble increasingly the former Soviet war in Afghanistan. In both cases, Russian troops found themselves defending unpopular communist regimes.[24] An attempt by the head of the UN mission in Tajikistan to mediate the conflict during May 1995 did not seem to be making much progress, although the number of UN observers increased from seventeen to forty. That same month, the military command of the Islamic Revival Party declared a *jihad* (holy war) against Russian troops in Tajikistan.

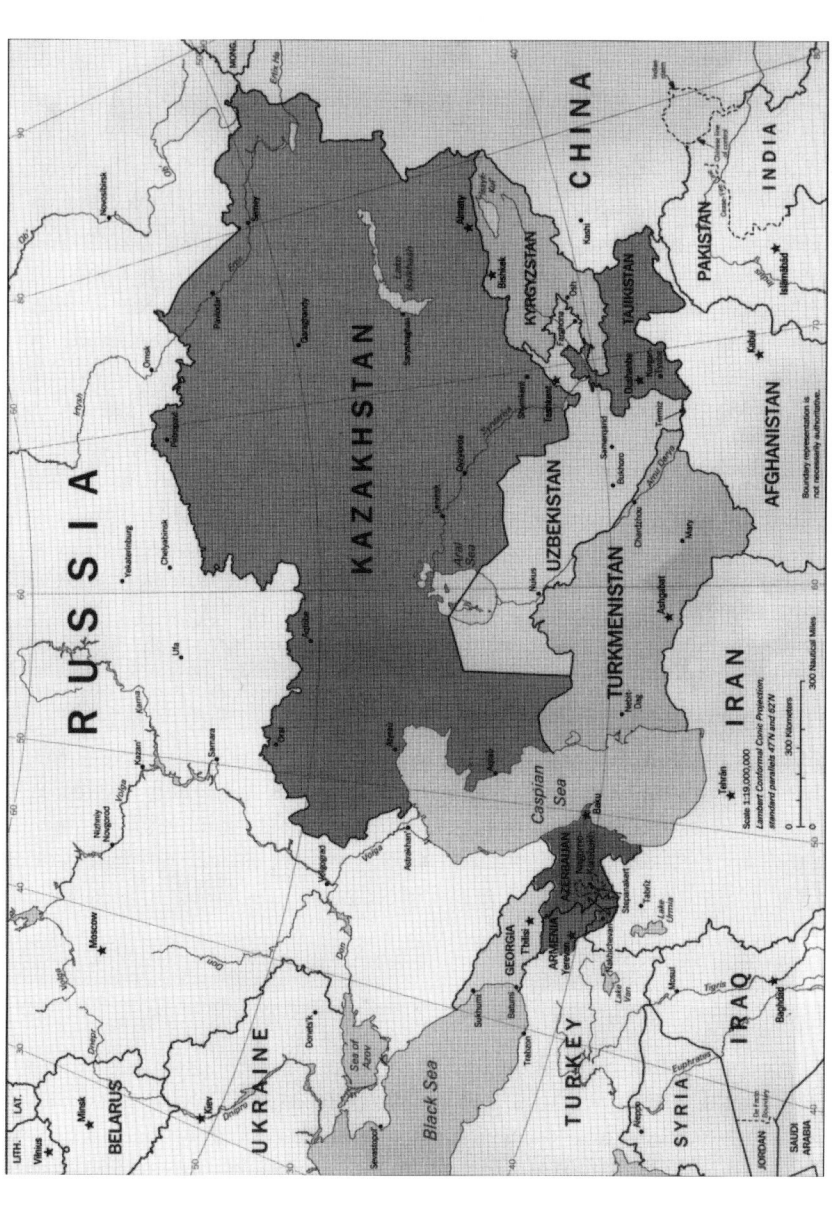

MAP 6.3: The Caucasus and Central Asia *(Central Intelligence Agency)*

South Ossetia

Commencing in 1989, the conflict throughout this province of Georgia has involved the Russian Federation, to which the bordering republic of North Ossetia belongs. Ossetians are descendants of Persian tribes who speak a Farsi language. A trilateral agreement for a ceasefire took effect in June 1992. The initial Russian peacemakers (950 men) were larger than the combined total in the Georgian (300 men) and South Ossetian (400–500 men) battalions, which belonged to the joint force. On 18 November 1992, the South Ossetian parliament formally requested its counterpart in Moscow to grant the province admission into the Federation of Russia.[25]

A complicating factor involves the existence of Ossetian refugees in the tens of thousands, many of whom have been resettled in areas from which the Ingush ethnic group had been expelled. From time to time, the small Organization for Security and Cooperation in Europe mission at Tbilisi attempts to send representatives to the South Ossetian capital at Tshkinvali, for the purpose of restoring communications between the two sides. However, Russia is most likely to become the only effective mediator.[26]

Among the 90,000 total population, only two-thirds are Ossetians. They had received Russian automatic weapons and missile launchers, which permitted them successfully to defend Tshkinvali and several villages from more numerous Georgian troops. An agreement signed at Dagomys established a monitoring commission and a joint military command. By early 1994, the original 1,000 Russian peacemakers had been cut in half with the 1st Battalion, 129th Regiment, 45th Motorized Rifle Division from the Leningrad Military District manning forty-eight observation posts.[27]

Abkhazia

One other province of Georgia seems to have achieved de facto independence. During the second half of 1992, up to 7,000 volunteers from the Confederation of Peoples of the Caucasus reportedly fought on the insurgent side. The small province of Abkhazia includes as many Russians as it does ethnic Abkhazians, approximately 100,000 of each. However, about the same number of former Georgian inhabitants have fled to Georgia and 35,000 to Russia. If this territory and that of South Ossetia succeed in maintaining independence and/or are annexed by Russia, not much will be left of Georgia. Two parachute units, the 345th Regiment of the 7th (Guards) Airborne Division, and one battalion, for a total of

3,000 peacemakers remain under command of Lt. Gen. Vasilii I. Iakushev. To these should be added another regiment, guarding the railroad in Georgia. Their mandate is extended every six months by the Federation Council in Moscow.

The two antagonists sent representatives to Geneva in January 1994 for talks organized by Russia and the United Nations. Disillusioned with the lack of progress, the government of Georgia appealed to the Commonwealth for assistance. An agreement between the two sides for repatriation of refugees had been signed on 4 April 1994 in Moscow. In the meantime, Abkhazians continue to install a barbed-wire fence and mine fords across the Inguri River, which borders on Georgia. The parliament of Abkhazia adopted a new constitution and elected the country's first president on 26 November 1994. The talks in Moscow ended in failure during May of the following year.[28]

North Ossetia–Alania and Ingushetia

In contrast with the foregoing, these two republics are parts of the Russian Federation. The North Ossetians began forming a national guard comprised of three battalions and three separate companies during February 1992, with the goal of recruiting a total of 2,000 men. When Ingush militia attempted to occupy the Prigorodnyi *raion,* annexed by North Ossetia in 1944 on Stalin's orders, Russian troops created a two- to three-kilometer corridor between the sides and established an emergency administration in November 1992. Martial law has been extended periodically ever since.

Yeltsin's decree of 13 December 1993 ordered return of Ingush refugees to four villages in the Prigorodnyi region, without any effect. The North Ossetians had appropriated all Ingush possessions and housing almost half a century earlier, after the latter were deported en masse to Kazakhstan because some of them allegedly had collaborated with the Germans during World War II. About 5,500 Russian peacemakers continue to patrol the area between the two sides. There appears to be little hope that the 74,000 refugees (97% Ingush) will be permitted to reoccupy their former homes.[29] North Ossetia adopted a new constitution on 12 November 1994 and changed its name to Republic of North Ossetia–Alania.

Nagorno-Karabakh

The Karabakh war between traditionally Christian Armenians and Muslim Azeris received an added impetus during 1992, four years after it had started, when the former Soviet 7th Army in Armenia and the 4th

Army in Azerbaijan were disbanded. The Azeris obtained more heavy equipment than the Armenians by acquiring armaments from four motorized rifle divisions plus naval guns, attack helicopters, and other warplanes. The Armenians received no aircraft,[30] although they did take the equipment and weapons from withdrawing Russian formations. (See chapter 7, "Commonwealth Armies Support Russia.")

By February 1993, two Azeri armies had closed a ten-mile gap which cut the supply route between Armenia and the province of Karabakh, an autonomous region in Azerbaijan that is claimed by both countries. As a result, Armenians were forced to rely on the Russian army for fuel and spare parts. They appointed as their military commander a former deputy chief of staff for USSR ground forces. The tide of war turned when professional Russian army officers began to plan military operations. Only threats from Turkey stopped the successful Armenian offensive after two months. Combat resumed, however, and by mid-October the Azeri 3rd Army Corps had been defeated. In addition to "liberating" virtually all of Nagorno-Karabakh, the Armenians also occupied about 20 percent of Azerbaijan proper. (See Map 6.4.)

The leaders of Nagorno-Karabakh who are ethnic Armenians, as is most of the population, demand independence from Azerbaijan, which would result in absorption of the province by the Republic of Armenia. They will probably continue to fight until a future government in Baku agrees to accept the reality of the situation. Otherwise, major powers throughout the region could become involved overtly in a military sense: Turkey's entrance into the war might provoke full-scale Russian intervention, and Iran might then also join Turkey in support of Muslim Azerbaijan.[31] It is not inconceivable that the unsuccessful attempt to oust Pres. Heydar Aliyev of Azerbaijan in September 1994 had been orchestrated by Moscow. Aliyev remained opposed to providing the Russians with base rights in his country, and six months later another attempt was made to overthrow him.[32]

In the meanwhile, Russia had offered to deploy a peacemaking force at forty-nine observation posts which would be guarded by two regiments and a rapid-reaction group from the 127th Motorized Rifle Division based in Armenia. The talks did lead to a ceasefire agreement on 12 May 1994. Some two years earlier, the Conference on Security and Cooperation in Europe (CSCE) had mandated establishment of the so-called Minsk Group of eleven member states, including the United States and Russia, to resolve the Karabakh problem. A former American ambassador

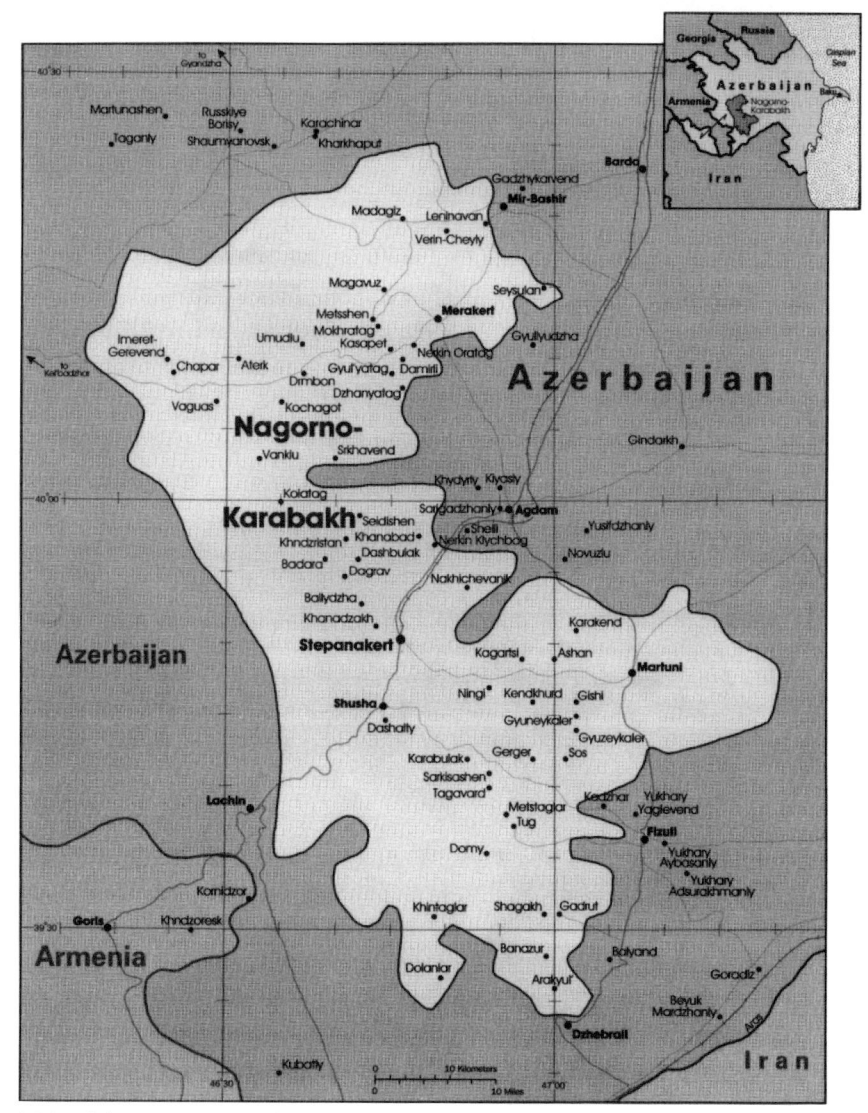

MAP 6.4: Nagorno-Karabakh *(Central Intelligence Agency)*

to CSCE presented a plan for accomplishing just that. However, the Russians apparently did not want such neutral observers in the Caucasus region.[33]

Even without a settlement, the Nagorno-Karabakh parliament elected a president of its self-proclaimed republic before year's end. He appointed a defense minister on 9 January 1995 and the rest of his cabinet two days later. The plan to send 600 peacekeepers by the renamed Organization for Security and Cooperation in Europe has remained unimplemented, just like the idea to hold an international conference on Karabakh. It appears obvious that Russia does not wish any outside interference with its own plans for the region.

The Future

The government in Moscow made a concerted effort during the fall of 1993 to convince the other UN Security Council members that Russia should be provided with a UN mandate for its peacemaking operations in the above-discussed regions of the former USSR. The Russian foreign minister also suggested establishment of a special fund, to which other UN member states would contribute, for financing these Russian activities.[34] Both appeals failed.

Toward the end of that same year, the Commonwealth of Independent States also rejected President Yeltsin's proposal that the 25 million Russians living in other SNG member states be given special status. Meeting at Ashgabat in Turkmenistan, eleven leaders from post-Soviet republics did sign agreements on tax policies, a joint SNG military headquarters, and technical cooperation. Only the host government's president initialed a statement confirming dual citizenship for ethnic Russians residing in his country.[35] (See Table 6.4.)

Regardless of whether the other Commonwealth members agree under pressure to provide their Russian minorities with special status, conflicts like the ones discussed above probably will spread. The director of a nongovernmental analysis center in Moscow cited an alleged U.S. Defense Intelligence Agency report as projecting twelve local wars throughout the "near abroad," with the following human casualties:[36]

- about half a million (523,000) killed;
- more than four million (4.2) deaths from disease;
- approximately 20 million refugees;
- and 88 million (well over one-half of the 130 million non-Russian population) affected by famine.

Such tremendous losses could be the price for implementing Russia's strategic objectives in the "near abroad." According to a Harvard University study, these goals include establishment of buffer zones against Turkey, Iran, and China; resumption of hegemony throughout the former USSR; and acquisition of control over raw materials such as oil, natural

TABLE 6.4
Percentages of Russians in SNG Countries

Republic	Inhabitants	Indigenous	Russians
Armenia	3,305,000	93.3%	1.6%
Azerbaijan	7,021,000	82.7	5.6
Belarus	10,152,000	77.9	13.2
Georgia	5,401,000	70.1	6.3
Kazakhstan	16,464,000	39.7	37.8
Kyrgyzstan	4,258,000	52.4	21.5
Moldova	4,335,000	64.5	13.0
Russia	147,022,000	81.5	—
Tajikistan	5,093,000	62.3	7.6
Turkmenistan	3,523,000	72.0	9.5
Ukraine	51,471,000	72.7	22.1
Uzbekistan	19,810,000	71.4	8.3
Total	*277,855,000*	*c. 70.0%*	*c. 12.4%*

Source: Stephen K. Batalden and Sandra L. Batalden, *The Newly Independent States of Eurasia* (Phoenix, Ariz.: Oryx Press, 1993), 8–167, passim; based on the most recent census in 1989.

gas, and strategic minerals.[37] All of this appears aimed at re-creation of the former military and economic union which collapsed at the end of 1991.

When Presidents Snegur and Yeltsin met on 28 June 1995 in the Kremlin, the latter reportedly demanded the right to station Russian troops in Moldova as well as politico-economic integration of the two countries. He announced that the time for withdrawal of the former 14th Army (three years) could be extended, that the location of this military contingent might be transformed into a Russian base, and that the status of forces in Moldova should parallel that in Georgia, where Russians are stationed in different parts of the country. Snegur had met with Defense Minister Grachëv at Chisinau two days earlier and probably was alerted to Yeltsin's subsequent demands.

What may be the objective is establishment of a second Kaliningrad region in Moldova, that is, bypassing Russia's immediate neighbors like Ukraine. By leap-frogging about 1,000 kilometers into Moldova, the Kremlin would be in a strong position to exercise its power more effectively throughout East-Central Europe. Kaliningrad already has more Russian troops per square kilometer than any other part of the country. At least, such is the thinking among certain Moscow analysts.[38]

An attempt will be made in the next chapter to answer the question whether any of the former Soviet republics will be capable, in the near future, to support such Russian objectives.[39]

Notes

1. This introductory section is based on Sergei M. Rogov et al., "Commonwealth Defense Arrangements and International Security," *CNA Occasional Paper* (Alexandria, Va.: Center for Naval Analyses, June 1992), 1–15.

2. Vasilii Kononenko, "SNG ukrepliaetsia…," *Izvestiia*, 25 September 1993, 1–2. See also Aleksandr Gavriliuk, "Tamozhennyi tranzit," *Rossiiskaia gazeta*, 27 December 1994, 3.

3. Central Intelligence Agency, *Kazakhstan: An Economic Profile* (Washington, D.C.: CIA, 1993), 18. See also Karen Dawisha and Bruce Parrott, *Russia and the New States of Eurasia* (New York: Cambridge University Press, 1994), esp. 161–94.

4. Moscow Radio, TASS, 26 December 1991, in FBIS-SOV-91-249 (27 December 1991), 9, broadcast the original declaration adhered to by the eleven governments.

5. Elizabeth Teague, "The CIS: An Unpredictable Future," *RFE/RL Research Report*, no. 1 (7 January 1994): 9. By the time of the SNG summit at Moscow on 10 February 1995, the number of unimplemented decisions had risen to about 400.

6. "Ustav Sodruzhestva Nezavisimykh Gosudarstv," *Rossiiskaia gazeta*, 12 February 1993, 6.

7. Interview with Shevardnadze by Misha Glenny in *Profil* (Vienna), 15 November 1993, 69, in FBIS-SOV-93-219 (16 November 1993), 103–4. The Kuchma quotation is from Steven Erlanger, "War in Russia Clouds Pact by Former Soviet Republics," *New York Times*, 11 February 1995, A-5.

8. Aleksandr Sabov, "Kirgiziia: spory o fasade?" *Literaturnaia gazeta*, no. 8 (22 February 1995): 11; interview with Bolotbek Shamshiev, opposition leader in parliament.

9. Viktor Litovkin, "Ministry oborony likvidirovali…," *Izvestiia*, 26 August 1993, 2.

10. Leonid Kravchenko, "Granitsy pishutsia krov'iu," *Rossiiskaia gazeta*, 12 November 1994, 1–2; interview with Col. Gen. Andrei I. Nikolaev. At the 25 January 1995 summit meeting in Moscow, representatives of Azerbaijan, Turkmenistan, and Ukraine refused to sign an agreement for protection of SNG external borders.

11. Dmitrii Orlov, "Neobkhodima blokovaia sistema bezopasnosti," *Rossiiskiie vesti*, 28 June 1994, 3; interview with Lt. Gen. Ivashov. See also OMRI *Daily Digest*, no. 33 (15 February 1995): pt. 1, p. 4, on implementation of proposals by Ivashov.

12. Col. O. A. Bel'kov, "Etnopoliticheskie faktory voennoi opasnosti v SNG," *Voennaia mysl'*, no. 7 (July 1992): 19.

13. Irina Kobrinskaia, "Mirotvorchestvo: kontseptsiia," *Krasnaia zvezda*, 7 December 1994, 3.

14. Interview with Col. Gen. Georgii G. Kondrat'ev, "Mirotvorchestvo-delo gosudarstvennoe," *Chest' imeiu*, no. 5–6 (May–June 1994): 2–6. See also Susan L.

Clark, "Russia in a Peacekeeping Role," in Leon Aron and Kenneth M. Jensen, eds., *The Emergence of Russian Foreign Policy* (Washington, D.C.: U.S. Institute of Peace Press, 1994), 119–47.

15. Moscow Radio, ITAR-TASS, 18 July 1994, in FBIS-SOV-94-138 (19 July 1994), 1.

16. Total troop strength is from Defense Minister Grachëv, quoted by Aleksandr Pel'ts, "Reformirovannaia 14-ia armiia," *Krasnaia zvezda*, 29 June 1995, 1.

17. Nikolai Peroskov, "Sud'ba 14-i armii reshena," *Krasnaia zvezda*, 4 May 1995, 4.

18. "Yeltsin's Envoy in Moldova Reveals Cards," RFE/RL *Daily Report*, no. 56 (23 March 1994): 2; emphasis added.

19. Dmitrii Trenin, "Blazhenny mirotvortsy…," *Novoe vremia*, no. 24 (June 1993): 11; Irina Lagunina, "Kto dast golubuiu kasku…?" *Novoe vremia*, no. 46 (November 1993): 23.

20. Chisinau Radio, 1 June 1995, in FBIS-SOV-95-108 (6 June 1995), 71.

21. Sergei Kniaz'kov, "Soglashenie o vyvode 14-i armii podpisano," *Krasnaia zvezda*, 26 October 1994, 3; Natal'ia Prikhod'ko, "Moldova," *Nezavisimaia gazeta*, 7 February 1995, 1.

22. Aleksandr Antoshkin, "Golubye kaski Sodruzhestva," *Rossiiskie vesti*, 11 January 1994, 3; "[Kyrgyz] Reinforcements Being Sent to Tajik-Afghan Border," Moscow Radio, ITAR-TASS, 25 January 1995, in FBIS-SOV-95-016 (25 January 1995), 42.

23. Trenin, "Blazhenny mirotvortsy…"; Kjell Engelbrekt, "Kolesnikov: Bulgaria Faces Islamic Threat," RFE/RL *Daily Report*, no. 223 (22 November 1993): 4; Tehran Radio, 27 June 1995, in FBIS-SOV-95-124 (28 June 1995), 77.

24. Leonid Mlechin, "Za osobuiu rol' Rossii v Tadzhikistane…," *Izvestiia*, 12 February 1994, 3; Semën Bagdasarov, "Voenno-politicheskaia obstanovka v Tadzhikistane," *NZ Voennoe obozrenie*, 22 April 1995, 1–2.

25. Moscow Radio, 19 November 1992, in FBIS-SOV-92-224 (19 November 1992), 39; Lagunina, "Kto dast golubuiu kasku…?" 23.

26. Trenin, "Blazhenny mirotvortsy…," 12. See also Neela Banerjee, "Russia Combines War and Peace to Reclaim Parts of the Old Empire," *Wall Street Journal*, 2 September 1994, A-1, 4.

27. Viktor Litovkin, "Mir na shtykakh…," *Izvestiia*, 19 January 1994, 1, 7.

28. Pëtr Karapetian, "4 aprelia v Moskve podpisany soglasheniia," *Krasnaia zvezda*, 5 April 1994, 3; Iaroslav Shimov, "Poteriannyi krai," *Izvestiia*, 31 January 1995, 4; "Postanovlenie Soveta Federatsii," *Krasnaia zvezda*, 23 June 1995, 3.

29. Ol'ga Churakova, "Opasnyi povorot…," *Novoe vremia*, no. 32 (1993): 7; Peter Jarman, "Ethnic Cleansing in N. Caucasus," *Moscow News*, no. 6 (11–17 February 1994): 13.

30. Lt. Col. Kirill Petrov, "Konflikt v Karabakhe…," *Krasnaia zvezda*, 19 January 1994, 2.

31. Trenin, "Blazhenny mirotvortsy…," 10; Mlechin, "Za osobuiu rol' Rossii v Tadzhikistane…."

32. Vladimir Gavrilenko, "Za chto pogib Bovshan Dzhavadov?" *Krasnaia zvezda*,

21 March 1995, 3. See also Radii Fish, "Nefteprovod pobedit voinu?" *Novoe vremia,* no. 5 (February 1995): 12–14, on role played by petroleum.

33. John J. Maresca, "War in the Caucasus," *Special Report* (Washington, D.C.: U.S. Institute of Peace, 1 July 1994), 7. See also Boris Vinogradov, "Rossiia ne khochet videt' nabliudatelei OBSE na Kavkaze," *Izvestiia,* 11 January 1995, 3.

34. Andrei Kozyrev, "OON: Trevogi i nadezhdy mira," *Rossiiskaia gazeta,* 30 October 1993, 1, 7; Igor' Rotar', "Voennye dolzhny ovladet' iskusstvom mirotvorchestva," *Nezavisimaia gazeta,* 24 November 1993, 1, 3.

35. Vasilii Kononenko, "Rossiia-Turkmenistan: podpisano soglashenie o dvoinom grazhdanstve," *Izvestiia,* 24 December 1993, 3.

36. Aleksei I. Podberëzkin, *Natsional'naia bezopasnost': Rossiia v 1994 godu* (Moscow: Rossiisko-amerykanskii universitet, 1994); summary only translated as *Russian National Security Concept for 1994* by FBIS-SOV-94-038-S (25 February 1994), 10. The office of the DIA director could not find any such report which may mean that the estimates were Russian.

37. Fiona Hill and Pamela Jewett, *Back in the USSR* (Cambridge, Mass.: Kennedy School of Government at Harvard University, 1994), 3; mimeographed. See also Banerjee, "Russia Combines War and Peace to Reclaim Parts of the Old Empire."

38. Vladimir Socor, "Yelsin-Sinegur Meeting…," *Prism,* pt. 2 (30 June 1995): 1–5; Jamestown Foundation. See also T. V. Trapeznikova, "Russkie v Moldavii," *Diplomaticheskii vestnik,* no. 4 (April 1995): 42–46.

39. Jan S. Adams, "Will the Post-Soviet Commonwealth Survive?" *Occasional Paper* (Columbus: The Mershon Center at Ohio State University, 1994), 19; Claudia Rosett, "Along Many Borders, the Russian Empire Stirs," *Wall Street Journal,* 27 February 1995, A-8.

Myth No. 7
Commonwealth Armies Support Russia

> Integration of SNG armed forces is realistic.
> *Gen. Pavel Grachëv* (9 February 1995)

The attempt to preserve unified armed forces under the Commonwealth of Independent States (SNG) did not succeed. At its second summit in Minsk on 30 December 1991, three of the members—Ukraine, Moldova, Azerbaijan—were permitted to establish their own armies. By the following month, only five member governments still supported the SNG unified command. Even that minority was soon to disintegrate.

The Western States

Ukraine had commenced planning for a national army well before establishment of the SNG. Already in August 1991, the parliament subordinated to itself all armed forces located on its territory. At the beginning of January 1992, Kiev announced that former Soviet conventionally armed troops (about 500,000) would henceforth be under command of the president and the defense minister. Before the end of that month, half of these officers and men reportedly had sworn an oath of allegiance to Ukraine.

Numbers alone made this defense establishment the second largest in Europe, after that of Russia. About 4,000 tanks and 1,000 aircraft enhanced its numerical strength. One problem, however, involved the fact that ethnic Russian officers outnumbered their Ukrainian counterparts by 60,000 to 40,000. They also occupied most of the higher ranks. An unofficial survey in the fall of 1992 reportedly concluded that most of the officers would not defend Ukraine if Russia were to attack.[1] An attempt has been made to instill national patriotism through a Main Administration for Educational and Socio-Psychological Work, which employs about 1,000 native officers to rebuild morale in the Ukrainian spirit.

Col. Gen. Konstantin Morozov had served as chief of the Soviet 17th Air Force Army before appointment as the first defense minister on 3 September 1991. He was succeeded by General of the Army Vitalii H. Radetsky two years later. The new defense minister had commanded the Odessa Military District, where only 25 to 30 percent of his indigenous officers could speak their native language. Therefore, Radetsky believed that Ukrainization would take several years to complete.[2]

It should be noted that Radetsky had served in the Soviet army for thirty years. Only eleven days after his appointment had been confirmed, the same session of parliament approved a national military doctrine. It states that "Ukraine will consider its potential adversary to be any state whose consistent policy constitutes a military danger to Ukraine."[3] This was obviously directed against Russia.

Toward the end of the month, after his election on 10 July 1994 as president, Leonid D. Kuchma appointed a new defense minister. He is a civilian, Valerii N. Shmarov, who retains his deputy premiership and oversight responsibilities for the military-industrial complex. (See Table 7.1.) The president had already announced[4] a 10 percent reduction of the armed forces to 450,000 by the end of 1995, and a cut of another 100,000 two or three years later. Due to the high number of deferments, a manpower shortage among inductees from a population of 52 million has forced the government to extend compulsory military service from eighteen to twenty-four months.

The new defense minister is also faced with other problems. Some 100,000 servicemen have no quarters, about 10,000 positions for officers remain unfilled, and only 10 percent of the 700,000 eligible draftees could be inducted. Shmarov calls this a "peasant" army, because anyone with money can bribe his way out of the military obligation. Russian traditions have remained, with *dedovshchina* responsible for almost 1,700 privates and sergeants being killed as well as about 10,000 severely beaten during one recent year.[5] Lately, unit commanders have been attempting to break this "tradition."

On 8 February 1995, the respective first deputy prime ministers signed an agreement at Kiev which states that Ukraine intends to lease the Sevastopol naval base in the Crimea and a few other installations on its territory to Russia as well as agree to an unspecified division of the Black

TABLE 7.1
Defense Ministers in Near Abroad

Republic	Name (ethnic origin)	Appointed
Armenia	Vazgen Z. Sargisiyan[a] (Armenian)	26 July 1995
Azerbaijan	Lt. Gen. Safar A. Abiev (Azeri)	6 February 1995
Belarus	Lt. Gen. Leonid S. Mal'tsev (Belarusian)	11 October 1995
Georgia	Lt. Gen. Vardiko M. Nadibaidze (Georgian)	27 April 1994
Kazakhstan	Lt. Gen. Alibek Kh. Kasymov (Kazakh)	16 October 1995
Kyrgyzstan	Lt. Gen. Murzakan U. Subanov (Kyrgyz)	17 December 1993
Moldova	Div. Gen. Pavel Creangà (Moldovan)	7 April 1992
Tajikistan	Maj. Gen. Sherali Kh. Khairullaev (Tajik)	7 April 1995
Turkmenistan	Army Gen. Danatar A. Kopekov (Turkmen)	28 January 1992
Ukraine	Valerii N. Shmarov[a] (Ukrainian)	28 August 1994
Uzbekistan	Lt. Gen. Rustan U. Akhmedov (Uzbek)	July 1992

Sources: Foreign Broadcast Information Service, *Directory of Military Organizations and Personnel: States Other Than Russia* (Washington, D.C.: JPRS Report, March 1994), 17, 23, 64, 87, 96, 101, 143; OMRI *Daily Digest*, no. 27 (7 February 1995): pt. 1, p. 4. Dushanbe Radio, 7 April 1995; FBIS-SOV-95-067 (7 April 1995), 72–73, for Tajik appointment; fax from Armenian embassy, Washington, D.C. (24 August 1995).

[a] Civilian, i.e., without military rank.

Sea fleet. In mid-March 1995, Ukrainians announced the sale to Russia of nineteen Tu-160s (Blackjacks), twenty-three Tu-95 MS strategic bombers, and 600 cruise missiles for $192.6 million, which would be used to write off the debt for natural gas.[6]

An eleven-article agreement was initialed by Presidents Yeltsin and Kuchma on 9 June 1995 at Sochi. The 635 ships in the Black Sea fleet are to be divided equally, although Russia is permitted to purchase up to 81.7 percent of the total number.[7] It will continue to lease the base at Sevastopol in return for energy supplies and reduction of Ukraine's debt. Since this is only an agreement and not a treaty, presumably no ratification by respective parliaments is required. During the summer, there still seemed to be differences between the two sides regarding interpretation of the document. The respective prime ministers met on 26 July and were scheduled to do so again on 2 August in order to reconcile views on practical implementation.

Belarus, on the other hand, has fewer problems, perhaps because of its smaller size and population of only 8 million. It resolved to preserve the armed forces remaining on its territory in March 1992 and established a defense ministry two months later. The 243,000 men in Soviet uniform had modern weapons and equipment. Three army corps have replaced former combined-arms and tank armies. By mid-1995, total manpower strength had been brought down to 153,000. Because of poor living conditions, many officers reportedly were leaving the service or joining armies in other SNG states.[8] Despite two military schools, cadets must be sent to Russia for training in many unavailable specialties.

On 12 April 1994, the respective prime ministers signed an agreement that will lease two military installations for Russian personnel. Belarus will receive petroleum and natural gas at subsidized prices, and currencies will become exchangeable. Another source states that contacts with Moscow most frequently pertain to the "presence of Russian troops on Belarus' territory and their withdrawal."[9]

Even more significant is the alleged existence of a draft (*proiekt*) tripartite agreement, dated 7 February 1995, and supposedly sent from Moscow to Minsk and Almaty. It reportedly includes sixteen articles and would make the Belarus and Kazakh military establishments part of the Russian armed forces. By 1 September 1995, "the [three] sides will examine and approve the aforementioned proposals at the highest level," according to a photographic copy of this document.[10] The newspaper reproduction includes the signatures of two Russian generals, which cannot be deciphered.

Col. Gen. Anatolii I. Kastenka, appointed defense minister on 25 July 1994, is a Russian by birth, who received his military education in Odessa as well as at the Frunze and General Staff academies in Moscow. He served as commanding officer for the Belorussian Military District between 1989 and 1992, then as first deputy defense minister of Belarus. His promotion came from the newly elected president, Alyaksandr G. Lukashenka,[11] who also fired him in early June 1995 for corruption.

The army is undergoing reorganization into three corps headquarters. Subordinate to them will be three brigades and several battalions. The four services remain directly subordinated to the ministry of defense: one of these (artillery) carries reserve status, whereas the airborne and motorized rifle formations are manned at 50 percent strength. Those men who completed their military obligation and had not reached their thirty-fifth birthday may be offered two-year contracts. The latter can be extended another three or six years. In May 1995, there were 9,000 contract servicemen on duty.

Emphasis is being placed on creating airborne assault and airborne ground-attack units, mechanized brigades, and air regiments. Heavy equipment includes tanks (1,800), armored combat vehicles (2,600), artillery systems (1,615), aircraft (716), and helicopters (80). Most of these armaments were inherited from the former USSR.[12] It should be mentioned that the remaining thirty-six SS-25 Topol intercontinental ballistic missiles were to be withdrawn from Belarus to Russia by 31 July 1995. Support equipment should have been transferred by the end of that year.[13]

Moldova's chief of state, Mircea I. Snegur, issued a decree on 16 November 1991, following the examples set by Georgia and Azerbaijan, which nationalized all property belonging to Soviet army units stationed on his country's territory. During March–April 1992, legislation on the new defense establishment[14] and a decree introducing conscription were adopted. Moldovan citizens serving in the armed forces of other Newly Independent States were invited to return home. Almost two years later, about 10,000 men had been recruited out of a population numbering 4.3 million. This has been declared the optimum number required. Moldova also controlled a regiment of MiG-29s (offered for sale in May 1994) and one squadron of eight helicopters with 1,400 airmen.[15]

Apart from the twenty-seven MiG-29 fighters and five transport aircraft, the armed forces included three motorized infantry brigades, one artillery brigade, and some air defense troops. Beginning in 1991, alternative service for pacifists and members of certain religious groups was introduced. Three thousand youths, who could prove neither affiliation, were nevertheless not drafted. Another 12,804 worked in agriculture, communal services, construction, hospitals, and road maintenance in lieu of conscription.[16]

By the year 2000, it is planned to achieve an all-volunteer army patterned after the Italian *carabinieri*. Due to the breakaway Trans-Dniester Republic, protected by a limited contingent of Russian forces (see chapter 6, "Peacemaking Equals Peacekeeping"), Moldova cannot obtain any weapons from Moscow. Instead, it relies on deliveries by the neighboring Romanians with whom it is linked ethnically and historically as well as by the same language. Division General Pavel Creangà, a Moldovan national who served with the Soviet army in both Afghanistan and Cuba, became defense minister in 1992. Three years later, parliament approved a military doctrine that defines the army as a state structure outside politics and under the control of legislative and executive authorities. The national security concept stipulates neutrality and does not permit foreign troops on Moldovan territory.[17]

The Trans-Caucasus

Prior to independence, the countries in this region, totaling 15.7 million inhabitants, had developed paramilitary forces that identified with different political groups. The majority of draftees into the Soviet army were absorbed by construction battalions rather than combat units. Hence, relatively few of the indigenous conscriptees who were ethnics became officers. This explains the difficult and complicated process of organizing regular armed forces in Armenia, Azerbaijan, and Georgia as well as the heavy reliance on Russians to fill field-grade positions.[18]

Armenia's legislature adopted a resolution on 18 March 1992 which banned removal of equipment, arms, and munitions of the former Soviet 7th Guards Army at that time being withdrawn from its territory. By leaving these supplies behind, the Russians contributed substantially to the Armenian military establishment. It was decided that half or even two-thirds of the future army (by law only 30,000 men from a population of 3.3 million) would comprise light infantry or mountain units because of the terrain.[19]

In developing their plan, the Armenians were fortunate initially to obtain as their commander retired Lt. Gen. Norat Ter-Grigoryan who had served in Afghanistan and held senior staff positions with the Soviet ground forces. The draft began during August 1992 and a new defense minister, Serzh G. Sargisiyan, appealed for Russian officers from the 7th Guards Army to serve in the new Armenian forces. Also conscripted were local reserve officers up to the age of 65, depending on rank.[20] In mid-December 1993, it was announced that the call-up had been filled by just over 100 percent and that the army would be at full strength by the spring of the following year.

However, ethnic Russians residing in Armenia are drafted by the Group of Russian Forces in the Trans-Caucasus. They comprise about 80 percent of the recruits in such units, some of which will defend the country's borders. A joint Russian-Armenian military base was to be fully staffed during January and February 1995. Defense Minister Sargisiyan (appointed national security advisor in May 1995) is quoted as having said that such military installations "would mean a strengthening of the Armenian national army." General Grachëv announced a plan to send a squadron of jet fighters to protect the five Russian bases in Armenia and Georgia.

Presidents Yeltsin and Levon Ter-Petrosyan met in Moscow on 14 March 1995 to sign an agreement that authorized a Russian army base at the northwestern Armenian town of Gyumri for the 127th Motorized Rifle Division and a Russian command group in the capital city of Yerevan. The latter will include a motorized rifle regiment of troops. The treaty also provides for joint air defense of the country and will be valid during a period of twenty-five years, with automatic extension unless one side does not agree.[21]

Azerbaijan, on the other hand, adopted a law concerning its future armed forces on 9 October 1991.[22] It placed them under the republic's president as commander-in-chief. The following day, the legislature nationalized all property of the Soviet 4th Army and called for the return of 140,000 Azeri draftees from other parts of the USSR. It was not until the Tashkent Agreement (15 May 1992) that 4th Army assets were promised by the Russians, and only a year later did the last former Soviet division withdraw from Gandzha.

The agreement at Tashkent divided military equipment equally among Azerbaijan, Armenia, and Georgia. Each country was to receive 100 combat aircraft, 50 attack helicopters, 220 tanks, 220 armored vehicles, and 285 artillery systems. However, the latter two states received at most one-half of their share because Azerbaijan had "privatized" or seized most of the heavy armaments.[23] (See Table 7.2.) This did not help the Azeris in the fighting throughout Nagorno-Karabakh, where they were defeated by the Armenians. (See chapter 6.)

Despite these setbacks, the Azeri army is planned to comprise half contract volunteers and half conscripts. In 1996 it should total about 30,000 men (from a population of 7 million), although only one-third will be in the ground forces. A National Guard of 5,000 men will provide internal security. The June 1993 revolution brought to power former Azeri KGB chief and subsequently first secretary of the Communist Party of Azerbaijan Heydar A. Aliyev, who installed the seventh and eighth successive defense ministers.[24] The Azeris have organized their own border guards to protect frontiers with Iran and Turkey, refusing to do so jointly with the Russians or even allow the latter access to military bases on their territory.

Georgia's first free elections in October 1990 had already been preceded by establishment of paramilitary organizations like *Mkhedrioni* (Horsemen) headed by Jaba K. Ioseliani and numbering about 2,000 men; *Tetri Giorgi* (White George), whose members supported President Zviad K. Gamsakhurdia and his Round-Table–Free Georgia Movement, which had won the elections; and *Shevardeni* (Falcons). After the turn of the year, a parliamentary decree established a National Guard of up to 12,000 men for maintenance of internal order.

Two months following Gamsakhurdia's ouster in early 1992, the former Soviet foreign minister, Eduard Shevardnadze, returned to his native

TABLE 7.2
Azeri and Armenian Heavy Weapons

Category	Azerbaijan	Armenia
Tanks		
T-55	116	—
T-72	163	129
Infantry Fighting Vehicles		
IFV-1	104	192
IFV-2	191	9
IFV-3	3	—
IFV-1k (command)	—	7
BRM-1 (reconnaissance)	34	22
BMD-1	90	12
BMD-2	2	—
Armored Personnel Carriers		
APC-60PB	8	27
APC-70	76	67
APC-80	9	4
APC-152	—	6
APC-A (amphibious)	22	—
Multipurpose Tracked Vehicles		
MT-LB	198	—
Artillery Systems		
122mm howitzer D-1	—	2
D-20	36	31
D-30	153	63
152mm self-propelled 2S-1 *Gvozdika*	14	10
2S-3 *Akatsiia*	36	32
gun 2A-36B *Giatsint*	24	20
mortars	—	19
multiple-rocket launcher LV 21 *Grad*	66	48
Aircraft		
MiG-21 fighter	6	—
MiG-25 reconnaissance	35	—
Su-17 bomber	2	—
Su-24 tactical bomber	7	5
Su-25 assault and reconnaissance	3	—
Mi-24 assault helicopter	6	13

Source: Irakli Aladashvili, "Caucasus—The War Continues," *7 Dghe* (4–9 June 1994), 6, in FBIS-SOV-94-119 (21 June 1994), 1–2.

Note: Since there is no corroboration for the above, one should be cautious in accepting these figures as being absolutely accurate.

Georgia. It was then that the legislature approved a national army of 10,000 men, with total forces to reach 20,000 based on universal conscription from a population of 5.4 million. The first defense minister, Tengiz K. Kitovani, led a unit of the National Guard to Sukhumi (capital of Abkhazia). An exchange of fire precipitated a war, which in turn led to a massive flight of Georgians from the Abkhaz province.[25] A new defense minister, 27-year-old Brig. Gen. Giorgii Karkarashvili (identified as a veteran of Afghanistan and commander of National Guard formations in Abkhazia), took over prosecution of this civil war on 27 May 1993. (See chapter 6.)

The former deputy commander for armaments from the Group of Russian Forces in the Trans-Caucasus, Lt. Gen. Vardiko M. Nadibaidze (born in Georgia), was appointed defense minister by President Shevardnadze exactly eleven months later. The latter stated at the time that "without cooperation and friendship with Russia at this stage, it is impossible to make a truly national Georgian army." The new defense minister gives interviews in Russian, having forgotten his native language.[26]

Shevardnadze next issued an edict on "special purpose, rapid reaction, and mobile units" that are being planned for the new army of Georgia. He also banned all military formations and groups that were not part of the armed forces. Their staffs and weapons will be transferred to national motorized rifle brigades.[27] Lieutenant General Nadibaidze has announced that the military establishment would be brought down to 15,000 men.

Subsequently, Generals Grachëv and Nadibaidze initialed an agreement on 22 March 1995 which provided for five Russian bases in Georgia to be maintained over a twenty-five-year period. If approved in both parliaments, the treaty will be signed by Presidents Yeltsin and Shevardnadze. Two weeks earlier, an agreement had been reached for joint protection of Georgia's frontiers. This also allowed the Russians to recruit from among the local population for duty with their own guard units. In effect, Moscow now has control over Georgia's borders with Turkey.[28]

Central Asian States

It would have appeared initially that all five newly independent governments throughout Central Asia (total population over 54.1 million in 1995) had been willing to place their defense under the Commonwealth of Independent States. However, only four signed the SNG collective security treaty at the May 1992 summit in Tashkent. Turkmenistan preferred bilateral defense relations and suggested establishment of joint military units with Russia, which rejected the proposal. The only state outside the

SNG that has offered acceptable defense assistance is Turkey, where Turkmenistan sent 300 officers for training.[29]

On 8 July 1994, three of the Central Asian republics (Kazakhstan, Kyrgyzstan, and Uzbekistan) agreed in Almaty—the former Alma-Ata—to establish an economic and defense union. The president of Kazakhstan, Nursultan A. Nazarbaev, called these measures a first step and announced that the union would remain open to other SNG member states. He expressed hope that such a small-scale model of his planned Eurasian Union would enhance or even replace the SNG.[30]

Kazakhstan, which has a 2,000-km border with Russia, is the second largest former Soviet republic in terms of territory. It established a Republican Guard in March 1992 for protection of the country's president and legislature, with a projected total of 2,500 men. The government assumed control two months later over all former Soviet military personnel, property on its territory, and bases as approved by the SNG collective security treaty. After a presidential decree on establishing border troops (for the boundary with China) in August, legislation at year's end concerning the army's structure[31] also allowed for peacemaking in other countries. Parliament in April 1993 gave approval for such a mission in Tajikistan. (See chapter 6.)

During the previous month, agreements with Russia on military cooperation had envisaged a joint defense zone as well as coordination of industrial production for the armed forces. Some of the 6,000 Russian troops (remnants of the former Soviet 40th Army) in Kazakhstan, including 1,500 at the Baikonur cosmodrome, have been involved with training the local army. Despite this close relationship, a separate pact on military cooperation was signed in early February 1994 by Kazakhstan, Uzbekistan, and Kyrgyzstan. The Russians, reportedly, had not been told about this in advance.[32]

The following month, President Nazarbaev approved eighteen bilateral agreements in Moscow. Some 500 officers attend military schools in Russia each year, and 700 indigenous officers from other SNG countries had returned during 1993 to serve in the Kazakh armed forces. Two dozen cadets were sent to attend academies in Turkey because the only such native institution is not large enough to supply an adequate number of graduates.[33] It will take many years before the authorized strength of 70,000 men in uniform (from a 16.7 million population) can be reached and most Russian officers (97 percent) replaced with native ones.

During early 1994, the Kazakh government decided not to withdraw its token "peacemaking" battalion from Tajikistan. At the same time, an agreement signed at Almaty provided for joint defense with Russian border guards of Kazakhstan's frontiers.[34] Another document, initialed on 1 June 1994, laid the basis for interaction between Russian and Kazakh air defense systems. One of the problems facing the new republic's army stems from departure of many nonindigenous officers, resulting in a cadres' shortage exceeding 50 percent. The complement of enlisted personnel and sergeants is claimed to be filled.[35]

The defense minister, General of the Army Sagadat K. Nurmagambetov, is a native Kazakh who had served in the Soviet Army since World War II. He attended the Frunze Military Academy, performed duties in Turkestan and then in Hungary, retiring from command of the Central Asian Military District in 1989. Two years later, he became chairman of the Kazakhstan state defense committee and from May 1992 to October 1995 served as defense minister.[36]

After talks in Moscow, Presidents Nazarbaev and Yeltsin issued a joint declaration on 20 January 1995 concerning establishment of a combined military force later during the year. They signed a separate agreement on the legal status of Russian citizens living in Kazakhstan and Kazakhs in Russia. Also announced was a treaty for joint defense of external frontiers, subsequently signed on 10 February. Respective prime ministers placed their signatures to agreements on the status of Russian troops located in Kazakhstan and their use of military facilities in that country.[37] On 24 April 1995, the last nuclear warheads from SS-18 intercontinental ballistic missiles were transported to Russia—four years ahead of schedule.

Kyrgyzstan has only 4.5 million inhabitants and permits Russian border troops to guard its frontier with China. President Askar A. Akaev had wanted to avoid establishing an indigenous army, although he did promise a contribution to the joint SNG peacemaking force in Tajikistan to which 500 of his troops were dispatched. Despite presidential hopes, during 1992 there were already 4,000 men in the Kyrgyz army, although the planned target is 18,000.

In 1995, the ground forces alone totaled 12,281 men, with the 8th (Guards) Motorized Rifle Division stationed at Bishkek as their core. It included thirty tanks and seventy-five armored vehicles. A Border Guards Command will number some 2,000 men when recruited. A joint force with Russia currently protects the frontiers. Kyrgyzstan boasts twenty-two major generals and three lieutenant generals for a total of 14,000 men in its armed forces (including an air force that numbers 200 planes and also an air defense). Toward the end of 1993, a new defense minister was appointed, Lt. Gen. Murzakan U. Subanov, who has been identified as having been cleared of corruption charges.[38]

An interstate treaty allows Russian soldiers to serve in the military forces of Kyrgyzstan on a contract basis. Automatic transfer will be processed through the end of 1999. About 8,000 Russians, or 90 percent of the new officers' corps, found themselves in the Kyrgyz army when former USSR units were "privatized" by the new republic.[39] More than 200,000 Soviet military personnel at one time held assignments in what was then called Kirgizia.

Uzbekistan's army has developed slowly, despite a population of more than 22.6 million. Parliament adopted a law on defense during the summer of 1992, when Russian-speaking personnel comprised 70 percent of the officers' corps.[40] Apart from a small National Guard of about 1,000, the Uzbek target for its armed forces is 30,000 men.

About 7,000 Uzbek soldiers and noncommissioned officers were still serving in the Russian army during summer 1992 as volunteers. When their contracts expired, it was hoped that they would return home. In addition, Uzbeks being trained at officer candidate schools in Russia are called back after graduation. On 2 March 1994, Presidents Boris Yeltsin and Islam A. Karimov signed in Moscow a treaty on military cooperation which provides for delivery of Russian weapons and logistics.[41]

This cooperation extends to sending about 500 Uzbek servicemen for guard duty along the Tajik-Afghan border, announced on 21 August 1994. Just prior to that, a biographic sketch appeared of Lt. Gen. Rustan U. Akhmedov, the new defense minister. He was born in Uzbekistan and served with Soviet armored troops, graduating from the Frunze Military Academy. This same source indicates that Uzbek armed forces maintain 280 tanks, 780 armored vehicles, 265 fixed wing aircraft, and 24 helicopters.[42]

Despite the foregoing, U.S. Secretary of Defense William Perry signed an agreement with his counterpart on 6 April 1995 which provides for a working group to study cooperation that would include training of Uzbek officers in the United States. It is interesting to note that President Karimov, former first secretary of the communist party, identified three threats to Uzbek independence as follows:[43]

    Imperialist ambitions rearing up in Russia…which are intensifying daily;
    the threat from the south, of [Muslim] fundamentalism;
    and the problem of how to ensure…the forced advance of political and economic reform.

This list of threats may have been for American consumption, especially the last item.

Turkmenistan, with a population of 4.5 million, made an agreement with Russia in mid-1992 for the latter to assist in organization of an indigenous army. By the following April, about 60,000 soldiers were stationed inside the country, based on the former Soviet 52nd Army, only one-fourth of them Russian. Lacking native officers, however, President Saparmurad A. Niyazov sent 300 soldiers to Turkey for training.[44]

It was reported on 2 September 1993 that a bilateral agreement had been signed with Moscow on military cooperation between the two countries. This treaty permits Russian citizens (2,000 officers) to carry out their service in Turkmenistan's armed forces on a contract basis and the latter's indigenous officers to be trained at Russian military schools. Since 1 January 1994, Turkmenistan has been paying the entire cost of Russia's military expenses on its territory. This includes guarding the southern border with Afghanistan.[45] In addition, Turkmenistan maintains 750 tanks, about 1,400 armored vehicles, and 25 aircraft of its own.

The local defense minister is a native Turkmen, Army Gen. Danatar A. Kopekov. Ashgabad has signed the most complete package of defense agreements with Moscow. However, Russian officers remain unhappy with pay and living conditions, which should result in a mass exodus once their contracts have expired. The first class of 500 indigenous lieutenants graduated from the military academy at Ashgabad and joined the army during summer 1994. It will take many years before they become field grade officers,[46] that is, with the rank of major through colonel.

Tajikistan's civil war has been discussed in chapter 6. Perhaps little known is the fact that about 90 percent of the Russian 201st Motorized Rifle Division protecting the 500-km border with Afghanistan is comprised of Tajik nationals as enlisted personnel.[47] Apart from a plan for 1,200 native border troops and a 1,000-man National Guard, then-President Rakhman A. Nabiev announced toward the end of 1992 that indigenous armed forces also would be established from a population of around 5.8 million.

The decree adopted by the Tajik parliament's presidium on 19 December 1992 provided a legal basis for conscription.[48] Assistance was offered by a group of SNG high command experts. In the meanwhile, the brunt of war against infiltrators from Afghanistan is being borne by Russian officers and Tajik soldiers. The 201st Division will remain in Tajikistan until at least the year 1999, according to Defense Minister Grachëv.

The Tajik armed forces in April 1995 comprised a total of 11,500 men organized into one incompletely manned *spetsnaz* unit, four battalions, and two motorized rifle brigades. These units do not seem to be effective, even against insurgents within the country's borders.[49]

TABLE 7.3
Conventional Military Power: Russia versus Ukraine

Category	Russia	Ukraine
Manpower	1,500,000	700,000
Tanks	6,400	4,080
APCs	11,480	5,050
Artillery systems	8,415	4,040
Aircraft	3,450	1,900
Attack helicopters	890	330

Source: Dos'e MN, "Kazhdomu-svoiu nepobedimuiu," *Moskovskie novosti*, no. 8 (20–27 February 1994): 9A.

Note: APC = armored personnel carrier

In conclusion, it seems obvious that the "other armies" represent no threat to Russia's armed forces. Their support, if any, will be negligible over the next twenty years. The precedent of combining Kazakhstan's fledgling military establishment with that of the Russian Federation could be applied to a few of the other SNG member states, and may be next implemented with Belarus. The same pattern could indeed repeat itself with other Central Asian republics during the near future. In the optimistic words of Russia's defense minister, Army General Pavel S. Grachëv, "Integration of SNG armed forces is realistic."[50]

That would still leave Ukraine (with 52 million inhabitants) as a potential enemy and a formidable one, if it receives membership in NATO around the year 2000. (See Table 7.3.) As a full member of that alliance, Kiev could become an important actor in its own right within the post-Soviet region of East-Central Europe. Even though they had dismantled only forty of the 176 ICBMs on their territory by the end of April 1995, Ukrainians apparently are living up to their obligations undertaken through various conventional arms reduction treaties, which are discussed in chapter 8.

Notes
---

1. *Komsomol'skaia pravda,* 29 October 1992, 1; as cited by Stephen Foye, "Civilian-Military Tension in Ukraine," RFE/RL *Research Report* 2, no. 25 (18 June 1993): 63.

2. Ustina Markus, "No Longer as Mighty," *Transition* 1, no. 13 (28 July 1995): 24–29.

3. American Embassy Kiev, "Military Doctrine of Ukraine," unclassified dispatch

to Department of State (3 November 1993); translated from *Narodna armiia* (26 October 1993). Source courtesy of Maj. Gen. Nicholas Krawciw, U.S. Army (ret.).

4. Moscow Radio, ITAR-TASS, 22 July 1994, in FBIS-SOV-94-142 (25 July 1994), 42. The military received only 16.9 percent of funds it had requested for 1995. See also Taras Kuzio, "The Ukrainian Armed Forces in Crisis," *Jane's Intelligence Review* 7, no. 7 (July 1995): 305–6.

5. Anatolii Poliakov, "Armiia Ukrainy," *Krasnaia zvezda*, 10 November 1994, 3. See also chapter on "Oboronnyi potentsial Ukrainy," in Evgenii M. Kozhokin, ed., *Ukraina: vektor peremen* (Moscow: Rossiiskii Institut Strategicheskikh Issledovanii, 1994), 42–65.

6. Ianina Sokolovskaia and Viktor Litovkin, "Ukraina budet sotrudnichat' s Rossiei," *Izvestiia*, 10 February 1995, 1; Vladimir Sergeev, "Vozvrashchenie strategicheskoi aviatsii," *Segodnia*, 14 March 1995, 3.

7. "Soglashenie mezhdu R.F. i Ukrainoi po Chernomorskomu flotu," *Krasnaia zvezda*, 14 June 1995, 3.

8. Col. Valerii Kovalëv, "Kto pod belo-krasno-belym znamenem idët?" *Krasnaia zvezda*, 27 April 1994, 2; interview with acting defense minister Mal'tsev over Moscow Radio, 26 June 1995, as translated in FBIS-SOV-95-123 (27 June 1995), 73.

9. Mikhail Berger, "Belorussiia obmenila chast' svoego suvereniteta," *Izvestiia*, 14 April 1994, 1; Lt. Gen. Leonid S. Mal'tsev, "Voennye kontakty s Rossiei…," *Krasnaia zvezda*, 22 February 1995, 2.

10. Ivan Sidar, "Nas utsiagvaiuts' u raseiski 'katsël'," *Svaboda* (Minsk), 22 February 1995, 1.

11. Valerii Kovalëv, "Prezident Belorussii formiruet pravitel'stvo," *Krasnaia zvezda*, 26 July 1994, 3.

12. International Institute for Strategic Studies, *The Military Balance 1994–1995* (London: Brassey's, October 1994), 78. See also Mark Galeotti, "The Belarusian Army," *Jane's Intelligence Review* 7, no. 6 (June 1995): 258–60.

13. Dos'e MN, "Kazhdomu-svoiu nepobedimuiu," *Moskovskie novosti*, no. 8 (20–27 February 1994): 9A. Minsk Radiostantsia Belarus, 16 March 1995, in FBIS-SOV-95-052 (17 March 1995), 67.

14. Defense Law, issued on 17 March 1992, *Moldova suverana*, 4 April 1992; JPRS-UMA-92-018 (20 May 1992), 41–45.

15. Vladimir Socor, "Moldova Advertises MiG-29s for Sale," RFE/RL *Daily Report*, no. 100 (27 May 1994): 8.

16. "Defense Ministry Against Alternative Service," Radio Chisinau, 27 July 1994, in FBIS-SOV-94-148 (2 August 1994), 43–44.

17. "Parliament Approves Military Doctrine," Moscow Radio, 17 March 1995, in FBIS-SOV-95-053 (20 March 1995), 66. See also "Parliament Adopts National Security Concept," Radio Moscow, 5 May 1995, in FBIS-SOV-95-088 (8 May 1995), 65.

18. Elizabeth Fuller, "Paramilitary Forces Dominate Fighting in Transcaucasus," RFE/RL *Research Report*, no. 25 (18 June 1993): 74.

19. Nelson Aleksanyan, "Reflections on a National Army," *Respublika Armeniia*, 3 April 1992, 2; translated in JPRS-UMA-92-020 (3 June 1992), 44.

20. Lt. Col. Konstantin Petrov, "V Armenii sygrali 'v ruzh'e!'" *Krasnaia zvezda,* 5 December 1992, 3.

21. Vitalii Denisov, "Pod rossiiskimi znamenami sluzhat ne tol'ko rossiiane," *Krasnaia zvezda,* 7 July 1993, 1; "Joint Armenian-Russian Command Post for 1995," Yerevan Radio, 3 January 1995, translated in FBIS-SOV-95-002 (4 January 1995), 48; Moscow Radio, INTERFAX, 16 March 1995, in FBIS-SOV-95-052 (17 March 1995), 5–6.

22. "Zakon o vooruzhënnykh silakh Azerbaidzhanskoi respubliki," *Krasnaia zvezda,* 31 October 1991, 2.

23. Fuller, "Paramilitary Forces Dominate Fighting in Transcaucasus," 79–80. See also Shireen T. Hunter, *The Transcaucasus in Transition* (Washington, D.C.: Center for Strategic and International Studies, 1994), 58–96.

24. Colonel Talekh by Nurani, "Models for Republic's Armed Forces," *Zerkalo,* 15 April 1993, 3; JPRS-UMA-95-020 (2 May 1995), 69.

25. Fuller, "Paramilitary Forces Dominate Fighting in Transcaucasus," 79–80.

26. Moscow Radio, INTERFAX, 2 May 1994, in FBIS-SOV-94-085 (3 May 1994), 39; Pëtr Karapetian, "Vot pridët russkii general...," *Krasnaia zvezda,* 4 June 1994, 3.

27. Tbilisi Radio, 8 June 1994, in FBIS-SOV-94-113 (13 June 1994), 84; *Sakartvelos Respublika,* 17 June 1994, 1, as translated in FBIS-SOV-94-123 (27 June 1994), 72.

An attempt to assassinate the previous defense minister, Maj. Gen. Giorgii Karkarashvili, and his former first deputy took place outside the General Staff hotel at Moscow in late January 1995. Only Karkarashvili survived.

28. "U rossiiskikh i gruzinskikh pogranichnikov rabota odna," *Krasnaia zvezda,* 16 November 1994, 2; Moscow Radio, 9 March 1995, in FBIS-SOV-95-047 (10 March 1995), 96; Tbilisi Radio, 22 March 1995, in FBIS-SOV-95-056 (23 March 1995), 66. See also Richard Woff, "Russia Strengthens Ties with Georgia and Armenia," *Jane's Intelligence Review* 7, no. 7 (July 1995): 294.

29. Bess Brown, "Central Asian States Seek Russia's Help," RFE/RL *Research Report* 2, no. 25 (18 June 1993): 83. See also Capt. O. Odnokolenko, "Rossiia-Kazakhstan: sozdan oboronitel'nyi soiuz," *Krasnaia zvezda,* 27 May 1992, 1.

30. "Central Asians Form Union," RFE/RL *Daily Report,* no. 129 (11 July 1994): 2; "Central Asian States Planning Economic Integration," Moscow Radio, 5 July 1995, in FBIS-SOV-95-130 (7 July 1995), 2–3.

31. William E. Odom and Robert Dujarric, *Commonwealth or Empire? Russia, Asia, and the Transcaucasus* (Indianapolis: Hudson Institute, 1995), 51–52.

32. "Trilateral Central Asian Military Pact," Baku Radio, 10 February 1994, translated in FBIS-SOV-94-030 (14 February 1994), 1.

33. Dimitry Vërtkin, "Prospects for Stability—the View from Kazakhstan," *Jane's Intelligence Review* 6, no. 6 (June 1994): 287.

34. Col. Oleg Falichev, "Rossiiskie pogranichniki na kazakhstanskoi granitse," *Krasnaia zvezda,* 23 February 1994, 1.

35. Aleksandr Gribanov, "The Army of Kazakhstan," Almaty ABV, 30 May 1994, in FBIS-USR-94-059 (8 June 1994), 101.

36. *Karavan,* no. 35 (2 September 1994): 6; JPRS-UMA-94-038 (14 September 1994), 16. For an interview, see Col. Anatolii Ladin, "Sagadat Nurmagambetov," *Krasnaia zvezda,* 18 February 1995, 5.

37. Igor' Spiridonov, "Rossiia i Kazakhstan…," *Segodnia,* 28 January 1995, 3.

38. Boris Vladimirov, "Kirgiziia," *Rossiiskaia gazeta,* 1 September 1994, 6; Odom and Dujarric, *Commonwealth or Empire?* 64–66. See *Vechernii Bishkek,* 4 April 1995, 1, in FBIS-SOV-95-067 (7 April 1995), 71, for charges against Subanov.

39. Ekmat Baibakpaev, "Sluzhi, soldat, gde khochesh'," *Trud,* 15 March 1994, 2, discusses the draft treaty, initialed at Bishkek on 4 March. See also Lt. Gen. Murzakan U. Subanov's article (no title) in *Krasnaia zvezda,* 4 May 1995, 3.

40. For identification of senior Russian officers in the Uzbek military, see Richard Woff, "Independence and the Uzbek Armed Forces," *Jane's Intelligence Review* 5, no. 12 (December 1993): 567–71.

41. Interview with deputy chief of staff, Col. Arslan Khalmatov, "Pod krylom ptitsy Khumo," in *Krasnaia zvezda,* 20 May 1993, 2. The treaty text appeared in *Narodnoe slovo* (Tashkent) on 10 March 1994, 1–2; translated in FBIS-SOV-94-050 (15 March 1994), 40–43.

42. Moscow Radio, 21 August 1994, in FBIS-SOV-94-162 (22 August 1994), 60. "Vooruzhënnye sily Respubliki Uzbekistan," *Nezavisimaia gazeta,* 15 July 1994, 2. For an interview with the new defense minister, see Tursunbai Batyrberkov, "Tri goda srochnoi sluzhby," *Rossiiskaia gazeta,* 21 January 1995, 6.

43. Tashkent TV, 6 April 1995, in FBIS-SOV-95-067 (7 April 1995), 76.

44. Brown, "Central Asian States Seek Russia's Help," 86–87. See also Vladimir Kuleshov, "Sozdaiutsia sovmestnye voiska," *Izvestiia,* 2 July 1992, 1.

45. Richard Woff, "The Armed Forces of Turkmenistan," *Jane's Intelligence Review* 6, no. 3 (March 1994): 132–35; for the border force treaty text, see *Rossiiskaia gazeta,* 28 January 1995, 15.

46. Lt. Col. V. Mukhin, "Slavianskii faktor v armiakh musul'manskikh gosudarstv SNG," *Armiia,* no. 10 (1994): 22–24.

47. Moscow Radio, INTERFAX, 5 November 1992, translated in FBIS-SOV-92-215 (5 November 1992), 62–63.

48. Aleksandr Karpov, "Tadzhikistan formiruet vooruzhënnye sily," *Izvestiia,* 10 February 1993, 1. See also Oleg Falichev, "Armii Tadzhikistana trebuiutsia professionaly," *Krasnaia zvezda,* 16 February 1993, 3.

49. "Russian 201st Army Division to Remain until 1999," FBIS-SOV-93-029 (16 February 1993), 57, as cited by Odom and Dujarric, *Commonwealth or Empire?* 73; Nikolai Plotnikov, "Vsë idët po planu," *Nezavisimaia gazeta,* 2 November 1994, 3, for an interview with then–Minister of Defense Maj. Gen. Aleksandr V. Shishliannikov.

50. Vladimir Mariukha and Anatolii Ladin, "General armii Pavel Grachëv: Integratsiia vooruzhënnykh sil SNG real'na," *Krasnaia zvezda,* 10 February 1995, 1.

Myth No. 8
Arms Treaties Are Observed

> Hardware used in [the Chechnya] war region...should not be counted under CFE.
> Gen. *Pavel Grachëv* (3 April 1995)

Although nuclear missiles have attracted more attention, the fact remains that Russia has applied exclusively conventional weapons in its conflicts throughout the "near abroad." Such arms are also more likely to be used than their nuclear counterparts through the turn of the century and beyond. Discussion in this chapter will center on international treaties reducing the number of main battle tanks, armored combat vehicles, artillery systems, combat aircraft, and assault helicopters as well as chemical and biological weapons. Comments will also be made about the ABM and START agreements. Clearly, military strategists in Moscow may have misgivings about the reduction or elimination of weapons that are of most use to them.

The CFE Agreement

Commencing on 30 October 1973, under the name of Mutual and Balanced Force Reductions (MBFR), formal negotiations at first included nineteen delegations: seven Warsaw Pact states from the East and twelve NATO members from the West. It should be noted that the Western alliance had invited its Eastern counterparts to initiate such talks more than five years earlier, that is, in June 1968 during the Reykjavik conference of NATO foreign ministers.[1]

Only three weeks after the MBFR talks had started in Vienna, Austria, the West suggested reductions to a common ceiling of 700,000 ground troops for each side. In view of the East's numerical preponderance, this would have involved withdrawal by one Soviet army of 68,000 men. Only after a second phase of reductions could the above common levels be attained. The East refused to discuss this proposal.

In December 1975 NATO offered to remove 54 aircraft (F-4s) capable of delivering nuclear ordnance, 36 Pershing I intermediate-range nuclear missile launchers, and 1,000 battlefield nuclear warheads, if the original proposal was accepted. The response again was negative, demonstrating an intransigence that continued almost until the end of these talks.

Four years later, in 1979, the West offered to begin the process with smaller reductions, namely the removal of 30,000 Soviet and 13,000 American ground troops from Eastern and Western Europe respectively. It also proposed a comprehensive set of associated (confidence-building and verification) measures. Although the East finally did accept the principle of reducing each side to 700,000 ground troops as well as 900,000 ground and air force manpower combined, the inaccurate and incomplete data released by the Warsaw Pact concerning its strength appeared to doom these negotiations to failure.

After almost a decade of frustrating talks, the first Western draft treaty ever prepared was offered to the East in July 1982. It took the form of a comprehensive agreement under which both sides would reduce their military manpower to the above-mentioned common collective ceilings over a period of seven years. This process would be accomplished in stages. Associated measures (exchange of data, verification, on-site inspection, and so on) comprised an integral part of the draft document. All of this remained predicated on release of truthful beginning manpower totals which would be written into the final treaty.

According to NATO estimates, if one included air force manpower, the Warsaw Pact disposed of 200,000 more troops in the reduction area than it admitted having. (See Table 8.1.) Without resolving this huge discrepancy, a treaty would be unverifiable, unworkable, unenforceable, and thus politically unacceptable. Instead of a response to the foregoing estimates, the East had submitted its own treaty in February 1982 which offered nothing new and represented merely a compilation of known Warsaw Pact positions. Then, after criticizing the July 1982 NATO document over the course of a full year, the East finally rejected it as the basis for a treaty.

Culminating after more than one and one-half decades of talks, MBFR held its last session in early February 1989. The following month, a renamed Conference on Armed Forces in Europe, or CFE, opened with

TABLE 8.1
Disparity between Forces in the Reduction Area (1 January 1981)

According to NATO Estimates

	NATO estimates for WTO forces	Western figures for NATO forces	Disparity
Ground	960,000	790,000	170,000
Air	230,000	200,000	30,000
Total	*1,190,000*	*990,000*	*200,000*

According to Warsaw Pact Data

	Eastern figures for WTO forces	Western figures for NATO forces	Disparity
Ground	800,000	790,000	10,000
Air	180,000	200,000	-20,000
Total	*980,000*	*990,000*	*-10,000*

Source: U.S. Delegation to MBFR talks in Vienna, Austria. Unclassified.

twenty-three delegations (France, Iceland, Portugal, and Spain joined the original twelve NATO negotiators). By mid-year, the West had presented a new proposal with subsequent additions during the fall.[2] The CFE talks probably would have continued without progress had events in East-Central Europe and the USSR itself not affected the East's negotiating power.

In June 1989, the Warsaw Treaty Organization dissolved. By the following January, the cycle of East-Central European revolutions had run its course. Hence, in mid-1990, Presidents George Bush and Mikhail Gorbachëv committed themselves to a CFE treaty by the end of the year. After unification between East and West Germany on 30 October, military holdings of the former were added to NATO totals. Secretary of State James Baker and Foreign Minister Eduard Shevardnadze resolved the remaining issues by 9 November, and ten days later the CFE treaty was signed by heads of state in Paris.[3]

However, the accuracy and completeness of Soviet data submitted at that time were still being challenged by NATO. The same applied to USSR claims that equipment with coastal defense units, naval infantry, strategic rocket forces, and civil defense within the reduction area should not be counted under treaty limits. Another example involved transfer of three "Guards" divisions (3rd at Klaipeda, 77th at Arkhangel'sk, and 126th at Simferopol) to naval infantry. In addition, between the time CFE talks began in March 1989 and signature of the treaty on 19 November 1990, the Soviet armed forces withdrew more than 75,000 weapons systems from the reduction area and transported them to locations east of the Ural Mountains, which remain outside the CFE applicable region. (See Table 8.2.) The spirit, if not the letter, of the CFE agreement had been violated.

The CFE treaty was signed at Paris by sixteen NATO and six former WTO heads of government, the number of signatories increasing to thirty with later inclusion of successor states to the USSR and Czechoslovakia. The treaty's principal objectives were listed as follows:

- Establishment of a secure and stable balance of forces in Europe at lower levels
- Elimination of historic inequalities between East and West
- Removal of the potential for a surprise attack and for large-scale offensive operations.

Implementation began on 16 November 1992 and has included inspection of destruction sites as well as other treaty-related facilities. During the first year of these activities, 154 such visits were carried out in Russia and 185 in NATO countries. Reportedly, a total of 4,500 main battle tanks, almost 5,000 artillery systems, and 60 attack helicopters were destroyed over the first twelve-month period.[4]

Army Gen. Mikhail A. Moiseev, chief of the USSR General Staff, visited Washington, D.C., during late May 1991 and attempted to explain why more than 75,000 units of treaty-limited heavy military hardware had disappeared before the CFE agreement could be signed. Secretary of State James Baker and Foreign Minister Aleksandr Bessmertnykh reached a

TABLE 8.2
Soviet CFE-Limited Equipment in East-Central Europe

Category	Mid-1988	End of 1990	Moved beyond Urals
Main battle tanks	41,500	21,000	20,500
Armored combat vehicles	45,000	29,600	19,300
Artillery systems	53,000	14,000	28,400
Combat aircraft	11,000[a]	5,150[a]	5,850[a]
Attack helicopters	2,900[a]	1,500[a]	1,400[a]
Total	150,700[a]	71,250[a]	75,450[a]

Sources: Marshal of the Soviet Union Dmitrii T. Iazov, "Vysokii rubezh istorii," *Krasnaia zvezda*, 29 November 1990, 3, for all figures in the first three categories; Richard F. Staar, ed., *East-Central Europe and the USSR* (New York: St. Martin's Press, 1991), 8, for estimates.

Note: Last two columns for armored combat vehicles and artillery systems do not add up to the totals in the first column.

[a] Estimated.

settlement on other aspects of the dispute by early June. In the middle of that month, the Soviets presented an official statement to a CFE extraordinary conference, which reportedly brought them "into *practical* compliance with treaty ceilings, sub-ceilings, and other provisions."[5]

And then the counting began in earnest. NATO inspectors found that approximately 2,000 tanks, armored personnel carriers, and artillery pieces were missing from Russia, Armenia, Azerbaijan, Georgia, and Moldova. These weapons systems should have been among those scheduled for destruction by the end of November 1993 in accordance with the CFE treaty.[6] Nothing has been reported subsequently about this discrepancy which, apparently, has been accepted as a *fait accompli* by the West.

Early in June 1993, Russian Defense Minister Pavel S. Grachëv approached his U.S. counterpart, Les Aspin, at a meeting in Garmisch-Partenkirchen, Germany, about revising the CFE treaty provisions that specified numbers of heavy weapons allowed in certain geographic regions west of the Urals. These totals had been divided among seven newly independent republics on 15 May 1992. (See Table 8.3.) The CFE agreement had set limits on tanks, artillery, and armored personnel carriers within the northeastern and southeastern flanks of European Russia.

Grachëv, in requesting a revision of the treaty, also brought up the "threat" of Islamic fundamentalism to the south of Russia. He claimed that the ceilings of 700 tanks, 580 armored personnel carriers, and 1,280 artillery pieces applying to both southern and northern flank areas (to take effect in November 1995) would place his armed forces at a disadvantage.[7] The request was rejected by NATO signatories to the treaty in September 1993, with Turkey being the most adamant opponent of any CFE revisions. Two months later Moscow dropped its threat to take unilateral actions, although these seem to have been adopted in connection with the invasion of Chechnya discussed below.

More than half a year later, after NATO had rejected Moscow's request to lift the flank restrictions in the CFE treaty, the chief of the General Staff wrote a long article on this subject to support his contention that "deployment of troops on its own territory, in accordance with the state's view on defense tasks and guaranteeing its own security interests [remain the] inalienable right of every sovereign state. This contradicts neither [CFE] treaty conditions nor Article 51 of the UN charter."[8]

That is exactly what happened when the high command ordered the invasion of Chechnya on 11 December 1994 by 40,000 troops, over 1,000 main battle tanks and armored fighting vehicles, hundreds of

TABLE 8.3
Maximum Levels for CFE Treaty-Limited Equipment[a]
(Tashkent, 15 May 1992)

Category of Weapons	Russia	Ukraine	Belarus	Moldova	Georgia	Armenia	Azerbaijan	Totals
Tanks	6,400	4,080	1,800	210	220	220	220	13,150
Armored combat vehicles	11,480	5,050	2,600	210	220	220	220	20,000
Artillery	6,415	4,040	1,615	250	285	285	285	13,175
Combat aircraft	3,450	1,090	260	50	100	100	100	5,150
Attack helicopters	890	330	80	50	50	50	50	1,500

Source: Amedeo de Franchis, "The CFE Treaty—the Role of the High Level Working Group," *NATO Review* 5, no. 20 (October 1992): 16.

[a] Kazakhstan has agreed to have no holdings in the CFE area of application.

artillery systems and rocket launchers, and more than 100 jet bombers and attack helicopters.

The CFE treaty specifies that Russia could station much less heavy equipment in active units throughout the southern flank area of the North Caucasus military district, which includes Chechnya and the other six small Muslim republics in the region.[9] Neither was any notice given of these large troop movements, as mandated by the CFE treaty. The regional limitation does not extend to combat aircraft or attack helicopters. Apparently flaunting what he had done in Chechnya, Defense Minister Grachëv announced another *fait accompli* during an interview on 3 April 1995 over Moscow Radio in these words: "Russia proposes that in fulfilling CFE, areas of combat operations be designated as outside the framework condition of this treaty." The Russian military commander in Chechnya, Lt. Gen. Anatolii V. Kvashnin, stated openly that "only a complete idiot would comply with the CFE treaty's flank limits."[10]

Chemical-Weapons Treaties

An international agreement (the Geneva Protocol) had placed a ban on chemical warfare already in 1925, although it did not prevent either development or production of such armaments. All major powers produced these weapons during World War II as insurance in case the other side used them first. Since that time, about twenty-four countries have produced a chemical warfare arsenal or are in the process of developing one.[11] President Gorbachëv finally admitted in April 1987 that the Soviet Union did have such weapons. The first agreement between the United States and the USSR, signed in 1989, obligated both parties to exchange data on stockpiles and production facilities as well as introducing verification. A second agreement the following year called for destruction of excess weapons (and inspections), leaving each side with 5,000 tons.[12]

At the same time, a multilateral chemical-weapons treaty was being negotiated. Opened for signature in Paris on 13 January 1993 by representatives of 140 countries, the treaty prohibits development, production, stockpiling, and use of chemical weapons, as well as obligates the signatories to destroy them and their production facilities.[13] Several countries, suspected of already possessing or developing such weapons, did not sign the agreement. They include Egypt, Libya, Iraq, Syria, North Korea, and Taiwan, although the last country is ineligible to become a treaty signatory as a nonmember of the United Nations. By June 1995, a total of 159 countries had signed the treaty although only 29 had ratified it, with

17 others planning to do so.[14] Sixty-five ratifications are needed to begin implementation of the agreement. Neither Washington, D.C., nor Moscow has ratified the treaty, as of this writing, although entry into force is expected during mid- or late 1996.

By far the largest stockpile of chemical weapons belongs to Russia, which in October 1993 claimed to have about 40,000 agent metric tons stored at seven locations. (See Table 8.4.) Some are probably being destroyed surreptitiously in order to have the admitted stockpile when the treaty enters into force. One destruction facility had been built at Chapaevsk, although it never opened due to strong protests by the local population concerning impact on the environment. The bilateral 1990 treaty, however, called for weapons destruction to commence during November 1992 at the latest and to be completed within ten years. Agreements to build experimental destruction units at Gornyi and Kambarka reportedly have been reached.[15]

In July 1992, the United States agreed to allocate up to $25 million for chemical weapons–elimination assistance to Russia; in March 1994, an additional $300 million or more was offered to help build a pilot

TABLE 8.4
CW Stockpiles in Russia

Location	Contents	Metric Tons
Pochep, S.W. Russia	Nerve agent; air-delivered munitions	7,500
Maradykovskiie, Kirov *oblast'*	Nerve agent; air-delivered munitions	7,000
Leonidovka, Penza *oblast'*	Nerve agent; air-delivered munitions	7,000
Kambarka, East Udmurtiia	Lewisite (L); bulk storage containers	6,000
Kizner, West Udmurtiia	Nerve agent; projectiles and rocket warheads	6,000
Gornyi, east of Saratov	Mustard (HD), Lewisite (L), and HDL mixture in bulk containers	1,160
Shchuche, east of Cheliabinsk	Nerve agent; projectiles and rocket warheads	5,440
Total		*40,100*

Sources: Aleksandr Piskunov, deputy chairman of the *Duma* defense committee (26 September interview with INTERFAX); cited by Doug Clarke, "Chemical Weapons Storage Sites," RFE/RL *Daily Report*, no. 185 (28 September 1994): 2. Brad Roberts, ed., *Ratifying the Chemical Weapons Convention* (Washington, D.C.: Center for Strategic and International Studies, 1994), 111, for map with locations and contents.

destruction plant that would take eight years or longer to become operational.[16] The United States has insisted that a detailed plan for exchanging specific data on stockpiles of chemical weapons be agreed upon before most of the assistance financing can be obligated.

There is good reason for such an approach, in view of the mid-1994 statement by chemical scientist Dr. Vil Mirzaianov, who had been imprisoned during the previous eighteen months. He announced the following over Ostankino TV: "In the 60 years that chemical weapons have been produced, according to the most modest estimates, over 600,000 tons of chemical agents [probably including the weight of weapons also] should have been manufactured. Yet for treaty and elimination purposes, only 40,000 tons were declared [by Russia]."[17] Lt. Gen. Anatolii D. Kuntsevich, immediate past chairman of the Committee for Treaty Problems Relating to Chemical and Biological Weapons, agreed on the same Moscow television program that the amount produced certainly exceeded 40,000 tons, although he challenged Mirzaianov's estimate as being exaggerated. By contrast, the United States has declared 31,000 agent tons of chemical weapons, and is already testing how to destroy them.[18]

Mirzaianov and another chemical scientist, Dr. Vladimir Uglev, provided corroboration that during the late 1980s a secret Soviet research program had produced a toxic agent five or six times more powerful than any other known poisonous substance. This project involved binary weapons for advanced warheads with two different chemicals which form a deadly poison gas when exploded together. Yet the Russian exchange of weapons-research data during early June 1994 did not mention this work. The U.S. government subsequently requested specific information about Russia's alleged binary weapons.[19] Moscow officially denied the existence of such weapons or any research program to develop them.

In the meantime, Russian officials stated in early 1994 that the January 1993 CW treaty would not be ratified until the $1 billion in foreign assistance promised for destruction of their chemical weapons stockpile had been received. There appears to be a strong movement against accepting such funds, although the condition mentioned could be eliminated by the State *Duma*, which had not commenced the treaty ratification process as of mid-1995.

However, a destruction site has been selected near the settlement of Gornyi, in the Krasnopartizanskii district of Saratov region. About 1,200 tons of toxic substances (mustard gas and lewisite) are stored here in drums and tanks. The process of destroying these poisons, as well as those at other sites, is scheduled to begin in 1997. Although construction should start on 1 September 1995 and funds reportedly have been earmarked for this work, no one had received any money as of mid-June.[20]

Biological and Toxin Weapons (BWC) Convention

Although a treaty on the above had been ratified by a sufficient number of governments to enter into force during 1975 and currently includes 130 states as parties, there appears to be evidence that some of the signatories have not abided by its provisions. The agreement prohibits development, production, and stockpiling of microbial or other biological agents or toxins (chemical substances produced by living organisms but not themselves living) as well as weapons, equipment, or means of delivery designed to use such agents or toxins for hostile purposes or in armed conflict.[21]

An epidemic of anthrax, the deadliest known naturally occurring pathogen, resulting from an explosion on 2 April 1979 at Military Compound No. 19 some thirty miles from Sverdlovsk, proved that the Soviets were testing vaccines on large animals.[22] Several hundred people were affected. Three years later, the United States formally accused the USSR of violating the BW convention. It was not until April 1992 that President Yeltsin issued a decree prohibiting research and development of bacteriological weapons. He also admitted that such experiments had been taking place clandestinely.[23]

Even after that presidential decree, a BW center reportedly existed on Vozrozhdeniie Island in the Aral Sea. It had been established forty years earlier as the secret city of Aral'sk-7 and focused on developing different strains of bubonic plague. Two epidemics broke out on the island during the late 1980s and early 1990s. The latter of these is reported to have killed approximately 434,000 animals. The entire human population was transferred to a military compound at Aral'sk-5 as a precautionary measure.[24] In other words, the Russian high command continued to violate the BW convention, Yeltsin's decree notwithstanding.

Although he assured Pres. George H. Bush in February 1992 that Russia's BW program had been closed down and repeated this to Pres. William J. Clinton in April 1993 at their meeting in Vancouver, Boris Yeltsin may have been misled by his own ministry of defense, although that cannot be confirmed. According to three recent Russian defectors, work not only continued but even expanded. Dr. Vladimir Pasechnik, director of two BW manufacturing plants and three research laboratories under the *Biopreparat* conglomerate, defected to Britain's MI-6 toward the end of 1989. Documents he gave to the British foreign intelligence service clearly proved awareness and support for such work by President Mikhail Gorbachëv. In June 1990, however, President Bush and Prime Minister Margaret Thatcher had met separately with Gorbachëv and specifically raised the BW question. Despite being shown copies of the above documentary evidence, Gorbachëv categorically denied any knowledge of such weapons.[25]

Six months later, the Soviets permitted Anglo-American visits to four of the six sites named by Pasechnik. At Obolensk, sixty miles south of Moscow where a new strain of the tularemia pathogen (super-plague) had been developed, the British found one BW testing chamber and a second area for trying out delivery systems. Another site had rows of fermenting units that could mass-produce BW agents in hundreds-of-kilogram batches. During September 1991, that is, one month after the abortive coup in Moscow, Prime Minister John Major confronted Gorbachëv in his office at the Kremlin with new evidence concerning the secret biological weapons program. The Russian leader still denied knowledge of anything concerning BW.

It was not until February 1992 that Yeltsin admitted to Bush at their meeting in Camp David that the program existed and promised that he would shut it down. The man put in charge of dismantling *Biopreparat* was Lt. Gen. Anatolii D. Kuntsevich, the same individual who had supervised the chemical warfare program. In mid-1992, the United States and Great Britain requested a list of all BW research production and storage sites as well as access to them. Although the Russians agreed to provide the foregoing, verification has been almost impossible to implement.[26] BW research, in any case, is easy enough to disguise.

In order to put more pressure on the Russians, the CIA announced in late 1993 that it had yet another defector from the *Biopreparat*. He apparently revealed how the Russian military had been able to keep this program operational. At each site visited by U.S. and British officials, elaborate deception arrangements were prepared to look as if agricultural research and manufacturing of vaccines were taking place. In actual fact, the secret work continued in parts of each site off-limits to the Anglo-American teams. A new clandestine facility was even under construction at Lakhta, near St. Petersburg, around the same time.[27]

It was not until 7 April 1994 that Yeltsin finally dismissed Lieutenant General Kuntsevich from chairmanship of the Presidential Committee on the CBW (Chemical and Biological Weapons) Convention for "numerous and rude violation of duties" as well as "a single gross violation of duties."

Two days before this event, a Russian expert who had inspected former BW sites in the United States and Britain told *Izvestiia* that those two countries, and not Russia, were ready to produce biological weapons.[28]

The deputy chief of radiation, chemical, and biological defense forces, Maj. Gen. Viktor Kholstov, claimed in an interview over Moscow Radio that all biological (weapons) installations were being inspected on a trilateral basis by Russia, the United States, and Britain. However, the October 1993 statement on confidence-building measures, although it did provide for mutual inspections, had failed to establish an agreed framework and assessment criteria. Before visits can take place at Russian military installations, General Kholstov revealed that a new document must specify exactly which sites would be subject to inspection, principles and assessment criteria, as well as the expected interpretation of inspection results. No visits to Russian installations will be permitted until such a document has been signed.[29]

In conclusion, Col. Gen. Stanislav V. Petrov, who commands the CB Troops, was quoted by Moscow Radio as stating that "storage of certain kinds of chemical poison built in the 1950s needed overhaul." He also admitted that the government had allocated only one-fourth of the funds needed to destroy such weapons during 1994 and that financing for 1995 would cover only half of the needs. And yet, the U.S. Defense Intelligence Agency's director testified before a Senate Committee on 10 January 1995 that "they [the Russians] have *active* biological and chemical warfare programs."[30]

The ABM and START Agreements

On 26 May 1972, the United States and Russia signed a treaty on limitation of antiballistic missile systems, followed two years later by a protocol. The original treaty permitted each country to maintain such defensive systems in two areas that were 1,300 kilometers apart (which would prevent nationwide protection) and 100 interceptor missiles as well as 100 launchers at each site. Development, testing, and deployment at sea, air, and space-based ABM defenses were prohibited. The 3 July 1974 protocol limited each side to one defensive site only.[31] Russia chose to protect Moscow, the United States its missile fields.

Even though the above treaties represent an anachronism, now that the Cold War is supposedly over, Presidents Clinton and Yeltsin reaffirmed both agreements at their summit meeting in May 1995. They issued a joint statement that has the effect of placing restraints on the U.S.

Theater Missile Defense (TMD) systems and allowing Russia a clear advantage in both numbers and geographic limitations. The ostensible reason for such disparity is explained by the alleged absence of a TMD threat to the United States, whereas the opposite supposedly applies to Russia.

This summit also eliminated cooperation on a global protective system which had been accepted by Yeltsin in January 1992. The relationship has been changed to joint work on TMD defense only. It probably will mean "transfer of extremely sensitive [U.S.] technical information, software and hardware that could lead to its irreparable compromise."[32] The above-mentioned constraints will prevent deployment of missile defenses on AEGIS cruisers as a first step toward effective global protection for the United States.

In the meanwhile, Russia is continuing to build a more effective ABM system of its own. The A-35 antiballistic missile defense system around Moscow will be superseded by the second-generation A-135 already before the end of 1995. "According to [Russian] specialists, it represents the most modern *strategic* ABM system, ensuring interception (both 'close' and 'from a distance') of enemy warheads and their destruction by means of nuclear explosions in the atmosphere."[33]

Russia's strategic missile forces are also being modernized. They reportedly include 1,603 carriers (ICBMs, SLBMs, and long-range bombers) for a total of 7,000 weapons allocated among four armies. A military railroad system moves the mobile missiles, which are concealed within what look like refrigerator cars, traveling at 80 kilometers per hour. Although the silo-based and mobile ICBMs are no longer aimed at the United States, "the necessary target coordinates can be tapped into a computer within a very short period of time."[34]

The *Topol* (poplar tree) represents a modification of the earlier mobile SS-25 "Sickle." Since the latter must be phased out and replaced with a silo-based ICBM under the START-II treaty, deployment of the new weapon should take place between 1996 and 2005. The new *Topol* M has a service-life of fifteen years compared to ten for its predecessor. "M" is larger in diameter, launch-weight, and throw-weight. The circular error probable (CEP) has been brought down to 350 from 650 meters.[35]

The State *Duma* has taken up ratification of the START-II treaty. Defense committee deputy chairman Aleksandr A. Piskunov stated that parliament will support the new agreement only if the United States offers "unconditional" compliance with the 1972 ABM treaty. The upper chamber or Federation Council opposes START-II, reportedly because it does not provide "equal military security" for the United States and Russia.[36] According to the constitution, treaties must be ratified by both houses of parliament.

How all of this fits into a national security concept will be discussed in the next chapter.

Notes

1. Richard F. Staar, "The MBFR Process and Its Prospects," in R. F. Staar, ed., *Arms Control: Myth versus Reality* (Stanford, Calif.: Hoover Institution Press, 1988), 47–58 (paperback ed.). This source covers the first ten years of conventional arms reduction talks.

2. U.S. Arms Control and Disarmament Agency (hereafter ACDA), "Treaty on Conventional Armed Forces in Europe: Chronology," *Fact Sheet* (Washington, D.C., 1 July 1991), 6, lists events until signing of the CFE treaty.

3. ACDA, *Treaty on Conventional Armed Forces in Europe* (Washington, D.C.: U.S. Information Agency, November 1990), pp. 110.

4. Lt. Gen. Vladimir M. Zhurbenko, first deputy chief of the General Staff, "Dogovor ob OBSE: god spustia," *Krasnaia zvezda,* 16 November 1993, 2.

5. ACDA, "Treaty on Conventional Armed Forces in Europe: Chronology," 6, italics added. See also P. Terrence Hopmann, "From MBFR to CFE," in Richard D. Burns, editor-in-chief, *Encyclopedia of Arms Control and Disarmament,* 3 vols. (New York: Scribner's, 1993), 2:967–98.

6. Iurii Kovalenko, "NATO interesuetsia 'ischeznoveniem'…," *Izvestiia,* 19 November 1993, 1.

7. Aleksandr Chërtkov, "Rossii ne khvataet tankov…," *Izvestiia,* 29 October 1993, 3.

8. Col. Gen. Mikhail P. Kolesnikov, "Problema flangov i budushchee dogovora…," *Krasnaia zvezda,* 19 April 1994, 3.

9. ACDA, *Treaty on Conventional Armed Forces in Europe,* Article 5, pp. 9–10.

10. Zhurbenko, "Dogovor ob OBSE." Kvashnin quote is from former CFE chief negotiator and later CIA director R. James Woolsey, "Say Nyet to Russian Treaty Breaking," *Wall Street Journal,* 8 May 1995, A-14.

11. John Ellis van Courtland Moon, "Chemical Weapons and Deterrence: The World War II Experience," *International Security* 8, no. 4 (Spring 1984): 3–35. U.S. General Accounting Office (hereafter GAO), *Status of U.S.–Russian Agreements and the Chemical Weapons Convention* (Washington, D.C.: GPO, 15 March 1994), GAO/NSIAD-94-136, 2, for a list of countries with CW arsenals.

12. ACDA, *Agreement between the United States of America and the Union of Soviet Socialist Republics on Destruction and Non-Production of Chemical Weapons* (Washington, D.C.: ACDA, 1 June 1990), 8.

13. ACDA, *Convention on the Prohibition of the Development, Production, Stockpiling, and Use of Chemical Weapons and Their Destruction* (Washington, D.C.: ACDA, October 1993), 187 pp.

14. *Status of U.S.–Russian Agreements,* 11; Valentin Volkov, "Konventsiia po

khimoruzhiiu poka ne ratifitsirovana," *Krasnaia zvezda,* 14 January 1995, 2; *Chemical Weapons Convention Bulletin,* no. 28 (June 1995): 3.

15. Viktor Litovkin, "Rossii ne khvataet deneg...," *Izvestiia,* 27 September 1994, 5; Iurii Golotiuk, "Rossiia pristupaet k unichtozheniiu boevykh OV," *Segodnia,* 28 March 1995, 3.

16. See, however, Dmitrii Gusev, "Khimicheskoe oruzhie unichtozhaetsia po planu," *Krasnaia zvezda,* 19 July 1994, 2, who erroneously claimed that the destruction process had commenced. President Yeltsin signed a decree on 25 March 1995 to begin destroying chemical weapons as soon as possible.

17. "Shikany Knot," Moscow Ostankino Television (2 July 1994), translated in FBIS-SOV-94-129 (6 July 1994), 28. Sergei Kudriashov, "Sklad kozhno-naryvnogo deistviia," *Izvestiia,* 1 July 1994, 4, discusses the 6,400 tons of old chemical weapons stored in four different areas of Russia since World War II.

18. GAO, *Chemical Weapons Disposal* (Washington, D.C.: GPO, December 1994), GAO/NSIAD-95-55, Appendix IV, p. 24.

19. Michael R. Gordon, "Russia Hides Effort to Develop Deadly Poison Gas, U.S. Says," *New York Times,* 23 June 1994, A-3.

20. *Status of U.S.–Russian Agreements,* 22. See also Brad Roberts, *Ratifying the Chemical Weapons Convention* (Washington, D.C.: Center for Strategic and International Studies, 1994), 116–26, on verifying the chemical weapons convention. See Lev Fëdorov, "Khimicheskoe razoruzhenie...," *Segodnia,* 30 March 1995, 9, for the statement that the USSR had produced 120,000 tons more than the 40,000 admitted today and that these other chemical weapons have been "lost" somewhere. Igor' Deriugin, "Vesti" newscast, Moscow TV Network, 16 June 1995, in FBIS-SOV-95-117 (19 June 1995), 27–28.

21. "Convention on...Bacteriological (Biological) and Toxin Weapons and on Their Destruction," in ACDA, *Arms Control and Disarmament Agreements: Texts and Histories of the Negotiations* (Washington, D.C.: ACDA, 1990), 133–37. See also Charles C. Flowerree, "Chemical and Biological Weapons and Arms Control," in Burns, *Encyclopedia of Arms Control and Disarmament,* 999–1019.

22. Aleksandr Pashkov, "Voennye otritsaiut svoiu prichastnost' k zagadochnoi bolezni," *Izvestiia,* 17 April 1992, 7. See also Matthew Meselson et al., "The Sverdlovsk Anthrax Outbreak of 1979," *Science* 266 (18 November 1994): 1202–8, for a similar conclusion based on an American investigation.

23. Viktor Litovkin, "El'tsin zapretil raboty po bakteriologicheskomu oruzhiiu. Eto znachit: oni velis', a nas obmanyvali," *Izvestiia,* 25 April 1992, 1.

24. Sergei Kozlov, "Uchënye pokinuli sekretnuiu laboratoriiu," *Nezavisimaia gazeta,* 23 June 1992, 6.

25. James Adams, "The Untold Story of Russia's Secret Biological Weapons," *Sunday Times* (London), 27 March 1994, sec. 4, p. 1. Two other Russian BW scientists subsequently defected to the United States with corroborating evidence.

26. Ibid., 2. See also Edward J. Lacey, "Tackling the Biological Weapons Threat," *Washington Quarterly* 17, no. 4 (Autumn 1994): 53–64.

27. James Adams, *The New Spies: Exploring the Frontiers of Espionage* (London:

Hutchinson, 1994), 270–83. On compliance problems, see also Brad Roberts, ed., *Biological Weapons: Weapons of the Future?* (Washington, D.C.: Center for Strategic and International Studies, 1994), 78–81.

28. Nikolai Burbyga, "Ne my, a SShA i Velikobritaniia gotovy k proizvodstvu biologicheskogo oruzhiia," *Izvestiia,* 5 April 1994, 2.

29. Interview by Anatolii Iurkin over Moscow Radio, ITAR-TASS, 14 June 1995, in FBIS-SOV-95-115 (15 June 1995), 6–7.

30. Moscow Radio, INTERFAX, 24 January 1995, in FBIS-SOV-95-017 (26 January 1995), 37. Lt. Gen. James R. Klapper Jr., "The Worldwide Threat to the United States and Its Interests Abroad," *Statement for the Senate Committee on Intelligence* (Washington, D.C., 10 January 1995), 10; emphasis added.

31. The texts of these documents appear in ACDA, *Arms Control and Disarmament Agreements,* 155–66, 181–83.

32. Frank J. Gaffney Jr., "The Clinton Missile Gaffe," *Wall Street Journal,* 19 May 1995, A-10.

33. Fëdor Emechenko, "Naletai, pokupai," *Trud,* 18 April 1995, 2.

34. R. Babaian, "Report on Strategic Missile Troops," Moscow TV Network, 16 April 1995, in JPRS-UMA-95-020 (20 May 1995), 17–18.

35. Stephen J. Zaloga, "The Topol (SS-25)," *Jane's Intelligence Review* 7, no. 5 (May 1995): 195–200.

36. OMRI *Daily Digest,* no. 138 (18 July 1995), pt. 2, p. 3, citing the *Washington Post.*

Myth No. 9
A National Security Concept Exists

There is a need to draw up a national security program.
Evgenii M. Primakov (20 April 1995)

A recent study, published in Moscow, claims that great power status is a natural right due Russia, because of its economic potential as well as achievements in science, culture, and military power. National security centers on guaranteeing stability throughout Eurasia, without which the country would be adversely affected. For this reason, any attempt by a single power or coalition to dominate Eurasia will be considered a serious threat. The same considerations apply to all states bordering on Russia, since the military factor still dominates international power relations.[1]

Although no serious external military threat is perceived at this time, the authors cited above suggest establishment of closer relations with Germany and a new policy vis-à-vis East Asia. In the latter case, China and Russia should maintain a coordinated policy in support of the changes that resulted from World War II throughout the Far East.

More recently, the above-cited Foreign Intelligence Service director enumerated three specific threats to national security:[2]

- the desire of certain forces to deprive Russia of great-power status
- the aggravation of regional conflicts and
- attempts by a number of states to acquire weapons of mass destruction.

North Atlantic Treaty Organization

Even prior to the demise of the Warsaw Treaty Organization, Russian civilian strategists had been discussing the need for a new security system in Europe, under UN auspices. Article 53 of that organization's charter envisages regional agreements that would allow coercive action under UN Security Council leadership.

One such regional arrangement has existed since 1 August 1975, when the "Final Act" was signed by heads of state from thirty-five initial members who met at Helsinki. Known as the Organization for Security and Cooperation in Europe (OSCE) since January 1995, it now encompasses West and East European countries, Canada and the United States in North America, as well as all former Soviet republics, including those of Central Asia, for a total of fifty-three members.

The director for all-European cooperation in the foreign affairs ministry has suggested that Russia should play an exceptional role in OSCE, due to its geopolitical location as a Eurasian power and link between security systems from "Vancouver to Vancouver," in effect creating a "space for stability, security and cooperation."[3] Justification for the above would appear to be the perception that NATO is attempting to expand eastward, which forces Russia to rethink its own security concepts.

Moscow's objective appears to be subordination of NATO to what was then the CSCE, which would become *the* political and military structure for the European continent, according to Russia's foreign minister. CSCE would also have under its domain the Commonwealth of Independent States (SNG).[4] SNG, thus, is equated with NATO, even though there is little to compare between these two regional alliance systems. Russia sent a formal letter to the then CSCE chairman on 30 June 1994 proposing the above arrangement, which was placed on the agenda for the 5–6 December 1994 summit meeting in Budapest.

As part of Moscow's proposal, the expanded fifty-three-member CSCE would become more effective after introduction of an executive committee and a standing body of permanent as well as rotating members, with Russia one of the former. Most of the SNG states reportedly had lined up in support of the Russian initiative, although not all endorsed the formal letter.[5]

In the meanwhile, members of the North Atlantic Cooperation Council—the military framework that engages sixteen NATO states, fifteen former Soviet republics, and seven former members of the Warsaw Treaty Organization in East-Central Europe—were invited to join the U.S.-inspired "Partnership for Peace" (PfP) program on 11 January 1994. It envisaged the following objectives:[6]

- Facilitation of transparency in national defense planning and budgeting
- Ensuring democratic control over defense processes

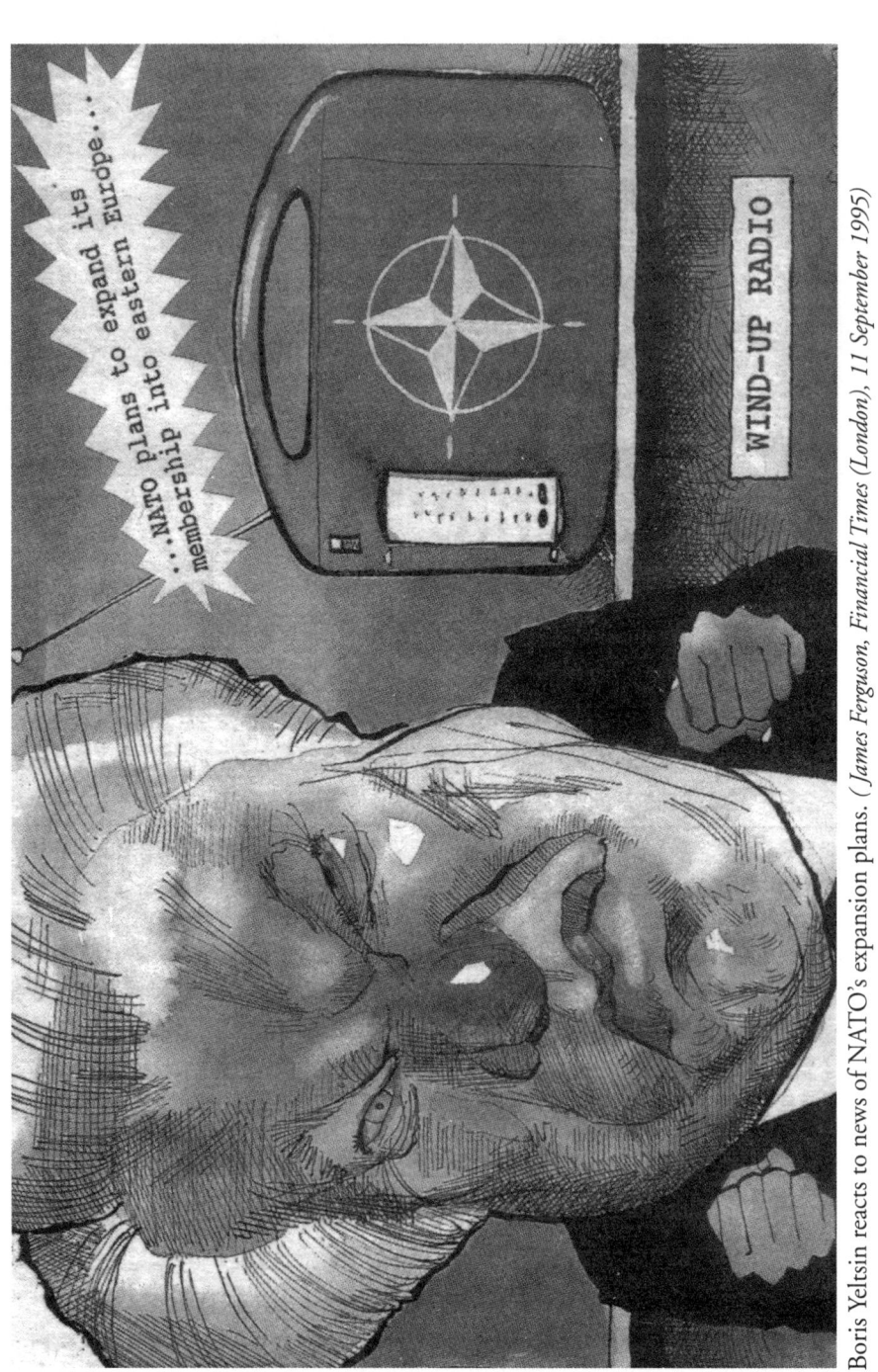

Boris Yeltsin reacts to news of NATO's expansion plans. (*James Ferguson, Financial Times (London), 11 September 1995*)

- Maintenance of capability and readiness to contribute, subject to constitutional considerations, to operations under authority of the United Nations and/or responsibility of the CSCE
- Development of cooperative military relations with NATO, for the purpose of joint planning, training, and exercises in order to strengthen the ability to undertake missions in the fields of peace-keeping, search and rescue, humanitarian operations, and others
- Development, over the longer term, of forces that would be better able to operate with those of North Atlantic alliance members.

This last objective will take considerable time and funding because of differences in military equipment (NATO versus the former Warsaw Pact), standard operating procedures, languages, and training.

Moscow's response to this Partnership for Peace invitation came from Pres. Boris Yeltsin, who demanded a special agreement with NATO which would recognize the "appropriate place of and role played by Russia in the world as well as in European affairs, its military power, and nuclear status of our country."[7] This announcement was followed six weeks later with a visit to Brussels by Defense Minister Pavel Grachëv who assured his audience that Russia would indeed join the PfP.

However, the next day this leading military commander proposed the following:

1. Creation of a Eurasian security system, at the political top of which would be the CSCE and not NATO;
2. Transformation of the North Atlantic Cooperation Council into the military arm of the new system; and
3. Establishment of an effective mechanism for consultation between Russia and NATO on European and world security issues which could function in an emergency and on a regular basis.

General Grachëv reportedly also had brought with him eight pages of "parameters" that appeared to represent preconditions for Russia's membership in PfP.[8]

Finally on 22 June 1994, almost five months after many other governments had done so, Russia signed the framework document as the twenty-first member state to join the PfP program. No preconditions apparently were granted by NATO. Moscow may have thought that PfP could serve as a useful vehicle to block East-Central European countries from becoming NATO members. The U.S. intention apparently was to buy time and postpone such membership into the indefinite future.

However, on 1 December 1994, Foreign Minister Kozyrev announced to his counterparts at a NATO meeting in Brussels that Russia would defer its participation in PfP because conditions for new members in NATO's enlargement had been announced that same day.[9]

Even before this event, joint NATO-Russian naval maneuvers code-named POMOR-94 took place during the latter part of March off the northern coast of Norway in the Barents Sea. Helicopters from Germany, Great Britain, the Netherlands, and the United States took part. Four months later, BREEZE-94 naval exercises were conducted on the Black Sea, with warships from the United States, Turkey, Greece, Ukraine, Romania, Bulgaria, and Russia. Also during July a five-day NATO exercise, BALTOPS-94, took place in the Baltic Sea with participation of a Russian destroyer.

Russian-American Maneuvers

In July 1988, the United States and the then–Soviet Union instructed their representatives to discuss an expanded exchange of data, military doctrine concepts, and other hitherto-restricted subject matter. The joint military working group also established a program of contacts among individual officers and reciprocal visits by warships.

Between 1991 and 1993, approximately ninety meetings took place: at U.S. Joint Chiefs of Staff and Russia's General Staff levels, in the form

Sovremennyi-class guided-missile destroyer under way in the Mediterranean. *(U.S. Naval Institute photo collection)*

of educational exchanges, and during military exercises. However, in calendar year 1994, the number of contacts dropped to twenty-six.[10] One reason involved the cost in dollars to the ministry of defense at Moscow; another could have been unwillingness by the high command to expose the Russian army's low state of readiness. Certainly, the 1994–95 war in Chechnya revealed the latter.

U.S. Defense Secretary William J. Perry's "talking points" when he visited Moscow in mid-March 1994 probably included the holding of war games on land with participants from both countries.[11] As a matter of record, more than fifty bilateral programs were envisaged by the Pentagon during 1994, including exchanges of senior officers and experts, joint military maneuvers, and other events. The Russians agreed only to about half of this number, not because they objected to participation as such but rather due to the possible embarrassment mentioned above.

One week after Dr. Perry's trip to Moscow, ARCTIC-94 took place in Alaska during 20–26 March, with Canadian, Russian, and American participation. These were search-and-rescue exercises, with only fifty-five men from each country.[12] One year earlier, U.S. Air Force and National Guard aircraft had flown from Alaska to Tiksi for a two-day search-and-rescue operation involving the crew of a downed plane simulation some 370 kilometers north of the Siberian base. Four helicopters flew to the mock crash site. Crew members landed by parachute and prepared the "victims" for evacuation.[13]

A much larger exercise, based on an agreement signed at the Pentagon on 8 September 1993 by Minister of Defense Grachëv, involved bilateral peacekeeping maneuvers to be held with units from the 3rd U.S. Army (Mechanized) Infantry Division based at Würzburg, Germany, and the 27th (Guards) Motorized Rifle Division stationed at Totskoe, Orenburg province, in the Volga Military District. Nobody apparently had informed the Germans that these war games were scheduled to be held at a NATO training base in Hohenfils. Reportedly, Bonn protested strongly and a decision was made to move the exercises elsewhere.[14]

Early the following year, it was announced that the training area at Totskoe would host the peacekeeping maneuvers. Americans would deliver by air about seventy wheeled vehicles, ammunition, and food; Russians would provide engineer support, fuel, some food, and bedding. Protests did not begin until the communist daily newspaper printed articles giving the false impression that the entire 3rd U.S. Army with 18,000 men and all of its equipment would be arriving.[15]

President Yeltsin ordered his ministry of defense on 26 April 1994 to reconsider holding the maneuvers. At the end of May, the last alternative was to move the war games to the United States. Subsequently, about 250 U.S. marines and 180 Russian naval infantrymen did conduct a training exercise between 18 and 23 June for rescue and humanitarian missions near Vladivostok,[16] which had been planned without any connection to the other ones in the Volga Military District.

After a delegation from the Russian parliament visited the Totskoe testing range during mid-July, these legislators seemed convinced that a few hundred Americans minus any heavy equipment and armed only with automatic handguns would not do any damage to the environment. The war games were to be conducted as an "ordinary planning exercise that would be carried out to a major extent on maps" and were rescheduled for 8–16 September 1994.[17] They did take place, despite a xenophobia that loathed the specter of an American flag anywhere in Russia's heartland.

Code-named PEACE MAKER-94 (*Mirotvorets-94*), this command post exercise was criticized for including Ranger "intelligence units" that allegedly comprised one-third of the 250 Americans who participated in the maneuvers. The source for such disinformation supposedly came from Russian military intelligence (GRU). If so, this attempt at sabotage failed. The principal newspaper in Moscow provided objective coverage and did not mention these false accusations. The next joint exercise in the United States has been scheduled for late in 1996, with the United States paying for transportation from and back to Alaska as well as all Russian expenses during the maneuvers.[18]

CSCE and UN Endorsements

Russia may have considered joining the Partnership for Peace in order also to receive that organization's approval of its own peacemaking involvement throughout the "near abroad," even though this was never NATO's intention. The other two instruments capable of such endorsement were the Conference on Security and Cooperation in Europe and the United Nations. A comprehensive program to make the CSCE more effective emerged from the Russian ministry of foreign affairs in Moscow during mid-1994.

This proposal recommended transforming the CSCE into a truly international organization. That would mean adopting a charter and a decisionmaking procedure. CSCE would then play a central coordinating role for the "Commonwealth of Independent States, the North Atlantic Cooperation Council, the European Union, the Council of Europe, NATO, and the Western European Union," according to Iurii V. Ushakov, director of the all-European cooperation department in the foreign ministry of Russia.[19]

According to this same official, Moscow believes that CSCE should focus on "protecting human rights from ethnic and religious intolerance and any manifestation of aggressive nationalism." Ushakov proposed formation of an executive committee, with ten to twelve permanent and rotating members. He stated that President Yeltsin had approved such a program, which was transmitted to all other member governments in the Commonwealth of Independent States for their signature as cosponsors.

Ten days later, Russia's chief delegate to the Vienna arms-control talks, Vladimir V. Shustov, stated that a recent letter from Foreign Minister Andrei Kozyrev to the fifty-three CSCE member governments had been "misunderstood."[20] Russia only wanted CSCE to become "the leading partner of the U.N. in settling conflicts in the region," and it should be given "overriding responsibility for maintenance of peace and strengthening democracy and stability in the Euro-Atlantic area."

In the former Soviet republics, the CSCE had been requested by Moldova (not Russia) to monitor a ceasefire with the Trans-Dniester forces. The Joint Russian-Moldovan-Dniesterian Control Commission allowed a CSCE representative to observe the peacemaking operation only two years after it had commenced.[21] Such inspection had been blocked previously by the Russians and Dniesterians. Moldova also has requested that the United Nations play a role in resolving this dispute.

Although both CSCE and the United Nations have special envoys stationed in this region, Russia's request that the SNG peacemaking force in Tajikistan be endorsed has not been approved. One obvious reason for the absence of such a mandate is that the Russians have engaged in counterinsurgency operations against the opposition forces. Their 26,000 troops also patrol the border with Afghanistan, protect power plants as well as other important installations, and "periodically help the Tajik government enforce security in Dushanbe."[22] In practice, this means that the regime in Tajikistan probably would fall if Russian soldiers were withdrawn.

However, the UN Security Council unanimously endorsed the Russian peacemaking operation in Abkhazia, since it involved a request by both Georgian and Abkhazian authorities that Moscow send troops for this purpose. The resolution also increased the number of UN observers in the conflict zone.[23] No peacemakers from any other SNG states are in Abkhazia.

Finally, the CSCE/OSCE has been active in the six-year war between Azerbaijanis and Armenians over Nagorno-Karabakh. Its proposed 300-man peacekeeping force was rejected by the Azeris. This small group would have been entrusted with monitoring a ceasefire, observing respect for human rights, and providing humanitarian assistance. The United Nations has sent fact-finding missions to the area, whereas the SNG and Russia have not responded to requests for peacekeepers.[24]

It should also be mentioned that the Minsk Group, an eleven-member subunit of the CSCE, made a two-year effort to stop the Nagorno-Karabakh war. This initiative ceased when Moscow proposed an open-ended deployment of its forces, the costs for which would be shared equally by Armenia, Azerbaijan, and Nagorno-Karabakh. Only after Russian troops arrived could political negotiations to end the conflict begin. It has been suggested that Moscow's motive may have been to bring its own "peacemakers" into the region rather than to offer a realistic solution to the problem.[25]

The Russians appear unwilling to allow OSCE to enter Nagorno-Karabakh, because this would introduce different rules. First of all, OSCE-sponsored peacekeeping forces do not engage in military operations. Second, their activities must be based on strict impartiality. Finally, the OSCE requires the full prior consent of all parties to a conflict before becoming involved. This is not the case with the Russians, who wish to receive a UN or OSCE *imprimatur* and funding without any constraint on their peacemaking activities.

Although authoritative spokesmen such as Yeltsin, Grachëv, and Kozyrev have requested a UN mandate for SNG (i.e., Russian) armed forces to operate within the so-called near abroad and receive hard currency for expenses, the deputy chairman of the Federation Council (upper house of parliament) has strongly opposed the deployment of NATO troops as peacekeepers in former Yugoslavia. Valerian N. Viktorov stated that "NATO is not a peace-keeping organization. Its tasks and objectives are quite different. NATO should by no means get involved with this conflict." Otherwise, he said, "a serious war may result."[26]

At the 5–6 December 1994 meeting of the CSCE in Budapest, Russians blocked a proposed declaration condemning Serb forces for the fighting at Bihac. President Yeltsin charged NATO with attempting to split the continent and that accepting East-Central European countries as members would isolate Russia. President Clinton denied these charges and said that expansion of membership would promote international security. NATO was to announce its decisions in November or December 1995.[27]

Relations with the United States

The transition in status from enemy to friend was formally endorsed on 17 June 1992, although probably a premature move, when Presidents Bush and Yeltsin signed the Russo-American Partnership and Friendship Charter in Washington, D.C. Both parties affirmed their respect for the independence, sovereignty, and existing borders of all CSCE members. The document ends with the following sentence: "The Russian Federation and the United States of America intend to accelerate their joint work to transfer the defense sectors to civilian output production."[28]

Some eighteen months later, on 24 January 1994, the Agency for International Development's (AID) administrator testified before a subcommittee of the U.S. Senate Appropriations Committee that AID had shipped $1.5 billion worth of food and medicine to the Newly Independent States of the former Soviet Union. Furthermore, American technical advisors had assisted the privatization program in seventy-seven of Russia's eighty-nine administrative units. Other projects dealt with economic reform, energy, the environment, and health care.

A more comprehensive survey came from the U.S. Department of State at hearings before the Committee on Foreign Affairs, U.S. House of Representatives. Although only $704 million had been requested for the Newly Independent States of the former USSR during fiscal year 1994, an additional $1.8 billion in supplemental funding brought the total to about $2.5 billion. Two-thirds would be spent in Russia. Some of these funds were to pay for "increased assistance to provide housing for demobilized Russian officers being brought home from the Baltics and elsewhere."[29]

On its own, in late November 1993, Congress passed the Friendship Act, which removed earlier laws and regulations adopted to protect the United States from the "world-wide communist conspiracy." Henceforth, Russia would be allowed to import even some American military technology. Other trade restrictions also have been lifted. The objective of the Friendship Act is to support economic and democratic reform in Russia. During 1995, Moscow planned to purchase 400,000 tons of American grain with funds from the Food for Progress program passed by the U.S. Congress the preceding year.[30]

However, results from an All-Russian Center for Public Opinion poll concluded that only 4 percent of policymakers and experts in Moscow considered the United States their country's best friend, whereas 22 percent placed Germany in that category. Germany had pledged more than $9 billion in support of the Soviet troop withdrawal, which was completed on 31 August 1994, although investors from Bonn (with around 1,500 joint ventures) are only second after the United States.[31]

Apart from the foregoing, Russian negotiators attempted to obtain $13 billion in new credits from the International Monetary Fund or IMF (where the United States has considerable influence) and other Western sources. The IMF had already provided some $3 billion in special standby loans. This money restrained the Central Bank in Moscow from issuing billions of dollars worth of credits in rubles to failing industry between July and September 1994 which would have added to the budget deficit. That did not seem to affect negotiations during 1995 for another $6.8 billion from IMF (allocated), $2 billion each from the World Bank and Eurodollar loans, and $3 billion from other sources.[32]

Despite such largess, making Moscow the largest recipient of American aid after Israel and Egypt, Russia violated the Missile Technology Control Regime (MTCR) by selling Brazil critical information on how to build a rocket capable of delivering nuclear or chemical arms. A classified memorandum sent by the White House to the U.S. Congress reportedly waived sanctions, because both parties had promised to abide by the MTCR rules in the future. The end of that same month, Moscow announced that it would become cofounder of two international organizations: one on export controls and the other on nonproliferation of missile technology.[33]

The Far East

Japan remains reluctant to assist Russia with substantial financing until at least the southern Kuriles have been returned, as promised by Moscow in 1956, after a peace treaty is signed. All forty MiG-23s stationed on one of these (Iturup Island), together with their ground-support staff, were withdrawn in mid-1994, which did not represent a preliminary move toward a settlement. However, Japanese fishing boats reportedly violated Russian territorial waters in the Kuriles about 7,000 times and caught 12,000 tons of sea products during a one-year period.[34]

On the other hand, Foreign Minister Kozyrev visited Tokyo in early March 1995 and agreed to begin negotiations on where the Japanese would be permitted to fish around the Kurile Islands. More important was the presence of (former deputy defense minister) Boris V. Gromov in his new capacity as chief military advisor to the ministry of foreign affairs. He proposed exchanging observers at military exercises, reciprocal flights of air force planes, and visits by naval vessels. The Japanese refused to initial a memorandum of understanding, stressing that their National Defense Board never signs such documents.[35]

North Korea was an ally of the Soviet Union ever since its establishment as a puppet state at the end of World War II. The most recent Treaty of Friendship, Cooperation, and Mutual Assistance was signed in 1961 and has been automatically extended every five years thereafter. According to President Yeltsin, amendments made in 1990 no longer provide for automatic assistance to North Korea in case of war. He reportedly told the South Korean president that Russia will not renew the treaty when it comes up for extension on 10 September 1996. This probably means that Moscow will refrain from supporting the North in another war on the peninsula, although notice must be given one year before the treaty expires.[36]

South Korea has already invested $1.4 billion in Russia, which was discussed when Pres. Kim Yong-sam visited Moscow in early June 1994. A joint declaration outlined further areas of cooperation between the two countries. At the same time, both sides agreed to intensify international efforts to convince North Korea that it should comply with the Non-Proliferation Treaty to which it is a signatory. According to the nuclear power minister, Viktor N. Mikhailov, North Korea owes Russia about $5 million for development of its nuclear engineering projects. Moscow wants equal status in the international consortium to modernize Pyongyang's nuclear power system.[37]

Mongolia had been established in 1921 as the first Soviet satellite. Some 95 percent of Ulanbator's foreign trade is still controlled by the former metropole. Practically all energy imports as well as hardware and equipment come from Russia. A new treaty on friendship and cooperation, concluded in January 1993 at Moscow, provides for continuing export of meat, copper, and molybdenum concentrates from Mongolia.[38] All Russian forces were withdrawn from this country, although Moscow agreed two years later (1994) to train indigenous border troops.

China has a 4,300-kilometer-long frontier with Russia; negotiations to delimit it have been under way for several years and will continue until at least 1997. The Russian population of Khabarovsk, the Krasnoiarsk territory, and the Amur region has been declining. On the other hand, local police reports indicated the presence of nearly 370,000 Chinese, presumably registered. If so, there may be up to 2 million altogether, including illegal aliens in the Far East and Siberia.[39]

Russian border guards are also stationed in Kyrgyzstan and Tajikistan, which have frontiers with China. Kazakhstan is "cooperating" with Moscow in protecting its own border. An interview with Col. Gen. Andrei I. Nikolaev, commanding officer of the Federal Border Service, provided this information. He also revealed that three sectors of the Chinese frontier remain disputed. The border itself had been "very open" during all of 1992 and the first nine months of 1993. Nikolaev concluded that cooperation with China remains among Russia's strategic interests.[40]

Fifteen rounds of Sino-Russian talks (expanded to include Kazakhstan, Kyrgyzstan, and Tajikistan) had taken place through mid-May 1995. The objective is to reduce troops and armaments within a 100-kilometer zone on each side of the border. Chinese proposals for manpower ceilings had been unacceptable to the Russians who have a high concentration of their own armed forces in this region, according to Defense Minister Grachëv. He did say that China had agreed to support a collective security system in North Asia which hypothetically would include both countries as well as the United States, Japan, and North and South Korea. Grachëv's offer to co-police Asia reportedly was turned down by the Chinese. However, on 28 June 1995, seven agreements were signed in Moscow by the two prime ministers.[41]

Is There a National Security Concept?

In his annual message to the Federation Council (upper house of parliament) on 16 February 1995, President Yeltsin presented a *tour d'horizon* about domestic and foreign policies. He devoted only 5 percent, if that much, of his report to relations with countries outside the former Soviet Union.[42] The survey was striking for its superficiality and reminiscent of speeches by pre-1991 leaders of the USSR.

This becomes understandable when one recalls the statement by Foreign Minister Kozyrev during an interview the previous month. He stated the following: "There has been no reform in the ministry of foreign affairs.... If anybody considers that the former communist diplomats can become democrats within two or three years, he is a naive person."[43] Hence, one should not be surprised at the pedestrian and even dismissive style of that part of Yeltsin's speech, apparently written by *apparatchiki* (former communist bureaucrats) in the current foreign ministry.

Since an official national security concept has not been released by the government in Moscow, and indeed there is none, it becomes necessary to fall back on a study prepared by experts at the Russian-American University (RAU) in Moscow. Of particular relevance to national security are the short-, medium-, and long-term national interests discussed in this analysis.

Short-term interests over the next two to four years (1996–2000) will center on the following:

The termination of interethnic conflicts along Russia's border in the Caucasus

An agreement on a common economic space and a border regime among SNG member states

An accord with the same governments on defense against nuclear attack and strengthening of the nonproliferation treaty (NPT).

The first of these interests is the most urgent, and the authors admit that it will be impossible to secure borders between SNG countries without the use of armed forces. Furthermore, "it is unfair for Russia alone to bear the responsibility and costs."[44]

American and Ukrainian defense officials, including U.S. Defense Secretary William J. Perry, discuss the removal of nuclear warheads from ICBMs at an empty missile silo in Ukraine. *(U.S. Naval Institute photo collection)*

Medium-term interests, five through ten years ahead (2000–2005), will involve stabilization and normalization of relations with

- SNG member states, especially regarding mutual security
- NATO countries in the defense area
- Japan vis-à-vis the southern Kurile Islands
- The People's Republic of China regarding an accord on absence of respective territorial claims
- The Afghanistan-Pakistan-Iran triangle on recognition of borders as inviolable and cooperation also in defense, without affecting Russia's close ties to India
- States emerging in place of the former Yugoslav federation.

Conflicts within and between SNG countries, including armed ones, will require special attention. An effective system for collective defense must become a reality in pursuance of these objectives.[45]

Long-term interests, ten to twenty years ahead (2005–2025), call for

- Maintenance of stability throughout the world
- Elimination of conflict near Russian borders
- Normal relations with all states, especially European and Asian ones, developing into partnerships
- Strengthening UN, OSCE, and other "peacemaking" efforts to prevent armed conflict
- Deepening the process of disarmament, so Russian armed forces can be reduced to a necessary minimum
- Reestablishment of Russia's international prestige and recognition by the world of its status as a great power.

The probability of local wars for religious or nationalistic reasons can not be excluded along the southwestern and southern borders of the former Soviet Union. That is why Russia will support the political aspects of "peacemaking" by the United Nations and the OSCE in other parts of the world. This same pattern of rapidly eliminating the sources of potential conflict through negotiation should be followed.

External Threats to Stability

The RAU study excludes any possibility, for the time being, of an attack from the West.[46] It does not rule out a spillover effect of the armed conflict from Yugoslavia into neighboring countries. That protracted war has a religious dimension involving Islamic (Bosnia), Roman Catholic

(Croatia), and Eastern Orthodox (Serbia) believers. Similar divisions exist in other states, like the Federation of Russia, where a civil war along related lines is potentially replicable.

Other countries in East-Central Europe are vulnerable to the outbreak of conflict because of large ethnic minorities. The idea of *terra irredenta* is implicit in the "Greater Romania" movement, which would incorporate Moldova (its former province of Bessarabia) and the Dniester region (now protected by Russia's limited army contingent). Such attempts might trigger claims against Romania by Bulgaria (Dobrudja), Hungary (Transylvania), and even Russia (Trans-Dniester Republic).

The most dangerous potential military threat is centered on the Caucasus and Central Asia. This "threat from the South" (*ugroza s iuga*) would be sponsored by Iran and Pakistan (possibly also by Turkey), in order to establish a bloc of countries that would include Azerbaijan, Turkmenistan, Uzbekistan, and Tajikistan. This so-called Islamic fundamentalism may also spread to Kyrgyzstan and Kazakhstan.

In the Middle East, normalized relations with Israel have resulted in "sustenance" for that country because of Jewish emigration from Russia. This has caused increasing anti-Russian feelings among the Arab countries. Alienation from Libya and Iraq is due to Moscow's support for the UN embargo against these countries. Once these restrictions have been lifted, Russia will reestablish trade in weapons.

Finally, the contributors to the RAU study contend that it would be a mistake to dismiss the possibility of military pressure from the southeast, that is, from China. Factors other than the demographic one, not specified, would come into play.

The future role of Russia's military is summarized as follows: "At present we can not rely on the armed forces alone," because they are "not adequately capable of meeting the changed spectrum of threats to our national security."[47] It is proposed that a system of collective responsibility be established by the SNG member states to maintain peace, eliminate sources of conflict, and resolve armed confrontation throughout the region.

The RAU study also proposes establishment of a Regional Security Council for conflicts occurring *within the zone of Russian interests* (emphasis added). This demarcation is supposedly accepted by belligerent parties when they appeal to Russia for mediation. Therefore, it is imperative that the United Nations provide Moscow's "peacemaking" forces with a mandate to function under UN auspices, with "blue helmet" status.

According to the chairman of the Science Council (see Chart 2.3), work on a national security concept by an interdepartmental group has made some progress. It will apply to the next five to ten years, on the basis of which annual national security strategy documents should be adopted by parliament. The overall concept will consist of three sections.[48]

Russia in the Modern World:
    external and domestic aspects;
    claim to world power status based on location, natural resources, economic and military potential;
    negative trends include sociopolitical aspects, demographic stratification, production decline, crime

Russia's National Interests
    at home: require political stability
    at subregional level: strengthen ties with former USSR republics
    at regional level: ensure Russian national interests within countries bordering on SNG
    at global level: prevention of major conflicts and wars

Ensuring Russia's National Security
    foreign threats include actions that
        undermine state sovereignty
        weaken ties with former Soviet republics
        violate rights and freedoms of Russian-speaking people (*sic*) in other states
    domestic threats center on
        development of local separatism
        nonobservance of laws and growth of crime
        decline in standard of living
        sharp reduction of scientific, technical, and cultural potential

The foregoing represents merely an outline for a draft national security concept that will be revised and expanded by the interdepartmental group. Apparently, there is no timetable for completion of this work.

Finally, in an address to graduates of military academies held at the Kremlin, President Yeltsin listed the following national security tasks that have the highest priority:[49]

1. Final restoration of a constitutional order in Chechnya.
2. Completion of a collective security system throughout the SNG.
3. Establishment of an all-European security system.
4. Russia's foreign policy mandates creation of an Asian Pacific security system.

The next chapter will conclude this book with three possible scenarios, each of which would impact differently on future developments.

Notes

1. Aleksei I. Podberëzkin, ed., *Natsional'naia bezopasnost' Rossii v 1994 godu* (Moscow: "Obozrevatel'," 1993), 112–13; excerpts translated in FBIS-SOV-94-038-S (25 February 1994), 56 pp.

2. Eduard Ryzhkin, "Evgenii Primakov ukazal na tri istochnika…," *Segodnia*, 21 April 1995, 3.

3. Iurii V. Ushakov, "Diplomatic Panorama," Moscow Radio, 27 March 1995, in FBIS-SOV-95-062 (31 March 1995), 8.

4. Andrei Kozyrev, "The Lagging Partnership," *Foreign Affairs* 73, no. 3 (May–June 1994): 65.

5. Victor-Yves Ghebali, "After the Budapest Conference," *NATO Review* 43, no. 2 (March 1995): 24–27.

6. "Partnership for Peace: Framework Document," *NATO Review* 42, no. 1 (February 1994): 29–30.

7. INTERFAX, "Boris El'tsin—za spetsial'noe soglashenie s NATO," *Izvestiia*, 7 April 1994, 1. See also Mark Galeotti, "Decline and Fall—Can Russia Be a Partner?" *Jane's Intelligence Review* 6, no. 7 (July 1994): 290.

8. Bruce Clark, "Old Enemies Make Tricky Friends," *Financial Times* (London), 9 June 1994, 15.

9. The consequences of NATO expansion were intepreted as leading to a "new division in Europe" by Aleksandr Konovalov, "K novomu razdelu Evropy?" *Nezavisimaia gazeta*, 7 December 1994, 5. See also Vladimir Nadein, "Budushchee NATO reshaetsia v Moskve," *Izvestiia*, 14 February 1995, 3.

Russian generals believe that NATO would send five divisions to defend the Baltic States if they were attacked. Igor' Korotchenko, "Genshtab somnevaetsia," *Nezavisimaia gazeta*, 17 May 1995, 1.

10. Col. Jerry Morelock, U.S. Army, "Evolving U.S.-Russian Military-to-Military Contacts," *Seminar Report* (Alexandria, Va.: Center for Naval Analyses, June 1994).

11. Dorofeia Getmanenko, "Rossiia-SShA: voennoe sotrudnichestvo luchshe 'kholodnogo' mira," *Krasnaia zvezda*, 18 March 1994, 1.

12. See coverage by Col. Aleksandr Andriushkov, "Nad Aliaskoi…," *Krasnaia zvezda*, 25 March 1994, 1; and his "Arktika Sareks-94," in the same paper for 1 April 1994, 3.

13. Col. Aleksandr Andriushkov, "Tiksi-93; Vmeste vyzhit' legche," *Krasnaia zvezda*, 7 May 1993, 3.

14. Michael R. Gordon, "U.S.–Russia War Games Plan for Germany Halted by Bonn," *New York Times*, 5 November 1993, A-4.

15. Iurii Nikiforenko, "Iz arabskoi pustyni—v orenburgskie stepi," *Pravda*, 15 March 1994, 2. See also Ivan Bondarev, "A ne stoit li nashim generalam provesti ucheniia v shtate Aiova?" *Pravda*, 6 April 1994, 1.

16. Moscow Radio, 20 June 1994, in FBIS-SOV-94-119 (21 June 1994), 4.

17. Vladimir Ermolin, "Poligon, proveriaiushchii nas na zdravyi smysl," *Krasnaia zvezda,* 21 July 1994, 3; Pavel Anokhin, "Vzryvy strastei vokrug Totskogo poligona," *Rossiiskie vesti,* 22 July 1994, 1.

18. Mikhail Urusov, "U.S. Rangers under Cover of Peacekeepers," *Moscow News,* no. 37 (16–22 September 1994): 2; "Rossiiskaia i amerikanskaia armii uchatsia…" *Izvestiia,* 3 September 1994, 1–2. (The U.S. infantry battalion at Totskoe included only one S-2 [intelligence] captain which represents the regular complement.) See also "Grachëv on Funding for Joint U.S. Exercises," Moscow Radio, 4 July 1995, in FBIS-SOV-95-128 (5 July 1995), 3.

19. "Diplomatic Panorama," Moscow Radio, INTERFAX, 14 July 1994, in FBIS-SOV-94-136 (15 July 1994), 21–22.

20. Quoted by Stephen Foye, "Backtracking on Role of CSCE?" RFE/RL *Daily Report,* no. 139 (25 July 1994): 2.

21. Vladimir Socor, "CSCE Examines Russian Peacekeeping in Moldova," RFE/RL *Daily Report,* no. 140 (26 July 1994): 3.

22. U.S. Central Intelligence Agency, *Worldwide Peacekeeping Operations, 1995* (Washington, D.C.: Directorate of Intelligence, April 1995), EUR 94-10002.

23. Elizabeth Fuller, "UN Endorses Russian Peacekeeping Mission in Abkhazia," RFE/RL *Daily Report,* no. 138 (22 July 1994): 2.

24. U.S. Central Intelligence Agency, *Worldwide Peacekeeping Operations.*

25. Editorial, "Russian Interventions," *Wall Street Journal,* 10 August 1994, A-10.

26. Interviewed by Aleksandr Krylovich over Moscow Radio, ITAR-TASS, 29 July 1994, in FBIS-SOV-94-147 (1 August 1994), 8–9.

27. Elaine Sciolino, "Yeltsin Says NATO…," *New York Times,* 6 December 1994, A-10; Aleksei Pushkov, "Krizis 'otlozhen' do zimy," *Moskovskie novosti,* no. 38 (28 May–4 June 1995): 13.

28. Moscow Radio, ITAR-TASS, 17 June 1992, in FBIS-SOV-92-119 (18 June 1992), 18–22, at p. 22.

29. House of Representatives, Committee on Foreign Affairs, "U.S. Policy Toward the Newly Independent States," *Hearings* (Washington, D.C.: GPO, 1994), 9.

30. "The Laws Catch Up to the New Russia," *New York Times,* 29 November 1994, A-8. Moscow Radio, INTERFAX, 29 September 1994, in FBIS-SOV-94-190 (30 September 1994), 28, on grain purchases.

31. Alexei K. Pushkov, "Russia and America: The Honeymoon Is Over," *Moscow News,* no. 2 (13–19 January 1995): 2. See, however, Pëtr Emel'ianov, "Amerika Rossii podarila…," *Ekho planety,* no. 19 (April-May 1995): 5–8, for an optimistic assessment of U.S. assistance.

32. Steven Erlanger, "After Chechnya War…," *New York Times,* 27 January 1995, A-4.

33. R. Jeffrey Smith, "U.S. Waives Objection to Russian Missile Technology," *Washington Post,* 8 June 1995, 23, 27. See also "Diplomatic Panorama," Moscow Radio, 30 June 1995, in FBIS-SOV-95-127 (3 July 1995), 24–25; "Russia to Enter Post-COCOM Regime," *Arms Trade News* (July 1995), 1, 3.

34. "Russia Has Withdrawn All MiGs," *Aviation Week and Space Technology*

(2 August 1994): 17; Yelena Matveyeva, "Undeclared War in the Sea of Okhotsk," *Moscow News,* no. 44 (4–10 November 1994): 12.

35. "Gromov Tables Proposals," Moscow Radio, ITAR-TASS, 3 March 1995, in FBIS-SOV-95-044 (7 March 1995), 12–13.

36. Suzanne Crow, "Yeltsin on North Korea," RFE/RL *Daily Report,* no. 104 (3 June 1994): 1, quoting from a news conference held the previous day in Moscow. See also "On Selling Arms to North Korea," Moscow Radio, 27 June 1995, in FBIS-SOV-95-124 (28 June 1995), 11.

37. Moscow Radio, ITAR-TASS, 6 February 1995, in FBIS-SOV-95-025 (7 February 1995), 7.

38. Interview with President Punsalmaagiyn Ochirbat in *Komsomol'skaia pravda,* 3 December 1993, 7.

39. Vladimir N. Podoprigora, chairman of the Federation Council's international affairs committee, over Moscow Radio, INTERFAX, 6 May 1994, in FBIS-SOV-94-089 (9 May 1994), 17, for the 370,000 figure. See also PRC Foreign Minister Qian Qichen over Moscow Radio, ITAR-TASS, 4 September 1994, in FBIS-SOV-94-172 (6 September 1994), 21, for the two-million estimate.

40. Interview by Aleksandr Gol'ts, "Granitsa s Kitaem," *Krasnaia zvezda,* 17 November 1993, 3. See also Aleksei Voskresenskii, "Zona sotrudnichestva ili potentsial'nogo konflikta?" *Nezavisimaia gazeta,* 3 June 1994, 5, on the Sino-Russian border; Aleksandr Platkovskii, "Pogranichnyi spor mozhet vzorvat' otnosheniia s Kitaem," *Izvestiia,* 10 February 1995, 3.

41. Michael Mihalka and Doug Clarke, "Grachëv on . . . Collective Security," OMRI *Daily Digest,* no. 95 (17 May 1995): pt. 1, 3; Vadim Alekseev, "Diplomaticheskii voiazh generala," *Rossiiskaia gazeta,* 23 May 1995, 14, for Grachëv's offer; "Sovmestnoe Rossiisko-kitaiskoe kommunike," *Rossiiskaia gazeta,* 29 June 1995, 6.

42. Boris El'tsin, "Prioritety vneshnei politiki," *Rossiiskaia gazeta,* 17 February 1995, 5.

43. Quoted by Aleksandr Pumpianskii, "Rossiia i Zapad," *Novoe vremia,* no. 1 (January 1995): 22.

44. A. I. Podberëzkin, *Natsional'naia bezopasnost' Rossii v 1994 godu,* 116–17 of Russian version.

45. Ibid., 116.

46. Ibid., 115.

47. Ibid., 128.

48. Interview with Vladimir S. Piskunov in *Vooruzheniie, politika, konversiia,* no. 3 (6), (1994): 9–11; signed to the press on 24 January 1995.

49. Boris El'tsin, "Nam nuzhny kachestvenno novye armiia i flot," *Rossiiskaia gazeta,* 29 June 1995, 1.

===== *Myth No. 10* =====
The Future Is Ours, Comrades!

> We believe that the coming 21st century will be the century of Russia.
>
> *Natsional'naia doktrina Rossii*

A projection of future developments entitled "National Doctrine of Russia: Problems and Priorities" appeared recently in Moscow.[1] The fifty-three contributors, including two Russian generals, recommend that bilingualism and dual citizenship be introduced by all independent countries throughout the "near abroad" for their 25.3 million ethnic Russians. The coauthors believe the Kremlin should invoke economic sanctions against any former Soviet republic that refuses to implement such measures.

The heavy-handedness of this approach ignores one basic fact: the Commonwealth of Independent States (SNG) still remains more of a Russian ideal than a political or economic reality. If sanctions are applied by Moscow to enforce the above demands, it is doubtful they would encourage the recalcitrant republics willingly to accept Russian military domination in the name of collective security. Nor would it inspire confidence that Russia respects the sovereignty of individual SNG member states.

The same report warns that military manpower reductions in the United States and other NATO countries are more than being compensated for by introduction of the most advanced weapons systems. Upgrading of nuclear missiles (the third generation) and other means of mass destruction allegedly continues in the West. Such a loss of parity cannot help but cause anxiety within the Russian high command. The coauthors of this study recommend allocating a fixed percentage of the government's annual budget for military research on and development of futuristic weapons. Such funding would help to provide inducements for the best scientists to remain inside the country rather than emigrate.

Also echoing the country's military doctrine, the fifty-three-member study group believes that global war is not inevitable. Instead, "domestic instability, chaos, economic disintegration, and a loser mentality represent no less a threat to national security" than do external forces. The central problem facing Russia involves achievement of national unity and restoration of governmental authority. The final words of this report call for faith in the future, tremendous courage, and—most important—patient and selfless work as well as inspiration: *"We believe that the coming 21st century will be the century of Russia."*[2]

However, the path to a better future is not clear, and formidable obstacles must be surmounted along the way in order to achieve lasting stability.

Russia itself has been the hardest hit among all the constituent republics by collapse of the former USSR. "Authoritarian rule" is seen by many as the only means to solve the country's problems, according to recent public opinion polls. The political as well as economic situation is perceived to be unpromising, and public approval of Yeltsin's leadership had dropped to an all-time low at 6 percent during mid-1995. Among the threats to long-range stability is the trend toward breakup of the Russian Federation, as it now exists, including loss of regions that have relatively few ethnic minorities. Dangerous precedents have been established already within three of the constituent republics: Tatarstan does not recognize the Russian military draft and has asserted its right to wide-ranging autonomy; the large republic of Iakutiia-Sakha remits no taxes to Moscow; and the declaration of independence by small Chechnya in November 1991 remained a *fait accompli* for more than three years, until the sudden invasion by Russian troops.[3]

Fragmentation

Secessionist tendencies also can be observed in large economic regions inhabited mostly by Russians. Although they comprise some 83 percent of all federation peoples, Russians do not occupy even half of the land. The twenty-one ethnic republics with less than one-fifth of the total population hold more than half of the federation territory. (See Map 10.1.) Rich in natural resources, many of the ethnic republics actively seek independence

188　MYTH NO. 10

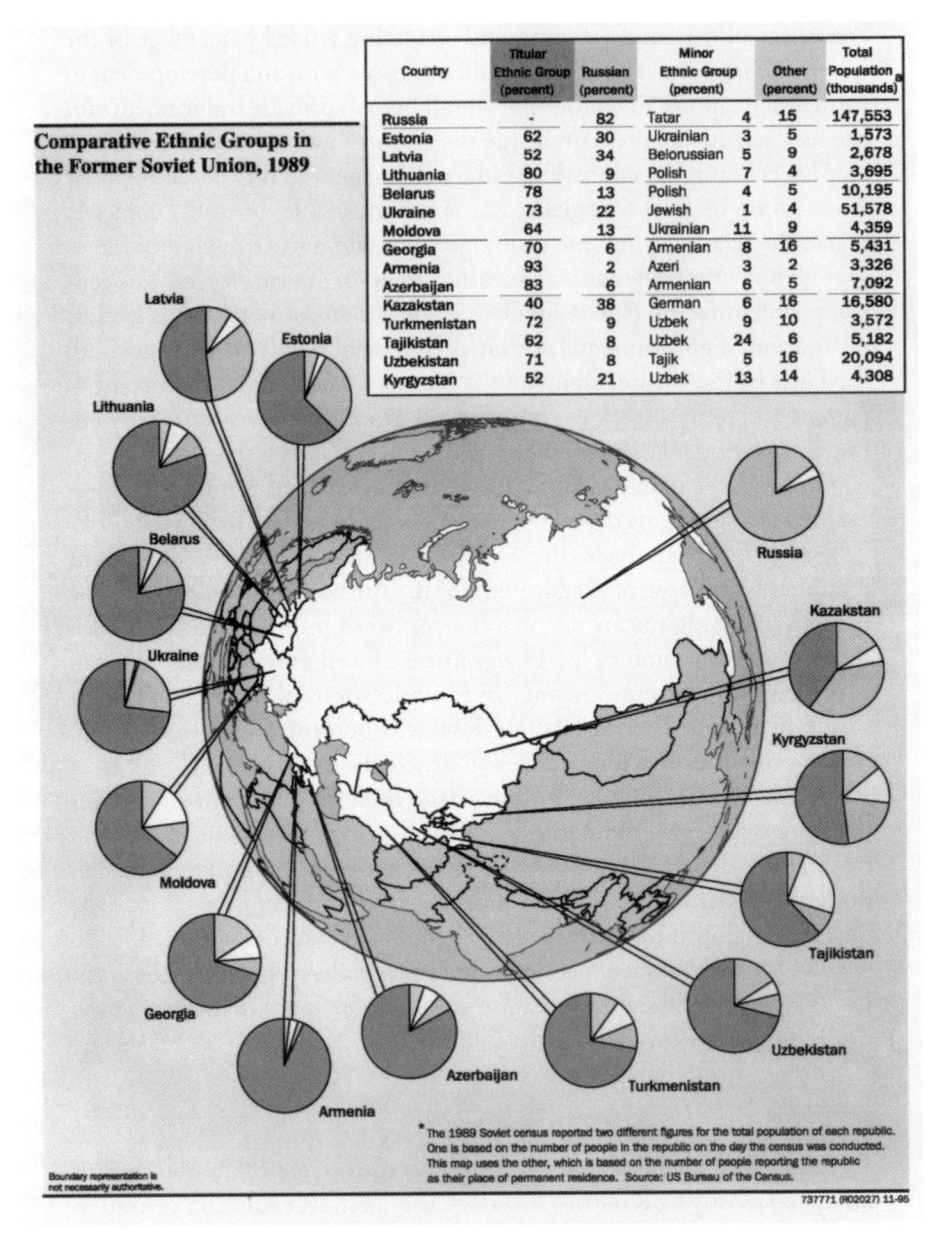

Comparative Ethnic Groups in the Former Soviet Union, 1989

Country	Titular Ethnic Group (percent)	Russian (percent)	Minor Ethnic Group (percent)		Other (percent)	Total Population[a] (thousands)
Russia	-	82	Tatar	4	15	147,553
Estonia	62	30	Ukrainian	3	5	1,573
Latvia	52	34	Belorussian	5	9	2,678
Lithuania	80	9	Polish	7	4	3,695
Belarus	78	13	Polish	4	5	10,195
Ukraine	73	22	Jewish	1	4	51,578
Moldova	64	13	Ukrainian	11	9	4,359
Georgia	70	6	Armenian	8	16	5,431
Armenia	93	2	Azeri	3	2	3,326
Azerbaijan	83	6	Armenian	6	5	7,092
Kazakstan	40	38	German	6	16	16,580
Turkmenistan	72	9	Uzbek	9	10	3,572
Tajikistan	62	8	Uzbek	24	6	5,182
Uzbekistan	71	8	Tajik	5	16	20,094
Kyrgyzstan	52	21	Uzbek	13	14	4,308

[a] The 1989 Soviet census reported two different figures for the total population of each republic. One is based on the number of people in the republic on the day the census was conducted. This map uses the other, which is based on the number of people reporting the republic as their place of permanent residence. Source: US Bureau of the Census.

Boundary representation is not necessarily authoritative.

MAP 10.1: Russia's Ethnic Republics *(Central Intelligence Agency)*

and frequently do so beyond their own geographic boundaries—on a regional basis. Such movements include the

Confederation of Peoples of the Caucasus (CPC)
United Nations of the Middle Volga and Urals (UN-MVU)
Siberian Independence Movement (SIM), and the
Far Eastern Republic (FER).

The northern Caucasus had its own autonomous mountain republic between 1921 and 1924. One of six contemporary mini-states (total ethnic population 3.5 million) in the region, Chechnya held its second independence anniversary parade on 9 September 1993 in the capital city of Groznyi. Moscow television filmed the weapons on display, which included what looked like a mobile SS-20 intermediate-range triple nuclear warhead missile launcher. Presumably the Kremlin had been impressed with this show of force which, in turn, the leaders of the other republics throughout the northern Caucasus probably applauded.

Five geopolitical regions exist in the Caucasus (see map 10.2):[4]

1. The Russian barrier—Krasnodar and Stavropol, Kalmykia and Astrakhan, with Cossack regions;
2. The CPC, which includes Adygeia, Cherkessia, Kabardino-Balkaria, North Ossetia, Ingushetia, Chechnya, Dagestan, as well as the adjoining Abkhazia, South Ossetia, and possibly the Lezgin areas of Azerbaijan;
3. Georgia and Azerbaijan, where the OSCE and NATO are active;
4. Armenia, with territorial claims against Georgia and Azerbaijan, and Adzhariia controlled by Russian troops; and
5. Turkey and Iran.

An organization of "united peoples" between the middle Volga River and the Ural Mountains proclaimed its existence on 18 August 1991 at a meeting in Kazan, capital of the Tatarstan republic. This movement unites several ethnic groups, although most important among them are the 6 million Tatars. It would resurrect the Idel-Ural Federation from the early 1920s. If this should materialize, the new region would have an external border with Kazakhstan and control major transportation as well as communication lines between European Russia and its energy base in Siberia. The UN-MVU is developing relations with Iran, which has helped restore some 350 mosques in Tatarstan alone, although the latter did receive special status in the Russian Federation by treaty on 15 February 1994.[5]

Interviewed about the Volga-Ural region, a state counselor to the president of Tatarstan suggested that if economic cooperation among republics

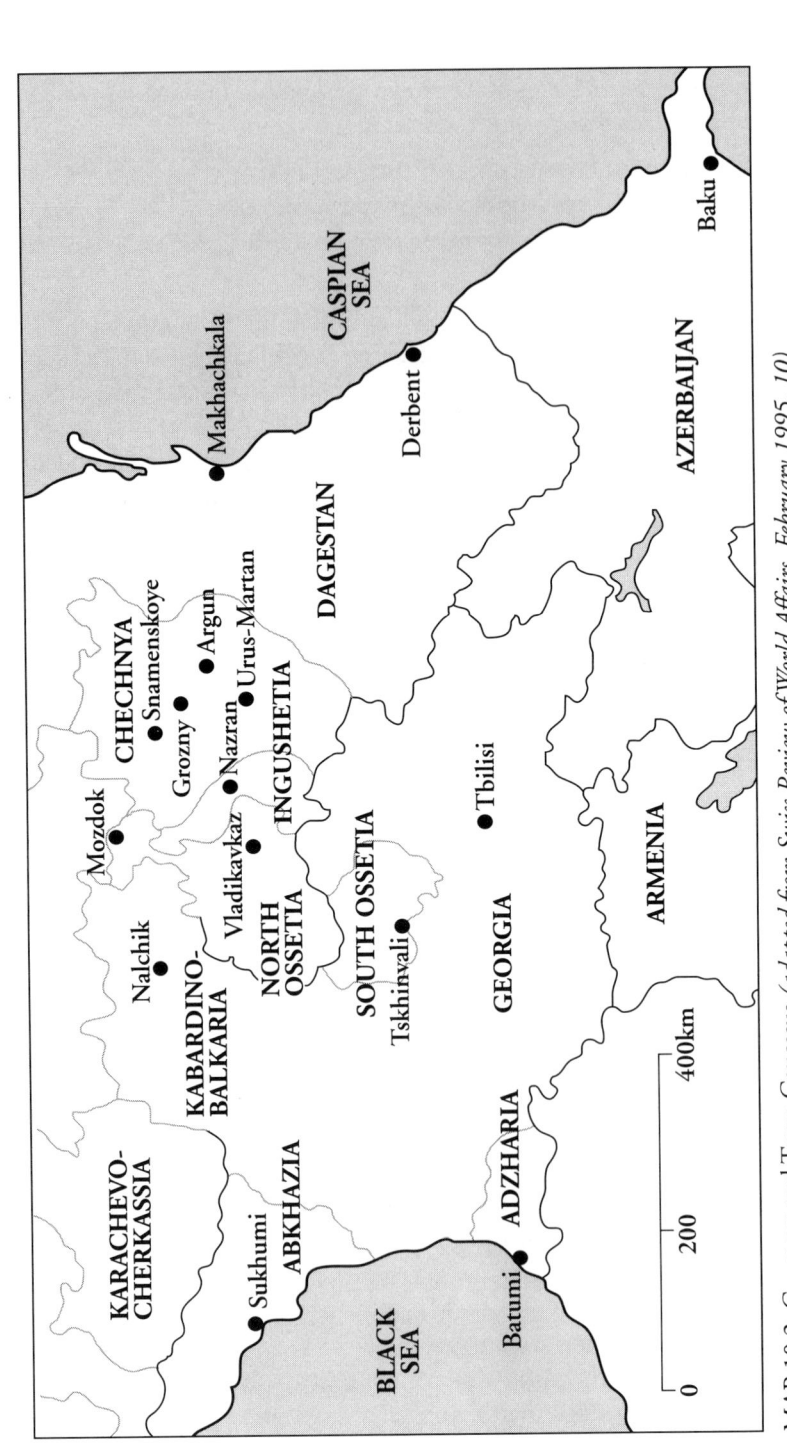

MAP 10.2: Caucasus and Trans-Caucasus *(adapted from Swiss Review of World Affairs, February 1995, 10)*

and *oblast*'s can be strengthened, then Moscow will be unable to dictate its will. Bashkortostan, a neighboring republic, has proclaimed itself a zone free from weapons of mass destruction, which is written into its constitution. The entire Volga-Ural region has a population of 20 million, and Tatarstan is located at the intersection of land and air routes. Both of these republics are building their own statehoods of a "presidential" type.[6]

At Novosibirsk on 29 September 1993, about 140 delegates from fourteen of the nineteen regions in Siberia (one-third of Russia, with 29 million people) sent an ultimatum to Russian Prime Minister Viktor S. Chernomyrdin. He was advised to rescind the presidential decree abolishing the national parliament. If he refused, the Siberian Independence Movement (SIM) threatened to stop all trains on the Trans-Siberian Railroad, withhold taxes, halt deliveries of coal and natural gas, and establish its own sovereign republic.[7] The central government did not respond and, after the rebels had been disarmed in Moscow, the dispute with SIM died down.

Siberia, the area between the Ural Mountains and Lake Baikal, produces two-thirds of all energy resources (90% of the natural gas, 75% of the petroleum, and 65% of the coal is under Moscow's control) and most of Russia's minerals. Export of these raw materials brings to the Center more than half of the hard currency it earns each year. Therefore, it would behoove the government in Moscow to offer Siberians some preference. The "Siberian agreement," an alliance of the nineteen regions, has decided to establish a common market for food, to lessen dependence on Moscow,[8] from which 50 percent of the imported food comes.

The Far East could also find historical support for its desire to exit from the Russian Federation, remembering the precedent of an independent republic at Vladivostok and the Maritime Province (1918–21). It could even be joined by Iakutiia-Sakha, with a relatively small population of 1 million (fewer than half are Iakuts) living on a huge expanse of 3 million square kilometers stretching north to the Arctic. Russia continues to take almost half the hard currency earned from diamonds and gold, even though the republic proclaimed its sovereignty in September 1990. The Far East is wealthy in timber, coal, high- and low-grade ores, and fish. It provides 15 percent of Russia's mining output and is already turning to Japan as a trading partner and developer.[9]

Apparently recognizing the implicit threat of a possible attempt to secede, Moscow negotiated seventeen documents with Iakutiia-Sakha in April 1995, including a treaty delineating powers between the two. Russia obligated itself to subsidize transportation of food and fuel to the far north. The treaty brings this republic into a political status similar to that of Tatarstan.[10]

Fragmentation of the "outer empire" began even prior to Christmas Day 1991, when the USSR was officially dissolved and replaced by fifteen independent republics. Tomorrow, the Federation of Russia may be in the process of losing its "inner empire" as well. Even if the central administrative structure holds, different economic forces at work in the various regions ultimately may support separatist tendencies. (See Map 10.3.)

The View of Future War

Having studied advanced weapons technologies applied by the United States in Operation Desert Storm against Iraq during 1991, the Russian General Staff is convinced that the next (sixth-) generation warfare will be determined by assault from aerospace with ground forces retained only in a supporting role. Maj. Gen. V. I. Slipchenko, head of research at the General Staff Academy, suggests that occupation of enemy territory may become irrelevant in future wars. By the turn of the century, Russia will have in its arsenal the following:[11]

Directed energy weapons
Automatic and automated high-precision systems
More powerful explosives
Deep-penetration ammunition
Super high-speed data-processing and electronic warfare equipment.

Scientists in Russia's secret cities continue to develop laser, incoherent light source, super high-frequency electronic, and electromagnetic pulse weapons—all of which are labeled "nonlethal." They may become perfected within the next ten years. A new plasma weapon is reportedly ready to be tested. Such a weapon ionizes the atmosphere, so that a missile or aircraft will be forced off its trajectory or glide path and "destroyed by enormous stresses."[12]

Since the new military doctrine signed by President Yeltsin on 2 November 1993 repudiated the "no first use" of nuclear weapons, the Russians are developing miniaturized nuclear devices with high energy yields. Researchers already claim to have produced one that generates twice the previous yield, while weighing only one one-hundredth of the earlier generation weapon.[13] This would suggest that, since it has lost conventional military superiority, Russia would probably not hesitate to use its "mini-nukes" if faced with imminent defeat or even as blackmail.

Finally, one should not forget the serious nuclear danger posed by the so-called dead-hand backup system in Moscow. It allows the General Staff to launch strategic weapons by issuing an emergency command to special

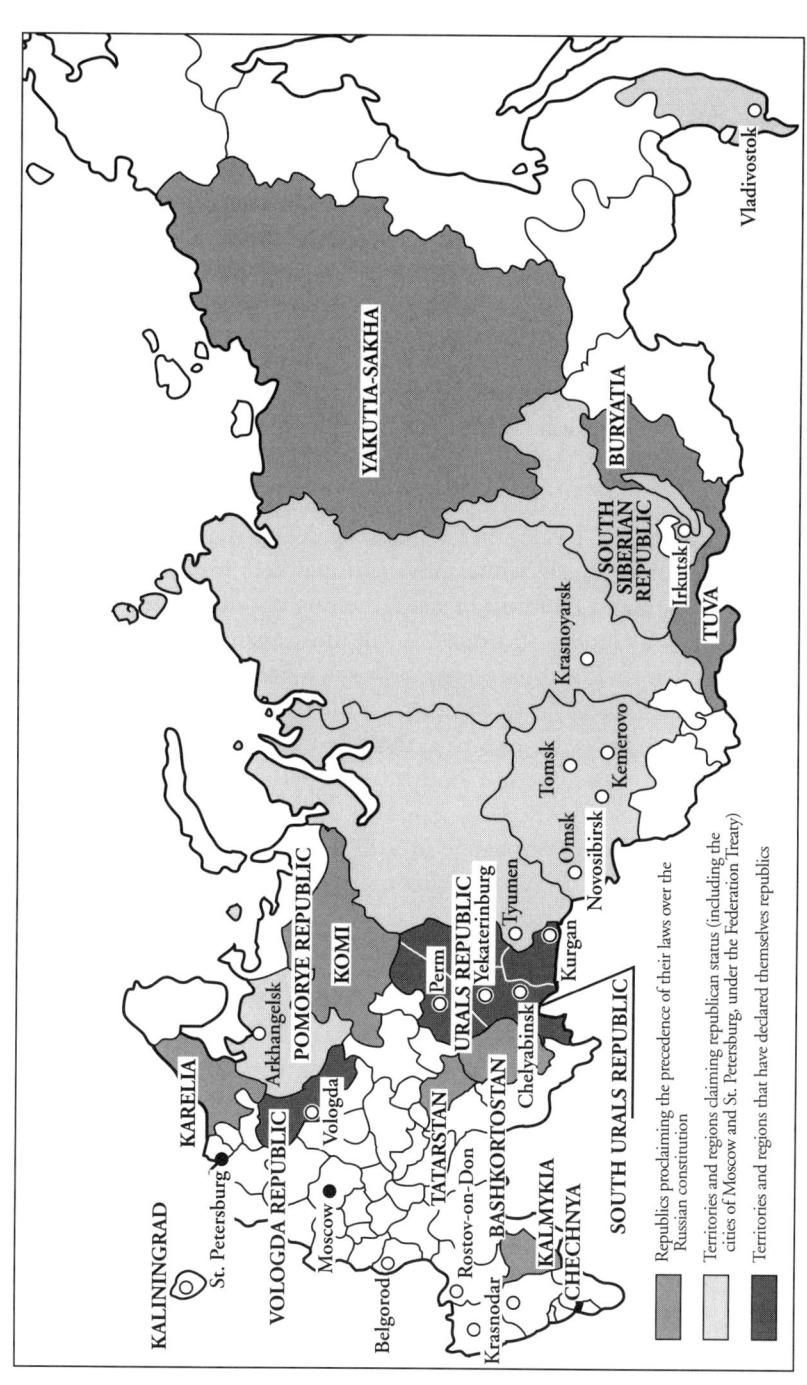

MAP 10.3: Fault Lines in the Russian Federation (*adapted from Moscow News, no. 40 [1 October 1993]: 6*)

radio nodes located far away from the capital itself. If communications have been broken and sensors detect a nuclear explosion in or near Moscow, the launch order is immediately transmitted to ICBM fields via special rockets. By contrast, the regular chain-of-command method takes approximately sixteen minutes.[14]

While accusing the United States of violating the Anti-Ballistic Missile Treaty of 26 May 1972 by testing a tactical ABM system in early 1995, the Russians themselves have admitted to having deployed the S-300 surface-to-air missile system ten years earlier. The most recent S-300PMU, a mobile version of the fixed-site S-300V, reportedly can shoot down stealth aircraft, cruise missiles, and "destroy warheads of operational-tactical and intercontinental ballistic missiles during the final phase of their flight."[15]

Toward the Twenty-first Century

The most significant developments that may decide the future of Russia include parliamentary elections and a national vote for president. The former, if held, may well result in strengthening opposition to the president, whereas the latter—if honest—will most assuredly end with the incumbent's defeat. The three scenarios below suggest different outcomes as well as consequences between now and the turn of the century.

A most important factor regarding these developments revolves around repercussions from the war in Chechnya and perhaps attempts by some of the other twenty non-Russian republics to break away from the federation. The central government in 1995 was receiving only half of expected tax revenue. The cost to Moscow of future "peacemaking" operations could result in a loss of Western financial assistance and removal of the current political leadership. The finance minister, Vladimir G. Panskov, announced that massive government corruption had broken the 1995 budget.[16]

Worst Case

The president becomes permanently incapacitated, either because of health deterioration or assassination. Since there is no vice-president, the constitutional successor for three months would be the prime minister or whoever occupies that position on an acting basis. After such an interregnum, elections for president must take place. Having managed only the natural gas industry since 1985, Viktor S. Chernomyrdin nevertheless became prime minister in December 1992 at age 54. However, he has neither the charisma nor the political experience of his mentor. The alleged acquisition of a 1 percent stake in the $100 billion natural gas conglomerate *Gazprom,* if true, would have made Chernomyrdin a billionaire and may have ruined his reputation among the electorate.[17]

Parliament becomes more forceful, and the military begins to make aggressive demands on the budget which cannot be met. Morale in the officers' corps reaches an all-time low after the supreme commander-in-chief blamed unnamed generals for the fiasco in Chechnya during his last annual State of the Russian Federation address. Although already deeply politicized, the high command has no strong leader who can take advantage of the imminent transition in the Kremlin.

History repeats itself when a new "Time of Troubles" (*smutnaia vremia,* the thirty years after Ivan the Terrible died in 1584) descends upon the land. Unemployment continues to grow, half the population sinks below the poverty level, the ruble suffers from hyperinflation, and republics in the "near abroad" begin to close their borders when faced with massive waves of Russian refugees. Many of the latter become boat-people and risk their lives to cross the Baltic Sea into Finland or Sweden. During the year 2000 alone such emigration is projected to encompass almost one million Russians.[18]

The country comes face to face with Mafia-type organizations assuming control over major cities. These gangsters had transferred almost $80 billion abroad during 1991–94, according to the Russian chief of Interpol. Many regions begin announcing their sovereignty, and the Federation seems headed toward chaos or civil war. The Commonwealth of Independent States (SNG) begins to unravel after mutual deliveries of coal drop by 20 percent; petroleum by 30 percent; ferrous metals, timber, and grain by 50 percent; trucks and tractors by 60 to 70 percent compared to the previous year. The underground economy evaded taxes on 20 to 22 percent of gross national product during 1995, according to the chairman of the State Committee on Statistics Iurii A. Iurkov.[19]

It is at this critical juncture that elections take place for a new president. In the meanwhile, various extremist organizations unite behind a single political movement: The Liberal Democratic Party of Russia or LDPR (200,000 members). Coalition components include the Russian National Council (100,000 members), headed by Aleksandr N. Sterligov, a former KGB major general. Another group calls itself the National Republican Party of Russia (45,000 members), led by Nikolai N. Lysenko, who had organized his stormtroopers into a Russian National Legion. Finally, the Russian National Unity Movement (150,000 members), controlled by Aleksandr P. Barkashov, becomes a major partner.[20] Communist Party of the Russian Federation leader, Gennadii A. Ziuganov joins the extreme nationalists to form a "Brown-Red" alliance.

Having founded his movement in 1989 (some say on KGB orders), LDPR leader Vladimir V. Zhirinovskii received 6.2 million votes when he ran third out of a field of six for president of Russia in June 1991 as a relatively unknown politician. His party doubled that number of supporters at the December 1993 parliamentary elections and gained the largest number of seats in the State *Duma*. The coalition that backs Zhirinovskii for president receives a plurality of 24 million votes, enough to make him chief of state. After all, about 70 percent of Russians agreed with him that the "long-awaited order must be introduced at any price and even with an iron fist."[21]

Zhirinovskii had published a tract in 1993 that in many respects resembled Hitler's *Mein Kampf*. He appealed to members of the Russian armed forces, police, blue-collar workers, and especially men below 25 as well as those between 40 and 54 years of age, according to public opinion polls. He was able to capitalize on the steady decline in both gross domestic product and industrial production each year since 1991. The 20 million unemployed, or one-fourth of the working-age population, also helped his cause. Zhirinovskii became supreme commander-in-chief of the armed forces with the military rank of reserve lieutenant colonel, bestowed by Defense Minister Grachëv, who had promoted him directly from captain.[22]

Most Hopeful
Realistic plans for transition to democracy and Western-style economic development finally begin to take hold. The economy shows the first signs of stabilization, and the Central Bank at last appears to be operating reliably. Reform of the armed forces provides hope that volunteers will find the military an attractive profession. Having harvested 84 million tons of grain (18% less than the previous year) and exported over 400,000 tons during 1994, the prognosis for only 131.5 million inhabitants in 2005 (a ten-year decline of 16.5 million) appeared to augur the elimination of future grain imports.[23] Life expectancy will have dropped to an average of 58 years by the turn of the century.

Conversion from arms production to consumer goods begins to succeed, when regions are developed around the needs of the former city-factories in the military-industrial complex. Unemployment declines. Leaders agree that a strong economy will make Russia a superpower. The rate of exchange between ruble and dollar starts to improve.

After the young economist Grigorii A. Iavlinskii has been elected president of the Russian Federation, an enormous rescue effort is launched by the West which dwarfs the $50-billion bailout of Mexico in 1995. The World Bank, International Monetary Fund, European Bank for Reconstruction and Development, the G-7 organization of seven leading economic powers, and private banks in the West and Japan all join to help Russia surmount its difficulties.

The new leadership proposes to transform the Federation of Russia with its twenty-one constituent republics into a new United States of Russia (*Soedinënnye shtaty Rossii*) that would more than double these territorial units. Five of the latter are Cossack republics, named after historic military settlements in the Don, Kuban, Terek, Orenburg, and Kurgan regions. (The Cossacks resume their tsarist function of guarding Russian borders.) All future constituent republics send representatives to a continental congress, convened at St. Petersburg for the purpose of drafting a new constitution and bill of rights.

Most Likely

Parliamentary elections are postponed indefinitely. A presidential decree opens up and distributes to the population the vast, once "untouchable" food reserves already tapped by the military. Another order allocates mobilization reserves, comprising huge stocks of machinery and raw materials, to military-industrial complex factories that have embarked successfully on producing the next generation of weapons systems.

The legislature protests the de facto state of emergency, after censorship begins to control the flow of information between Moscow and the various regions. When the military is given the task of maintaining law and order on the streets,[24] the lower house of parliament or State *Duma* votes to dissolve itself in protest and does so. This leaves the upper chamber or Federation Council as a figleaf of respectability. It consists of individuals, half of whom represent executive branches of the eighty-nine governmental units comprising the Federation of Russia.

The struggle between reformers and past members of the Soviet *nomenklatura,* or the old communist administrative apparatus, intensifies. An attempt is made to resurrect the efficient production of military hardware that can be sold abroad for hard currency. That also permits maintenance of a robust research and development program, built around the most advanced design bureaus, which allows Russia to keep up with the West in producing future weapons systems. Such an effort succeeds in slowing down the "brain drain" that already has resulted in thousands of scientists emigrating from the country.

In his annual address to the nation, the president redefines his concept of national security to include not only the right to intervene militarily throughout the Federation, but also to station Russian troops in all of the former Soviet republics comprising the "near abroad." The purpose is to defend external SNG borders, with the threat being defined by Moscow. What had been based hitherto on bilateral agreements between Russia and the protected sovereign republics, henceforth, is decided unilaterally by Kremlin fiat.

The blackmail effort to withdraw from various arms reduction agreements (like CFE and START or the CW and BW treaties), unless the Western partners offer more aid, does not succeed. The effect is counterproductive, and East-West relations become noticeably cooler. The only exception is Japan, which agrees to provide Russia with $50 billion in assistance over a ten-year period in exchange for return of the Kurile Islands.

The former acting prime minister and subsequent leader of the largest democratic faction in parliament, Egor T. Gaidar, had been quoted in an interview with the *Wall Street Journal* on 11 January 1995 as follows: "In the situation we are facing, you do not need an army to make a coup. You need one regiment." This understatement of the year suggested that Gaidar may not have understood the power of the president. He can call on troops from the Federal Border Service, Internal Affairs Ministry, Federal Security Service, Main Protection Directorate, and a newly created National Guard, among others.[25] (See Table 10.1.) The loyalty of regular army divisions, brigades, and regiments stationed around Moscow may not be significant so long as they remain neutral.

As a last resort, the president or prime minister as acting president may even call for a referendum on suspending elections until the year 2000. On the other hand, results could be rigged by means of the Central Electoral Commission, which has developed a nationwide propaganda apparatus. It allegedly represents a huge "brain-washing machine."[26] A Russian Center for Training in Electoral Technology would prevent "untrained" individuals from counting votes. The program is also funded and controlled by the executive branch of government. Thus the old Soviet aphorism will have been resurrected: "It is not important who wins an election: it is only important who counts the votes."

The Central Electoral Commission had not disclosed returns from the December 1993 parliamentary elections or the simultaneous referendum on the constitution through mid-1995, which suggests that the

TABLE 10.1
Regular and Other Armed Forces (1995)

Category	Number	Agency Budget (trillions of rubles)
Ministry of Interior (MVD), Army Gen. Anatolii S. Kulikov	300,000[a]	10,408,730
Federal Border Service (FPS), Army Gen. Andrei I. Nikolaev	250,000	2,331,073
Federal Security Service (FSB), Army Gen. Mikhail V. Barsukov	130,000	1,470,001
Military Space Forces (VKS), Col. Gen. Vladimir L. Ivanov	16,000	1,027,733[d]
Civil Defense and Disaster Relief (MChS), Lt. Gen. Sergei K. Shoigu	40,000	869,873
Communication and Information Agency (FAPSI), Col. Gen. Aleksandr V. Starovoitov	50,000	722,447
Special Military Construction Directorate (SSMO), Col. Gen. Aleksandr V. Tumanov	97,000	663,000
Main Protection Directorate for Individuals and Installations (GUO),[b] Lt. Gen. Iurii V. Krapivin (acting)	40,000	479,094
Defense Highway Construction (FDSU), Maj. Gen. Ivan D. Marchuk	170,000	397,526
Railroad Troops Agency (AZhV), Col. Gen. Grigorii Io. Kogat'ko	100,000	328,323
Foreign Intelligence Service (SVR), Evgenii M. Primakov	15,000	208,921
Presidential Security Service (SBPR),[c] Lt. Gen. Aleksandr V. Korzhakov	4,000	33,710
Total	*1,212,000*	*18,940,391*
Ministry of Defense, Army Gen. Pavel S. Grachëv	1,900,000	65,855,130
Grand Total	*3,112,000*	*84,795,521*

Sources: Evgenii Bovkun, "Nemetskie uchënye korrektiruiut...," *Izvestiia*, 29 October 1994, 1; Maksim Isaev, "Moskovskie adresa spetssluzhb," *Voennoe obozrenie*, insert with *Nezavisimaia gazeta*, 2 February 1995, 6; "O federal'nom biudzhete na 1995 god," *Rossiiskaia gazeta*, 7 April 1995, 1–2; Vladimir Lopatin, "Manevry generalov," *Izvestiia*, 27 April 1995, 4; interview with Maj. Gen. S. K. Shoigu, "My vsegda tam gde sluchilas' beda...," *Voennye znaniia*, no. 5 (May 1995): 32–33; Ivan Ivaniuk, "Biudzhet strany ne idealen," *Krasnaia zvezda*, 11 July 1995, 2, interview with a recent chief of the main directorate for cadres in the defense ministry, Col. Gen. Iurii N. Rodionov.

Note: The above are all "soft" figures, at times based on official data.

[a] This includes only Internal Troops and not the 570,000 uniformed police (*militsiia*) throughout Russia. See interview with then–MVD minister Viktor F. Erin, "Ne tol'ko detektiv...," *Argumenty i fakty*, no. 6 (February 1994): 3.
[b] GUO was subordinated to SBPR by presidential decree on 29 July 1995.
[c] These do not represent the new elite presidential units, reportedly being organized in early 1995. See "Lidery rossiiskogo gosudarstva...," *Nezavisimaia gazeta*, 15 December 1994, 1–2, for a document proposing establishment of such a national guard.
[d] Space agency budget.

announced results were fraudulent. Although the ballots were destroyed long ago, aggregate total returns may still be located in the commission's archives, which could be compared with published regional figures.[27] An order for 5,000 computers at a cost of $32 million has been placed abroad, possibly to manipulate national election results.

After the Year 2000

It is conceivable that the armed forces high command will become truly apolitical and not attempt to exert any influence on the future of Russia, but this remains highly unlikely in view of its previous actions during the 1991 and 1993 coup attempts and the 1994–95 war in Chechnya. More probable is the emergence from chaos of a military dictatorship headed by a charismatic general.[28] The armed forces maintain a nationwide organization, sufficient manpower, and a monopoly over weapons of mass destruction to successfully challenge any civilian government.

Their military doctrine envisages "no enemies," which does not necessarily mean that Russia has only "friends." Sending troops into former Soviet republics no longer is based on any external threat. It suffices if decisionmakers in the Kremlin announce that Russians throughout the "near abroad" are subject to "ethnic cleansing" or even discrimination.[29] Thus, national interests are rationalized by formulations in a military doctrine that does not even have the force of law.

What will become of reform in the armed forces? It is agreed by Russian analysts that no reform commenced until after the war in Chechnya had been unilaterally declared to have been won. Only then did retired General of the Army Vladimir N. Lobov, former chief of the General Staff, receive orders to active duty and a *carte blanche* for implementation of his program. He immediately made the following recommendations:[30]

> Restructuring from division-army to brigade-corps
> Preparation of military units, technical equipment, and weapons capabilities for local conflicts
> Retirement for half of the 1,793 generals, streamlining command and control
> Subordination of the General Staff to the president as supreme commander-in-chief
> Appointment of a civilian defense minister to control use of funds and represent the armed forces with other government agencies.

In order to further these objectives, a new government program will centralize the administration for converting less-efficient plants in the military-industrial complex—in effect decreeing that they either adapt successfully or declare bankruptcy. No more bailouts from Moscow. Support would be provided only to those defense plants that prove that they can produce weapons for competitive sale abroad. The myth that these exports are for "defensive" purposes only has fooled no one.

The Commonwealth of Independent States (SNG) did not develop into the equivalent of a West European Union due to the tremendous disparity among its twelve member states.[31] Moscow's attempt to dictate alliance-wide political, economic, and military objectives remained unsuccessful. The original concept of joint SNG armed forces failed, and the idea was discarded. Russia's peacemaking efforts resulted in a continuing economic drain on the budget.

The armies of other SNG countries never grew to the extent that they could individually or collectively support Russia. The development of "defensive" armed forces in the Central Asian republics suggests a fear of Moscow, especially after brutal attempts to suppress the 1.3 million also-Muslim inhabitants of Chechnya by federal military units in which orders emanate from predominantly Slavic officers and NCOs. (See Table 10.2.)

This spreads into guerrilla warfare with the other mountain peoples in the Northern Caucasus and repeated Russian punitive expeditions that are less than successful. The 20 million Muslims residing within the Federation of Russia—a majority of whom are located in the Central Asian republics, Tatarstan, and Azerbaijan—begin to support their coreligionists. The "threat from the South" materializes when Turkey and Iran commence dispatching volunteers and shipping weapons to the insurgents. The General Staff Academy in Moscow had projected that such peripheral conflicts might result in 500,000 combatants and 8 million civilians being killed.[32]

Military relations between Russia and the West center on treaties to reduce weapons systems. The war in Chechnya and its aftermath involved breaching the Conventional Forces in Europe (CFE) agreement. It appears that the Cold War mindset of "trust but verify" had not been taken seriously or perhaps was completely forgotten in the West. The fact of the matter remains that no one outside Russia knows for certain whether even one ICBM warhead has been dismantled. That is because foreigners are not permitted to witness the procedure.

Russia is violating all six conditions established by the U.S. Congress

TABLE 10.2
Ethnic Composition of Military Officers

Nationality	Commissioned Officers	Noncommissioned Officers
Russian	79.70%	73.10%
Ukrainian	11.70	15.50
Belarusian	3.80	4.00
Armenian	0.40	0.80
Moldovan	0.20	0.50
Cossack	0.13	0.40
Azerbaijani	0.15	0.30
Georgian	0.12	0.30
Uzbek	0.08	0.10
Tajik	0.05	0.07
Latvian	0.04	0.03
Kyrgyz	0.02	0.03
All others	3.61	4.87
Total	*100.00%*	*100.00%*

Source: Oleg Falichev, "Navestit' starushku mat'," *Izvestiia*, 3 June 1995, 3.

for assistance in demilitarizing the former Soviet Union under Public Law 103-160, the "Cooperative Threat Reduction Act," as follows:[33]

Making substantial investments of its resources. The United States agreed to provide $15 million for a fissile materials storage facility, although Russian designers were not being paid to do this work (GAO report).

Forgoing replacement of destroyed weapons. The CIA expects Russia to flight-test and deploy three new ICBMs during this decade and launch a new SLBM submarine soon thereafter.

Forgoing use in new weapons of components from destroyed nuclear weapons. Russia has failed to agree to "specific transparency measures to ensure…that stored materials are…not used in new weapons" (GAO report).

Facilitating U.S. verification of any weapons destruction carried out under this title. The United States has no means to inspect or account for destruction of any Russian nuclear warheads.

Complying with all relevant arms control agreements. Russia is in violation of treaties on biological (and toxin) weapons, conventional forces in Europe, chemical weapons, strategic arms, and possibly antiballistic missile defense.

Observing internationally recognized human rights, including protection of minorities. The 40,000 civilians killed in Chechnya, resulting from indiscriminate bombing and shelling, showed a complete disregard for this restriction and for the Geneva convention.

When Helen Thomas from United Press International asked President Yeltsin about the "continuing murder of civilians in Chechnya" at the 10 May 1995 press conference in Moscow, the supreme commander-in-chief responded that "there are no military operations in Chechnya.... The armed forces are not participating there, and now the internal affairs ministry is simply confiscating weapons that some small bandit groups still have."[34]

Since that encounter, naval infantry units from the Pacific and Northern Fleets have been airlifted to replace their comrades in Chechnya. Fresh airborne units have done the same. Defense Minister Grachëv apparently gave a more accurate assessment when he stated that "we will withdraw all units [in Chechnya] from other military districts and fleets, leaving only those which will become part of the newly created [58th] army in the North Caucasus Military District," established on 1 June 1995. The following month, President Yeltsin issued a decree mandating a permanent Russian military base in Chechnya.[35]

Perhaps the president and his defense chief do not talk to each other, or the problem may involve the kind of information received by the Kremlin. Such data is reported by the Federal Security Service (FSB), which is staffed primarily by former KGB personnel. One of its reports, dealing with activities of American scholars in Russia, was released to the public.[36] After listing some of the specialized research centers and organizations in the United States (like the American Association for Advancement of Slavic Studies, the Hoover Institution, Rand, the Peace Corps, American Council of Learned Societies, the Soros and Ford foundations, Harvard, and Yale), the FSB examines their funding.

Support allegedly comes from the Pentagon, U.S. Naval Academy, Foreign Service Institute, U.S. Congress, National Security Council, and U.S. Department of Education, the last as a conduit for funds from private foundations. Intelligence acquisition by the United States is also supported by Rotary and Lions Clubs as well as America House (a library attached to the embassy in Moscow and operated by the U.S. Information Agency).

Scientists, especially those in secret cities, are allegedly paid $500 per document delivered to American "scholar-agents." It is these Russian individuals, working for the military-industrial complex, who are invited to do their research in the United States. Thousands of scientists have accepted. The ensuing "brain drain" is being orchestrated allegedly to weaken the combat effectiveness of the Russian armed forces.

Based on such "disinformation," it should not be surprising that Yeltsin would decide to abandon his earlier reliance on partnership with the United States and turn toward a country that will become a superpower in the twenty-first century. He had already signed a joint declaration with Pres. Jiang Zemin at the Kremlin on 3 September 1994 which proclaimed "new relations based on constructive partnership" between Russia and the People's Republic of China (PRC). The document supported multilateral cooperation in the Asia–Pacific Ocean region. A secret report from the military council of the Chinese Communist Party reportedly included a reference to more than 1,000 experts from Russia's military-industrial complex, assisting China to modernize its armed forces.[37]

One day after the Chinese underground nuclear test, Defense Minister Grachëv left for Beijing to explore closer military cooperation, including PRC manufacture of Su-27 aircraft. He announced on 16 May 1995 that the two countries had agreed on the need for developing a collective security system in northeast Asia. Grachëv claimed that the question of an alliance had not been raised. He also denied that the sale of weapons to China posed a threat to Russian security.[38]

On the other hand, a report from the press conference in Beijing states that Grachëv told Russian journalists about the following proposal he had made to virtually every Chinese official who had met with him: Moscow and Beijing should coordinate their security policies. The Chinese replied that they have no intention to join an alliance and would not do so. It was unclear to the correspondent who reported the foregoing whether or not Grachëv had any authority from the Kremlin to make these proposals.[39]

Not only the current Chinese colonization of the Far Eastern regions of Russia, which apparently continues unabated, but also the concept of Beijing's sphere of influence represent long-range problems. The latter includes the Great North-East Area, the Great North-West Area, and Mongolia in between. The two former regions had been ceded to tsarist Russia in 1858 and 1864. The last region became a people's republic and Soviet satellite in 1924. These dormant claims do not necessarily mean that Beijing will remain adamantly opposed to an alliance with Moscow.

In conclusion, it would appear that there exists no national security concept in Russia today, according to Viktor I. Iliukhin, chairman of the committee for security in the State *Duma*. He predicts that there will be none before mid-1997, because the president's closest advisors are working overtime on keeping him in office with or without an election.[40]

Anticipating mass disorders throughout the country, if results are falsified or the presidential election is postponed, interior troops are being strengthened and reequipped. A regional regiment of mobile gendarmerie will be responsible for every two or three *oblast*'s, in order to suppress any widespread protest demonstrations. If need be, the new National Guard (directly subordinated to the president) can be called out. It will represent an armed organization and function "as an instrument in the battle for political power."[41]

It is at such a point that the military may become an active player in the midst of a civil war during the course of which Russian will be killing Russian.

Notes

1. Aleksei I. Podberëzkin, ed., *Natsional'naia doktrina Rossii: problemy i prioritety* (Moscow: "Obozrevatel'," 1994), 501 pp.

2. Ibid., 491, 494; emphasis added.

3. See, however, interview with Pres. M. E. Nikolaev, "Novyi etap federalizma," *Rossiiskie vesti,* 16 June 1995, 3; Leon Gouré, "The Russian Federation: Possible Disintegration Scenarios," *Comparative Strategy* 13, no. 4 (October–December 1994): 401–17.

4. Vadim Shorokhov, "Chechenskoe protivostoianie…," *Nezavisimaia gazeta,* 20 January 1995, 3.

5. For discussion of this treaty, see Nail' Aminov, "Tatarskaia model'," *Nezavisimaia gazeta,* 18 February 1995, 2.

6. Vladimir Kuznechevskii, "Komu ne po dushe edinaia Rossiia," *Rossiiskaia gazeta,* 6 April 1995, 2.

7. "Siberian Agreement, Association Meets in Novosibirsk," Moscow Radio, ITAR-TASS, 1 October 1993, in FBIS-SOV-93-190-S (4 October 1993), 82.

8. Sergei Strokan, "Siberian Discontent," *Moscow News,* no. 16 (28 April–4 May 1995): 3.

9. Boris Reznik, "Dalnii Vostok stavit tsentru ultimatum," *Izvestiia,* 3 February 1995, 1. See also Susan L. Clark and David R. Graham, "The Russian Federation's Fight for Survival," *Orbis* 39, no. 3 (Summer 1995): 329–51.

10. Oleg Kriuchek, "Iakutiia khochet razdelit' s Moskvoi…," *Segodnia,* 5 April 1995, 2.

11. Mary C. FitzGerald, "The Russian Image of Future War," *Comparative Strategy* 13, no. 2 (April–June 1994): 167–80; her interview with Slipchenko is on 168.

12. Ibid., 171–73, 176. See also A. Prishchepenko, "Elektro-magnitnoe oruzhie v boiu budushchego," *Morskoi sbornik,* no. 3 (March 1995): 71–72, for electromagnetic radio frequency radiation in future warfare.

13. Mikhail Rebrov, "Bomby trekh pokolenii," *Krasnaia zvezda,* 27 October 1992, 2; cited by FitzGerald, "Russian Image," 177. See also Aleksandr Pikaev, "Arsenal-XXI," *Novoe vremia,* no. 39 (September 1994): 12–14, which discusses this topic of weapons for the next century.

14. Bruce G. Blair, "Doomsday Machine and Other Nuclear Dangers in the Former Soviet Union," *CNA Seminar Report* (Alexandria, Va.: Center for Naval Analyses, May 1994), 3. See also his book, *The Logic of Accidental Nuclear War* (Washington, D.C.: Brookings Institution, 1993), 364 pp.

This information had appeared also on the op-ed page of the *New York Times,* 8 October 1993. A reply four months later corroborated Dr. Blair's contention. See Col. Valery Yarynich, "The Doomsday Machine's Safety Catch," *New York Times,* 1 February 1994, A-15.

15. Sergei Oznobishchev and Anton Surikov, "Novaia PRO: panatseia ot ugroz…," *Segodnia,* 6 May 1995, 9, for charges that U.S. is violating the ABM treaty; Igor' Korotchenko, "Bolshoi uspekh voennoi razvedki SShA," *Nezavisimaia gazeta,* 27 December 1994, 2, on Russian ABM capability. The author is grateful to William T. Lee for the second source.

16. Quoted by J. Michael Waller, *Russia Reform Monitor,* no. 14 (26 May 1995): 1. For violation of tax laws, see "Nalogovaia politsiia nabiraet moshch'," *Delovoi mir,* 4 April 1995, 8. See also Steven Erlanger, "A corrupt tide in Russia…," *New York Times,* 3 July 1995, 1, 5.

17. "Boris Fëdorov znaet…," *Kommersant-Daily,* 30 May 1995, 3.

18. Unemployment from Vitalii Golovachev, "Kazhdyi piatyi—lishnii?" *Trud,* 1 April 1995, 1–2; projections by Evgenii Balatskii, "Perspektivy vneshnetrudovoi migratsii," *Delovoi mir* (19–25 December 1994): 27.

Out of 24 million Russians in the "near abroad," labor ministry official Aleksandr Tkachenko predicts that up to 4 million will return from Central Asia and the Caucasus (2 million), the Baltic States (300,000), and Moldova (100,000). Alaina Lemon, "Labor ministry predicts," OMRI *Daily Digest* 1, no. 159 (16 August 1995): 2.

19. Interview with Finance Minister Vladimir G. Panskov, "V mesto 60 nalogov budet vvedën odin…," *Trud,* 14 March 1995, 2, for Mafia money; Evgenii Vasil'chuk, "Neudachi ekonomicheskoi integratsii…," *Finansovye izvestiia,* no. 15 (2 March 1995): IV, for trade statistics.

20. Vladimir Ostrosvetov, "The Russian Order of Alexander Barkashov," *Moscow News,* no. 15 (15–21 April 1994): 3; Vladimir Sirotini, "The Fuehrer Is with Us!" *Moscow News,* no. 22 (3–9 June 1994): 6; and his "The Russian National Council," *Moscow News,* no. 26 (1–7 July 1994): 6; Igor' Baranovsky, "From KGB to LDPR: The Rise of a Fascist," *Moscow News,* no. 37 (16–22 September 1994): 1, 7. See also Valerii Kornev, "Chernosotentsy zovut v pokhod na Kreml'," *Izvestiia,* 6 July 1995, 5.

21. On his presidential plans, see interview "Vladimir Zhirinovskii: Rossiiu ne budut grabit'…," *Delovoi mir,* 25 March 1995, 2. The 70 percent figure is cited by

Sergei Gryzunov, "Fashizmu v Rossii poka nichto ne grozit," *Izvestiia,* 6 June 1995, 5.

22. See Vladimir V. Zhirinovskii, *Poslednyi brosok na iug* (Moscow: Pisatel' i Bukvitsa, 1993), 143 pp.; Oleg Savel'ev, "Opiat' griadut vybory," *Moskovskaia pravda,* 8 February 1994, 1, for opinion poll results; Viktor Litovkin, "Polku podpolkovnikov pribylo," *Izvestiia,* 31 March 1995, 1, for promotion of Zhirinovskii.

23. INTERFAX, "V blizhaishie 10 let Rossiia mozhet poteriat' 16.5 mln. chelovek," *Izvestiia,* 22 December 1994, 1; Aleksandr Gavriliuk, "Tak bogatym ne stanesh'," *Rossiiskaia gazeta,* 25 April 1995, 1.

24. A total of 36,000 military personnel, including 15,000 paratroopers, were on patrol in Moscow. See Igor' Cherniak, "V Moskvu vvodiat voiska," *Komsomol'skaia pravda,* 21 June 1995, 1.

25. Nikolai Troitskii, "Pretoriantsy tret'ego Rima," *Obshchaia gazeta,* no. 12 (12–18 January 1995): 8; interview with president's chief of staff, Sergei A. Filatov, "Sleduiushchuiu vnutrennuiu voinu…," *Argumenty i fakty,* no. 7 (February 1995): 2; Valerii Vyzhutovich, "Tenevye sovetniki Kremlia…," *Izvestiia,* 24 January 1995, 1–2, on the National Guard.

26. Sergei Chugaev, "Vse na bor'bu s konstitutsionnoi bezgramotnost'iu?" *Izvestiia,* 11 April 1995, 5.

27. Tat'iana Skorobogat'ko, "Tsentrizbirkom: ni shagu nazat," *Moskovskie novosti,* no. 36 (21–28 May 1995), 7.

28. For a different view, see Mikhail Tsypkin, "Will the Military Rule Russia?" *Security Studies* 2, no. 1 (Autumn 1992): 38–73.

29. Emil A. Pain, presidential council member, estimates that only two or three million Russians will return from the "near abroad" because of economic conditions and not ethnic discrimination. Michael Mihalka, OMRI *Daily Digest,* 14 April 1995, 4–5.

30. General armii Vladimir Lobov, "Kak reformirovat' rossiiskuiu armiiu," *Rossiiskaia gazeta,* 25 January 1995, 1–2.

31. Vitalii Tret'iakov, "Pochemu Evropeiskii soiuz—real'nost', a SNG—mif?" *Nezavisimaia gazeta,* 22 April 1995, 1.

32. Vadim Solov'ëv, "Pavel Grachëv po novomu stroit oboronu Rossii," *Nezavisimaia gazeta,* 7 May 1993, 1, for number of Muslims; Oleg Vladykin, "Ugroza s iuga," *Krasnaia zvezda,* 3 February 1995, 2, for General Staff predictions.

33. GAO, *Weapons of Mass Destruction* (Washington, D.C.: October 1994), NSIAD-95-7; J. Michael Waller, *Foreign Aid Advisory,* no. 5 (19 May 1995).

34. "Question & Answer Session," Moscow Public TV, 10 May 1995, in FBIS-SOV-95-090 (10 May 1995), 5.

35. "Grachëv: Troops Remain until 'Bandits' Give Up," Moscow Radio, 13 May 1995, in FBIS-SOV-95-093 (15 May 1995), 30.

36. "Dokument: FSK obespokoena aktivnost'iu amerikanskikh issledovatelei v Rossii," *Nezavisimaia gazeta,* 10 January 1995, 3.

37. *Zhen Ming* (Hong Kong); cited by Vladimir Skosyrev, "Aziia napugana rasshireniem voennogo sotrudnichestva Rossii s Kitaem," *Izvestiia,* 9 November 1993, 1, 4.

38. "Grachëv Cited on Results of Visit," Moscow Radio, 18 May 1995, in FBIS-SOV-95-097 (19 May 1995), 11–12.

39. Vladimir Skosyrev, "Pekin otverg 'soiuznicheskie' predlozheniia Grachëva," *Izvestiia,* 20 May 1995, 1.

40. Interview by Oleg Zhirnov, "Sostoianie natsional'noi bezopasnosti—kriticheskoe," *Moskovskaia pravda,* 29 April 1995, 1, 7.

41. Valerii Vyzhutovich, "Tenevye sovetniki Kremlia…."

Appendix A
Biographical Information on Key Military Figures

Abiev, Safar Akhundbala-ogly (Lieutenant General). Born 1950: Azeri. Baku Combined Arms Command School (1971); Frunze Military Academy (1982). Served with Western Group of Forces (Germany), the Baltic States, Trans-Baikal, and Trans-Caucasus MDs. February 1992: joined Azerbaijan armed forces; 6 February 1995: defense minister, Azerbaijan. *Source: Krasnaia zvezda,* 4 May 1995, 2.

Achalov, Vladislav Alekseevich (Colonel General). Born 1945: Russian. Kazan Tank Academy (1966); Malinovskii Academy of Armored Troops (1973); General Staff Academy (1984). 1984: first deputy CO, 2nd Tank Army, Western Group of Forces (Germany); 1987: chief of staff, first deputy CO, Leningrad MD; 1989–91: CO, Airborne Troops, and deputy minister of defense for public disturbances. Dismissed for coup involvement in September 1991; acting "defense minister" during October 1993 mutiny; amnestied in 1994. *Source:* Vasilevskii and Pribylovskii, *Kto est' kto v rossiiskoi politike,* 51–52.

Akhmedov, Rustan Urmanovich (Lieutenant General). Born 1943: Uzbek. Kokand Technical School for Mechanization and Electrification of Agricultural Farms (1961); Tashkent Armor School (1965); Armored Forces Military Academy (1985). In command positions and political education work with troops. Samarkand Higher Armor Command and Tashkent Higher Combined Arms Command Schools. 1986–91: chief of staff, deputy chief for civil defense in Tashkent *oblast';* 1991–92: minister

209

for defense affairs and CO, National Guard; July 1992: defense minister, Uzbekistan. *Source: Krasnaia zvezda,* 4 May 1995, 3.

Akhromeev, Sergei Fëdorovich (Marshal of the Soviet Union). Born 1923: Russian. Red Army Higher Officers' School (1945); General Staff Academy (1967). World War II veteran: Leningrad, Stalingrad, Southern and 4th Ukrainian fronts. 1974–83: deputy chief of staff, General Staff. Four years as chief of operations in Afghanistan. 1983: Marshal of the Soviet Union; Hero of the Soviet Union. 1984–88: chief of General Staff; first deputy minister of defense; December 1988: adviser to President Gorbachëv. 24 August 1991: suicide. *Source:* Krotov and Tsyganov, *Voennye Rossii,* 126–28.

Baltin, Eduard Dmitrievich (Admiral). Born 1936: Russian. Caspian Higher Naval School (1958); Naval Academy (1975); General Staff Academy (1980). 1981: Hero of the Soviet Union. 1987–90: first deputy CO, Pacific Fleet; 1990–93: chairman, Department of Strategic Naval Studies, General Staff Academy; 1993– : CO, Black Sea Fleet. *Sources: Morskoi sbornik,* no. 2 (February 1993): 21; no. 6 (1995): 6–9.

Bogdanov, Anatolii Anatol'evich (Colonel General). Born 1945: Russian. Kharkov Tank School; Malinovskii Armored Troops Academy; General Staff Academy. Commanded from platoon in Trans-Caucasus MD to deputy CO, Western Group of Forces (Germany). 1994: deputy chief of General Staff. *Source: Krasnaia zvezda,* 15 April 1995, 3.

Burlakov, Matvei Prokopevich (Colonel General). Born 1935: Russian. Omsk Military Academy (1957); Frunze Military Academy (1968); General Staff Academy (1977); advanced course (1986). 1983–88: chief of staff and first deputy CO, Trans-Baikal MD; 1988–90: CO, Southern Group of Forces (Hungary); 1990–94: CO, Western Group of Forces (Germany); 1994: deputy minister of defense; January 1995: dismissed for corruption. *Source: Military News Bulletin,* no. 9 (September 1994), published in Moscow.

Chechevatov, Viktor Stepanovich (Colonel General). Born 1945: Cossack. Joined army in 1963. Ul'ianovsk Guards Tank School (1966); Armored Troops Academy (1973); General Staff Academy (1984). Commanded platoon to army; chief of staff for Central Asian MD (1987); first deputy CO, Carpathian MD (1989); CO, Kiev MD (1991–92); CO, Far East MD (April 1992). *Source: Military News Bulletin,* no. 10 (October 1992): 18.

Chernavin, Vladimir Nikolaevich (Admiral of the Fleet). Born 1928: Russian. Leningrad Higher Naval School (1951); Naval Academy (1965);

General Staff Academy (1969). 1959: CO, nuclear submarine; 1977–81: CO, Northern Fleet; 1981–85: chief of Navy Main Staff, first deputy CO of Navy; 1985: commander-in-chief, Navy; deputy defense minister; 1991: Hero of the Soviet Union; commander-in-chief, SNG Navy; 1992: honorary president for preparation of 300th anniversary of Russian Navy (1996). *Source:* Gazukin, *Vooruzhënnye sily Rossiiskoi Federatsii*, 58–59.

Chindarov, Aleksandr A. (Lieutenant General). Born 1948: Tatar? Riazan Higher Airborne Command School (1971); Frunze Military Academy (1980); General Staff Academy (1991). Served from platoon to division CO, including Afghanistan, Ossetia-Ingush, and Abkhazia conflicts. 1991: deputy CO, airborne troops; 1994: commanded airborne group in Chechnya; January 1995: first deputy CO, airborne troops. *Sources: Moskovskii komsomolets*, 2 December 1994, 1; *Kommersant-Daily,* 13 May 1995, 3.

Churanov, Vladimir Timofeevich (Colonel General). Born 1945: Russian. Volsk Military School (1966); Rear Services and Transport Academy (1979); General Staff Academy (1987). 1979: service in Kiev MD; 1991: deputy CO for rear services and chief of Moscow MD rear services; 1992: chief of armed forces rear services; 1995: deputy defense minister for rear services. *Source: Krasnaia zvezda*, 21 January 1995, 1.

Deinekin, Pëtr Stepanovich (Colonel General). Born 1937: Russian. Balashov Military Flying School (1957); Gagarin Air Force Academy (1969); General Staff Academy (1982). 1988: CO, Long Range Aviation; 1990: first deputy CO, Air Forces; 1991– : commander-in-chief, Air Forces. *Sources: Krasnaia zvezda*, 6 October 1992, 1; 28 November 1995, 3.

Dudayev, Djokar Musaevich (Major General). Born 1944: Chechen. Tambov Higher Military Aviation School; Gagarin Air Force Academy (1977). First Chechen general in Soviet air force. Served in Siberia, Afghanistan (1985–86), and Estonia (1987–90). Retired, May 1990. Elected president of Chechnya, 27 October 1991. *Source:* Krotov and Tsyganov, *Voennye Rossii*, 38–44.

Egorov, Vladimir Grigorevich (Admiral). Born 1938: Russian. Frunze Higher Naval School (1962); Naval Academy by correspondence (1984); General Staff Academy by correspondence (1990). 1986–88: CO, Mediterranean flotilla; 1988–91: first deputy CO, Baltic Fleet; 1991: CO, Baltic Fleet. *Source:* Krotov and Tsyganov, *Voennye Rossii*, 45–46.

Erofeev, Oleg Aleksandrovich (Admiral). Born 1940: Russian. Kirov Caspian Higher Naval School (1961); Naval Academy (1976); General Staff Academy (1987). 1990: chief of staff; first deputy CO of Northern Fleet; 1992: CO, Northern Fleet. *Source: Morskoi sbornik*, no. 4 (April 1995): 11.

Evnevich, Valerii Gennad'evich (Lieutenant General). Born 1951: Russian. Riazan Airborne School (1972); Frunze Military Academy (1983); General Staff Academy (1992). CO, 56th Guards Airborne Assault Brigade in Afghanistan; wounded; withdrew in February 1989 with last troops. 1992–95: CO, 2nd Taman Motorized Rifle Div.; brought units into Moscow to suppress October 1993 mutiny; "Hero of Russian Federation" award. 1 July 1995: CO, Group of Russian Forces in Trans-Dniester; 2 August 1995: promoted to lieutenant general. *Sources: Krasnaia zvezda*, 31 October 1992, 3; 5 October 1993, 3; 3 November 1994, 1.

Gareev, Makhmut Akhmetovich (General of the Army). Born 1923: Tatar. 1941: volunteer, Tashkent Infantry School; wounded in 1942 and 1944; 1945: senior officer for operations on staff of army in Far East. Frunze Military Academy; General Staff Academy with gold medal. CO of regiment, division; chief of staff, combined arms army, Belarus MD. 1971–72: chief of staff and principal military advisor to Egyptian army; 1972: chief of staff for Ural MD; 1974: chief of military science directorate; 1983: deputy for operations and (1985) deputy chief of General Staff; 1989: principal military advisor in Afghanistan and de facto CO of Afghan armed forces during two years; severely wounded. Order of Lenin and promoted to General of the Army; doctorate in military science; military theoretician. President, Russian Academy of Military Sciences. *Source:* Gazukin, *Voruzhënnye sily Rossiiskoi Federatsii*, 17; *Orientir*, no. 6 (December 1994): 17–23.

Golovnëv, Anatolii Andreevich (Colonel General). Born 1942: Russian. Moscow Combined Arms Command School (1963); Frunze Military Academy (1973); General Staff Academy (1980). Served in command and staff positions in Ukraine, Far East, and Western Group of Forces (Germany); first deputy CO, Moscow MD; August 1992: deputy commander-in-chief for combat training of ground forces; May 1995: first deputy commander-in-chief, Ground Forces. *Source:* Gazukin, *Voruzhënnye sily Rossiiskoi Federatsii*, 18.

Grachëv, Pavel Sergeevich (General of the Army). Born 1948: Russian. Riazan Higher Airborne Command School (1969); Frunze Military Academy (1981); General Staff Academy (1990). CO, airborne regiment; CO, airborne division in Afghanistan (1981–83; 1987–89). Hero of the Soviet Union. 1990–91: CO, Airborne Troops; August 1991: first deputy minister of defense, USSR; 1992: chairman of RSFSR state committee for defense questions and first deputy commander-in-chief of SNG Joint Forces; 1 April 1992: deputy defense minister of Russian Federation; May 1992: defense minister. *Source:* Gazukin, *Voruzhënnye sily Rossiiskoi Federatsii*, 19–23.

Grekov, Iurii Pavlovich (Colonel General). Born 1943: Russian. Leningrad Higher Combined Arms Command School; Frunze Military Academy (1974); General Staff Academy (1985). Served with Soviet Forces in Germany, Trans-Baikal, Trans-Caucasus, Leningrad, Baltic, and Turkestan MDs; 1986–88: chief of staff and first deputy CO, 40th Army in Afghanistan; 1990–92: first deputy CO, Trans-Caucasus MD; July 1992– : CO, Ural MD. *Source: Military News Bulletin,* no. 11 (November 1992): 4.

Gromov, Boris Vsevolodovich (Colonel General). Born 1943: Russian. Frunze Military Academy (1972); General Staff Academy (1984). Three tours of duty in Afghanistan (1980–82, 1985–86, 1987–89); CO, 40th Army, in charge of withdrawal. 1988: Hero of the Soviet Union. 1989–90: CO, Kiev MD; 1991: deputy minister of internal affairs; June 1991: vice-presidential candidate with Nikolai Ryzhkov, taking 17% of vote; 1992: first deputy commander-in-chief of ground forces/general purpose forces; 1992–94: deputy defense minister for troop reaction in emergencies and peacekeeping forces; February 1995: transferred as military expert to foreign ministry, with rank of deputy minister. *Source:* Vasilevskii and Pribylovskii, *Kto est' kto v rossiiskoi politike,* 172–73.

Gromov, Feliks Nikolaevich (Admiral). Born 1937: Russian. Pacific Higher Naval School (1959); Naval Academy by correspondence (1983); General Staff Academy by correspondence (1991). 1977–81: chief of staff for training division, Leningrad Naval Base; 1981–84: CO, operational squadron; 1984–88: first deputy CO, Northern Fleet; 1988–92: CO, Northern Fleet; 1992: first deputy and (August 1992) commander-in-chief, Navy. *Source: Morskoi sbornik,* no. 10 (October 1992): 19.

Gurinov, Georgii Nikolaevich (Admiral). Born 1939: Russian. Caspian Higher Naval School (1960); Naval Academy (1975); General Staff Academy (1984). Served four years with Strategic Missile Troops. 1964: CO, air defense artillery battery on warship of Baltic Fleet. Senior aide to CO; CO of destroyer; chief of staff for brigade of missile patrol boats; CO, destroyer brigade; 1984: chief of staff and (1986) CO, Kamchatka naval flotilla. 1989–92: chief of staff, Black Sea Fleet; 1992: deputy commander-in-chief of Navy. Since 1 April 1993, CO, Pacific Fleet. *Source: Krasnaia zvezda,* 3 April 1993, 2.

Haroutiunian, Michael (Major General). Born 1946: Armenian. Army Higher School for Commanders (1967); Frunze Military Academy (1973–76); General Staff Academy (1986–88). CO, platoon through corps. 1988–91: senior lecturer at GSA, Moscow; 1992–94: deputy chief and first deputy chief of General Staff, Armenia; 1994–95: first deputy minister of defense and chief of General Staff, Armenia; acting minister of defense between 17 May and 27 July 1995. *Source:* Embassy of Armenia, Washington, D.C.

Iazov, Dmitrii Timofeevich (Marshal of the Soviet Union). Born 1923: Russian. Moscow Infantry School (1942); Frunze Military Academy (1956); General Staff Academy (1967). World War II veteran; 1962: served in Cuba; 1972–80: first deputy CO, Far East MD and then CO, Central Group of Forces (Czechoslovakia); 1980: CO, Central Asia MD; 1984–87: CO, Far East MD; 1987: chief of main personnel directorate, General Staff; 1987–91: minister of defense. August 1991: arrested; 1994: amnestied. *Source:* Krotov and Tsyganov, *Voennye Rossii,* 123–25.

Ivanov, Vladimir Leont'evich (Colonel General). Born 1936: Russian. Caspian Higher Naval School (1958); Dzerzhinskii Military Engineering Academy (1973); General Staff Academy. Passed through all grades of military service up to deputy CO of a missile army. 1979–84: CO, Plesetsk space center (northern rocket test facility) in Arkhangel'sk *oblast';* 1984–86: chief of staff and first deputy chief of main directorate for military space forces; 1986–89: chief of staff and first deputy chief of military space forces; 1989; commander of military space forces USSR-SNG; September 1992: commander of military space forces, ministry of defense. Doctorate in military science. *Sources: Armeiskii sbornik,* no. 4 (October 1994): 8; *Krasnaia zvezda,* 16 August 1995, 2.

Kalinin, Nikolai Vasil'evich (Colonel General). Born 1937: Russian. Kirov Officers School; Frunze Military Academy; General Staff Academy. 1986: CO, Siberian MD; 1987–89: CO, Airborne Troops; 1989: CO, Leningrad and then Moscow MDs. 1991: relieved 24 August 1991, later exonerated; 1991–94: chief, Malinovskii Academy of Armored Troops. Retired. *Sources: Kommunist Voruzhënnykh sil,* no. 10 (May 1989): 9; *Moskovskii komsomolets,* 13 February 1992, 1.

Kapitanets, Ivan Matveevich (Fleet Admiral). Born 1928: Russian. Joined Navy in 1946. Caspian Higher Naval School, Naval Academy, and General Staff Academy graduate. Commanded naval units, destroyers, division of ships. 1978: first deputy commander and (1981) CO of Baltic Fleet; 1985: CO of Northern Fleet; 1988–92: first deputy commander-in-chief of Navy; 1994: first deputy director, Naval Center attached to government of Russia. *Source: Krasnaia zvezda,* 24 June 1995, 6.

Kasatonov, Igor' Vladimirovich (Admiral). Born 1939: Russian. Black Sea Higher Naval School (1960); Naval Academy (1972); General Staff Academy (1979). Lieutenant on destroyer *Gnevnyi;* CO of missile battery during cruise from Black Sea, around Europe, across northern seas to the Pacific Ocean. 1970: CO of large ASW ship, *Provornyi;* 1975: CO of new ASW ship, *Ochakov;* 1980–82: CO of surface division; 1982–88: CO, Kola Flotilla; 1988–91: chief of staff and first deputy CO, Northern Fleet; September 1991–92: CO, Black Sea Fleet; September 1992: first deputy commander-in-chief, Navy. *Sources: Morskoi sbornik,* no. 12 (December 1992): 11; *Krasnaia zvezda,* 5 December 1995, 2.

Kasymov, Alibek Khamidovich (Lieutenant General). Born 1954: Kazakh. Higher General Military Command School named after Marshal I. S. Konev in Alma-Ata (1975); Frunze Military Academy (1985). Served in the Baltic States MD; after graduation from the Academy, sent to Transcaucasus MD; early 1992; 1st deputy chief of staff, 40th Army Headquarters at Almaty; November 1992: 1st deputy minister of defense and chief of general staff, Kazakhstan armed forces; 16 October 1995: minister of defense. *Sources: Kazakhstanskaia pravda,* 17 October 1995, 1; *Krasnaia zvezda,* 20 October 1995, 1; embassy of Kazakhstan in Washington, D.C.

Khairullaev, Sherali Khairullaevich (Major General). Born 1949: Tajik. State University of Tajikistan (1970). Served as police officer, USSR MVD; 1977–88: held responsible positions in Tajikistan MVD; 1980–April 1995: deputy internal affairs minister, Tajikistan; 7 April 1995: defense minister, Tajikistan. *Source: Krasnaia zvezda,* 4 May 1995, 3.

Kharchenko, Dmitrii Konstantinovich (Colonel General). Born 1947: Russian. Ordzhonikidze Radio-Technical School of Air Defense; Zhukov Air Defense Command Academy (1977); General Staff Academy (1990). Since 1965 served with various PVO units and group of Soviet military specialists in Egypt. 1990: division commander; August 1992: chief of international treaty directorate at Ministry of Defense regarding CFE, START, and CW agreements; January 1995: also deputy chief of General Staff. Daughter married to Sergei Grachëv, son of the defense minister. *Sources: Komsomol'skaia pravda,* 12 May 1994, 1; *Krasnaia zvezda,* 12 July 1995, 3.

Kharnikov, Viacheslav Timofeevich (Vice Admiral). Born 1945: Russian. Black Sea Higher Naval School (1962); Naval Academy; General Staff Academy. 1990: joined Pacific Fleet; August 1993: CO, Kamchatka Flotilla. *Source: Krasnaia zvezda,* 18 October 1994, 2.

Khmel'nov, Igor' Nikolaevich (Admiral). Born 1949: Russian. Pacific Higher Naval School (1969); higher specialized course for officers (1973); Naval Academy (1981). 1981–87: commands in Northern Fleet; 1993: first deputy CO, Pacific Fleet; August 1994: CO, Pacific Fleet. *Source: Morskoi sbornik,* no. 8 (August 1994): 28.

Kobets, Konstantin Ivanovich (General of the Army). Born 1939: Russian. Kiev Military Communications School (1959); Budënnyi Communications Academy (1967); General Staff Academy (1978). Doctor of military science; Hero of the Soviet Union (1982). 1986: participated in clean-up of Chernobyl; 1987: oversaw restoration of communications in earthquake-devastated regions of Armenia. 1987–91: chief of Signal Troops and deputy chief of General Staff; 1991: chairman, RSFSR committee on defense and security; chairman, military reform committee; 1991: organized defense of White House; promoted to General of the Army by Gorbachëv in August 1991; August–September 1991: acting defense minister. 1991: head of commission to investigate role of military during August coup; 1992: briefly at SNG headquarters; chief military inspector of armed forces; 1993: deputy defense minister. *Source: Krasnaia zvezda,* 4 June 1993, 1.

Kokoshin, Anatolii Afanas'evich (civilian). Born 1945: Russian. Bauman Higher Technical School (1969); USA and Canada Institute (1972); candidate of sciences (1973); doctorate in history (1982); professor (1987); member, Russian Academy of Sciences. Reserve commission, although never served; son of an officer. 1989: dealt with arms control treaties as deputy director for disarmament and conversion at USA and Canada Institute; deputy chairman, Committee of Soviet Scientists in Defense of Peace. 3 April 1992: first deputy minister of defense. *Source:* Vasilevskii and Pribylovskii, *Kto est' kto v rossiiskoi politike,* 2:284–85.

Kolesnikov, Mikhail Pëtrovich (General of the Army). Born 1939: Russian. Omsk Tank Technical School (1959); Malinovskii Academy of Armored Troops (1975); General Staff Academy (1983). 1983–87: CO, army in Trans-Caucasus MD (Armenia); 1987: chief of staff and first deputy CO, Siberian MD; 1988: chief of staff and first deputy commander-in-chief, Southern Theater of Operations (HQ, Baku, Azerbaijan); 1989: briefly commanded "Baku special region"; 1990: chief of main staff, first deputy commander-in-chief, Ground Forces; 1991: deputy chief of General Staff, chief of organization and mobilization directorate; 1992: same position in SNG; 1992: first deputy defense minister and chief of General Staff; promoted to general of the army on 7 May 1995. *Source:* Gazukin, *Voruzhënnye sily Rossiiskoi Federatsii,* 38–39.

Komoedov, Vladimir Pëtrovich (Vice Admiral). Born c. 1952: Russian. Naval Academy; General Staff Academy. Successively commanded a ship; chief of staff and CO, surface division; chief of staff and CO, Baltiisk naval base in Kaliningrad *oblast',* which includes warships and coastal defense. *Sources: Morskoi sbornik,* no. 11 (November 1992): 17; *Krasnaia zvezda,* 22 July 1995, 3.

Kondrat'ev, Georgii Grigorevich (Colonel General). Born 1944: Russian. Kharkov Guards Tank Command School (1965); Malinovskii Academy of Armored Troops (1973); General Staff Academy (1985). 1986–88: first deputy CO of 40th Army in Afghanistan; 1989: first deputy CO and (1991) CO, Turkestan MD; 1992: CO, peacekeeping forces, South Ossetiia; 1993: CO, same in Abkhazia; 1992–95: deputy defense minister. 1995: chief MChS military expert. *Source: Izvestiia,* 4 October 1995, 1.

Kopylov, Viktor Andreevich (Colonel General). Born 1940: Russian. Kharkov Guards Tank School; Malinovskii Armored Troops Military Academy (1970); General Staff Academy (1979). Commanded tank platoon and company. 1970: CO, tank battalion, then chief of staff and first deputy CO of tank regiment, regiment CO, deputy division CO; 1979–83: CO, tank division; 1983–88: chief of staff and deputy CO of a tank army; 1985–88: CO of a tank army; 1988: first deputy CO, Central Asian MD; 1988–91, directed Soviet military advisors in Syria; August 1991: CO, Siberian MD. *Sources: Krasnaia zvezda,* 6 September 1991; 7 July 1992, 1.

Kulikov, Anatolii Sergeevich (Army General). Born 1946: Russian. Ordzhonikidze Higher Military School of MVD (1966); Frunze Military Academy (1974); General Staff Academy (1990). Command posts in MVD. 1993: deputy interior minister; CO, Internal Troops Directorate; October 1993: CO, Moscow Emergency District; March–July 1995: CO, Joint Command, Federal Group of Forces in Chechnya; July 1995: minister of internal affairs. *Sources: Krasnaia zvezda,* 30 December 1992, 1; *Izvestiia,* 8 July 1995, 1; *Krasnaia zvezda,* 10 November 1995, 1.

Kuz'min, Fëdor Mikhailovich (Colonel General). Born 1937: Russian. Leningrad Higher Combined Arms Command School; Frunze Military Academy; General Staff Academy. 1986–89: first deputy CO, Leningrad MD; 1989–91: CO, Baltic States MD; 1991: relieved briefly after August coup; 1991: first deputy commander-in-chief, Far Eastern Theater (TVD); July 1992– : commandant, Frunze Academy. *Sources: Kommunist Vooruzhënnykh sil,* no. 10 (May 1989): 13; *Krasnaia zvezda,* 13 July 1994, 2.

Kuznetsov, Leontii Vasil'evich (Colonel General). Born 1938: Russian. Leningrad Higher Combined Arms Command School; Frunze Military Academy (1974); General Staff Academy (1981). Held command and staff positions, from platoon to army. 1988–90: chief of staff and first deputy CO, Moscow MD; 1990–92: chief of staff and first deputy commander-in-chief, Western Group of Forces (Germany); 1992: chief of main operational directorate, SNG General Staff; July 1992: appointed CO, Moscow MD. *Source:* Gazukin, *Voruzhënnye sily Rossiiskoi Federatsii,* 40.

Kvashnin, Anatolii Vasil'evich (Colonel General). Born 1946: Russian. Malinovskii Armored Troops Academy; General Staff Academy. Served from deputy CO of tank company to first deputy CO of tank army. 1992–95: deputy and first deputy chief of General Staff operations directorate; December 1994: CO for military operations in Chechnya; February 1995: CO, North Caucasus MD. *Sources: Krasnaia zvezda,* 21 June 1995, 2; *Orientir,* no. 6 (June 1995): 26.

Lebed', Aleksandr Ivanovich (Lieutenant General). Born 1950: Russian. Riazan Airborne Command School (1973); Frunze Military Academy (1985). 1981–82: CO, airborne battalion in Afghanistan; 1985: CO, Tula Airborne Division (helped defend White House in August 1991); 1991–92: deputy CO, Airborne Troops; 1992: CO, 14th Army in "Trans-Dniester Republic" of Moldova. Submitted resignation and transferred to reserves 15 June 1995. *Sources:* Vasilevskii and Pribylovski, *Kto est' kto v rossiiskoi politike,* 2:326–27; *Krasnaia zvezda,* 16 June 1995, 1.

Lobov, Vladimir Nikolaevich (General of the Army). Born 1935: Russian. Frunze Military Academy (1968); General Staff Academy (1978); professor and doctor of military sciences (1987). 1981: first deputy CO, Leningrad MD; 1984: CO, Central Asian MD; 1987: first deputy chief of General Staff and chief of main operations directorate; 1987–91: CO, Combined WTO Armed Forces and first deputy chief of General Staff, USSR Armed Forces. Refused to command Moscow region during August 1991 coup; 1991–92: three months as chief of General Staff; 1992: transferred to commandant of Frunze Academy for two months. Retired. 1993: head of "Military Security and Defense" section in Academy of Natural Sciences. *Source:* Krotov and Tsyganov, *Voennye Rossii,* 66–69.

Makashov, Al'bert Mikhailovich (Colonel General). Born 1938: Russian. Tashkent Higher Combined Arms Command School (1960); Frunze Military Academy; General Staff Academy. 1988: served in region of Armenia devastated by earthquake; military commandant of Yerevan, Armenia, for NKAO conflict; 1989: CO, Ural MD; 1989–91: CO, Volga-Ural MD. June 1991: as candidate for president of Russia, received less than 4% of vote. August 1991: active supporter of GKChP; "retired" seven years early. October 1993: led attack on Ostankino television station with c. 100 men; arrested; 1994: amnestied. *Source:* Vasilevskii and Pribylovskii, *Kto est' kto v rossiiskoi politike,* 2:350–52.

Mal'tsev, Leonid Semënovich (Lieutenant General). Born 1949: Belarusian. Suvorov Academy, Minsk (1967); Higher Combined Arms Command School, Kiev (1967–71); Frunze Military Academy (1976–79); General Staff Academy (1990–92). CO, platoon through army corps. 1994: chief of General Staff and first deputy defense minister; 11 October 1995: minister of defense, Belarus. *Source:* American Embassy, Minsk.

Mironov, Valerii Ivanovich (Colonel General). Born 1943: Russian. Moscow Higher Combined Arms Command School (1965); Frunze Military Academy (1973); General Staff Academy (1984). 1979–82: as CO, 108th Motorized Rifle Division, led first troops into Afghanistan; 1984–89: deputy CO of army, Western Group of Forces (Germany); 1989–91: first deputy CO, Leningrad MD; 1991: CO, Northwestern Group of Forces (Baltic States); 1992–94: deputy defense minister (for personnel training and placement); January 1995: suspended; April 1995: reassigned as chief military adviser to prime minister. *Sources: Krasnaia zvezda,* 10 June 1992; *Izvestiia,* 4 October 1995, 1.

Miruk, Viktor Fëdorovich (Colonel General). Born 1941: Russian. Yaroslav School of Air Defense Forces (1963); Zhukov Air Defense Academy for Commanders (1975); General Staff Academy (1987). Candidate in military science. Pre-August 1991: CO, Air Defense Army and deputy CO for Leningrad MD; after August 1991: first deputy commander-in-chief, Air Defense Troops. *Source: Military News Bulletin,* no. 5 (May 1993): sec. 2, p. 1.

Mitiukhin, Aleksei Nikolaevich (Colonel General). Born 1945: Russian. Omsk Technical Tank School; Malinovskii Tank Troops Academy (1974); General Staff Academy (1986). Commanded a regiment, division, corps, and army. 1991: first deputy commander-in-chief, Western Group of Forces (Germany); July 1993–December 1994: CO, Northern Caucasus MD. *Source:* Gazukin, *Voruzhënnye sily Rossiiskoi Federatsii,* 42.

Moiseev, Mikhail Alekseevich (General of the Army). Born 1939: Russian. Far Eastern Tank Academy (1962); Frunze Military Academy (1972); General Staff Academy (1982). 1987: CO, Far East MD. December 1988: chief of General Staff and first deputy minister of defense; 21 August 1991: appointed post-coup minister of defense; replaced after one day; November 1991: retired; 1992: at Center for Military-Strategic Research of General Staff. *Sources: Krasnaia zvezda,* 3 December 1992 and 29 October 1994.

Nadibaidze, Vardiko Mikhailovich (Lieutenant General). Born 1939: Georgian. Ordzhonikidze School for Working Youth (1958), Riazan Military Automobile School (1961); Military Supply and Transport Academy (1972). Served from platoon leader to deputy CO for armaments, Trans-Baikal MD. 27 April 1994: defense minister, Georgia. *Source: Krasnaia zvezda,* 4 May 1995, 2.

Nikolaev, Andrei Ivanovich (Army General). Born 1949: Russian. Moscow Higher Combined Arms Command School (1971); Frunze Military Academy (1976); General Staff Academy (1988). 1982–86: chief of staff and then CO, motorized rifle training division in Ural MD; 1988: chief of staff and then army CO; 1990–92: CO, 11th Guards Army (Baltic States MD); June 1992: first deputy chief, main operations directorate of General Staff; December 1992: first deputy chief of General Staff; 1993: deputy minister of internal affairs and CO, border guards; 1994: director, Federal Border Guards Service. *Source: Izvestiia,* 7 October 1995, 5.

Nurmagambetov, Sagadat Kozhakhmetovich (Lieutenant General). Born 1924: Kazakh. Fought in World War II with troops capturing Berlin. Hero of the Soviet Union (27 February 1945) for battle along Vistula River. Frunze Military Academy (1949). Served in various command posts; 1961–89: deputy CO, Central Asian MD and then first deputy CO, Southern Group of Forces (Hungary); 1989: chairman, Council of War Veterans; December 1991: chairman, State Committee for Defense Affairs; 7 May 1992: minister of defense, Kazakhstan. 16 October 1995: advisor to the president. *Source: Krasnaia zvezda,* 4 May 1995, 2.

Patrikeev, Valerii Anisimovich (Colonel General). Born 1938: Russian. Frunze Military Academy (1967); General Staff Academy (1977). 1985–89: CO, Volga MD; 1989–92: CO, Trans-Caucasus MD; 1992–94: at disposal of commander-in-chief, Ground Forces; 1994–95: CO, joint peacekeeping forces of SNG in Tajikistan; 1995: general inspector attached to Main Military Inspectorate. *Sources: Moskovskie novosti,* no. 14 (5 April 1992): 19; *Krasnaia zvezda,* 22 April 1995, 1.

Petrov, Stanislav Veniaminovich (Colonel General). Born 1939: Russian. Saratov Chemical School (1959); Chemical Defense Academy (1971); General Staff Academy (1980). 1980–86: CO, chemical troops for Siberia and Belorussian MDs, first deputy and chief of chemical troops for Western Group of Forces (Germany); 1986: first deputy chief and (1989) chief of radiation, chemical, and biological protection troops. *Source: Voennyi vestnik,* no. 1 (January 1992): 12.

P'iankov, Boris Evgenevich (Colonel General). Born 1935: Russian. Far

East Tank School (1959); Armored Academy (1969); General Staff Academy (1979); served in Afghanistan. 1960–65: with Strategic Missile Forces; 1986: first deputy CO, Odessa MD; 1987: CO, Siberia MD; 1991–92: chief of civil defense and deputy minister of defense; 1992: deputy commander-in-chief of SNG; 1992–94: CO, joint SNG peacekeeping troops in Tajikistan; 1994: first deputy chief of staff for coordinating military cooperation in SNG. *Source: Krasnaia zvezda,* 10 November 1993, 1.

Podkolzin, Evgenii Nikolaevich (Colonel General). Born 1936: Russian. Alma-Ata Airborne Service School (1958); Frunze Military Academy (1973); General Staff Academy (1982). 1976: CO, Guards Airborne Division; 1982: first deputy chief of staff, Airborne Troops; 1986: chief of staff and first deputy CO, Airborne Troops; August 1991: CO, Airborne Troops. *Source: Krasnaia zvezda,* 7 December 1995, 2.

Prudnikov, Viktor Alekseievich (Colonel General). Born 1939: Russian. Armavir Flying School (1959); Gagarin Air Force Academy (1967); General Staff Academy (1981). 1975: CO, air defense division; 1978: first deputy CO, independent air defense army; 1983: CO, air defense army; 1989–91: CO, Moscow Air Defense District; 31 August 1991: commander-in-chief, Air Defense Troops. *Source: Armiia,* no. 24 (December 1991): 7–11.

Rodionov, Igor' Nikolaevich (Colonel General). Born 1936: Russian. Orël Tank Academy (1957); Malinovskii Armored Troops Academy (1970); General Staff Academy (1980). 1980: CO, army corps and then of an army; 1986: CO, Soviet forces in Afghanistan; 1987: first deputy CO, Moscow MD; 1988: CO, Trans-Caucasus MD; 1989: commandant, General Staff Academy. *Sources: Armiia,* no. 22 (November 1991): 20; *Orientir,* no. 7 (July 1995): 3.

Romanov, Anatolii Aleksandrovich (Lieutenant General). Born 1948: Russian. Saratov Military Command School (1972); Higher Command School; General Staff Academy (1991). CO, platoon through army corps. 1993: deputy CO, internal troops. 1994–95: led one of three main assault formations in Chechnya and, as deputy, supported commander of all Russian forces. 19 July 1995: CO, internal troops and deputy ministry of interior (MVD). *Source: Krasnaia zvezda,* 10 October 1995, 1–2.

Rutskoi, Aleksandr Vladimirovich (Major General). Born 1947: Russian. Gagarin Air Force Academy; General Staff Academy (1990). Two tours of duty in Afghanistan (1985–86, 1988), flew 428 combat missions as helicopter pilot. Deputy CO, 40th army air troops, during second tour. Hero of the Soviet Union. June 1991: elected vice-president of Russia; supervised defense of White House during August 1991 coup; 1993: "acting president" of Russia in October mutiny; arrested; 1994: amnestied. *Source:* Krotov and Tsyganov, *Voennye Rossii,* 91–100.

Samsonov, Viktor Nikolaievich (Colonel General). Born 1941: Russian. Pacific Higher Combined Arms Command School (1962); Frunze Military Academy (1972); General Staff Academy (1981). 1985: CO, 7th Army in Armenia; 1987: deputy CO, Trans-Caucasus MD; 1988: commandant of Yerevan after earthquake; 1988–90: chief of staff, Trans-Caucasus MD; 1990: CO, Leningrad MD; 1991: during coup, appointed military commandant of Leningrad city but refused to deploy troops. December 1991: chief of General Staff; 1992: transferred to SNG as chief of staff for coordination. *Source:* Krotov and Tsyganov, *Voennye Rossii,* 101–2.

Seleznëv, Sergei Pavlovich (Colonel General). Born 1944: Russian. Odessa Combined Arms Command School; Frunze Military Academy; General Staff Academy. 1974–78: deputy CO, motorized rifle regiment; 1978–85: CO, regiment, then deputy CO and CO, Pacific motorized rifle division; 1985–89: deputy CO of army; 1989–91, CO of army; 1991: chief of staff and first deputy CO, Leningrad MD. *Source: Krasnaia zvezda,* 13 December 1991, 1.

Selivanov, Valentin Egorovich (Admiral). Born 1936: Russian. Higher Naval School (1958); Higher Naval Course for Officers (1965); Naval Academy (1971). CO, brigade and then division of surface warships; 1985: chief of staff and first deputy CO, Black Sea Fleet; 1989: CO, Leningrad Naval Base; October 1991: chief of Main Staff and first deputy commander-in-chief of Navy. *Source: Military News Bulletin,* no. 7 (July 1993): 1–3.

Semënov, Vladimir Magomedovich (Colonel General). Born 1940: Karachaivets. Baku Higher Combined Arms Command School (1962); Frunze Military Academy (1970); General Staff Academy (1979). 1988–91: CO, Trans-Baikal MD. 1991: replaced Varennikov as commander-in-chief of Ground Troops; 1992: CO, General Purpose Forces, SNG. *Sources: Krasnaia zvezda,* 28 April 1993, 1; *Orientir,* no. 4 (October 1994): 27–30.

Sergeev, Anatolii Ipatovich (Colonel General). Born 1940: Russian. Far East Tank Service School (1963); Malinovskii Armored Troops Academy (1973); General Staff Academy (1982). Commanded platoon through army; 1983–86: chief of staff and first deputy CO, 40th Army in Afghanistan; 1986: CO, army in Odessa MD; 1988: chief of staff and first deputy CO, Odessa MD; 1991: CO, Volga-Ural MD; July 1992: CO, Volga MD. *Sources: Military News Bulletin,* no. 4 (April 1994): 5; *Armeiskii sbornik,* no. 2 (August 1994): 2–5.

Sergeev, Igor' Dmitrievich (Colonel General). Born 1938: Russian. Nakhimov Black Sea Higher Naval School (1960); Dzerzhinskii Military Engineering Academy Command Faculty (1973); General Staff Academy (1980). 1960: various engineering command positions in Strategic Missile Forces; 1980: chief of staff and then CO of missile army; 1983: chief of operations, deputy chief of Strategic Missile Forces main staff; 1989: deputy CO for combat training of Strategic Missile Forces; January 1992: deputy commander-in-chief, Strategic Missile Forces, SNG; August 1992: commander-in-chief, Strategic Missile Forces. *Source: Krasnaia zvezda,* 25 August 1992, 1.

Shaposhnikov, Evgenii Ivanovich (Air Marshal). Born 1942: Russian. Kharkov Higher Aviation School (1963); Gagarin Air Force Academy (1969); General Staff Academy (1984). 1987–88: CO, aviation for Western Group of Forces (Germany); 1988–90: CO, air army; first deputy commander-in-chief, Soviet Air Forces. 1990–91: commander-in-chief, Air Forces and deputy minister of defense. 23 August 1991: appointed USSR Minister of Defense; 1992: commander-in-chief, SNG Joint Armed Forces; 1993: appointed secretary of Security Council; 1994: presidential representative to *Rosvooruzhenie;* 1995: Aeroflot chief. *Source:* Vasilevskii and Pribylovskii, *Kto est' kto v rossiiskoi politike,* 3:623–24.

Shmarov, Valerii Nikolaevich (civilian). Born 1945: Ukrainian. Kiev Radio-Electronics Technical School (1966); Shevchenko State University (1972). Twenty years at Kiev *Radio-zavod* as engineer, head of laboratory, and factory manager; 1987: director, defense industry plant; 1992: first deputy director-general of Ukraine's national space agency; June 1993: first deputy prime minister for military-industrial complex; 28 August 1994: also defense minister, Ukraine. *Source: Krasnaia zvezda,* 4 May 1995, 3.

Skuratov, Ivan Sidorovich (Colonel General). Born 1940: Russian. Black Sea Higher Naval School (1964); Naval Academy (1974); General Staff Academy (1987). Military service with Black Sea, Pacific Ocean, and Baltic Sea fleets. CO, coastal defense troops for Baltic Fleet; September 1992: CO, coastal troops of Navy. Doctorate degree in military science; member, International Academy of Information Sciences and Russian Academy of Military Science. *Source: Krasnaia zvezda,* 17 May 1995, 2.

Solomatin, Anatolii Vasil'evich (Colonel General). Born 1939: Russian. Pushkino Military Construction and Technical School (1962); Leningrad Higher Military Engineering and Technical School (1969). 1987: chief, Air Defense Forces main engineering directorate; 1991–93: deputy chief and (1993) chief of construction and billeting; January

1995: deputy defense minister and chief of construction and billeting. *Source: Krasnaia zvezda,* 21 January 1995, 1.

Subanov, Murzakan Usurkanovich (Lieutenant General). Born 1944: Kyrgyz. Tashkent Higher Combined Arms Command School (1966); Frunze Military Academy (1977); General Staff Academy (1984). CO, platoon to corps. Served in Afghanistan. 1991: chief of staff, Turkestan MD; 1991–93: first deputy chairman and chairman, State Committee for Defense Affairs; 17 December 1993: defense minister, Kyrgyzstan. *Source: Krasnaia zvezda,* 4 May 1995, 3.

Toporov, Vladimir Mikhailovich (Colonel General). Born 1946: Russian. Odessa Artillery School (1968); Frunze Military Academy (1975); General Staff Academy (1984). 1968: next twenty years in Airborne Troops; 1987: first deputy CO, army; 1988: CO, army; 1989–91: chief of staff and first deputy CO, Far East MD; September 1991: CO, Moscow MD; 1992: deputy defense minister for troop billeting. *Source: Krasnaia zvezda,* 10 June 1992, 1.

Tret'iakov, Valerii Stepanovich (Colonel General). Born 1941: Russian. Tashkent Higher Combined Arms Command School (1963); Frunze Military Academy (1972); General Staff Academy (1985). Served from platoon to army CO; 1988–91: first deputy CO, Trans-Baikal MD; August 1991: CO, Trans-Baikal MD. *Source: Krasnaia zvezda,* 16 May 1995, 2.

Varennikov, Valentin Ivanovich (General of the Army). Born 1923: Russian. Frunze Military Academy (1954); General Staff Academy (1967). World War II veteran: artillery and intelligence officer. 1973–79: CO, Carpathian MD; 1979: chief of main operations directorate and first deputy chief of General Staff; 1984–89: first deputy chief of General Staff, while serving as head of Operational Group in Afghanistan and supervising withdrawal; 1989–91: commander-in chief, Ground Forces and deputy minister of defense; August 1991: arrested after coup; 1994: refused amnesty and found innocent after trial. Awarded 80 million rubles as compensation. *Sources:* Krotov and Tsyganov, *Voennye Rossii,* 19–20; *Izvestiia,* 21 July 1995, 3.

Volkogonov, Dmitrii Antonovich (Colonel General). Born 1928: Russian. Orlov Tank School (1952); Lenin Military Political Academy (1963); doctorate in history and philosophy; professor. 1964–70: lectured at Lenin Military Political Academy; 1974–87: deputy chief of propaganda directorate, employed by Main Political Administration (MPA) of Soviet Army and Navy; head of administration for special propaganda ("psychological warfare"); 1984: deputy chief of MPA; 1987–90: director,

Institute of Military History at defense ministry academy of sciences and chief editor for multivolume *History of the Great Patriotic War.* May 1991: resigned from the communist party or CPSU. July 1991– : advisor on defense matters to President Yeltsin; 1992: cochairman of Russian-American Commission on POWs. Died, 6 December 1995. *Sources:* Krotov and Tsyganov, *Voennye Rossii,* 21–23; *New York Times,* 7 December 1995, C-19.

Vorob'ëv, Ed'uard Arkad'evich (Colonel General). Born 1938: Russian. Baku Higher Combined Arms School (1961); Frunze Military Academy (1971); General Staff Academy (1981). 1987: CO, Central Group of Forces (Czechoslovakia); 1991–92: deputy commander-in-chief for combat training of Ground Troops; 1992–94: representative for Russian forces in Moldova, Tajikistan; January 1995: as first deputy commander-in-chief of ground troops, transferred to army reserves for refusal to accept command of forces invading Chechnya. *Sources: Kommunist Vooruzhënnykh sil,* no. 10 (May 1989): 6; *Orientir,* no. 3 (September 1994): 22–25.

Vysotskii, Evgenii Vasil'evich (Colonel General). Born 1947: Russian. Tashkent Higher Tank Command School (1970); Frunze Military Academy (1978); General Staff Academy (1988). 1970–77: commanded platoon, company and staff of tank battalion with Southern Group of Forces in Turkmenistan. 1978: CO, motorized regiment, Odessa MD; 1988–89: chief of staff and first deputy CO of army; 1989–91: CO of army in Far East MD; 1991: first deputy CO, Trans-Baikal MD; August 1992: chief of main directorate for cadres and military education at defense ministry. *Source:* Gazukin, *Vooruzhënnye sily Rossiiskoi Federatsii,* 16.

Zherebtsov, Viacheslav Vladimirovich (Colonel General). Born 1947: Russian. Far East Higher Armored Command School (1968); Malinovskii Tank Troops Academy (1979); General Staff Academy (1990). Various command positions. 1993: chief of staff and first deputy CO, Trans-Baikal MD. 30 August 1994: chief of main organizational-mobilization directorate and deputy chief of General Staff. *Source: Orientir,* no. 4 (April 1995): 3.

Zhurbenko, Vladimir Mikhailovich (Colonel General). Born 1939: Russian. Omsk Higher Combined Arms School (1962); Frunze Military Academy (1977); General Staff Academy (1982). 1971: various command positions in Turkestan MD; 1982: deputy chief for operations on staff at Southern Group of Forces (Hungary); 1985: deputy chief, and (1987) chief of operations directorate on staff of the South-Western

TVD; 1989: deputy chief of main operations directorate for General Staff. 24 September 1993: appointed first deputy chief of the General Staff. *Source:* Gazukin, *Voruzhënnye sily Rossiiskoi Federatsii,* 29–30.

Zinin, Boris Mikhailovich (Vice Admiral). Born 1941: Russian. Leningrad Higher Naval School of Engineers (1967); Naval Academy by correspondence (1979). Commenced service in Pacific Fleet, where he became CO of a surface warship division. 1988: chief of staff and first deputy CO for the Caspian Naval Flotilla; 1991: CO of the flotilla. *Source:* Gazukin, *Voruzhënnye sily Rossiiskoi Federatsii,* 30.

Appendix B
Russian Newspapers and Journals

All news publications in Russia were required to reregister after the August 1991 abortive coup. Certain publications, such as *Komsomol'skaia pravda,* retain their original titles for ease of recognition, and not necessarily because they maintain their earlier political outlook.[1]

Monthly or Quarterly Publications

Armeiskii sbornik ("Army Journal"): Moscow, est. 1994. Monthly. Subtitle: "Journal for military professionals." Founded by General Staff of armed forces. More technical than *Armiia*; created as merger of *Armiia, Voennyi vestnik, Aviatsiia i kosmonavtika, Vestnik PVO,* and *Voenno-ekonomicheskii zhurnal.* Copies printed: 12,150.

Armiia ("The Army"): Moscow, 1991–94. Continuation of *Kommunist Vooruzhënnykh sil.* Subsidized by Russian defense ministry. Included articles of technical and popular interest. Merged with *Armeiskii sbornik.*

Aviatsiia i kosmonavtika ("Aviation and Astronautics"): Moscow, 1962–94. Covered civilian as well as military topics; popular information on space program. Considered sophisticated and reliable. Merged with *Armeiskii sbornik.*

Chest' imeiu ("I Have Honor"): Moscow, est. 1993. Superseded *Sovetskii voin.* Published by ministry of defense. Covers popular topics of military interest. Copies printed: 125,075.

Khimiia i zhizn' ("Chemistry and Life"): Moscow, est. 1965. Publication of Soviet/Russian Academy of Sciences. Scientific-popular magazine. Circulation unknown.

Kommunist Vooruzhënnykh sil ("Communist of the Armed Forces"): Moscow, 1960–91. Semimonthly publication of the Soviet army and navy. Provided detailed information on personnel changes in armed forces. Continued by *Armiia* in 1991.

Mezhdunarodnaia zhizn' ("International Life"): Moscow, est. 1954. Monthly journal on problems of world politics, diplomacy, and international relations. Published by ministry of foreign affairs. Continuation of *Biulleten' Narodnogo Komissariata Inostrannykh Del*. English language edition titled *International Affairs*. United Nations documents and articles by foreign authors routinely published. Copies printed: 71,620.

Mirovaia ekonomika i mezhdunarodnye otnoshenia ("World Economics and International Relations"): Moscow, est. 1957. Monthly publication of Soviet/Russian Academy of Sciences. Special issues. Copies printed: 26,000.

Morskoi sbornik ("Naval Journal"): Moscow, est. 1848 (*sic*). Monthly. Publication of Russian navy. Targets wide range of readers; covers current and historical events, technical matters, foreign navies. Circulation unknown.

Na boevom postu ("At the Battle Station"): Moscow, est. 1958. Subtitle: "Monthly military-journalistic and literary-artistic magazine of interior troops"; supplemented by newspaper *Situatsiia* ("Situation") and magazine of "scholarly-methodological materials," *Boevoi vestnik* ("Battle Herald"). Copies printed: 7,500.

Obozrevatel' ("The Reviewer"): Moscow, est. 1992. "Journal of problems, analyses, prognoses." Published by Russian-American University Corporation. English language summary. Copies printed: c. 500.

Orientir ("Reference Point"): Moscow, est. June 1994. Monthly journal of the defense ministry. Replaced *Armiia, Argument,* and *Sobesednik voina* ("Soldier's Companion"). Copies printed: 15,391.

Rodina ("Motherland"): Moscow, est. 1989. Monthly. Subtitle: "Russian historical journal." Popular appeal, with illustrations. Government-subsidized. Copies printed: 90,000.

Rossiiskaia Federatsiia ("Russian Federation"): Moscow, est. 1994. Semimonthly. Subtitle: "Socio-political journal" which targets a popular readership. Publisher: Russian government. Copies printed: 50,000.

SShA: ekonomika, politika, ideologiia ("USA: Economics, Politics, Ideology"): Moscow, est. 1970. Social science magazine; published by

Institute of USA and Canada, Soviet/Russian Academy of Sciences. Copies printed: 9,998.

Sluzhba bezopasnosti ("Security Service"): Moscow, est. 1993. Semimonthly. Subtitle: "News of intelligence and counterintelligence." Targets popular audience. Published through FSB. Copies printed: 10,000.

TV-Tekhnika i vooruzhenie ("Equipment and Armaments"): Moscow. Monthly scientific and technical journal. Color-illustrated. Published by ministry of defense. Discontinued in 1994.

Vestnik granitsy ("Border Herald"): Moscow, 1988–94. Subtitle: "Monthly journal of border troops." Popular publication, included articles on ecology and culture, as well as border concerns.

Voennaia mysl' ("Military Thought"): Moscow, est. 1918. Subtitle: "Monthly military-theoretical journal." Organ of defense ministry. Sophisticated treatment of military topics. Copies printed: 5,000.

Voenno-ekonomicheskii zhurnal ("Military-Economic Journal"): Moscow, 1989–95. Continued *Tyl Vooruzhënnykh sil* ("Supply of the Armed Forces"). Published by ministry of defense. Merged with *Armeiskii sbornik* in 1995. Copies printed: 11,875.

Voenno-istoricheskii zhurnal ("Military History Journal"): Moscow, est. 1939. Semimonthly. Scholarly articles and documents on a variety of historical and contemporary subjects; publication of General Staff. Copies printed: 12,500.

Voennyi vestnik ("Military Herald"): Moscow, est. 1921. All-service monthly publication; popular and technical articles. Merged with *Armeiskii sbornik* in 1995.

Weeklies

Argumenty i fakty ("Arguments and Facts"): Moscow, est. 1992. Targets urban population. Rated no. 1 among weekly papers, according to *Nezavisimaia gazeta* in November 1992. Independent, democratic publication. Copies printed: 3.2 million.

Literaturnaia gazeta ("Literary Newspaper"): Moscow, est. 1929. Liberal newspaper, targets politicized sector of society; covers wide range of cultural subjects. Copies printed: 280,000.

Megapolis-ekspress: Moscow, est. 1990. International weekly newspaper. Similar in style to *Kommersant*. Business as well as social issues covered. Reviewed as universal, democratic, and neoconservative publication. Copies printed: 400,000.

Moskovskie novosti ("Moscow News"): Moscow, est. 1930. Independent since 1990. Rated second in overall quality of weekly papers. Antiestablishment. Linked with leaders of Democratic Reform and Democratic Russia parties until 1993. English language version, *Moscow News*. Copies printed: 161,367.

Novoe vremia ("New Times"): Moscow, est. 1943. For politicians, businessmen, journalists, and those in academia. Reputation for investigative reporting; covers national and international events in sophisticated way. Similar in scope to many Western news weeklies. English-language edition *New Times*. Copies printed: 25,000.

Ogonëk ("Little Flame"): Moscow, est. 1899. Similar to German popular magazine *Bunte Illustrierte*, which subsidizes *Ogonëk*. Copies printed: 100,000.

Rossiia ("Russia"): Moscow, est. 1990. Originally democratic orientation; more conservative stance after October 1993. Known for "fair" interviews with government officials. Popularity diminished in recent times. Copies printed: 76,200.

Rossiiskie vesti ("Russian News"): Moscow, est. 1991. Three times per week. Considered more informative and of higher quality than other government papers, *Rossiiskaia gazeta* and *Rossiia*. Special supplement, *Reformy* ("Reforms"), also carries decrees and other public announcements. Copies printed: 130,000.

Dailies

Delovoi mir ("Business World"): Moscow, est. 1991. Six times per week. Targets managers and engineer/managers; extensive advertising. Supplement: *Rynok* ("The Market"). Subtitle: "Daily newspaper of Commonwealth of Independent States (SNG)." Copies printed: 76,000.

Izvestiia ("News"): Moscow, est. 1917. Six times per week. Until August 1991, official organ of government; today, solid information network with general democratic orientation. Circulation dropped by one million after beginning of 1992. Supplement *Finansovye izvestiia* ("Financial News") appears once or twice a week. Copies printed: 604,765.

Kommersant-Daily ("Businessman's Daily"): Moscow, est. 1990. Targets young Russians—wealthy, intellectual part of society involved in business. Known for interesting interviews. Copies printed: 104,400.

Komsomol'skaia pravda ("Young Communist League Truth"): Moscow, est. 1925. Five times per week. Change in editorship led to less orientation toward youth and radicalism. Name retained for purposes of identification, not ideology. Copies printed: 1,547,000.

Krasnaia zvezda ("Red Star"): Moscow, est. 1924. Five times per week. Central organ of the defense ministry; conservative stance, covers mostly military news. Source for information on personnel changes in armed forces. Copies printed: 107,350.

Moskovskii komsomol'ets ("Moscow Young Communist League Member"): Moscow, est. 1919. Five times per week. Targets youth; easy reading and informative. Rated no. 1 in quality by *Nezavisimaia gazeta* poll in November 1992. Criticizes opposition and youthful dissipation. Subtitle: "Socio-political youth newspaper." Copies printed: 857,502.

Moskovskaia pravda ("Moscow Truth"): Moscow, est. 1918. Five times per week. Draws from a variety of news services. Copies printed: 377,000.

Nezavisimaia gazeta ("Independent Newspaper"): Moscow, est. 1990. Five times per week. Treatment of social topics straightforward. Never subsidized by government. Supplement: *Nezavisimoe voennoe obozrenie* ("Independent Military Review"). Copies printed: 50,000. Last issue appeared on 24 May 1995; resumed 3 October 1995 with help of *Obedinennyi bank.*

Pravda ("Truth"): Moscow, est. 1912. Six times per week. Now seen as slightly eccentric: unusual slant on international events. Continues to purvey the communist world outlook. In opposition to direction of current government. Copies printed: dropped from over one million to 165,000.

Rabochaia tribuna ("Labor Tribune"): Moscow, est. 1990. Five times per week. Similar to newspaper *Trud* in targeting interests of workers. Subtitle: "Social partnership and social defense." Previously progovernment; by 1994, more conservative editorial position. Supplement: *Promyshlennyi vestnik* ("Industry Herald"). Copies printed: 175,000.

Rossiiskaia gazeta ("The Russian Newspaper"): Moscow, est. 1990. Five times per week. Official documents and interviews with leaders. More progovernment than *Rossiiskie vesti,* although official editorial stance not well defined. Copies printed: 500,500.

Segodnia ("Today"): Moscow, est. 1993. Daily political and business paper, which includes television listings, articles on weather, art, fashion. Alleged FSB connection to paper's financial backing. Copies printed: 100,000.

Sovetskaia Rossiia ("Soviet Russia"): Moscow, 1956. Subtitle: "Independent national newspaper." Reflects both communist and nationalist viewpoints. Copies printed: 250,000.

Trud ("Labor"), Moscow; est. 1921. Subtitle: "Newspaper of professional [trade] unions." Rated as number 2 among daily newspapers by *Nezavisimaia gazeta* in November 1992; quality seen as diminished since that time. Copies printed: 1,215,000.

Note: Only 216 of the approximately 10,000 publications received government subsidies during 1994. The State *Duma* reduced these funds from 237 billion down to 89 billion rubles for 1995, specifying that only *Rossiiskie vesti, Rodina,* and *Rossiiskaia Federatsiia* would be supported. The rest would subsidize publications for the blind, children, and other social categories. Natalia Arkhangel'skaia, "Ekonomika i politika," *Kommersant-Daily,* 24 March 1995, 3. Of the 23,000 newspapers that had been established since 1991, only about 10,000 existed four years later. "Vsled za 'Kurantami' gazety budut ostanavlivat'sia eshchë i eshchë," *Moskovskaia pravda,* 7 June 1995, 1.

Notes

1. Sources for this appendix include: L. Alenicheva and A. Suetnov, eds., *Gazety Rossii, Moskovskie izdaniia* (Moscow: Arkhiv netraditsionnoi pechati, 1992), 55 pp.; "Periodicheskie izdania," *Novoe vremia,* no. 35 (September 1994): 94; Natal'ia Zhelnorova's interview with Vsevolod Bogdanov, chairman of Russian Journalists' Union, in *Argumenty i fakty,* no. 17 (April 1995): 8. Most figures for copies printed are from "Pre-election Survey of Major Russian Media," FBIS-SOV-95-223-S (5 December 1995), 20 pp.

Bibliography

Primary Sources

Anikin, V. I. *Konversiia: problemy, teoriia, metodologiia.* Moscow: Diplomaticheskaia Akademiia MID, 1993. 303 pp.

Bakatin, Vadim V. *Izbavlenie ot KGB.* Moscow: Novosti, 1992. 267 pp.

Batalden, Stephen K., and Sandra L. Batalden. *The Newly Independent States of Eurasia: Handbook of Former Soviet Republics.* Phoenix: Oryx Press, 1993. 205 pp.

Bekmurzaev, Bekmurza A. *Vooruzhënnye konflikty v SNG i mirotvorcheskaia deiatel'nost' Rossii.* Moscow: Diplomaticheskaia Akademiia MID, 1994. 32 pp.

Belanovskii, S. A., and S. N. Marzeeva, comps. *Dedovshchina v armii.* Moscow: Institut narodno-khoziastvennogo prognozirovaniia, 1991. 215 pp.

Belousova, Galina A., and Vladimir A. Lebedev. *Partokratiia i putch.* Moscow: "Respublika," 1992. 48 pp.

Bogoliubov, Ieroskhimonakh Moisei, N. A. Bulgakov, and A. A. Iakovlev-Kozyrev. *Pravoslavie, armiia, derzhava.* Moscow: Russkii vestnik, 1993. 111 pp.

Boldin, Valery. *Ten Years That Shook the World.* Trans. Evelyn Rossiter. New York: Basic Books, 1994. 310 pp.

Burns, Richard Dean, ed. *Encyclopedia of Arms Control and Disarmament.* New York: Scribner's, 1993. 3 vols.

Buzzalin, Aleksandr, and Andrei Kolganov. *Krovavyi oktiabr' v Moskve.* 2nd rev. ed. Moscow: "Erebus," 1994. 177 pp.

Chernomys, V. A., ed. *Svod voennykh zakonov Rossiiskoi Federatsii.* Moscow: Voennoe izdatel'stvo, 1993. 192 pp.

El'tsin, Boris N. *Zapiski prezidenta.* Moscow: "Ogonëk," 1994. 416 pp.
Gaidar, Egor T. *Gosudarstvo i evoliutsiia.* Moscow: "Evraziia," 1995. 208 pp.
Gareev, Makhmut A. *Esli zavtra voina?* Moscow: VlaDar, 1995. 239 pp.
Gazukin, Pavel, comp. *Vooruzhënnye sily Rossiiskoi Federatsii: biograficheskoi spravochnik.* 2d rev. ed. Moscow: Panorama, 1995. 81 pp.
Grimmett, Richard F. *Conventional Arms Transfers to Developing Nations, 1987–1994.* Washington, D.C.: Congressional Research Service at the Library of Congress, 4 August 1995. 92 pp.
Gromov, Boris V. *Ogranichënnyi kontingent.* Moscow: Progress, 1994. 352 pp.
Gul'binskii, Nikolai, and Marina Shakina. *Afganistan...Kreml'...Lefortovo....* Moscow: "Lada-M," 1994. 352 pp.
Iakovlev, Nikolai N. *Zhukov.* Moscow: "Molodaia gvardiia," 1992. 464 pp.
International Institute for Strategic Studies. *The Military Balance, 1995–1996.* Oxford: Oxford University Press, October 1995. 322 pp.
Ivashov, Leonid G. *Marshal Iazov: Rokovoi avgust 91-go.* Moscow: "Muzhestvo," 1992. 112 pp.
Jones, David R., ed. *The Military Encyclopedia of Russia and Eurasia.* Vol. 20. Gulf Breeze, Fla.: Academic International Press, 1995. 430 pp.
Karasik, Theodore W., ed. *Russia and Eurasia: Facts and Figures Annual.* Vol. 20. Gulf Breeze, Fla.: Academic International Press, 1995. 439 pp.
Karpenko, A. V., and I. A. Povarenkov, eds. *Rossiiskoe raketnoe oruzhie, 1943–1993.* 2nd rev. ed. St. Petersburg: "PIKA," 1993. 180 pp.
Khasbulatov, Ruslan I. *Chechnia: mne ne dali ostanovit' voinu.* Moscow: Paleia, 1995. 80 pp.
Kotenev, Aleksandr. *Neokonchennaia voina.* Moscow: Soiuz veteranov Afganistana, 1994. 159 pp.
Kozhokin, Evgenii M., ed. *Ukraina: vektor peremen.* Moscow: Rossiiskii Institut Strategicheskikh Issledovanii, 1994. 461 pp.
Krivokhizha, V. I., et al. *Problemy vneshnei i oboronnoi politiki Rossii.* Moscow: RISI, 1994. 119 pp.
Krivosheev, G. F., chief ed. *Grif sekretnosti sniat: poteri Vooruzhënnykh sil SSSR v voinakh, boevykh deistviiakh i voennykh konfliktakh.* Moscow: Voennoe izdatel'stvo, 1993. 416 pp.
Krotov, N. I., and A. A. Tsyganov. *Voennye Rossii.* Moscow: "RAV-Pres," 1992. 131 pp.
Kruglikova, T. V., ed. *Konversiia v Rossii.* Moscow: Mezhvedomstvennyi analiticheskii tsentr, 1993. 120 pp.
Lebed', Aleksandr I. *Spektakl' nazyvalsia putch.* Tiraspol': "Lada," 1993. 49 pp.
Luk'ianov, Anatolii I. *Perevorot mnimyi i nastoiashchii.* Voronezh: Soiuz zhurnalistov Rossii, 1993. 142 pp.
Maksimov, Iurii P., ed. *Raketnye voiska strategicheskogo naznacheniia.* Moscow: TsIPK, 1994. 185 pp.
Masliukov, Viktor, and Konstantin Truevtsev, eds. *V avguste 91-go: Rossiia glazami ochevidtsev.* Moscow: Limbus-Press, 1993. 236 pp.

Medvedev, N. P. *Mezhnatsional'nye konflikty i politicheskaia stabil'nost'*. Saransk: NII regionologii, 1992. 59 pp.
Mel'nikova, M. A., ed. *Oboronnyi kompleks narodnomu khoziaistvu*. Moscow: VIMI, 1993. 56 pp.
Men'shikov, V. L. *Baikonur: Moia bol' i liubov'*. Moscow: Garant, 1994. 232 pp.
Nazarbaev, Nursultan A. *Nursultan Nazarbaev: bez pravykh i levykh*. Moscow: "Molodaia gvardia," 1991. 256 pp.
Nedelciuc, Vasile. *Respublika Moldova*. Kishinëv: Universitas, 1992. 185 pp.
Nenashev, Mikhail F. *Poslednee pravitel'stvo SSSR*. Moscow: AO Krom, 1993. 224 pp.
Pavlov, Valentin S. *Gorbachëv-putch: Avgust iznutri*. Moscow: Delovoi mir/Business World, 1993. 126 pp.
Plekhanov, Sergei N. *Zhirinovskii: Kto on?* Moscow: Evraziia-Nord, 1994. 215 pp.
Podberëzkin, Aleksei I., ed. *Kontseptsiia natsional'noi bezopasnosti Rossii v 1995 godu*. Moscow: "Obozrevatel'," 1995. 224 pp.
———. *Natsional'naia doktrina Rossii: problemy i prioritety*. Moscow: "Obozrevatel'," 1994. 501 pp.
———. *Rossiiskaia Federatsiia: Bezopasnost' i voennoe sotrudnichestvo*. Moscow: "Obozrevatel'," 1995. 396 pp.
Ponomarëv, A. K., et al., eds. *Konversiia v Rossii*. Moscow: MATs, 1993. 120 pp.
Poroshina, N., ed. *Kto est' kto v Rossii i Blizhnem Zarubezh'e: Spravochnik*. Moscow: "Novoe Vremia," 1993. 782 pp.
Pustobaev, Mikhail. *Khronika agressii*. Vil'nius: Amzius, 1994. 239 pp.
Rutskoi, Aleksandr V. *Lefortovskie protokoly*. Moscow: Paleia, 1994. 177 pp.
Safonov, B. S., and V. I. Murakovskii, eds. *Osnovnye boevye tanki*. Moscow: Arsenal Press, 1993. 192 pp.
Sarychev, V. A., et al. *Novaia Evraziia*. Moscow: RISI, 1994. 126 pp.
Shaposhnikov, Evgenii I. *Vybor: zapiski glavnokomanduiushchego*. Moscow: PIK, 1993. 248 pp.
Shebarshin, Leonid V. *Iz zhizni nachalnika razvedki*. Moscow: Mezhdunarodnye otnosheniia, 1994. 192 pp.
SINUS Moskau. *Militaereliten in Russland 1994*. Munich: Friedrich-Ebert-Stiftung, August 1994. 77 pp.
Sislin, John, and Siemon Wezeman. *1994 Arms Transfers: A Register of Deliveries from Public Sources*. Monterey, Calif.: Monterey Institute of International Studies, 1995. 80 pp.
Sobchak, Anatolii A. *Tbilisskii izlom*. Moscow: Sretenie, 1993. 225 pp.
Stepankov, Valentin G., and Evgenii K. Lisov. *Kremlëvskii zagovor*. Moscow: "Ogonëk," 1992. 319 pp.
Stepanov, L. V., and A. I. Chicherov, eds. *Nekotorye uroki voiny v Persidskom zalive*. Moscow: RAU, 1992. 63 pp.
Sterligov, Aleksandr N. *Opal'nyi general svidetel'stvuet*. Moscow: Paleia, 1992. 62 pp.

Stockholm International Peace Research Institute. *SIPRI Yearbook 1995: World Armaments and Disarmament.* Oxford: Oxford University Press, 1995. 925 pp.

Sverdlov, Fëdor D. *Evrei-generaly Vooruzhënnykh sil SSSR.* Moscow: Moskovskaia tipografiia no. 9, 1993. 272 pp.

Timofeev, Timur T., et al., eds. *Perekhodnye protsessy: Problemy SNG.* Moscow: "Nauka," 1994. 241 pp.

Ukraine, Ministerstvo Oboroni Ukraini. *Timchasovi statuti Zbroinikh Sil Ukraini.* Kiev: Narodna armiia, 1993. 132 pp.

U.S. Arms Control and Disarmament Agency. *Arms Control and Disarmament Agreements: Texts and Histories of the Negotiations.* Washington, D.C.: ACDA, 1990 ed. 459 pp.

———. *Convention on the Prohibition of the Development, Production, Stockpiling and Use of Chemical Weapons and Their Destruction.* Washington, D.C.: ACDA, October 1993. 187 pp.

———. *Treaty on Conventional Armed Forces in Europe.* Washington, D.C.: ACDA, November 1990. 110 pp.

———. *World Military Expenditures and Arms Transfers, 1993–1994.* Washington, D.C.: ACDA, February 1995. 172 pp.

U.S. Central Intelligence Agency. *Global Humanitarian Emergencies.* Washington, D.C.: Directorate of Intelligence, January 1995. 36 pp.

———. *Worldwide Peacekeeping Operations, 1995.* April 1995. 1 sheet.

Urban, V., ed. *Zakony Rossii: voennyi paket.* Moscow: "Krasnaia zvezda," 1993. 126 pp.

Vagan, Oleh. *Natsionalizm i natsionalistychnyi rukh.* Drohobych: "Vidrodzhennia," 1994. 192 pp.

Vandenko, Andrei, and Evgenii Dodolev. *Ikh Kreml'.* Moscow: "Novyi Vzgliad," 1992. 110 pp.

Vasilevskii, Andrei, and Vladimir Pribylovskii, eds. *Kto est' kto v rossiiskoi politike.* 3 vols. Moscow: Panorama, December 1993.

Verkhovnyi Sovet. Komissiia po rassledovaniiu prichin i obstoiatelstv gosudarstvennogo perevorota. *Stenogramma.* Moscow, 18 February 1992. 220 pp.

Volkogonov, Dmitrii A. *Triumf i tragediia: Politicheskii portret I. V. Stalina.* 2 vols. Moscow: Novosti, 1989.

Yeltsin, Boris N. *The Struggle for Russia.* New York: Random House, 1994. 316 pp.

Zhirinovskii, Vladimir V. *O sud'bakh Rossii.* Moscow: Raït, 1993. 3 vols.

———. *Poslednii vagon na sever.* Moscow: Conjou Ltd., 1995. 233 pp.

———— *Secondary Sources* ————

Adams, James. *The New Spies: Exploring the Frontiers of Espionage.* London: Hutchinson, 1994. 380 pp.

Altman, Jürgen, et al., eds. *Verification at Vienna: Monitoring Reductions of Conventional Armed Forces.* Philadelphia: Gordon and Breach Science Publishers (in cooperation with the Peace Research Institute, Frankfurt), 1992. 396 pp.

Banuazizi, Ali, and Myron Weiner, eds. *The New Geopolitics of Central Asia and Its Borderlands.* Bloomington: Indiana University Press, 1994. 284 pp.

Bernstein, David, ed. *Defense Industry Restructuring in Russia.* Stanford, Calif.: Center for International Security and Arms Control, December 1994. 223 pp.

Blank, Stephen J., and Jacob W. Kipp, eds. *The Soviet Military and the Future.* Westport, Conn.: Greenwood Press, 1992. 318 pp.

Brusstar, James H., and Ellen Jones. *The Russian Military's Role in Politics.* McNair Paper 24. Washington, D.C.: National Defense University, 1995. 62 pp.

Brzezinski, Zbigniew, and Paige Sullivan, eds. *Russia and the Commonwealth of Independent States.* Armonk, N.Y.: M. E. Sharpe, 1996. 820 pp.

Chorbajian, Levon, Patrick Donabedian, and Claude Mutafian. *The Caucasian Knot: The History and Geopolitics of Nagorno-Karabagh.* London: Zed Books, 1994. 198 pp.

Cooper, Julian. *The Soviet Defence Industry.* London: Royal Institute of International Affairs, 1991. 111 pp.

Danopoulos, Constantine P., and Daniel G. Zirker, eds. *Civil-Military Relations in Soviet and Yugoslav Successor States.* Boulder, Colo.: Westview Press, 1995. 288 pp.

Davis, Christopher, Hans-Hermann Hoehmann, and Hans-Henning Schroeder, eds. *Ruestung, Modernisierung, Reform.* Cologne: Bund-Verlag, 1990. 274 pp.

Dawisha, Karen, and Bruce Parrott. *Russia and the New States of Eurasia.* New York: Cambridge University Press, 1994. 437 pp.

Ehrhart, Hans Georg, Anna Kreikemeyer, and Andrei V. Zagorski, eds. *Crisis Management in the CIS: Whither Russia?* Baden-Baden: Nomos Verlag, 1995. 256 pp.

Ferdinand, Peter, ed. *The New States of Central Asia and Their Neighbors.* London: The Royal Institute of International Affairs, 1994. 120 pp.

Galeotti, Mark. *The Age of Anxiety: Security and Politics in Soviet and Post-Soviet Russia.* New York: Longman, 1995. 219 pp.

Glantz, David M. *The History of Soviet Airborne Forces.* London: Frank Cass, 1994. 446 pp.

Hunter, Shireen T. *The Transcaucasus in Transition.* Washington, D.C.: Center for Strategic and International Studies, 1994. 223 pp.

Krause, Joachim, and Charles K. Mallory. *Chemische Waffen in der Militaerdoktrin der Sowjetunion: Historische Erfahrungen und militaerische Lehren, 1919–1991.* Baden-Baden: Nomos Verlag, 1993. 238 pp.

Kuzio, Taras. *Ukrainian Security Policy.* Westport, Conn.: Praeger, 1995. 168 pp.

Lee, William T., and Richard F. Staar. *Soviet Military Policy since World War II.* Stanford, Calif.: Hoover Institution Press, 1986. 263 pp.
Mesbahi, Mohiaddin, ed. *Central Asia and the Caucasus after the Soviet Union.* Gainesville: University Press of Florida, 1994. 353 pp.
Odom, William E., and Robert Dujarric. *Commonwealth or Empire? Russia, Asia, and the Transcaucasus.* Indianapolis: Hudson Institute, 1995. 292 pp.
Parrott, Bruce, ed. *State Building and Military Power in Russia and the New States of Eurasia.* Armonk, N.Y.: M. E. Sharpe, 1995. 319 pp.
Potter, William C., and Leonard S. Spector. *Nuclear Successor States of the Soviet Union.* Monterey, Calif.: Monterey Institute of International Studies, July 1995. 88 pp.
Raevsky, A., and I. N. Vorob'ëv. *Russian Approaches to Peacekeeping Operations.* Geneva: U.N. Institute for Disarmament Research, 1994. 182 pp.
Roberts, Brad, ed. *Biological Weapons: Weapons of the Future?* Washington, D.C.: Center for Strategic and International Studies, 1993. 101 pp.
———. *Ratifying the Chemical Weapons Convention.* Washington, D.C.: Center for Strategic and International Studies, 1994. 128 pp.
Sapir, Jacques. *The Soviet Military System.* London: Polity Press with Basil Blackwell, 1991. 362 pp.
Scott, Harriet Fast. *Scott's Bird Count: Marshals, Generals, Admirals of Russia and FSU Republics.* McLean, Va.: Photocopy, 1993. 67 pp.
Scott, Harriet Fast, and William F. Scott. *The Armed Forces of the USSR.* 3rd rev. and updated ed. Boulder, Colo.: Westview Press, 1984. 455 pp.
———. *Soviet Military Doctrine: Continuity, Formulation, and Dissemination.* Boulder, Colo.: Westview Press, 1988. 315 pp.
Staar, Richard F. *Foreign Policies of the Soviet Union.* Stanford, Calif.: Hoover Institution Press, 1991. 352 pp.
———, ed. *Arms Control: Myth versus Reality.* Stanford, Calif.: Hoover Institution Press, 1988. 263 pp.
———, ed. *East-Central Europe and the USSR.* New York: St. Martin's Press, 1991. 264 pp.
Staar, Richard F., and Margit N. Grigory, eds. *1991 Yearbook on International Communist Affairs.* Stanford, Calif.: Hoover Institution Press, 1991. 689 pp.
Swietochowski, Tadeusz. *Russia and Azerbaijan.* New York: Columbia University Press, 1995. 290 pp.
U.S. Congress. Joint Economic Committee. *The Former Soviet Union in Transition.* 2 vols. Washington, D.C.: U.S. Government Printing Office, 1993. 1,187 pp.
U.S. Senate. Committee on Governmental Affairs. *Hearing: Proliferation Threats of the 1990s.* Washington, D.C.: U.S. Government Printing Office, 1993. 192 pp.
Zaloga, Steven J. *Inside the Blue Berets: A Combat History of Soviet and Russian Airborne Forces, 1930–1995.* Novato, Calif.: Presidio Press, 1995. 339 pp.

Name Index

Abiev, Lt. Gen. Safar A., 135, 209
Achalov, Col. Gen. Vladislav A., 3, 5, 6, 7, 8, 9, 10, 12, 13, 15, 209
Adamishin, Anatolii L., 41
Ageev, Col. Gen. Gennadii E., 3, 7
Akaev, Askar A., 116, 117, 143
Akhmedov, Lt. Gen. Rustan U., 135, 144, 209–10
Akhromeev, Marshal Sergei F., 2, 7, 8, 10, 210
Aliyev, Heidar A., 117, 126, 139
Arbatov, Aleksei G., 34
Aspin, Les, 154
'Aziz, Tariq, 107

Baker, James A., III, 152, 153
Baklanov, Oleg D., 3
Baltin, Adm. Eduard D., 52, 210
Barannikov, Army Gen. Viktor P., 13
Barkashov, Aleksandr B., 196
Barsukov, Army Gen. Mikhail V., 41, 199
Basaev, Shamil, 19
Baturin, Iurii M., 38, 39, 40, 41
Bazhanov, Mikhail N., 98
Beskov, Col. Boris P., 7
Bessmertnykh, Aleksandr A., 153
Bogdanov, Col. Gen. Anatolii A., 210

Boldin, Valerii I., 3
Brailovskii, Maj. Gen. Valerii G., 97
Brezhnev, Leonid I., 24
Burlakov, Col. Gen. Matvei P., 210
Bush, George H., 152, 159, 160, 175

Chechevatov, Col. Gen. Viktor S., 59, 210
Chernavin, Fleet Admiral Vladimir N., 210–11
Chernomyrdin, Viktor S., 19, 40, 194
Chernov, Stanislav P., 97
Chindarov, Lt. Gen. Aleksandr A., 8, 211
Chizhikov, Maj. Gen. Vladimir P., 6
Churanov, Col. Gen. Vladimir T., 58, 211
Clinton, William J., 159, 161, 175
Creangà, Div. Gen. Pavel, 135, 137

Deinekin, Col. Gen. Pëtr S., 12, 49, 58, 211
Demidov, Col. Gen. Aleksei A., 10
Denisov, Col. Gen. V. D., 10
Dmitriev, Maj. Gen. Gennadii, 35
Dudayev, Maj. Gen. Djokar M., 17, 39, 211
Dunaev, Col. Gen. Andrei F., 13

Egorov, Nikolai D., 42

239

240 Name Index

Egorov, Adm. Vladimir G., 52, 211
Erin, Col. Gen. Viktor F., 42
Ermakov, Army Gen. Viktor F., 10
Erofeev, Adm. Oleg A., 52, 211
Evnevich, Lt. Gen. Valerii G., 212
Evsienko, Lt. Gen. Dmitrii, 35

Frolov, Aleksandr V., 5, 7, 8–9

Gaidar, Egor T., 198
Gamsakhurdia, Zviad K., 139
Gareev, Army Gen. Makhmut A., 212
Generalov, Viacheslav A., 3
Glukhikh, Viktor K., 103
Glybin, Iurii A., 86–87
Golovnëv, Col. Gen. Anatolii A., 212
Gorbachëv, Mikhail S., 2, 5, 6, 14, 24, 31, 59, 152, 156, 160
Govorov, Army Gen. Vladimir L., 10
Grachëv, Army Gen. Pavel S., 1, 5, 6, 7, 8, 9, 11, 13, 14, 16, 17, 18, 27, 29–31, 34, 39, 40, 42, 47–48, 52, 58, 67, 83, 104, 109, 120, 129, 133, 138, 141, 145, 146, 150, 154, 156, 169, 171, 172, 174, 178, 196, 199, 203, 204, 212
Grekov, Col. Gen. Iurii P., 59, 213
Gromov, Col. Gen. Boris V., 4, 5, 7, 8, 12, 18, 71, 122, 177, 213
Gromov, Adm. Feliks N., 52, 58, 70, 213
Grushko, Viktor F., 3
Gurinov, Adm. Georgii N., 213

Haroutiunian, Maj. Gen. Michael, 213–14
Hussein, Saddam, 69

Iablokov, Aleksei A., 41
Iakushev, Lt. Gen. Vasilii I., 125
Ianaev, Gennadii I., 3, 5
Iaramenko, Iurii V., 77
Iavlinskii, Grigorii A., 197
Iazov, Marshal Dmitrii T., 2, 3, 4, 5, 6–7, 8, 10, 214
Iliukhin, Viktor I., 205
Ioseliani, Jaba K., 139
Iurkov, Iurii A., 195
Iushenkov, Sergei N., 42
Ivanov, Col. Konstantin, 36

Ivanov, Adm. Vitalii P., 9, 10
Ivanov, Col. Gen. Vladimir L., 199, 214
Ivashov, Lt. Gen. Leonid G., 117, 118

Jiang Zemin, 204

Kalinin, Col. Gen. Nikolai V., 4, 5, 6, 8, 10, 214
Kapitanets, Fleet Admiral Ivan M., 214
Karimov, Islam A., 117, 144
Karkarashvili, Maj. Gen. Giorgii, 141
Karpukhin, Maj. Gen. Viktor E., 7, 8
Kasatonov, Adm. Igor' V., 214–15
Kastenka, Col. Gen. Anatolii I., 136
Kasymov, Lt. Gen. Alibek Kh., 135, 215
Khadziev, Salambek N., 19, 39
Khairullaev, Maj. Gen. Sherali Kh., 135, 215
Kharchenko, Col. Gen. Dmitrii K., 215
Kharitonov, Col. Dmitrii, 36
Kharnikov, Vice Adm. Viacheslav T., 52, 215
Khasbulatov, Ruslan I., 16
Khmel'nov, Adm. Igor' N., 52, 104, 215
Kholstov, Viktor, 161
Khronopulo, Adm. Mikhail N., 10
Khrushchëv, Nikita S., 2
Kim Yong-sam, 177
Kirilenko, Maj. Gen. German V., 60
Kitovani, Tengiz Z., 141
Kobets, Army Gen. Konstantin I., 4, 9, 58, 216
Kochetov, Army Gen. Konstantin A., 10
Kogat'ko, Col. Gen. Grigorii Io., 199
Kokoshin, Anatolii A., 33, 41, 58, 59, 216
Kolesnikov, Army Gen. Mikhail P., 58, 122, 216
Komoedov, Vice Adm. Vladimir P., 216–17
Kondrat'ev, Col. Gen. Georgii G., 18, 217
Kopekov, Army Gen. Danatar A., 135, 145
Kopylov, Col. Gen. Viktor A., 59, 217
Korzhakov, Lt. Gen. Aleksandr V., 108, 109, 199
Kotelkin, Aleksandr I., 97, 106, 107, 109
Kovalëv, Valentin A., 41
Kozyrev, Andrei V., 41, 102, 107, 112, 170, 173, 174, 176, 178

Krapivin, Lt. Gen. Iurii V., 199
Kremlev, Col. Gen. Vitalii Ia., 71
Kriuchkov, Vladimir I., 3, 5
Kruchina, Nikolai L., 3
Kruglov, Anatolii S., 42
Kuchma, Leonid D., 116, 117, 134, 135
Kulikov, Army Gen. Anatolii S., 40, 42, 199, 217
Kuntsevich, Lt. Gen. Anatolii D., 158, 160
Kuz'min, Col. Gen. Fëdor M., 10, 217
Kuznetsov, Col. Gen. Leontii V., 59, 217–18
Kuzyk, Boris N., 97, 107, 109
Kvashnin, Col. Gen. Anatolii V., 156, 218

Lebed', Lt. Gen. Aleksandr I., 6, 7, 8, 15, 18, 120, 218
Lilley, James R., 81
Lobov, Oleg I., 38, 40
Lobov, Army Gen. Vladimir N., 24, 58–59, 200, 218
Lopatin, Vladimir N., 9, 218
Lukashenka, Alyaksandr H., 117, 136
Luk'ianov, Anatolii I., 3
Lysenko, Nikolai N., 195

Major, John, 160
Makashov, Col. Gen. Al'bert M., 8, 9, 10, 11, 13, 218
Malei, Mikhail D., 41
Mal'tsev, Lt. Gen. Leonid S., 135, 219
Manilov, Lt. Gen. Valerii L., 37, 40
Marchenkov, Maj. Gen. Valerii I., 6
Marchuk, Maj. Gen. Ivan D., 199
Markin, Col. Vladimir N., 40
Mel'nichuk, Lt. Gen. Fëdor I., 10
Mikhailov, Viktor N., 41, 177
Mironov, Col. Gen. Valerii I., 18, 97, 219
Miruk, Col. Gen. Viktor F., 9, 10, 219
Mirzaianov, Dr. Vil, 158
Mitiukhin, Col. Gen. Aleksei N., 59, 219
Moiseev, Army Gen. Mikhail A., 8, 10, 153, 219
Morozov, Col. Gen. Konstantin P., 134

Nabiev, Rakhman A., 145
Nadibaidze, Lt. Gen. Vardiko M., 135, 141, 220

Nazarbaev, Nursultan A., 117, 142
Nekrasov, Vice Adm. Vladilen P., 10
Nikolaev, Col. Gen. Aleksandr I., 41
Nikolaev, Army Gen. Andrei I., 116, 178, 199, 220
Niyazov, Saparmurad A., 117, 145
Novikova, Elena, 87
Nurmagambetov, Lt. Gen. Sagadat K., 143, 220

Opatov, Aleksandr, 41
Oslikovskii, Sergei N., 107
Ovcharov, Lt. Gen. Viktor D., 10

Panichev, Valentin N., 42
Panov, Aleksandr N., 94, 108
Panskov, Vladimir G., 41, 194
Parmokhov, Adm. Nikolai P., 52
Pasechnik, Dr. Vladimir, 159, 160
Pastukhov, Boris N., 42
Patrikeev, Col. Gen. Valerii A., 122, 220
Pavlov, Valentin S., 3, 5
Perry, William J., 87, 144, 171, 179
Petrov, Col. Gen. Stanislav V., 161, 220
P'iankov, Col. Gen. Boris E., 9, 10, 220–21
Pirumov, Adm. Vladimir S., 40
Piskunov, Aleksandr A., 162
Plekhanov, Iurii S., 3
Podkolzin, Col. Gen. Evgenii N., 18, 60, 63, 221
Primakov, Evgenii M., 41, 167, 199
Prudnikov, Col. Gen. Viktor A., 49, 58, 221
Pugo, Boris K., 3

Radetsky, Army Gen. Vitalii H., 134
Rakhmonov, Imamali S., 117
Rodionov, Col. Gen. Igor' N., 27, 33, 221
Romanov, Lt. Gen. Anatolii A., 221
Rubanov, Col. Vladimir A., 40
Rutskoi, Maj. Gen. Aleksandr V., 9, 12, 13, 15, 221–22
Rybkin, Ivan P., 40

Sadovnikov, Col. Gen. Nikolai G., 10
Samoilov, Lt. Gen. Viktor A., 104–5, 106, 107

Samsonov, Col. Gen. Viktor N., 10, 119, 222
Sargisiyan, Serzh G., 138
Sargisiyan, Vazgen Z., 135
Seleznëv, Col. Gen. Sergei P., 59, 222
Selivanov, Adm. Valentin E., 222
Semënov, Col. Gen. Vladimir M., 49, 58, 222
Sergeev, Col. Gen. Anatolii I., 58, 59, 222
Sergeev, Col. Gen. Igor' D., 48, 223
Shakhrai, Sergei M., 31, 40, 41
Shaposhnikov, Air Marshal Evgenii I., 4, 9, 37–38, 48, 105–6, 107, 108–9, 116, 223
Shenin, Oleg S., 3
Shevardnadze, Eduard A., 116, 117, 139–41, 152
Shevtsov, Maj. Gen. Vadim G., 15
Shibaev, Vladimir D., 97
Shirshov, Pëtr P., 42
Shliaga, Col. Gen. Nikolai I., 10
Shlykov, Col. Vitalii V., 107
Shmarov, Valerii N., 134, 135, 223
Shoigu, Maj. Gen. Sergei K., 41, 199
Shumeiko, Vladimir F., 40
Shustov, Vladimir V., 173
Skokov, Iurii V., 29, 37
Skuratov, Col. Gen. Ivan S., 53, 70, 223
Slipchenko, Maj. Gen. Vladimir I., 192
Snegur, Mircea I., 117, 122, 129, 137
Sokolov, Maj. Gen. Pëtr, 16–17
Solomatin, Col. Gen. Anatolii V., 58, 223–24
Soskovets, Oleg N., 97
Stalin, Joseph V., 1, 2
Starodubtsev, Vasilii A., 3
Starovoitov, Lt. Gen. Aleksandr V., 42, 199
Stepashin, Col. Gen. Sergei V., 17, 29, 42, 63
Sterligov, Maj. Gen. Aleksandr N., 13, 195
Studeman, Vice Adm. William O., 79
Subanov, Lt. Gen. Murzakan U., 135, 143, 224
Sukhanov, Vladimir I., 97
Svechnikov, Sergei I., 97, 108, 109

Tarasenko, Lt. Gen. Pavel, 122
Tarasov, Lt. Gen. Boris V., 11, 13
Terekhov, Lt. Col. Stanislav N., 13, 71
Ter-Grigor'yan, Lt. Gen. Norat G., 138
Ter-Petrosyan, Levon H., 117, 138–39
Thatcher, Margaret, 160
Thomas, Helen, 203
Tiziakov, Aleksandr I., 3
Toporov, Col. Gen. Vladimir M., 58, 224
Tret'iak, Army Gen. Ivan M., 11
Tret'iak, Valerii D., 97
Tret'iakov, Col. Gen. Valerii S., 59, 224
Trofimov, Maj. Gen. Valentin F., 97
Troshin, Aleksandr N., 40
Trushin, Lt. Gen. Vasilii P., 13
Tumanov, Col. Gen. Aleksandr V., 199

Uglev, Dr. Vladimir, 158
Ushakov, Iurii V., 173

Varennikov, Army Gen. Valentin I., 2, 3, 4, 7, 8, 11, 224
Vasev, Vladilen M., 120
Viktorov, Valerian N., 174
Vladimirov, Maj. Gen. Aleksandr I., 14
Volkogonov, Col. Gen. Dmitrii A., 224–25
Vorob'ëv, Col. Gen. Ed'uard A., 18, 66, 225
Vysotskii, Col. Gen. Evgenii V., 69, 225

Yeltsin, Boris N., 5, 7, 9, 11, 13–14, 15, 16, 17, 19, 26, 29, 36, 37, 38, 39, 40, 47, 56, 79, 82, 93, 96, 98, 99, 107, 112, 117, 118, 125, 128, 129, 135, 141, 143, 144, 159, 160, 162, 169, 172, 174, 175, 177, 178, 192

Zheludkov, Arkadii, 41
Zherebtsov, Col. Gen. Viacheslav V., 225
Zhirinovskii, Vladimir V., 196
Zhukov, Marshal Georgii K., 2
Zhurbenko, Col. Gen. Vladimir M., 225
Zinin, Vice Adm. Boris M., 52, 226
Ziuganov, Gennadii A., 196
Zverev, Andrei V., 41

Subject Index

Abkhazia, 124–25, 189
ABM and START agreements, 161–64
ABM system, Russian development of, 162
advanced weapon systems R and D, 186–87
Afghanistan, 35, 104
airborne troops, 6, 11, 63, 125
air defense systems, 100, 108
air defense troops. *See* Troops for Air Defense
"Al'fa" team, 7, 12, 15
All-Russian Center for Public Opinion polls, 175–76
American "scholar agents," 204
An-124 military transport, 49, 98
Antiballistic Missile Treaty (May 1972), 161–62, 194
antitank systems, 100–102
Arab states, 181
ARCTIC-94 joint maneuvers, 171
armaments deployed outside Russia, 54, 56
armed forces high command, future of, 200
armed forces reform, 19, 27, 35, 71, 191; and civilian control, 59, 60, 196; and Lobov's plan, 58–59; program of, 200–201
Armenia, 35, 37, 138, 139, 189; agreement on bases in, 14; and collective security treaty, 113, 114, 116, 117; and Russian presence, 56; and Soviet military equipment, 138
armored personnel carriers, 96, 101, 102
armored vehicles, 101
arms bazaars, 98, 99, 102
arms reduction agreements, 198
arms sales, 102, 107–8; black market in, 96, 98; and corruption, 107, 108–9; decline of, 103, 104
army, Russian, 69–70
August 1991 coup, 1–9; compared to October 1993 mutiny, 14–16; indictments after, 4; and investigative commission hearings, 2–3
Azerbaijan, 30, 35, 138–39, 189; and collective security treaty, 113, 116, 117; and Islamic fundamentalism, 181; Muslims in, 201; and Soviet military equipment, 139

Baltic Fleet, 53, 59, 70
Baltic states, 27, 30, 47, 112, 118

243

Basic Forces, functions of, 69
Basic Research Fund, 82
Belarus, 48, 56, 146; armed forces of, 135–37; and collective security treaty, 113, 114, 117; and major weapon systems production, 76; Russian military equipment in, 60; as SNG charter member, 112; and Soviet military equipment, 136
"Beta" team, 7, 15
Biological and Toxin Weapons Convention, 198; expanded program of, 161; ratification of, 159–61; violations of, 159–60, 202
Biopreparat, 159, 160
black market, 195; in arms, 96; and SNG countries, 98
Black Sea Fleet, 53, 134–35
"brain drain," 79–82; to China, 78–80; effect of, on Russia, 81; to U.S., 79, 204; and weapons development, 198
BREEZE 94 joint naval exercises, 170
Budapest summit (Dec. 1994), 168, 174
Budennovsk raid, 19, 42

Caucasus, the, 189
Center for Geopolitical and Military Forecasting, 32
Central Asian Republics, 142
Central Bank of Russia, 113, 176, 196
Central Electoral Commission, 198–200
Chechnya war, 49, 149, 154, 171, 189, 203; effects of, 60, 194; failure of, 18–19, 195; origins of, 2, 16–18, 154, 189; and Russian losses, 18–19; and the Russian military, 18, 39, 69; and weapons used, 16–17, 189; and Yeltsin, 39
Cheliabinsk-70, 87
chemical weapons: destruction of, 157–59; multilateral treaty on (Jan. 1993), 156, 198; stockpile of, 157
China, 35, 69, 82, 128; arms sold to, 94, 102; and border with Russia, 178; and military pressure, 181; and relations with Russia, 167, 178, 204; Yeltsin's visit to (Dec. 1992), 103
Chinese, in Russia, 177–78

citizenship status, 128, 143
Coalition of Defense Forces, 118
collective security concept between China and Russia, 177–78, 204
Collective Security Treaty (May 1992), 47, 117
collective security zones, 117–18
command, control, and communication capabilities, 69
Commission for Analysis of Activities by the Leadership of the USSR Armed Forces, 4
Commission on Senior Military and Special Ranks, 38
Committee for Treaty Problems Relating to Chemical and Biological Weapons, 158, 160
Commonwealth of Independent States. *See* SNG
communists: in SNG leadership, 116, 122; in Russia, 196
Confederation of the Peoples of the Caucasus, 124, 189
Conference on Security and Cooperation in Europe (CSCE), 126–27; and Moldova, 173; and Nagorno-Karabakh conflict, 174; and peacekeeping in the "near abroad," 172; Russian vision of, 173. *See also* Organization for Security and Cooperation in Europe
Congress of People's Deputies, Eighth (Dec. 1992), 47–48
Conventional Forces in Europe treaty (Nov. 1990), 56, 152–54, 198, 201
conversion, 82–84; case studies of, 87–88; and increases in weapons production, 89; and joint ventures, 88–89; obstacles to, 86–87, 89; predictions about, 88, 90; Stanford conference on, 87; success of, 196
Cooperative Threat Reduction Act, 202
corruption: in arms sales, 107–9; in government, 194, 195
Cossack republics, 197
Council of Border Troop Commanders, SNG, 114
Croatia, 108
Cuba, 47, 53, 60

dead-hand backup system, 192–94
defense budgets, 67, 68, 88–90; and deficits, 77, 82, 83, 87
Defense Ministers' Council, SNG, 114, 116
Defense Ministry, and arms sales, 98
defense plants, 87
"defensive armed force," 201
Desert Storm, Russian preoccupation with, 67–68
detargeting of nuclear weapons agreement (Jan. 1994), 35
dictatorship, possibility of, 200
draft, military, 64–66, 70–71

East-Central Europe, 35, 47, 146; and NATO membership, 35; Russian military equipment in, 60. *See also individual countries*
economic union treaty with Belarus (Sept. 1993), 113
elections, 194, 198
emigration from Russia, 195
Estonia, 53, 56, 112
ethnic conflicts, 30; in Baltic states, 56–58; in Moldova, 120
ethnic republics and independence, 187–89
ethnic Russians abroad, 128, 138; rights of, 26, 27; and Russian National Doctrine, 186
European Bank for Reconstruction and Development, 89, 197
extremist organizations, 195–96

Far East region, 189, 191
Federal Border Service, 53, 122, 143, 198
Federal Security Service, 198, 203–4
Federation Council, 17, 197; military members of, 37; and START II, 162
Foreign Counter-Intelligence Service, 17
Foreign Economic Relations Ministry, 96, 97, 106
Foreign Intelligence Service, 53
Fourteenth Army, 60, 120
future wars, projections about, 192

General Staff, and control of military, 59

Geneva Convention (1949), 17, 156
Georgia, 30, 35, 53, 112, 113, 116, 117, 138; armed forces of, 139, 141; civil war in, 119, 141; elections in, 139; and major weapon systems production, 76; and Russia, 141
Germany, 82, 167, 176
Government Committee for the State of Emergency, 4, 5
Grad multiple rocket launcher, 102
"Greater Romania" movement, 181
Group of Russian Forces, in Armenia, 138

hidden cities, 77–80

Iakutiia-Sakha, 187, 191
Iantar Shipbuilding Enterprise, 85
ICBMs, 48, 85, 87, 137, 162; dismantling of, 146, 201–2; in the "near abroad," 48
Idel-Ural Federation, 189
Igla antiaircraft missile systems, 99
independence efforts in non-Russian republics, 187–89, 194, 195
India, 95, 98, 104
Ingushetia, 125, 189
Interdepartmental Commission for Scientific and Technical Questions in the Defense Industries, 38
Interdepartmental Coordinating Council on Military-Technical Policy, 97
Internal Affairs Ministry troops, 70, 198
International Monetary Fund, 176, 197
Interstate Economic Committee, SNG, 113
Iran, 35, 82, 126, 128, 139, 181, 189; arms exports to, 94; and mosque restoration, 189; as "threat from the South," 201
Iraq, 35, 82, 181; arms exports to, 104; embargo against, 107
Islamic fundamentalism, 154, 181, 201
Islamic Revival Party, 122

Japan, 82, 176–77, 197, 198
Joint Armed Forces Command, 112, 116
joint defense of external frontiers agreement (Feb. 1995), 143
joint maneuvers, 170–71, 172

Joint Russian-Moldovan-Dniesterian Control Commission, 173
Joint Staff for SNG Military Coordination, 116

Kaliningrad, 87, 128; access to, 56; port of, 53
Kazakhstan, 37, 48, 56, 79; and airborne brigades, 63; and collective security treaty, 113, 114, 117; and Islamic fundamentalism, 181; and Russia, 136, 142
KGB, 8, 11, 53, 109
Kiev-class aircraft carriers, 104
Kiev Military District, 106
Kola Peninsula, 53
Königsberg. *See* Kaliningrad
Kurile Islands, 176, 198
Kyrgyzstan, 142; armed forces of, 143; and collective security treaty, 113, 114, 116, 117; economic and defense union of, 142; former Soviet military units in, 144; and Islamic fundamentalism, 181

Latvia, 53, 56, 112
League of Defense Enterprises, 77
Leningrad Military District, 60, 118
Liberal Democratic Party, 195, 196
Libya, 81; arms exports to, 104; and chemical weapons treaty, 156; embargo against, 107
Lithuania, 53, 56, 112

Main Administration for Educational and Socio-Psychological Work, 134
Main Protection Directorate troops, 198
Maritime Territory, 79
martial law, 18
MBFR. *See* Mutual and Balanced Force Reductions talks
military, Soviet/Russian: and civilians, 1; and law and order, 197; outside Russia, 53–54, 57; and politics, 1, 35–36, 47–48; SNG's nationalization of, 56. *See also* army, Russian
military cooperation pacts, 142, 204
military districts, 59, 60
military doctrine, 24–25, 27–29, 36–37, 200; assessment of, 29–30, 33–36; and ethnic conflicts, 30; and former Warsaw Pact countries, 35; and the military, 27; and nuclear weapons, 29–30, 31, 192–94; provisions of, 29, 31–32; publication of, 30–31; and the Security Council, 27, 37; tenets of, 24–26
military-industrial complex, 76; conversion of, 201; as employer, 87; privatization of, 87; and Russian assistance to China, 204
military-technical agreements, 104
"mini-nukes," 192
Minsk summits: of December 1991, 133; of February 1992, 11
mobile forces, 60, 63, 69, 205
mobilization stockpiles, 83
Moldova, 15, 34, 47; armed forces of, 137–38; and collective security treaty, 113, 117; and monitoring of ceasefire, 173; and peacemaking, 119; Russian withdrawal from, 177; and Soviet military equipment, 137
Moscow Military District, 4, 6, 60
Muslims, 122, 126, 201
Mutual and Balanced Force Reductions (MBFR) talks, 150–56

Nagorno-Karabakh, 35, 125–26, 127–28
National Guard, 198, 205
National Republican Party of Russia, 195
national security assistant, 38
national security concept, 198, 205
national security interests, 180
National Technological Base program, 89
navy, Russian (VMF), 52–53, 70–71
"near abroad" (*blizhnee zarubezh'e*), 32, 36, 49, 113, 128, 150, 198
"no first strike" pledge, 24, 26, 33
nomenklatura, 197–98
North Atlantic Cooperation Council, 168
North Atlantic Treaty Organization (NATO), 27, 35, 167–72; and East-Central European countries, 32; and MBFR, 150; and OSCE, 169; and the "Partnership for Peace," 169
North Caucasus Military District, 203
Northern Sea Fleet, 53, 59, 70

Subject Index 247

North Korea: arms exports to, 104; and chemical weapons treaty, 156; and Russia, 177
North Ossetia–Alania, 125, 189
Nuclear Nonproliferation Treaty (1968), 31, 35, 177
nuclear weapons development, 194

Oboroneksport, 96, 99, 106
October 1993 mutiny: and Grachëv's actions, 12, 14; plans for, 15–16; at the White House, 9–14
officers, military: and August 1991 coup, 1–9; decline in numbers of, 65; ethnic makeup of, 71; housing aid for, 175; and October 1993 mutiny, 12–13; and politics, 120; promotions of, 13–14; in Ukraine, 134
OMON *spetsnaz* (Interior Ministry special troops), 11, 15, 53; and the armed forces, 53–54; and police detachments, 7
Operation Thunder (*Grom*), 7
Organization for Security and Cooperation in Europe (OSCE), 124, 168, 180. See also Conference on Security and Cooperation in Europe
Ostankino radio and TV, 11, 14, 15
"outer empire," 192

Pacific Fleet, 59
parliamentary elections, postponement of, 197
"Partnership for Peace," 32, 168–70, 172
peacekeepers, in Yugoslavia, 174–75
peacemakers, 118–19; in Armenia, 126–27; in Moldova, 120–22; in North Ossetia, 125; in South Ossetia, 122
peacemaking (*mirotvorchestvo*), 118–20, 194; in the "near abroad," 26, 172; political aspects of, 180; regional principles of, 118, 119; and UN mandate, 128

Regional Security Council, 181
Republican Guard of Kazakhstan, 142
research and development, 49, 82, 89–90, 104–5

Reykjavik conference (June 1968), 150
Rosvooruzhenie, 96, 97, 104, 105; corruption in, 108–9; leadership of, 105–6; regulation of, 106; and representation abroad, 106
Russian Academy of Sciences, 81, 90
Russian-American Partnership and Friendship Charter, 175
Russian-American University, Moscow, 179–83
Russian bases: in Armenia, 14, 138; in Chechnya, 203; in Georgia, 138, 141
Russian Center for Training in Electoral Technology, 198
Russian constitution, 17
Russian Federation, dangers for, 187
Russian Military Brotherhood, 71
Russian military intelligence, 98, 172
Russian National Council, 195
Russian National Unity Movement, 195–96
Russian people, ethnic makeup of, 187–89

secessionist tendencies, 187–89
"secret cities," 192, 204
Security Council, 17, 27, 29, 37–42; decision of, on Chechnya, 17; expansion of, 37; restructuring of, 37–38; and Yeltsin, 39
Siberian Independence Movement, 189, 191
Siberian Military District, 9
SNG, 4, 26, 47, 112; armies of, 146; and arms allocations, 56; charter of, 114, 116; failure of, 113, 195, 201; joint defense forces in, 133, 141; military organization of, 48, 133; Yeltsin's chairmanship of, 118
SNG Collective Security Treaty (May 1992), 33, 141, 186
"soldier-internationalists," 48
South Ossetia, 189
stability, threats to, 180–83, 187
Stanford conference on conversion (1993), 87, 89
START, and ICBMs, 162, 198
State Committee for Defense Industry (*Goskomoboronprom*), 86

State Committee for Military-Technical Policy, 109
State Committee on Conversion, 98
State Company for Export and Import of Arms and Military Equipment. *See* Rosvooruzhenie
State *Duma,* 17, 29, 34, 39; dissolution of, 197; and Grachëv's testimony, 67; military members of, 37; and obligatory service, 65; and pardons for officers, 14; and START II, 162
Strategic Missile Forces (RSVN), 48, 162
strategic reserves, 83, 107, 197
strategic weapons, 48
Syria, 34, 95, 102, 104

Tajikistan, 34, 35, 66, 118, 143; armed forces of, 145; civil war in, 122, 145; and collective security treaty, 113; and Islamic fundamentalism, 181; and peacemaking, 173
Tashkent meeting and treaty (May 1995), 113
Tatarstan, 189–91; Muslims in, 201; and Russian stability, 187; and Volga-Ural region, 191
theater missile defense limits, 161–62
"threat from the South," 181, 201
Trans-Dniester Republic, 15, 34, 120, 137
Troops for Air Defense (PVO), 9, 49–52
troop withdrawals, 56–57, 177
Turkey, 35, 126, 128, 139, 181, 189; and officer training, 143, 144, 145; as "threat from the South," 201
Turkmenistan: and collective security treaty, 113, 114, 116, 117; and Islamic fundamentalism, 181; and peacemaking, 119; and Russian assistance, 144–45

Ukraine, 37, 48, 53, 56, 113, 114, 117; armed forces of, 133–34; arms sales to Russia by, 135; and major weapon systems production, 76; military doctrine of, 134; and peacemaking, 119; and post-Soviet East-Central Europe, 146; presidential elections in, 134; Russian military equipment in, 60; as SNG charter member, 112; and Soviet military equipment, 134–35
Unified Command for Troops in Southern Russia, 60
Union of Russian Veterans, 71
Union Treaty, 5, 14
UN and Russian peacemaking, 173, 174
UN embargoes: against Iraq, 181; against Libya, 181; Russian violations of, 107
United Nations of the Middle Volga and Urals, 189
United States, 128, 161, 175–76, 194, 198
"United States of Russia," 197
"untouchable" supplies, 107, 197
Uzbekistan, 142; and airborne brigades, 63; armed forces of, 144; and collective security treaty, 113, 114, 116, 117; economic and defense union of, 142; and Islamic fundamentalism, 181; and major weapon systems production, 76; and military cooperation treaty with Russia, 144

verification of treaty compliance, 201, 203
Volga River and Ural Mountains, United Peoples of, 189
Volga-Ural region, 189–91
Volga-Urals Military District, 8, 11, 60, 118
VPK: and conversion costs, 87; importance of, 77, 82; production ratio of, 107; technology level of, 90. *See also* military-industrial complex

Warsaw Pact, 150–52, 157
weapons as revenue source, 89, 90, 94, 95
Western Group of Forces, 108
World Bank, 89, 176, 197

About the Author

Richard F. Staar is a senior fellow at the Hoover Institution. He served as U.S. ambassador to the Mutual and Balanced Force Reductions (MBFR) negotiations in Vienna from 1981 to 1983. His areas of specialization include Russia, East-Central Europe, arms control, and public diplomacy. He earned an A.B. from Dickinson College, an A.M. from Yale University, and a Ph.D. in political science from the University of Michigan.

The **Naval Institute Press** is the book-publishing arm of the U.S. Naval Institute, a private, nonprofit society for sea service professionals and others who share an interest in naval and maritime affairs. Established in 1873 at the U.S. Naval Academy in Annapolis, Maryland, where its offices remain today, the Naval Institute has almost 85,000 members worldwide.

Members of the Naval Institute receive the influential monthly magazine *Proceedings* and discounts on fine nautical prints, ship and aircraft photos, and subscriptions to the bimonthly *Naval History* magazine. They also have access to the transcripts of the Institute's Oral History Program and get discounted admission to any of the Institute-sponsored seminars offered around the country.

The Naval Institute's book-publishing program, begun in 1898 with basic guides to naval practices, has broadened its scope in recent years to include books of more general interest. Now the Naval Institute Press publishes about 100 titles each year, ranging from how-to books on boating and navigation to battle histories, biographies, ship and aircraft guides, and novels. Institute members receive discounts of 20 to 50 percent on the Press's nearly 600 books in print.

Full-time students are eligible for special half-price membership rates. Life memberships are also available.

For a free catalog describing Naval Institute Press books currently available, and for further information about U.S. Naval Institute membership, please write to:

Membership Department
U.S. Naval Institute
118 Maryland Avenue
Annapolis, Maryland 21402-5035
Telephone: (800) 233-8764
Fax: (410) 269-7940